CHARLES K. McCLATCHY

and the

GOLDEN ERA

of

AMERICAN JOURNALISM

CHARLES K. McCLATCHY

and the

GOLDEN ERA

of

AMERICAN JOURNALISM

Steven M. Avella

University of Missouri Press

Columbia

ISBN: 978-0-8262-2068-4
Library of Congress Control Number: 2015955239

♾️™This paper meets the requirements of the
American National Standard for Permanence of Paper
for Printed Library Materials, Z39.48, 1984.

Typefaces: Century, Bembo, Garamond

To the Memories of James Henley
and
James Briggs McClatchy

Contents

◆

Acknowledgments

THIS BIOGRAPHY OF C. K. McClatchy was a long and exceedingly complex project. It began with an offhand comment made to me by the late James Henley, director of what was then called the Sacramento Archives and Museum Collection Center—today the Center for Sacramento History (CSH). Jim had been instrumental in bringing the McClatchy Papers to the center in 1982. While researching Catholicism in Sacramento, I perused many copies of the *Bee* and was struck by CK's familiarity with Catholic culture and his sensitivity to Catholic teachings. As I discovered, he was raised and educated as a Catholic but had fallen-away from the practice of his faith. However, unlike his brother, who became an Episcopalian and a Mason, CK was tethered to the Catholic Church by his wife, a devout and loyal communicant until her death. She even memorialized her husband and son in church decor at the chapel of a former orphanage, and after she died her two daughters donated an elaborate crucifix and altar to the city's majestic Cathedral of the Blessed Sacrament.

Henley invited me to examine the letter books that were part of the McClatchy Papers. Once I dipped into them, I was hooked, and I determined to study and write about C. K. McClatchy, whose editorial career (1883–1936) spanned a remarkable period in national, state, and local history. I thus began a multiyear study of the letter books and the voluminous McClatchy Papers, traveling often to Sacramento (my hometown) and using sabbatical time and any moments I could grab from my full-time job at Marquette University to keep the project moving forward. The task was onerous. CK was involved in many different issues, and the records were not always in good shape. But thanks to Jim and the kindness of the CSH staff, I was able to make uneven but steady progress. The first result was a thousand-page manuscript that required

ix

numerous revisions, rethinking, and paring down. What appears here has gone through a long process of research and writing and rewriting. Tempted to give it up at times, I always had the strong encouragement of Jim Henley to press forward. Jim died in 2014, but his spirit and quiet inspiration are among the motivating forces behind this book.

Jim Henley introduced me to James Briggs McClatchy, CK's grandson and the son of Carlos McClatchy. James and his wonderful wife, Susan, became good friends, and James shared many things with me—some of them very difficult for him—that were of great help. He also provided some financial assistance for travel and research. I imbibed some of the nuances of the McClatchy story from James—things that documents could not easily convey. Before his passing, James had been very concerned that the McClatchy newspapers might not carry on the ideals set out by his grandfather. I wish I could have helped him more with that, but I will always be grateful to him and Susan for their hospitality, encouragement, and the stimulating conversation that took place in their living room and around their table. Apart from James and Susan McClatchy, I have only met in passing some members of the family. Neither they nor the company has seen this text. It is solely my work.

No historian is totally objective. We all bring our "baggage" to how we reconstruct the past. Others have written about CK, but few have painstakingly studied the McClatchy Papers as well as materials in other related repositories. Standard accounts of his life and accomplishments come largely from people who worked for the *Sacramento Bee.* A 1960s doctoral thesis relied on the newspapers themselves and some oral history. These oral histories, of uneven quality, are to be found in the Center for Sacramento History. Also relying heavily on the oral histories and the newspapers were rejected drafts of manuscripts about the history of the newspaper by various authors and historians hired by the *Bee,* including the great Oscar Lewis. These research attempts produced interesting genealogical studies as well as rehashed accounts of the life of CK's father, James McClatchy. Various students at California State University, Sacramento, have pursued assorted topics related to the *Bee* or CK's editorials. I was able to use many of these sources and fully examine the breadth of this man's career—what influenced him and how in turn he influenced those who read his opinions and were shaped by his priorities.

I come to this project as an academic scholar who teaches courses in twentieth-century American history and have more than a passing knowledge of the wider epoch during which CK's life unfolded—the late nineteenth century and the first third of the twentieth. He knew Populists and Progressives, struggled with America's involvement in global politics, suffered under the conservatism of the New Era, and even met Franklin Roosevelt in the White House during the Hundred Days of his first term. As an editor, Californian, and American, CK took note of these movements and issues and commented on them all. I am also a scholar of Catholicism in the American West. My Catholic interests and perceptions have allowed me to understand how religious ideas and culture drove C. K. McClatchy, even though he was not formally affiliated with any religious denomination.

I was reared in Sacramento and was a newspaper carrier for the *Bee* from 1962 until I left for the seminary in 1965. I managed Route 3491, which encompassed a good bit of suburban Orangevale—a small community where, I have learned, Valentine McClatchy at one time had real estate interests. In those days the *Bee* was an afternoon paper and I was an "independent businessman" buying my papers from the *Bee* and then recouping my costs plus a tiny profit by collecting from my customers. I made little money, even though I grew the route from sixty-two customers to ninety daily and Sunday customers by the time I left for high school. The *Bee* would occasionally take all of us "*Bee* Boys" on trips to San Francisco to see exciting Cinerama movies like *How the West Was Won*. I think I even saw Eleanor McClatchy at one of these events. But the small profits (only about $300 for three years of hard work) were more than compensated by the tutorial they gave me in public affairs. Every day as I wrapped those papers I would read them from top to bottom (even the classified ads). I learned much about the world and how it works through the eyes of the *Bee*. In terms of current events, I was one of the best-informed young men in my grade school and junior high classes. I was the only one who knew who Chief Justice (and former California governor) Earl Warren and U.S. senators Clair Engle and Tom Kuchel were—as well as the columnist Katherine Kitchen, state senator Al Rodda, and the editor Walter Jones. I had some grasp of the water issues that divided the northern and southern parts of the state, the growth of the defense industry, and the rise of local suburbs. I regaled in the annual coverage of the state fair, which took place just before we went back to school. I loved the editorial page, which had the wonderful art of the great cartoonist Herblock and the prosaic common sense of the editorial writers. I remember so well the uncharacteristically bold headlines on the day John F. Kennedy died and the tears I shared with customers as I handed them their newspaper on that dark November day in 1963. The *Sacramento Bee* and I were good friends. The *Bee* taught me my politics, had a great comics page, and gave me an unending love for Sacramento.

A note about the McClatchy Papers—the primary source for this work. When they arrived at the Center for Sacramento History, they had some skeletal organization that had been preserved from their original filing. Charles Duncan, a former assistant to Eleanor McClatchy, had been assigned to work with the papers. He did some organizational work and created a rough database of its contents. Duncan also rearranged some files in an effort to impose some order on the collection. Others took steps to preserve the letter books. In 2005 a large number of documents were transferred to the CSH from the *Bee* vault. In 2014 another gift came from the estate of James B. McClatchy. C. K. McClatchy may be the best-documented newspaper editor in U.S. history. Over the years the status of the papers has changed, including their location in the center's large storage facility. The citations in this book are taken from the organizational structure as it existed in 2014, and some of the cataloging is inconsistent and confusing. The collection desperately needs reorganization and more consistent cataloging. Since its finding aids are imperfect, the researcher is compelled to go box by box. Linking these documents with what appeared in the *Bee* required careful examination of every issue of the paper CK edited. I was fortunate to be able to use bound copies of the *Bee* and microfilm. Since the microfilm copies were dark and poorly photographed, having access to both sources was helpful. CK also had voluminous correspondence with Hiram Johnson, California governor (1911–17)and U.S. senator (1917–45). I have tried to identify as many letters from CK to Johnson as exist in the Sacramento archives—although not a few are located in the "incoming files" of the Johnson Papers at the University of California's Bancroft Library in Berkeley. Johnson's replies to CK are there as well.

I accumulated many debts in writing this book. First and foremost, the patient and long suffering of the staff at the Center for Sacramento History. It has changed several times since I began this work—but I must single out Patricia Johnson who worked with me diligently for years. I could not find a better, more supportive, archival friend than the kindhearted and patient Pat. I also acknowledge the help of Stasia Wolfe, Lisa Prince, Carson Hendricks, Dylan McDonald, Charles Duncan, and the current director, Marcia Eymann. Rebecca Crowther helped prepare the pictures. All these folks have treated me like family over these many years. Librarians at the Bancroft in Berkeley and the Haynes Collection at UCLA were a great help. The able staff of the

California Room of the California State Library and its former director, Gary Kurutz, have been a port in every storm. The Marquette University Library has been wonderful in providing resources—especially by purchasing a nearly full run of the *Sacramento Bee* in a local research center library—a great boon for anyone living in the Midwest.

I wish also to thank the staff of the University of Missouri Press for their interest and help with this work. I would like to single out Clair Willcox, who first expressed interest when I met him at the Western History Association; Gary Kass, the acquiring editor assigned to me; Mary Conley, who has handled the details of preparing the manuscript for publication; and Sara Davis, the managing editor.

Individuals who have helped over the years include Susan Silva, who has edited many drafts; Annette Kassis, who traveled with me to the Bancroft; Joseph Pitti, perhaps the best Sacramento historian, who lent me his students' master theses on *Bee* topics; and my Marquette research assistants, Paula Dicks, Justin Hoffman, Edward Schmitt, and Beth Gabriel. Brigitte Charaus secured some desperately needed information from the Santa Clara University library. My good friend Dr. John Buenker read various drafts and gave it the kind of attention I hoped from a scholar as accomplished and insightful as he has always been. Chuck Wallenberg and Gary Kurutz were also kind enough to look over the manuscript. Generous grants of sabbatical time from Marquette University and the support of the Marquette library staff, especially Dr. John Jentz, were indispensable. I owe all these folks a great deal. I sincerely thank them.

But the inspiration and encouragement for this book is attributable mostly to the two Jims, Henley and McClatchy. These men befriended me and drew me into the labyrinthine world of the *Bee* and the McClatchy family. Their support and encouragement were critical. I regret that I disappointed both by not finishing this book before they died, and I dedicate it to their memories. Both Jims knew and loved Sacramento more than I do. In their own ways they were great friends and their memory is a blessing.

As any biographer knows, the subject often becomes a cherished, if at times maddening, friend. CK was a complex and often contradictory man whose formal and standoffish ways were balanced by a warm heart. A passage from Dickens or a rendition of Hamlet by the great Edwin Booth or Frederick Warde could easily move him. The majestic, if antiquated, English of the King James Bible inspired him. In his mind he was always David fighting Goliath, or a thundering Jeremiah, warning of dire dangers while also praying for the well-being of his city. In quiet ways not known to many, he was the image of the "Gentle Nazarene," dispensing kindness and charity. Yet, like all of us, he was a flawed human being. CK also had a misogynistic streak, could be relentlessly stubborn, especially concerning foreign policy issues—about which he knew little—and terribly vindictive to anyone who crossed him. He often glossed over the inconvenient truths about himself, his father, the *Bee,* and other people.

In the end CK helped to shape the collective mind and identity of thousands of people in his time—and did so motivated by a desire to help them and not just enrich himself. Like any biographer, I found myself feeling his emotions, agonizing for his woes, and cheering on his assaults on the various and sundry rascals he publicly pummeled. Knowing his foibles and inconsistencies does not dismay or shock me. Knowing his respect for the truth, I have tried to be as direct and honest as he would want a writer to be—even if what I wrote was not always complimentary to him. He could take the heat—and give it back when he felt he had to. Perhaps he would have quoted the King James Version of 2 Corinthians about himself: "But we have this treasure in earthen vessels, that the excellency of the power may be of God, and not of us." Such it is for a man of principle and passion—"excellency of power" in a weak human vessel. Such was CK. Such is the historian who writes about him.

A Note on Sources
The McClatchy Papers

◆

The multiple citations to the McClatchy papers may seem confusing. This large collection, held by the Center for Sacramento History (CSH), is imperfectly cataloged at present. It consists of the following components:

1. The letter books of the company, which include both professional and personal correspondence. These are generally indicated by the kinds of letters: "Editorial," "Personal," and some specialized files dealing with particular topics, for example, "Segregation and Scatteration." Each book has a number and dates of correspondence. I have tried to use this complex recording system to identify items cited.

2. Assorted personal and business-related materials. These items, generally given the title "McClatchy Papers," are in numbered boxes with haphazard organization. Some papers have no date but cover important moments in the history of the company and the life of the McClatchy family. A keyword database is available to researchers at the center but is not available online.

3. After these files were transferred to the CSH, Duncan, a longtime employee of the *Bee* who had extensive personal knowledge of the internal realities of the company, rearranged them. Although his efforts imposed some order, he had no professional archival experience, and his alterations created some challenges for research and proper identification.

4. The McClatchy Newspapers and Broadcasting Collection. These papers, transferred to the CSH in 2005, were materials found in vaults in the *Sacramento Bee* building. They contain a great deal of correspondence,

particularly between C. K. and Hiram Johnson. They are well organized and have a good finding aid, which is available online.

5. The James and Susan McClatchy Collection. These papers were received by the CSH in 2014 from the estate of the late James McClatchy. They have a good inventory guide and some materials relevant to Carlos and Phebe McClatchy.

6. Images used in the book are from the Center for Sacramento History, Eleanor McClatchy Collection. Images have assigned numbers; numbers for images in the photo section, in order, are as follows: 1982–005–9301, 9–064–002, 1982–005–4805, 1982–005–4605, 1982–005–4736, 1982–005–5697, 1982–005–4806, CDI 002098, 1982–005–4608, 1982–005–4738, 1982–005–9266, 1982–005–0788.

7. The *Bee* changed names several times over the years. A listing appears below:
    February 1857–January 1890: *Daily Bee*
    January 1890–March 1908: *Evening Bee*
    March 1908–present: *The Sacramento Bee*

CHARLES K. McCLATCHY

and the
GOLDEN ERA
of
AMERICAN JOURNALISM

Introduction

◆

CHARLES KENNY McCLATCHY (1858–1936) was a man of great importance in the history of California and of western journalism. His years as editor of the *Sacramento Bee* (1883–1936) bridged the nineteenth and twentieth
centuries—engaging its key public issues and the various transformations of
American journalism. His editorial influence was an amalgam of deeply held
principles and his inner drives and passions.

He lived in a golden age of journalism. This was the era of newspaper giants
like William Randolph Hearst, Joseph Pulitzer, and Robert McCormick. In
California he was a contemporary of Harrison Gray Otis, Fremont Older, and
Michael de Young. In those days the work of editors mattered in a way quite
different from today. For CK journalism was not just a job, it was a vocation,
as it was for his contemporaries.

His reputation grew in the fifty-three years he edited the *Sacramento Bee*.
Editors throughout California and elsewhere read him, politicians courted his
endorsement, and common people voted their affirmation by subscribing to
his paper. CK dictated newspaper policy without editorial boards or stock-
holders peering over his shoulder. It was a time when editors had time to go
deeply "into the weeds" on matters of public policy—local, state, national,
and international. C. K. McClatchy ruled with an iron hand. His subordinates
did not make a move without his consent. Those who transgressed his rules,
or dared to adopt a different tone or line, sometimes found themselves out the
door. He jealously guarded his right to dictate what the *Bee* said and what causes and candidates it stood for—not even allowing his own brother (ostensibly
the coeditor) to have a significant say. Although CK often declared his intention to turn over the direction of his papers to his only son, Carlos, CK never

1

let loose of the ideological direction of the *Bee*—even though it meant hamstringing his son on numerous occasions and making him endure a constant micromanagement that drove him to distraction.

CK's was one of the most influential voices of the state's vast Central Valley as his opinions were heard from Sacramento to Siskiyou and from Fresno to Bakersfield. Reared as the son of a prominent journalist, he understood that his words had influence and his position imposed a special moral duty on him: "There is considerable difference between the obligations resting upon the man who sells codfish, potatoes, and ham, and the man who edits a newspaper . . . it can be said that an editor occupies a position where it is his duty to battle for the right as God has given him to see that right."[1] At the ceremony dedicating a new high school posthumously named for CK, a Butte county assemblyman summed it up best: "I don't think a man ever lived who made a greater impression, who had a greater influence on the people of the community in the district he served than C. K. McClatchy."[2]

In counseling his son and heir, CK shared his belief that the written word should have "influence of a positive character" and ought to evoke "the admiration if not the love of the people generally."[3] He toasted the ideals of journalism at a banquet given at Santa Clara University in 1901: "There are still to be found earnest hearts and valiant hands among the workers in journalism, men who put the True and Right, the Good before them and follow as faithfully as the mariner the polar star . . . who . . . are guided by principle only."[4] He spoke of journalism as chivalrous and believed "the *Bee* [was] a tower of righteousness and a terror to evil doers . . . an unceasing friend to every great public cause of right, the unflinching foe of every monstrous public wrong. I have made it almost a Bible in our section of California. It is respected wherever it is read."[5]

Bee historians and the few others who have written about CK have characterized him as a crusading journalist, and this is partially true. Indeed he embraced populism and California-style progressivism; railed against urban corruption, land monopoly, venal politicians, monopolies, and trusts; favored public ownership of utilities and the end of the electoral college; and promoted efficiency, coordination, and order in local, state, and national life. He often stood courageously against the tide, proclaiming in one crusade: "As long as I am Editor of The *Bee*, The *Bee* will not follow along with the mob simply because the mob is running one way."[6] He was militantly anti-imperialist and often wondered how the United States would remain faithful to its belief in human freedom if it imposed its will, culture, and beliefs on other peoples of the world. He was critical of the dislocations created by industrialization and urbanization and derided the "malefactors of great wealth."

The positive aspects of his public persona, faithfully preserved by the *Sacramento Bee,* were cherished by his family (especially his daughter and successor, Eleanor) and even repeated by historians. This book does not fundamentally dissent from this oft-repeated narrative, but thanks to the availability of fairly extensive sources, we now have a more nuanced understanding of what motivated him. The forces that drove CK did not always flow from his deeply held beliefs, nor were they exclusively predicated on linear thinking, rationality, logic, or consistency. Other, more affective, forces contributed to his ideas and writing: his love of the theater, his reading, his associates, his love of family, and his alcoholism. To be sure, he often built intellectual bridges between his principles and his passions. Even when others questioned or debunked his views, or offered other perspectives, he often clung to his positions stubbornly—what he believed and what he knew as empirical fact were always one and the same. His world was an amalgam of principles and passions— clear and consistent in his mind, even if, at times, they seemed to clash with reality or created some cognitive dissonance. Some called this hypocritical, but for McClatchy they were a seamless robe. This fusion of the ideological and the personal offers a glimpse of the forces that drove McClatchy—and perhaps others—in the editorial fraternity of his times.

CK's affective side influenced his view of the world. He was a voracious consumer of, and expert on, the melodrama of the nineteenth-century stage—a genre known for its often simple verities of right and wrong, darkness and light, good and evil. A nonpracticing Catholic, he scorned organized religion but read the Bible faithfully, quoted it extensively, and gave evidence that Catholic life and tradition had left some imprint on his imagination. He traveled to the Holy Land, met at least two popes, and walked in the great churches of Christendom. He was attracted to clerics of depth and kindness but waged one of his worst verbal wars against a priestly antagonist in San Francisco, who could give as well as he received from McClatchy.

CK, like all of us, was a welter of contradictions—magnified in his case because of his public influence. He could rail against the depredations of big business but never questioned the fundamentals of capitalism. His rhetorical admiration for the common person and respect for the working class were points of pride, except when it came to workers in his own company or people of color. He hated monopoly but made sure that the *Bee* dominated the Central Valley. He waxed rhapsodic over the Declaration of Independence, the Bill of Rights, and his patriotic views of American history yet could be openly scornful of the civil liberties of those who disagreed with the government—or him—during times of war. He lashed hard-hearted or bigoted ministers, continually reproaching them for failing to live up to the standards of the "Gentle Nazarene." Yet forgiveness was not in his DNA and he could be distressingly spiteful. He believed in American exceptionalism, and no one could be more patriotic, even jingoistic, especially in times of national emergency. However, he failed to come to grips with America's transformation into a superpower that had to exist in an interdependent world. Indeed his harangues about isolationism and his disdain for any form of international cooperation reflected a distressing ethnocentrism fed by a filiopietistic view of American history. CK contributed to the nation's foreign policy consensus that kept the United States from taking the actions that might have forestalled the collapse of Europe to fascism in the 1920s and 1930s or checked the aggression of Japan. He even offered qualified praise for the dictator Benito Mussolini, whose ability to control the economic and social lives of Italians CK found congenial—and only reluctantly acknowledged Mussolini's repeated violations of human rights. CK could be a tender and sentimental husband and father—but an equally passionate hater of anyone who crossed him for personal or professional reasons. He was a colossus in his heyday, commanding the respect and attention of thousands of people in the Central Valley and beyond. But he was also sued repeatedly for libel.

What makes this biography possible is access to a rich trove of sources. Only one other person, Bernard A. Shepard, has attempted to write extensively about McClatchy; Shepard wrote a doctoral thesis in 1960. He, however, lacked access to the preserved letter books and correspondence donated to the Center for Sacramento History by CK's grandson, also C. K. McClatchy, and the McClatchy Company in 1982. The McClatchy Papers consist of ten thousand linear feet of records related to the McClatchy family and the company. The most important portion of this extensive collection are the 287 press letter books (books containing copies of correspondence between the McClatchys and various individuals and businesses. In the days before carbon paper or photocopying, copies were made by pressing a typed or written letter to a thin sheet of porous paper using a vise-like press), each containing hundreds of pages of personal and official correspondence between Charles Kenny (CK) and his older brother, Valentine, and hundreds of correspondents. A careful scrutiny of the letter books provides the core of what appears in this volume. Likewise, a similar cache of letters—some highly personal—exists in the papers of CK's close friend and confidant, Hiram W. Johnson of California. Johnson's papers are located at the Bancroft Library at the University of California, Berkeley. A comparable collection was also found in the vaults of the *Bee* in 2005. The CK-Hiram letters touch on many issues of moment before the nation but also lay bare the editor's fears, hopes, disappointments, and challenges. These letters also reveal how much Hiram Johnson relied on the *Bee* and CK personally to prop him up when he found himself in the sloughs of depression or facing harsh political realities. Johnson had many friends and correspondents, but a special bond of intimacy and trust marks these letters—CK and Hiram were truly brothers in spirit.

The McClatchys have left a powerful imprint on the city of Sacramento in many ways. They were among the founding fathers and mothers of Sacramento—a family that did not abandon the city for San Francisco or the East, as so many others of prominence did in the nineteenth century. The McClatchys were invested in the building up of the California capital and were among those who saw the dynamic potential of an economically integrated Central Valley. They created the links of communication that knit together the communities from Mount Shasta to Bakersfield. They pressed for critical infrastructure reforms that would transform the region, including centrally directed and funded irrigation, an end to environmentally destructive mining, clean and free-flowing water for city residents, public ownership of common transportation and utilities, trees to shade the city during searing valley heat, and realistic public policies that would curtail petty urban corruption and crime. Their contribution to the arts and local culture, especially theater, dance, and music, continue to be a gift to Sacramentans. From their catbird seat in the state capital, they offered Californians a critical view of the functions of their state government. Because the McClatchys dominated the newspaper market, they were able to imprint a standard narrative on Sacramento that comported with their views of history and progress. Many Sacramentans acknowledged the hegemony of the McClatchys and the *Bee*—agreeing with their politics and guided by their views.

Yet others regarded the McClatchys with bitterness. CK preserved one letter that summed up the feelings of many:

> The *Bee* has for years dominated this city. It has controlled the election of public officials and their conduct in office. It has forced extravagant expenditures upon the city. It has bullied and browbeaten business men and private citizens until they have been afraid to oppose the *Bee* policies for fear of reprisals. . . . They have come to look upon Sacramento, upon the people of Sacramento, upon the property of the people of Sacramento as theirs in fee simple. To defy them has been to defy the Gods, to commit lèse majesté and to invite destruction by thunderbolts hurled from the cavern on Seventh Street [*Bee* offices].[7]

Sacramento Bee history obviously intersects with this narrative; however, this is not primarily a history of the newspaper. Steve Wiegand, a journalist commissioned by the *Bee,* has written a sturdy account of the *Bee*'s evolution from early days to the present. He consulted many of the same sources used in this book, and his account is succinct and accurate, though I may differ with him on some issues. The wider context of this biography is the history of the United States, California, and Sacramento from the end of the nineteenth century through the first third of the twentieth. On these subjects CK had an opinion about nearly everything. Political issues loomed front and center at the *Bee.* The proximity of the *Bee* to the sources of state power lent a quality to its writing that other newspapers did not have. CK also took a deep interest in his native Sacramento—goading it constantly to rise above its status as a provincial backwater and fiercely defending it from detractors.

In a move that CK would have hated and fought against, the McClatchy newspapers have today become the kind of syndicate that extends nationwide. The company already had begun acquiring midsized regional papers in the 1980s and 1990s. In 2006 the McClatchy Company purchased the Knight Ridder chain of newspapers. Today McClatchy Newspapers is the second-largest newspaper chain in the United States, publishing twenty-nine dailies in fourteen states with an average weekday circulation of 2.2 million, 2.8 million on Sunday. The McClatchy News Service has one of the most respected press bureaus in the business, capturing the I. F. Stone Award for its courageous coverage of the Iraq War, and the *Sacramento Bee* alone has received five Pulitzer Prizes.

CK would not have approved. He saw himself as a counterpoint to syndicate editors like William Randolph Hearst who owned the huge newspaper chains that "left editorial conduct . . . to subordinates who have generally no respect for the newspaper, nor care at all about its principles."[8] CK would worry that a newspaper corporation of this size would lose touch with its local constituency—that it could no longer be part of the fabric of the particular region, alert to its distinctive needs and problems, and helpful in knitting together a community of common understanding or at least offering a forum for public debate.

CK had plenty of enemies but also legions of admirers in Sacramento, who showed their respect by not only subscribing to his paper but by naming Sacramento's second high school after him. C. K. McClatchy High School was dedicated one year after CK's death—a testimony to his influence in the city of his birth, a city that had grown from a gold rush–era community to a prosperous state capital during his lifetime and with his support. Today students pass between two recumbent lions perched at the formal entrance. CK also had lions at the entrance of his home in Sacramento. He liked the image of lions—fearless and ferocious, always the leaders. They could also be taken as metaphors for CK's inner life: one motivated by courageous principles he inherited from his father, the other reflecting the passions of his heart: dramatic, sentimental, and at times vengeful. Both roared from the pages of the *Bee* for nearly fifty-three years.

Chapter One
Sacramento's Son

CHARLES KENNY McCLATCHY, the second son of James and Charlotte Feeney McClatchy, first saw the light of day on November 1, 1858. Known as "CK" from his childhood, he and his brother inherited the *Sacramento Bee* in 1883, and it came to dominate the journalism of the Central Valley. With the dogmatism of a pulpit preacher, CK published an eclectic amalgam of positions on everything from tree planting to U.S. foreign relations. Virtually nothing of importance escaped his attention and comment. His influence reached beyond the city to encompass the state and even the nation.

CK's mastery of a multiplicity of topics was often astounding. California—especially Northern California, which one of his staffers christened "Superior California"—was first and always his point of reference. Although an introvert, CK became a lion when he took up his pen—inveighing in colorful Dickensian or Shakespearean English or the archaic prose of the King James Bible—against whatever affronted his own moralistic worldview. In similarly effusive language he lauded his heroes, including giants like Abraham Lincoln and William Jennings Bryan but especially his father. By the time CK died in 1936, his quaint prose had been superseded by a new journalistic argot that cast the news in cooler, more modern terms. Still, his moralizing and crusading vision persisted at the *Sacramento Bee* well into the 1980s, perpetuated by his son, his daughter, a faithfully trained acolyte (Walter Jones), and his namesake and grandson, also CK.

James and Charlotte: Patriarch and Matriarch

CK's father, James, was born in Northern Ireland in 1824 and emigrated to New York in 1841. He became involved with local politics and acquainted with journalism through the legendary Horace Greeley, editor of the *New*

York Tribune. Lured by the promise of instant riches, James McClatchy made his way to California during the gold rush and sent articles back to Greeley describing circumstances on the Pacific coast. James was typical of many who came to the state during the gold rush: he was young, unmarried, and Irish. However, as with many who came, he found the hard work and privations of mining too difficult and returned to more genteel pursuits—politics, law enforcement, and journalism. In 1849 he began working for an array of Sacramento papers that came and went in the "upstart city." He also became involved in local politics, running for mayor and later for sheriff. At one point he thrust himself into the city's violent squatter riots of the early 1850s—as a defender of the squatters.

For a time his interests vacillated between journalism and politics, but James finally settled on journalism. He was not a founder of the *Bee* (as his sons would later assert) but joined the newspaper shortly after it had been founded in 1857, serving first as an assistant editor and then later as editor. His attachment to the *Bee* was not secure, and he tried out other newspapers and politics. However, after a stint as sheriff of Sacramento County in the mid-1860s, he acquired enough money to purchase a controlling share of the *Bee.* In 1872 he became majority owner but still had a partnership with a helpful friend who had a journalism background, General John Sheehan. James, however, was the main voice of the *Bee* from 1871 to his death in 1883.

In 1856 James met and married a Sacramento widow, Charlotte McCormack Feeney. Charlotte McCormack, born April 21, 1830, was a native of Charlottetown, Prince Edward Island, a British island colony off New Brunswick. Devoutly Roman Catholic, Charlotte and her sister, Harriet, taught school to provide their family with its meager income. In 1852 Charlotte carried on a letter-writing courtship with Captain Edward Feeney, a Mexican War veteran who had become a hotelier in Sacramento and married him in a proxy ceremony. She arrived in Sacramento in late 1852 (shortly after a disastrous fire had wiped out much of its early commercial district), and the couple lived in a small country home but returned to Sacramento for the birth of her first child, Emily, on October 20, 1854.

Charlotte's dreams of domestic bliss were shattered when her husband died of blood poisoning in November 1855. Her grief multiplied when baby Emily, a frail infant who had never been able to lift up her head, died on January 6, 1856. James, already working as an editor for the *Bee,* entered her life shortly afterward and proposed to her at the end of May 1856. After securing the consent of her mother, Charlotte and James wed on November 4, 1856 (Election Day) at St. Rose of Lima Church at Seventh and K streets. The rival *Sacramento Age* quipped, "Mac is bound to serve the country—getting married on Election Day!" The *Sacramento Union,* which had once condemned James as a "rabid squatter," wished "long life and every happiness to the wedded couple."[1]

Charlotte bore her first son, Valentine Stuart, named for James's childless brother and one of Charlotte's friends on Prince Edward Island, on August 29, 1857. On November 1, 1858, Charles Kenny was born, named for a brother of Charlotte's. Their first daughter, Fanny, was born in 1861. Charlotte brought herself to name her final child Emily, born in October 1862, after the child lost in the tragic winter of 1855–56. Two other sons did not survive their first year, James, who was born in October 1863 and died in June 1864, and another unnamed boy, who may have died in childbirth. Eventually the family settled in a comfortable walk-up at Third and P streets. Charlotte's sister, Harriet, joined the young family and soon went to work as a teacher and administrator in the city's public schools. Charlotte played a secondary role in McClatchy business affairs, although she occasionally had to mediate differences between the two sons. Never overly fond of Sacramento, she spent her final years in the Bay Area, where she and her unmarried daughter, Emily, moved in 1901. Charlotte died in 1916. Emily lived until 1946.[2]

The Sacramento Matrix

Sacramento was still a work in progress when CK was born. The California capital was a product of the gold rush era, one of the "instant cities" created when the "world rushed in" to the Golden State in 1848–49. Its compact urban grid extended eastward from the Sacramento River, with numbered streets going north and south and lettered streets going east and west. Two main arteries, J and K streets, formed the nucleus of the commercial district. Sacramento grew slowly—it did not claim 100,000 citizens until the 1930s, and for most of CK's life the city retained a small-town atmosphere. It prided itself on its survival in a commercially convenient but hydrographically precarious location at the confluence of the Sacramento and American rivers. It suffered terrible bouts of flooding by the rivers that embraced it. It contended with waterborne plagues and urban violence. In the tinder-dry summer months its wooden structures often caught fire, and entire city blocks burned.

However, the city's inhabitants always rebuilt—erecting higher levees, redirecting the American River to the north, raising city streets, welcoming

physicians to help combat disease, and constructing brick buildings to reduce the devastations of fire. Sacramento became California's capital in 1854
and for many years was the most important city in the four-hundred-mile
Central Valley.[3] An early city motto said it all. Sacramento was Urbs Indomita
(Indomitable City).

The McClatchys were part of the informal cadre of merchants and middle-class citizens who became stakeholders in Sacramento's future. Unlike other families, who began poor in Sacramento and left once they struck it rich,
the McClatchys, although tempted, never abandoned the community for the
more cosmopolitan (and cooler) climes of the Bay Area or the East Coast. In
1863 Sacramento became the western terminus of the transcontinental railroad. The Central Pacific (later folded into the Southern Pacific) erected a
small industrial plant to the north of the city, where it repaired and built the
railroad's rolling stock, providing steady work at good wages. Local canneries
and box companies received the produce of the surrounding fields, and the
rails of the Southern Pacific shipped the Sacramento-canned and -boxed fruits
and vegetables of the Central Valley to national markets, making Sacramento
an economically viable urban center.

The meridian of C. K. McClatchy's life was Sacramento. Glued together
by its close personal associations, it regularly reinvented itself to meet new
economic and social conditions. CK's journalistic depictions of Sacramento
became part of the city's master narrative. He and his writers even branded
portions of the city with enduring names such as "The Homes" (residential districts) or "Superior California" (for Northern California). Aided initially by his
brother Valentine, CK soon presided over an important newspaper corporation—later a journalism empire that was one of Sacramento's leading businesses. In a day when print journalism was a significant social force, CK's words
carried great weight in shaping public opinion in the capital city and in the
tributary areas the *Bee* served.

His hopes for Sacramento also made him one of the region's major "boom-
ers" (i.e., boosters) to outsiders. In 1894 the *Bee* published an elaborate tract
called the *Souvenir*—a parlor-table book containing many photographs and
effusively describing every aspect of the city (although CK later admitted some
of the articles were "of a rose tint"). He urged local representation at national
agricultural fairs—showing off the region's produce and even insisting that the
citrus fruits of the north were far better than those of the southland. He gave

precious publicity to street fairs and touted the city's strengths. He eagerly supported and celebrated the electrification of the city. He continually pressed for the improvement of the city's water, streets, and public appearance. Sacramento was a place where families could settle in comfortable homes. Homeowners, he argued, had "an interest in the community . . . in good strong levees, clean, well-watered streets, beautiful public plazas, good, high, well-constructed and fine appearing public buildings, handsome gardens, plentiful shade trees . . . excellent public schools, good drinking water." He was also aware of its liabilities. In 1903, when legislators threatened to move the state capital to San Jose, he urged the city to shake off its provincialism and to stop acting like a backwater "of the hamlet order and the village persuasion."[4]

But woe to others who criticized Sacramento. CK fiercely defended his hometown and took umbrage at any public comment denigrating the community. He once even chastised the Rand McNally company for giving Sacramento short shrift in a guide to the Pacific coast. His favorite targets were various state legislators and public servants who lamented their exile to Sacramento during their terms of state service. When one San Francisco representative complained to the *San Francisco Examiner* that Sacramento was an eyesore, CK archly replied, "The various State Departments in the Capitol building are full of Roman-nosed young men who tip-tilt their nostrils at everything in this fair city of ours . . . and who are forever telling everybody how sorry they are that they are forced to live in Sacramento. We do not know that any lasso has been thrown around their necks." Reminding the legislators that "five trains leave here daily for San Francisco," he bluntly advised them to go home. "In the meantime, we suggest that they give Samson's traditional weapon (the jawbone of an ass) a rest." He verbally spanked ministers of religion who sometimes condemned the city as a new Sodom and Gomorrah in order to frighten congregants. He chided one local businessman, who faintly praised Sacramento as "simply the capital of the State and a nice place in which to live, nothing more," writing, "This is scarcely the way in which a merchant of Sacramento should speak of Sacramento on the outside." He acknowledged that "Sacramento is certainly not a Golconda in wealth, nor an Athens in architectural beauty and grandeur" but declared it was something more than "a nice place in which to live." He noted its many homes, its transportation (river and rail) facilities, railroad shops, magnificent art gallery, benign climate, broad drives, and arching trees. "Sacramento is as orderly, as quiet, as respectable a community as there is on God's green footstool, where the chime of the church bells sounds on the reverent and is never listened to by any but respectful ears."[5]

Throughout his life he praised the tree-lined streets of his youth. As a young boy he had climbed the remaining cottonwood and scrub oak stands that once dotted the city. When these disappeared, he endorsed efforts to plant the streets with trees to provide shade in the scorching summer heat. If merchants complained that the trees blocked the signage on their shops, he dismissed their concerns, pointing to the wide arboreal drives of Paris and Rome. In November 1915 he wrote to Senator James D. Phelan to report "the sentiment is growing that shade trees especially in warm climates, are not only an advantage but a positive comfort and almost a necessity on business streets. . . . These shade trees will lower the temperature in front of those places [city businesses] on the warmest summer day from twelve to eighteen degrees."[6] Whenever a tree was cut down, the *Bee* supposedly flew its flag at half-staff.

But concern for city and region was only part of his wider agenda. CK was also a California reformer. CK's editorials and reporting reflected the season of reform that swept California and the nation in the late nineteenth and early twentieth centuries. He eagerly supported California's version of the Populist movement and maintained a lifelong friendship with William Jennings Bryan, the Democratic Populist. CK aligned himself with the brand of California progressivism advanced by his close friend Hiram Johnson—so much so that the *Bee* was a virtual mouthpiece for Johnson. Although CK never accepted the agenda of any political party or movement in toto (for example, he hated Progressive-era prohibition), he nevertheless gave his readers a steady diet of crusading editorials. CK decried monopoly—first of land but also of transportation, communications, and power. He could scarcely conceal his contempt for the obscene fortunes of the elite—often ill-gotten by the exploitation of workers or the corruption of elected officials. In contrast "The People," which he always capitalized, had no more ardent champion than CK. He lionized those like Bryan and Johnson who shared his views—even for a time Franklin Roosevelt. Some of CK's journalistic crusades were prophetic and eventually met success—sometimes many years after he first espoused them; others were nothing more than stubborn rantings against reality and even tragically incorrect.

He was inconsistent in his application of these principles. He loved the worker but was suspicious of, and often hostile to, organized labor. He hated monopoly but did everything he could to make his newspaper the main news source in the Central Valley. He venerated the First Amendment, unless radical groups were using it to protest war or challenge corporate power. While personally kind and courteous, CK could also be vindictive. He rarely forgave a political or personal enemy. He crowed loudly when his enemies were vanquished or disgraced and kicked them when they were down. His dark side eventually led to a permanent estrangement from his brother (although the contempt was mutual). He loved his family and lavished on them every gift within his power. But they brought much sadness and tension into his life and he into theirs. His lowest moment came when he was forced to depose his son and heir from the leadership of the newspaper.

The Young McClatchy

CK grew up with the city of Sacramento. When he was a toddler, he and his family had to flee the city during the floods of 1861–62. He watched in awe as loads of dirt were dumped to raise streets and looked on as mudjackers cranked up buildings to the new city levels. Because his father was active in local politics and journalism, CK was present in January 1863 when the first shovels of dirt were turned at the foot of Third Street for the building of the Central Pacific. He observed the erection of the handsome state capitol complex begun in 1864 and finally completed in 1871. Walking around the small town with his father, CK became intrigued with politics—and the biannual meetings of the state legislature, which quickened city life as legislators poured into city hotels and boardinghouses to transact the state's business. He became a friend— but more often the mortal enemy—of governors, state officials, members of the legislature, and various local politicians.

From the few personal fragments about Charles's early life, we know he enjoyed good health and was quiet and shy although willing to engage in typical boyhood pranks such as stealing watermelons. Thomas Fox, a childhood companion, recalled spending the 1860s "learning to swim along with a kid named Charles K. McClatchy in the old brick yard."[7] He was close to his brother Valentine ("Vallie"), although even in childhood the two had very different temperaments. The more outgoing and athletic Valentine enjoyed competitive games and was better at his studies. Young CK was less athletic and far more introverted than his brother. Even as a little boy he was called CK—in the days before such initials were considered an informal shorthand for a person's full name. His close friends knew him as Charlie.

CK attended Sacramento's public schools where his aunt, Harriet McCormack, taught. His first lessons were taken in the city's first brick school-house, the three-story Franklin School, erected at Sixth and L streets and dedicated the year of McClatchy's birth.[8] The building held the city's high school on the top floor, a grammar school on the second floor, and in the basement, the primary school. Each floor had but one classroom—though the upper had separate rooms for art and music—and one teacher who drilled the students in roughly divided age groups in the curriculum of those days. Here CK learned to read and write a legible hand (penmanship was taught by two gentlemen whom CK praised in later years). He also acquired a patriotic version of American history that remained with him for his entire life. Later in life he waged verbal war on anyone who questioned this filiopietistic version of the American past; among those he attacked was one of the University of California's most respected historians, H. Morse Stephens, who offered a revisionist view of the causes of the American Revolution.

CK loved Franklin School because it gave him the opportunity to mix with the various social and ethnic groups living in Sacramento. Years later, when he was trying to talk his daughter-in-law out of sending his grandson to an elite boarding school in Colorado, CK extolled the democratic experience of rubbing shoulders with so many different types of people in Sacramento, as he had done at Franklin School.[9]

A Small Village

Franklin School brought him into close association with the relatively small company of men and women who lived in Sacramento their whole lives. Sacramento was a modest-sized town, where people intermarried and social contacts were easy to make and sometimes impossible to avoid. The compactness of the city grid brought people into physical proximity in ways not possible in larger metropolises. Common use of city institutions—churches, school, banks, retail houses, and the like—reinforced interpersonal bonds. The McClatchys knew everybody and everybody knew them. Sometimes CK made a blood sport of destroying his enemies—using information he acquired through local gossip or by private detectives. At the same time many knew that CK was an alcoholic and at times saw him staggering on the street. Some of the animosities stemmed from childhood feuds. Sometimes these feuds gave way to friendship, as in the case of CK and his closest friend, Hiram

Johnson. Others remained foes for life. McClatchy based his comments on local conditions—not only on the due diligence of the *Bee*'s reporters but also on long-standing networks of personal knowledge, intermarriage, and friendships made and broken over the years. Likewise his connections with various California politicians stemmed from personal interaction and visits with them at their homes, in taverns, or on vacations at California resorts.

In his years as editor of the *Bee,* McClatchy steadfastly refused to join local churches and clubs or to publicly lend his name to fund-raising or other projects for fear of jeopardizing his ability to speak critically about them. Yet CK knew well many of Sacramento's most prominent and humble citizens. He regularly eulogized the old-timers, contemporaries of his revered father's, and also noted the passing of ordinary citizens whom CK met through the years, for example, the boot black at a local corner, the barber who gave CK tips about legislators, and the gardener who planted flowers and trees in Capitol Park. On other occasions CK used what he knew about them to skewer those whom he considered hypocrites. For example, when a local lawyer lectured on public morality and railed against the city's red light district, CK reminded a correspondent that the lawyer's own sons were regular clients of a local madam.[10] When the legislature voted to suppress red light districts throughout the state (a fool's errand in CK's view; he advocated regulating them instead), CK decried the hypocrisy of the outraged moralists who pushed the legislation:

> I was born in the City of Sacramento, and I can point to a long list of distinguished names of the principal pew-holders in the Churches of this community who made their money from renting such [immoral] places; and I can show you the pedigree of some of the distinguished citizens of Sacramento the basis of whose fortunes were just that same proposition; and I can tell you that the ex-president of the Tuesday Club and an ex-Mayor of the city and one of the most devoted 'Christian women' who accepted these rents at an exorbitant figure and would today if it hadn't become so unpopular.[11]

From time to time he had to offend friends in order to be faithful to his profession. To one sorrowful soul CK noted: "As Editor of The *Bee*, I conceive it to be my duty to publish public news. . . . If such publication hurts my friends, I feel extremely sorry; but still I do not shirk from what I consider to be my duty."[12] However, in this as with other expressions of unflinching principles, he made exceptions.

Dear Old Santa Clara

If CK had been the son of a railroad worker or an employee of the canneries, his formal education would have ended long before his graduation from Franklin School. But because he had some money, and a strongly religious mother, McClatchy attended Jesuit Santa Clara College (just as his sisters attended the convent school run by the Sisters of Notre Dame in San Jose).[13] Founded on the grounds of the old Mission Santa Clara near San Jose in 1851, this college began in makeshift buildings that soon gave way to the ambitious plans of the Swiss-born Burchard Villiger, S.J., who built a campus complex around the old mission. A Southern Pacific rail line, extending south from San Francisco, ran through Santa Clara and provided a stop-off for students and their parents.

The school was a combination high school and college, mostly made up of boarders like the McClatchy brothers but also day students. Santa Clara's curriculum was governed by the Jesuit Ratio Studiorum, a sixteenth-century program of studies used worldwide. The Ratio prescribed a rigorous course of studies devoted to the humanities: classical languages, history, and rhetoric. Valentine McClatchy entered the college in 1871. The next year, on August 5, 1872, CK entered. The college had an enrollment of 186 students when CK arrived and grew to more than 275 by the time he left. Both young men resided in the big dormitory called "the Ship," built by President Aloysius Varsi. A corps of Jesuit brothers performed most of the manual labor, including raising the food and produce for the table. Meals may not have been to everyone's liking, but the Italian-born Jesuits insisted on wine at lunch and dinner—perhaps beginning CK's lifelong "affection for the grape." The college exercised in loco parentis control of student life, closely monitoring the personal behavior of their charges (with whom the Jesuits shared quarters in the large dormitory) and administering punishments for infractions of the rules. The most common punishment was enforced detention in a room called "Letter A"; it was held on either Thursday or Sunday afternoon, and there "delinquents in studies and discipline made reparation for their shortcomings." The punishments often involved memorizing passages from speeches or the Bible but also at times copying numbers of lines. Lines could apparently be assigned arbitrarily by professors, and if a student accumulated a thousand lines, he could be dismissed. CK came nowhere near receiving the dreaded thousand lines, but on one occasion he received eighty for smoking—a habit he later detested in others.[14]

The atmosphere resembled a Roman Catholic seminary where students could not leave the campus except for vacations or on monthly visiting days, when parents could pick them up but had to have them back by dark. Studies were demanding, and the college had an array of extracurricular events. CK was not interested in athletics (in fact the school did not have much in the way of intramural sports in the 1870s), but he joined the college's Philhistorian Debating Society, learning the rules of debate on issues of the day.[15]

Each month the lads received grades for both conduct and diligence—the latter referred to the amount of effort and seriousness they brought to their studies. CK's scores in both areas were average to low. His worst grades were in diligence, which reflected faculty opinion of his seriousness as a student. These were consistently in the sixties and seventies (out of one hundred), even dipping into the fifties on some occasions, although the first two months of 1875 found him in the nineties—perhaps the result of a scolding by his parents during the Christmas holidays.

CK had few positive things to say about Santa Clara until later in life, but some Jesuits, especially Edmund Young and Robert E. Kenna, left a definite impression. Young, from Maryland, had once served as a page in the U.S. Senate and formed the student debating society based on the rules of that body. Young's classwork in eloquence insisted on precision of expression in debating questions of the day. He also revolutionized the debating format used by the Philhistorians. Rather than follow the format of traditional debate, Young urged his charges to engage in the lively give-and-take reminiscent of the old-fashioned debates on the floors of Congress. He urged the young men to think on their feet, instead of preparing text, and to deliver ripostes and jabs as part of the exercise. "Father Young was an optimist," one former Santa Clara student recalled. "He saw the best in everyone, and by his warm and unstinted praise succeeded in promoting the natural talents of the debaters to a very high degree of cultivation." Young had a powerful influence on McClatchy's writing style.[16]

Robert E. Kenna was also an English teacher and became a close friend of McClatchy's. Kenna became president of Santa Clara on two different occasions—from 1888 to 1893 and again from 1899 to 1905. During his second presidency he reached out to the now prominent CK and brought him back in 1901 to receive an honorary degree when the school celebrated its fiftieth anniversary. Kenna's flattery and personal support transformed CK into an affectionate booster of "dear old Santa Clara." He relied on the priest as an adviser and friend and offered his paper's assistance in pushing Kenna's successful efforts to set aside a stand of redwoods in Big Basin Park.[17] However, after Kenna's death CK reverted to his former indifference to Santa Clara—especially its appeals for money. Responding in 1915 to an alumni survey card, he insisted, "I did not graduate from Santa Clara College. I missed my degree being . . . lacking in mathematics. Twenty-five years subsequently I was given an honorary degree. I do not think under the circumstances that I am entitled to be called a graduate of your university."[18]

Indeed academic troubles—especially with math—were the reason CK gave when asked why he left the college abruptly sometime during the 1875–76 academic year. The subject of his departure reveals a subtheme of CK's life: his propensity to make things up or embellish tales of his youth and family life. One wonders whether academic deficiency was the true cause of his departure, because, as the historian Gerald McKevitt has suggested, the flexibility of the Santa Clara curriculum at the time and the various options available for boys of different academic levels would have precluded dismissal for such a reason. CK probably did have trouble with mathematics, but his spotty diligence may tell us more about his departure. In all likelihood he was bored with formal education. Moreover, to the consternation of his pious mother, he had also distanced himself from the Catholic Church while still a student at Santa Clara. According to an 1896 letter written to friend and fellow editor James Barry, who mistook him for a non-Catholic, CK noted: "I was instructed in the Catholic Church"; however, "I had nothing to do with the Catholic Church long before I left college and long before I escaped the years of indiscretion."[19] Interestingly, religious instruction took up few classroom hours. Santa Clara students had one hour of catechism on Sunday and no formal classes in doctrine or other Catholic teachings. Yet CK did not become an atheist or even an agnostic—nor could he quite shake his Catholic heritage. He admitted as much when traveling abroad and observed Jews who tried to distance themselves from what he considered their racial and religious heritage: "I can understand how either [man or woman] can change a religion. But the conscientious Jews are like the conscientious Catholics—very few forsake their religion from principle."[20]

In place of organized religion CK adopted a highly personal moralistic religiosity similar to Charles Dickens's and rejected adherence to dogma in favor of kindness and generosity. CK had no use for hymn-singing moralists, pompous preachers, or prayer as a substitute for practical charity. He utterly detested missionaries, whom he considered ideological imperialists with no business imposing their faith on people who had their own religious beliefs. On some occasions he accepted the rather unusual view (for that time) that all religions were equal, "some of them more ancient [than Christianity] and not less moral." He enjoyed the company of certain clergy if they were charitable and good natured, such as the Catholic bishop of Sacramento, Thomas Grace, who was godfather to CK's daughter Eleanor, or Grace's Episcopalian counterpart, William Moreland. CK also doted on literary types such as Monsignor Thomas Capel, an expatriate British scholar and lecturer clouded by personal scandal who landed in Sacramento. To the annoyance of the city's pastors CK frequently praised the "infidel agnostic," Robert Ingersoll. CK had nothing but scorn for traditional preachers who made Christianity "repulsive by the dark and terrible superstitions which they evoke from [the pages of the Bible] and to which they attribute the absolute authority of a vengeful and jealous God."[21] Although he often evoked a sensitivity to the Catholic liturgy and culture he had known in his youth, he never looked back nostalgically on his childhood faith.

After leaving Santa Clara free of religion and formal education, CK gratefully returned home from college, and his father put him to work at the *Bee*. In November 1879, on his twenty-first birthday, CK became a partner in the paper.[22]

Valentine

Although CK had ingloriously exited Santa Clara, Valentine continued his higher studies at the Jesuit college. Unlike his brother, who wrote nothing for the college paper, Valentine published a series of articles in the *Owl*.[23] Although his topics were of a literary nature, Valentine's writing took a more scientific and rigorous bent than his dreamy brother's. Valentine finished his bachelor of science degree in June 1877 with honors. His final project was a demonstration of the physical (luminous) effects of voltaic electricity. Even though he, too, abandoned his childhood Catholic faith, he took the Owl Association's gold medal for his essay, "The Existence of God." However, Valentine's academic accomplishments apparently did not overly impress the self-educated James, who was in the Northeast and did not attend his elder son's graduation. Charles may have been papa's favorite, because of his desire to return to the *Bee* and to work his way up through the various departments of the newspaper. The proximity to James also helped shape CK's political opinions as he listened carefully to his father's take on various matters.

The Passing of the Patriarch

James McClatchy had been in ill health since 1877, gradually slowing in his workload and taking extended breaks from the relentless demands of the newspaper. CK had joined the staff in 1876 as a writer and sampled the array of jobs in the business. In mid-October 1883 James had gone to the thermal springs of Paraiso, California, leaving Charles behind to tend the day-to-day dealings of the *Bee*. On Monday, October 21, James suffered a slight stroke. Charlotte called Valentine and Emily to their father's bedside, and he appeared to rally on Tuesday. But by Wednesday of that week James's condition deteriorated, and a frantic telegram went to Charles and Fanny in Sacramento to hurry to Paraiso Springs. James died on October 25, 1883, at about four in the afternoon. Although he made no public statement, CK no doubt was crushed by his father's death.

James had acquired much since his penniless days in early Sacramento. Even before he died, he had begun to parcel out his holdings. In 1881 he had given his daughters, Fanny and Emily, his share of the *Bee* building. In 1882 he had turned over to Charlotte the family home and the lots he held on Fifteenth, Sixteenth, J, and K streets. In May 1882 he had given his sons the reclamation lands he owned north of Sacramento. He had appointed Valentine and Charles as executors of his estate, but the more business-savvy Valentine did most of the work to complete the arrangements. James had requested that his business ventures, which were valued at $18,837.05, be parceled out. He willed 280.75 shares in the Gas Company to his daughters, with the proviso that the income derived from them would go to Charlotte, who was also the beneficiary of a $5,000 life insurance policy. James left his twenty shares in the Union Building and Loan to his daughters, but since he had a debt of $3,250 to the D. O. Mills Bank and had left cash bequests to various relatives, these were sold to cover the debts and the bequests. The most important bequest, his half ownership of the *Bee*, was left to Charlotte, who received one-fourth of the whole, and to Charles and Valentine, who each received one-eighth.[24]

CK Marries

In 1885 CK married a portly young schoolteacher, Elizabeth Ellen "Ella" Kelly. Ella was born in Philadelphia on March 4, 1861, the youngest in the brood of the Irish immigrants Patrick and Eleanor McDermott Kelly.[25] Patrick Kelly died shortly after the Civil War, and Eleanor bundled the family and made her way to Sacramento by way of the Isthmus of Panama. She first appears in the city directories as residing at 82 N Street, between Second and Third. Tax records indicate she was a tenant and not the owner of the home. It is not clear how she supported herself and her young children, but most likely she took in wash and did domestic work. At some point she had her own lodgings and took in boarders and extended family members who paid some rent.

A large part of Ella's life revolved around the local Catholic church. Ella and her mother went to Mass faithfully, and both were involved with church picnics and women's groups the church sponsored. In 1879 Ella was inducted into the largest group of young Catholic women in her parish, the Children of Mary, and she treasured the fancy certificate handed out on that occasion. Ella attended St. Joseph Academy at Eighth and G streets, a small boarding and day school run by the Sisters of Mercy. After an expansion of the school's facilities in the 1870s, the state certified it as an academy, allowing the Sisters of Mercy to award teaching certificates to its graduates.[26] Ella was one of the first to receive this certificate in 1878. She excelled in her studies and was selected class valedictorian. Ella looked back on her years at St. Joseph's with gratitude and for her entire life cherished a warm loyalty to the school and to the Sisters of Mercy. Despite her husband's and children's withdrawal from the Catholic Church, she remained staunchly loyal to her faith. Always quite generous with the church, she raised money for St. Joseph's and various Catholic charities and contributed adornments to the chapel of St. Patrick Orphanage (later St. Rose Church) and to the Cathedral of the Blessed Sacrament.[27] CK's occasional feuds with Catholic clerics or periodic editorial swipes at Catholic beliefs and practices may have set her nerves on edge, but there is no evidence they argued over religion. He transported her to Mass every Sunday, and while she prayed he worked in his office. The children were all baptized and reared as Catholics, although like CK they ceased attending church when they attained the age of majority.[28]

Ella was at times an emotionally fragile and hypersensitive individual. Over the years CK learned that certain kinds of news had to be kept from her—or so he thought—especially minor injuries to the children or any kind of divergence from religious practice. On the other hand Ella also had a "she-who-must-be-obeyed" side to her personality—and in fact that is what most people who spoke about her remembered. CK accorded her broad leeway to run the home as she wished, and he was never miserly with money, allowing her to purchase what she needed for herself, the children, and the house; she made all the travel arrangements for the couple, who in later years spent many months at a time abroad. She managed the construction of the family home on U Street—overseeing every detail with the architect and making sure her plans were carried out to the last letter. She worried incessantly about her children and sometimes with good cause. While there were likely the normal tensions of marriage and no doubt consternation over CK's drinking, any kind of domestic tension would be impossible to know because the McClatchys were so intensely private. The veil of secrecy was lifted only once, when Ella challenged her husband's plans to turn the assets of the paper over to their son, Carlos, she demanded that their daughters receive a fair share of ownership and profits of the *Bee,* rather than the mere pension CK had planned. Ella prevailed.

CK was nearly three years her senior, and she may have met him through her brother Jim, an affable barfly who frequented some of the same watering holes as CK. The couple was married at St. Rose Church on February 12, 1885, by the Reverend (later Bishop) Thomas Grace. William McKenna, the foreman of the typographers at the *Bee,* stood up for CK, and Esther Green, a friend from school years, was maid of honor for Ella. CK recalled his financial condition at the time of his marriage, after his own daughter had eloped with a somewhat improvident young man: "The day I was married I hadn't a cent to my name and I owed some $1300."[29] The couple rented quarters at 1416 Third Street and lived there until they purchased a comfortable home at 1015 O Street, where Ella's mother joined them until her death at ninety in 1909. They remained at this address until 1913, when they built a new residence at Twenty-second and U streets.

Their first child, Charlotte, named for CK's mother, was born on October 3, 1887. A series of lost pregnancies may have followed, because the second child, Carlos, was not born until March 2, 1891. Eleanor, named for her Grandmother Kelly, arrived on September 27, 1895. As noted, all the children were baptized in the Catholic Church, and priests served as godfathers for both Carlos (Rev. Thomas McSweeney) and Eleanor (Rev. Thomas Grace, who also baptized her).

CK and Val at the *Bee*

Tall and mustachioed, forthright, and even brash, CK was perhaps a bit overawed by the thought of succeeding his father and was often in the shadow of his more extroverted elder brother. Nonetheless, as he grew in confidence CK brought all his readers into his carefully constructed world of heroes and villains. With him they stood at Armageddon and battled for the Lord; his sense of righteousness often gave his writing by turns a thundering or sarcastic tone. However, his blunt moralizing often created false straw men whom he either vilified or beatified—and he sometimes oversimplified the complexities of public issues.

The division of labor seemed to flow naturally from the two sons' particular gifts. Charles tended primarily to the editorial side of the paper—thereby giving the *Bee* its public persona. Valentine handled the business end of things— working with advertisers, improving circulation, and keeping an eagle eye on the evolving technology of newspaper production. He took the lead in personnel decisions but deferred widely to Charles in the selection of people who worked in the news department. Valentine also took a hand at editorial writing or at least influencing the content of *Bee* positions on certain issues. The delicate relationship between the news content and the economic viability of the paper was also subject to the informal give and take of the brothers' relationship. CK was by his choice less interested in the practicalities of running the paper—seeming at times befuddled by changes.[30] CK was always worried about any potential expansion of the paper because he believed it made the papers too cold and impersonal and not connected to local culture. Unlike his brother, CK was not much of a risk taker when it came to spending. He had an insecurity with finances that made him quite conservative.

In addition to his newspaper duties, Valentine managed extensive real estate holdings in the city of Sacramento and throughout the region—some of which he inherited from his father and others he managed for his brother. These property holdings were the source of a growing personal fortune and the origin of Valentine's later career in real estate. Real estate management must have consumed a lot of Valentine's extra time.[31] In 1887 he became a member of a consortium of land speculators led by David A. Lindley and bought up blocks of city property south of N Street and east to Thirty-first. Valentine also enticed his younger brother and even his mother to join these efforts to develop Sacramento. Like any good land speculator, he diversified his investments and purchased land in all parts of the state. Valentine also held substantial stock holdings.[32]

In the late 1880s Valentine became heavily involved in the creation of a fruit colony (a settlement among groves of fruit-bearing trees, often citrus) in eastern Sacramento County called Orange Vale (later Orangevale). Formerly known as the Rancho San Juan, Orange Vale was to be a developer's dream—with streets running east and west every quarter mile and north and south every half mile. The first families arrived from Canada in 1888, and the developers started building homes and the Hotel Villa. By 1895 all the avenues and parcels had been laid out, and on September 18, 1895, the county recorded the official map of the Orange Vale colony. However, the 1880s land boom ended in the Panic of 1893, and by 1896 land sales became nearly impossible and the company folded.[33]

Valentine also held a number of tenant properties. One was the McClatchy Ranch, six miles north of Sacramento—a pasturage area he owned with CK—that they rented out to a livestock farmer in 1906 and also to a hunting club. Valentine haggled over rents, oversaw the payment of mortgages and taxes, and in particular paid close attention to the flow of water on these properties.[34]

In an effort to promote newspaper circulation and the future prosperity of the McClatchy land holdings, the *Bee* consistently advertised the benefits of living in Northern California. In 1892 the *Bee* produced the elaborate multipage *Souvenir* book, which described the advantages of life in Northern California—depicting in glowing terms the climate, soil, economic possibilities of the region, and especially Sacramento as an up-and-coming metropolis that was shaking off its antiquated ways to embrace a new era of development.[35] These prodevelopment news stories and editorials also exposed the McClatchys to accusations of conflict of interest—or of advocating public policies that had the indirect effect of enhancing their personal wealth. As CK once boasted on the pages of the *Bee*: "The McClatchys own more real estate in the City of Sacramento than any other family . . . this is said not boastfully but simply to indicate their faith in the city and their permanent selfish interest in its prosperity."[36]

The Brothers McClatchy: A Loving but Intense Relationship

The rivalry that may have existed between the two brothers since their youth began to ooze out. Both brothers took monthlong vacations during the summer—Valentine went often to Tahoe, where he had purchased property, and CK to some cool spot along the ocean or in the mountains. When one was gone, the other had control of the absentee's department. But already in 1889, CK had begun his penchant for taking long trips and leaving work behind for his brother. In that year CK traveled to the Pacific Northwest with Ella and Charlotte. In fact for most of his career CK, Ella, and occasionally Eleanor were away from Sacramento and the business for extended periods. Valentine let it be known—especially to their mother—that he was becoming increasingly peeved with the work habits of his younger brother. As it turned out these trips were more than vacations for CK—he needed them in order to dry out.

In the aftermath of his father's death, CK may have resumed a drinking habit he probably picked up at Santa Clara. CK soon became a habitué of the circle of drinking establishments around the *Bee* building at Third and J, frequenting a series of taverns, including the Golden Eagle at Seventh and K, the Office Saloon on Fourth Street, the Capital Saloon at Second and J, and Gruhler's Saloon at Fifth and J, after the *Evening Bee* "was put to bed" around three o'clock in the afternoon. His drinking became the talk of small-town Sacramento as many people saw him inebriated and worried about his health and well-being, as well as that of his wife and children. CK's bluntly stated opinions and public ridicule often angered people in Sacramento and elsewhere. According to one urban legend, California Secretary of State Charles Curry was so offended by McClatchy for some unknown reason that he hit the editor over the head with a cuspidor at the Golden Eagle saloon.[37] Whether this was true or not, CK's drinking attracted some unfavorable opinion. One of his critics was the future father-in-law of his son, Carlos, Dr. William E. Briggs, whose daughter Phebe recalled in an interview: "He [Dr. Briggs] could look out of the window of his office every afternoon and CK would leave The *Bee* office which was just across the street and there was a saloon on the corner . . . he [Dr. Briggs] would see CK come out of the saloon staggering and go home and he did that so often that it was distressing." She further commented, "I think CK's countenance showed the effect of having been a heavy drinker."[38]

Liquor loosened his tongue, and with his confidants he swapped political gossip and shared good times. Drinking with male companions may also have provided this rather quiet and undemonstrative man with an outlet for pent-up emotions. But the drinking was excessive, for a time imperiling his work, family life, and public reputation.

Valentine confronted his brother on several occasions and eked out pledges for reform. Whatever CK promised Valentine was soon forgotten as CK shared good cheer with old childhood chums like Will Huntoon and Al Johnston (later the state printer of California), who frequently raised glasses with the young editor. Valentine often found himself bearing the brunt of work while his brother was indisposed by drunkenness or a hangover. In one attempt to cure his brother, Valentine banished Huntoon and Johnston and sent CK on a sea cruise along the coast then through Panama to New York in the summer of 1889. Writing bluntly to his brother in New York, Valentine gave CK an ultimatum: "1889 is the last year that I will maintain business relations that shall be a source of anxiety by day and worry by night . . . the only condition under which in fairness to myself (aside from my desire to save you) I can longer maintain our past business relations is that you become and remain permanently a total abstainer."[39]

Valentine also drafted a circular letter to the local taverns his brother frequented, informing them of the terms of a March 1889 law, which Valentine had personally lobbied to passage, preventing the sale of liquor to "persons addicted to the inordinate use of intoxicating liquors." He noted, "Charles K. McClatchy is a person addicted to the inordinate use of intoxicating liquors." He warned them that if they sold CK "any spirituous, vinous, or malt liquor, you will be guilty under the provisions of said act of misdemeanor, punishable by imprisonment not exceeding six months, or by fine not exceeding two hundred dollars or by both such fine and imprisonment."[40] In the end Valentine never saw a single tavern owner prosecuted—nor did he wean his brother away from liquor.

CK returned from his enforced 1889 vacation literally sobered to the realities of life. Valentine's skepticism about his brother's ability to conquer his addiction to alcohol was well founded—because he never did. CK regularly imbibed wine and other spirits with assorted cronies and chums, some of whom were his political and professional allies. In fact his personal regard for people seemed to increase once he found they shared his love of alcohol. In contrast he often discarded political allies when they differed with him on the question of liquor. The advent of Prohibition and the divided stands many of his friends took on the issue, often led him to break his bonds with them— with the possible exception of Hiram Johnson, who voted for the ratification of the Eighteenth Amendment. Liquor took its toll on his life and energy, and CK regularly traveled to spas and baths in California and abroad to detoxify for a time and clear his mind. But bouts of drinking recurred, no doubt when he was away from Ella and the children and often on the way home from work. McClatchy was particularly prone to pratfalls and accidents. In 1913 he was no doubt inebriated when his coat caught in the door of a streetcar that then dragged him several feet. This kept him at home for a number of weeks nursing a badly injured left arm. However, Valentine's threat to pull away from the management of the paper must have scared CK sober—or at least was enough to curtail his drinking and persuade him to pay more attention to his duties. At least at the outset of their partnership the two brothers realized they needed each other to make the *Bee* a success.

Chapter Two
An Editor's Vision

———————————◆———————————

CK'S DEBUT AS an editorial writer came shortly after the resolution of the tumultuous 1876 election and the inauguration of the Republican Rutherford B. Hayes (whom the *Bee* had supported). With CK's ascension James began to take time away from the paper, and CK not only wrote but took on some administrative responsibilities. He began with a short punchy column called "Notes," a compilation of wry and sometimes snide comments on local, state, and national issues. "Notes" first appeared on March 6, 1877, and continued for some years. Later he created a more extended column he called "Private Thinks" or "Merely Some Private Thinks" (or "Think" if it was a single-topic column) that allowed him to comment on several, sometimes disparate, issues.[1] In a review of CK's early writings the publicist Hugh Mohan compared CK's prose to the artistry of the English artist William Hogarth: "He will make you laugh when you least expect to do so, and so pungent sometimes is he and sarcastic, if you will that few imagine such deep reflection emanating from the brain of a young man of twenty-one summers."[2]

Initially CK labored over a piece, writing it out by hand and reworking it as time allowed. However, as deadlines and correspondence became more demanding, he took to dictating his editorials—with the exception of the "Thinks," which he always handwrote. No one exceeded C. K. McClatchy's love for the English language, which he admired for its firmness and directness. He flatly rejected the overly complex sentence structure of Latin. "A Latinized writer of English generally must become windy," he observed. "If a man have the proper material in him, the best way in which to bring it out so he will write good, clean, strong, clear English is to leave Latin alone; study and study and study the combined brevity and force of the English in the King James edition of the Bible; read and read and re-read Shakespeare—that is enough. It is about all Abraham Lincoln had from which to shape the masterly English that was his."[3]

The Mind of the Editor

As for the content of his writing, CK accumulated a vast storehouse of wisdom from extensive reading of magazines, the *Congressional Record,* the acts of the state legislature, and items he read in newspaper exchanges (often complimentary subscriptions) with contemporaries, as editors referred to their rivals near and far. His columns frequently goaded, needled, or ridiculed—often with a tone of self-righteousness, sarcasm, or exasperation. He delighted in exposing hypocritical actions by politicians or other public figures.

In 1917 a professor at the University of Missouri asked him to suggest books "general in character" that were "indispensable or at least eminently desirable for the library of a working newspaper man." CK urged a thorough familiarity with the U.S. Constitution and the "essential laws of his own State; with the general plan of municipal government of his own and other cities." He also advised a familiarity with the methods of government in other countries and other cities. To keep up to date, the newspaperman had to keep current with the "whys and wherefores, the pros and cons of the newer problems in the government of today." The journalist should be "at least fairly well informed on the subject of municipal playgrounds, parks, sanitation, housing, and public utilities generally." CK recommended "one or two histories of the United States." He also suggested the *Congressional Record* as a good source for "both sides of dominant American issues," urging "some conception of the newest things in modern science and general progress" from "current periodicals of high class."[4]

However, he also insisted that the sheer accumulation of practical knowledge was not enough. For CK a newspaper writer should also look to the example of great men, literary figures, and the sacred scriptures. "He should also have the lives of some of the greater Americans whose labors really added to the greatness of the country, and more particularly the Life of Abraham Lincoln. He should possess some of the speeches of our greatest Americans. . . . He should know the Bible thoroughly, and be saturated with Shakespeare. I do not suggest anything in the way of reading for the formation of a style but the Bible and Shakespeare. These are enough."[5] His attachment to Shakespeare, especially the tragedies, was especially formative. He loved the Bard of Stratford-on-Avon for his use of language, the subtlety of his plots, and his clear sense of good and evil. The characters of familiar Shakespearean plays offered apt analogies for the cast of villains and heroes that crossed the stage of CK's life.[6] His devotion to the literary works of Charles Dickens further amplified the often simple, sweet moralizing of the stage.

Dickens's Disciple

CK had a lifelong love of the works of Charles Dickens. In a letter to a contemporary in 1919, CK noted, "I read Dickens all the time—that is to say, there is not a month that goes by that I do not read something from him."[7] On the centenary of Dickens's birth CK lavishly eulogized the British writer as "the greatest novelist the world has ever seen—probably the greatest novelist the world will ever see." CK praised Dickens as the inspiration of his own reformist instincts, writing, "This globe's wizard novelist of all novelists was a 'muckraker' after the fashion set in Galilee, long before the word was invented. All he did was purposeful; all he wrote, for the betterment of mankind, for the throttling of oppression, for the estoppal [*sic*] of wrong, for the uplifting, protection and welfare of the poor."[8]

The drama of Shakespeare and the sentimental moralizing of Dickens left their imprint on CK's distinctive style—albeit leavened at times with an ironic twist or even sarcastic humor. CK also loved the quaint English and majestic cadences of the King James Version of the Bible. His columns were occasionally larded with obscure biblical references. The oft-repeated analogies and citations from the King James text were a tribute not only to its classical English but also to Abraham Lincoln, who relied on this version of the Bible as an inspiration for his own writing and public discourse.[9]

CK filtered virtually every issue through the prism of these sources. He never described his battles and crusades as journalists of the twenty-first century would, as objective stories according equal coverage to competing viewpoints. In the style of his day, his reporting and editorials always had clear antagonists and protagonists of the type found in many Shakespearean dramas or among the almost allegorical—yet human—characters of a Dickens novel or a contest between "Christ and Belial." The world truly was a stage.

McClatchy the Dramatist

CK also drew inspiration from the sometimes simple verities of the stage. From its origins Sacramento had an active theater culture. Even in its hardedged gold rush days, Sacramento offered alternatives to its saloons, dives, and gambling places. Beginning in 1849 with the Eagle, early Sacramento had a succession of popular theaters: the Tehama, American, Edwin Forrest, Sacramento, Diepenbrock, Metropolitan, and Clunie.[10] When the railroad connected the city with the rest of America in 1869, troupes of entertainers, musicians, opera singers, and actors made the California capital a stop en route to or from San Francisco. CK and his father loved the stage. "Papa says that we can go to the theater tonight if we want to," the eleven-year-old CK excitedly wrote his mother in 1870."[11] To encourage his son's love for the theater, James hired the deputy state librarian, the Jamaican-born Albert Hart, to tutor him on the history of drama.

CK's tastes were eclectic, but he preferred serious drama, and he often doubled as the theater critic for the *Bee*. He saved the programs of these plays and developed an encyclopedic knowledge of all the great stage actors of his day who appeared in Sacramento and elsewhere. In 1926 he produced a series of articles about the Sacramento stage that was later edited and reproduced in pamphlet form. On its pages were faithfully reconstructed chronologies and biographies of the major actors and plays that had come to the state capital. Some of these actors, such as the tragedian Frederick Warde, became close friends and frequent houseguests.[12]

Sacramento had indeed hosted some of the greats of the stage, including Junius Brutus Booth and his talented son Edwin. Edwin Booth was CK's beau ideal of an actor, and so much was CK moved by Booth's Hamlet that the editor had etched on his bookplate a figure of the melancholic prince of Denmark holding "poor Yorick's" skull. When Booth died in June 1893, CK tenderly eulogized him: "He was ever a manly, patient, tender, noble gentleman. The world as well as the stage owes him a debt it can never repay." In 1904 CK made a pilgrimage to the Players Club at 14 Gramercy Park South in New York, Booth's home and a repository of his memorabilia. With the permission of members CK spent hours savoring the atmosphere and fingering old programs and artifacts of the late actor—almost as though he were handling religious artifacts.[13]

CK absorbed the same lessons from the stage as he did from his literary sources: the expositions of human character; the nobility of some, the utter villainy of others; and at times the moral complexity of situations. The theatricals he watched both entertained and edified him. But his love for theater also had a civic purpose. He yearned for the day when Sacramento would have a respectable theater—owned by the city—that would uplift the values and morals of its citizens. "The theater could be made the great moral force of the nineteenth century," he wrote in late 1887. "It has within itself potentialities for good far in advance of those possessed by the pulpit. . . . The morality that is illustrated by action and scenic effects is far more persuasive than that which comes forth only from the dry, didactic reasoning of one man. . . . Properly regulated, the stage would be the greatest moral force of the age."[14] His attachment to the theater never waned, but his reception of newer forms of entertainment—vaudeville, the early musicals, and the movies—was always qualified, more tolerated than affirmed.

One might be tempted to dismiss CK's high-flown language as the artifact of an earlier generation of genteel journalism. But for McClatchy, Shakespeare, Dickens, the Bible, and stage melodrama provided a reliable window into human nature. It is significant that he wrote about both drama and public affairs—the latter more than the former. But there was a certain confluence of the two. With public issues as with drama, McClatchy was always crystal clear about what he liked and disliked. CK always threw everything—from tree planting to the entrance of the United States into the League of Nations—into his sometimes simplistic but never value-neutral world. From the theatrical and literary world he drew the archetypes for excellence and failure. For CK, William Jennings Bryan was a tragic yet heroic figure like Hamlet or King Lear. The editor's closest friend and political ally, Hiram Johnson, was a righteous judge of Israel or a latter-day David slaying the Goliath of the Southern Pacific. CK sentimentalized women as delicate and frail—like little Dora and Agnes in *David Copperfield*. His enemies, like Peter Yorke and Henry Gage, were Jack Cade or Black Bart or Rob Roy. A clergyman or public figure of whom CK approved became for him an emissary of Dickens's "gentle Nazarene" (Jesus), whereas a journalist with seemingly quirky or inconsistent writings was "an Ishmael in the fold." These three were enough—both in their contributions to cultural literacy and their high-mindedness.

CK and History

C. K. McClatchy had a filiopietistic conception of American history—one typical of many nineteenth-century historians, as it advanced a narrative of heroic leaders promoting civilization and democratic institutions across the North American continent. He cherished a Jacksonian reverence for "the people" and embraced an ethnocentric—my country right or wrong—patriotism, especially during times of war. He took an especially dim view of anyone who might take a revisionist view of the American past. Among the few public gifts he gave were two flagpoles—one that stood in front of the Cathedral of the Blessed Sacrament and another at Grant Union High School. He took a dim view of "hyphenated Americans" who refused to Americanize and unleashed the wrath of God on any foreigner who dared to criticize the U.S. government. He had little use for Asians (although he employed them as domestics and groundskeepers), deeming them unassimilable and even a menace to public health (though his brother's anti-Asian activities won more attention), and he treated African Americans and Latinos with paternalism at best and outright racism at worst.

The legacy he most closely guarded was that of his father. Protecting that and extending it to the issues of the day became the source of his crusading journalism.

"The Sons Have Builded a House to Their Father's Name"

Perhaps even stronger than the literary and dramatic sources CK revered were the ideas and examples of his late father, James McClatchy. James seemed to hover over CK's shoulder, especially when he penned his editorials and his personal column. In 1902, when a new *Bee* building was being erected on Seventh Street, CK insisted that the small half-rotunda at the entrance be emblazoned with these biblical-sounding words: "And the Sons Builded a House to Their Father's Name." The inscription was intended "to keep evergreen" the name of James McClatchy, from whom the *Bee* "still finds its best counsel and its safest advice," and to guide the agenda for his sons, who continued in their father's name.[15]

By the time of his death in October 1883, James McClatchy was a well-known and respected figure in Sacramento. Active in politics and journalism, dedicated to the economic and cultural advancement of the state capital, he was deeply invested in the life of the city and the region. "He was a MAN among men," wrote CK. "His conscience was as straight and towering as an Anak of the redwoods. As fearless as the mountains, he was as gentle as the doves. . . . Upon the rock of Eternal justice, James McClatchy built up The *Bee* in the very teeth of Adversity's wildest storms. Stone by stone he constructed it, fashioning it of the Truth and of the Right, until it became a beacon light to the manhood of state."[16]

CK's first writing was likely a letter to "papa" when he was six years old and staying with his mother for the summer in Vallejo. His father affectionately replied on June 28, 1865: "Your note of 20th instant in pencil came to hand. . . .

It is the first letter I ever had from you and it rejoiced me much." James's affection for his young son spilled out in another letter later that summer when he excused himself for not being able to join the family in Vallejo: "I had hoped to be in Vallejo with you this day," he wrote to CK in August, "to walk with you on the wharf, or go sailing, or playing, and to have been able to take you in my arms and kiss you." Later young CK would remain home with Papa while Mama and his sisters left the city. He reveled in the undivided attention he received from the father he already revered. He wrote to his mother in May 1870, "Today Papa took me down to the C.P.R. depot to see the excursion that came from Boston." When his mother was absent, James and the boys took care of the house. "I wash and wipe the dishes and make beds," reported a solemn CK during Charlotte's late spring trip. "Vallie empties the slopes [*sic*] while papa cooks." Another letter to his mother revealed his love of croquet and kitty cats, and it contained a request to subscribe to *Boys and Girls Weekly,* which was put out by Frank Leslie.[17] Memories of his father continually crowded in on CK throughout his life. In 1926, while traveling abroad, he witnessed a young woman helping a little boy who was struggling to drag a cart up a slope. "This brought back to mind a picture of my childhood days," he reminisced to his travel diary. "I was being taken up town along Third Street by my father. He always wore a stovepipe hat and carried a cane. A decrepit old Negro woman came along, staggering under a bundle of clothes she was trying to carry on her shoulders. . . . Tilting his hat back on his head in his characteristic fashion and handing me his cane, he took the bundle of clothes from the old Mammy, swung it over his own shoulder, and carried it to her little shack in an alley some blocks away."[18]

James mentored his son not only in simple acts of courtesy and kindness but also taught him to read the *Bee* from cover to cover. He also imparted his love of politics. In 1871 James took the twelve-year-old CK to a boisterous political rally and torchlight parade for Republican candidates led by Governor Newton Booth and former vice president Hannibal Hamlin. CK wrote his mother, "The meeting last night was the largest meeting I have ever seen. The street from J to K was a great mass of heads."[19]

James and the Journalism of Memory

Like his father—and perhaps with even more wit and sarcasm—CK hit hard at people and ideas that offended him and exalted (sometimes to the point of overstatement) the things James loved dearly: American exceptionalism, honest government, urban and regional development, and economic opportunity for white Californians. When CK left Santa Clara, he had plenty of time to examine old editorials and even more to discuss matters with his father, and the son deeply internalized the mind of his father. For many years CK's mother, Charlotte, clarified what James believed and stood for—although at times her memory could be faulty.

From the time they took over the *Daily Bee* in October 1883, CK and Valentine so venerated the memory of their father that they often encumbered his positions with a mélange of fact, romance, and myth that made it hard to disentangle fact from exaggeration or even from outright fiction. This type of hero worship is certainly understandable not only because of family loyalty but also because it represented a genre often used to describe figures from gold rush–era California. Indeed James himself belonged to the Sacramento branch of the Pioneers—an association of early settlers in California that often romanticized the "old days," smoothing out unpleasant parts of the past and wrapping its members with a nostalgic haze. James himself contributed to this by publishing effusive and tender obituaries of the old-timers—a task CK continued.

Indeed the facts of James's migration to California and subsequent career make a story worth retelling. He, like many other California pioneers, joined a gold rush "company" that chose as its travel route to the West a daunting journey through Texas to Mazatlán, Mexico; there they purchased the leaky ship *Dolphin,* which they hoped would carry them to San Francisco. At some point James and some of his companions abandoned the leaky vessel and completed the trek on foot, marching from Baja California to San Diego. They claimed to survive on a diet of cactus, rattlesnakes, and other varmints. When James arrived in San Francisco, he made for the gold fields near the Tuolumne River but soon discovered he had neither the resources nor the patience to dig gold out of the earth. He then made for Sacramento, where he participated in local civic affairs and then rose to respectability in the field of journalism.

Although forty-niner mythology was a powerful force in American California, James was seen as a member of one of the founding generation of Sacramento, not as an "old sour dough" miner. James was a proud member, and for a time president, of the Pioneers. His sons were proud of what he accomplished in his life and work in Sacramento—especially in the origins of the *Bee* and in public affairs. At times they embellished it. For example, even though James was only one of many who helped found the *Sacramento Bee,* his sons often depicted him as *the* founder. During the Civil War he was a devoted

Unionist, but his sons insisted he was also the unsung savior of California, delivering the state from a plot of secessionists. James was a foe of land monopoly, but his sons maintained he was the personal inspiration and patron of the social commentator Henry George, whose *Progress and Poverty,* published in 1879, was a significant manifesto of late nineteenth-century political reform. James was a foe of environmentally destructive hydraulic mining, but his sons maintained his was the "voice in the wilderness" that finally ended the practice. In CK's mind especially, James was not just an astute local journalist but a cracker-barrel philosopher who resembled Abraham Lincoln (although not in height), replete with chin whiskers and a stovepipe hat, and inspired his sons to be progressive newspapermen. The father had the wisdom of Shakespeare's Polonius, the integrity of Dickens's Sydney Carton, the magisterial presence of a biblical patriarch, and the common appeal of the martyred Lincoln.

Most of these assertions about James proved to be untrue or exaggerated. In fact James himself may have contributed to the misconceptions with his own faulty recollections. When questioned about these things, CK reacted defensively but in some cases was forced to concede he was wrong or did not have hard evidence for the claims. Yet he privately clung to them.

The McClatchy Myths

The mythologizing of James flowed easily from CK's pen as a harmonious blend of filial duty and his penchant for idealizing his heroes. There was also a business interest. Because James was so highly esteemed in Sacramento, he lent a patina of respectability to his two sons, who took over the *Bee* at twenty-three and twenty-four. Some regarded them as inexperienced and even impertinent. But invoking James, as CK often did, also carried liabilities, because sometimes opponents would use James's own words and actions to refute his sons—occasionally popping the bubble of the myth or at least revealing that James was far more complex and contradictory than his sons let on.[20]

The most persistent and oft-repeated myth was that James actually founded the *Bee.* CK advanced this particular untruth on virtually every occasion but especially at anniversaries of the paper.[21] He unfairly downplayed the role anyone else may have had in the early days of the *Bee.* Typical was his reaction in 1916 to an author who wanted to publish an essay on John Rollins Ridge, the actual first editor of the *Bee.* "I think you are mistaken in reference to John R. Ridge being the first Editor of The *Bee.* The first editor of The *Bee* was the late James McClatchy—John R. Ridge was an assistant, or you might call it an associate, with James McClatchy; and a very remarkable man too."[22] This was literally untrue if the standard was the "very first" editor. It was Ridge, although only for a short time.

In a similar fashion CK minimized the role of James's partners. A *San Francisco Call* article in 1890 praised the role of James's business manager, John F. Sheehan, in "raising it [the *Bee*] from a sickly sheet to a great and prosperous newspaper." In response CK wrote a huffy letter to the editor and reprinted it in full on the front page of the *Bee*, snorting: "John F. Sheehan . . . never was connected with The *Bee* in any journalistic capacity. . . . During all the time, then, that J. F. Sheehan was connected with the *Bee*, James McClatchy was its life, its force, its power, its vitality, its principle, its integrity, its manliness, its very soul of honor, and its innermost nobility of character."[23] In fact McClatchy did not "found" the paper in the sense that he originated it or bought it and directly operated it from its beginnings. In fact, although James had worked closely with the early owners, he did not finally decide to remain with the enterprise, or even in the state capital, until his defeat for a second term as Sacramento sheriff in 1865. The *Bee*-commissioned writer Steve Wiegand states it most succinctly: "James McClatchy was neither an original owner nor the lead editor of the *Bee* when it was founded."[24]

"Saving" California for the Union

Another myth involved James's role in a dramatic Civil War–era incident. CK, like his contemporary Theodore Roosevelt, grew up during the Civil War and was greatly affected by the memories of that conflict. James was a staunch Unionist and a supporter and member of the newly formed Republican Party. CK certainly heard the Union line from his father and read about the battles and heroes of the Civil War. Till his dying day CK was a perfervid admirer of the martyred Lincoln, whom he thought to be a demigod. James's son connected his father to the heroic efforts to preserve the Union by frequently repeating a story about his father's efforts to save California for the Union during the "great secession winter" of 1860–61. The gist of the story, as CK heard it from James, concerned rumors of a plot by California secessionists to detach California and seize federal arms. This was supposedly led by the commander of the Presidio in San Francisco, Albert Sidney Johnston, who later defected to the Confederacy. The alleged plot was detected and stopped by the appearance of Brigadier General Edwin V. Sumner, who replaced Johnston and thereby saved California for the Union.[25] The earliest account of this episode, related in

1866 by William G. Morris, a former general, insisted insurgents were going to seize the federal armories at Benicia and Mare Island and then the Presidio, Fort Alcatraz, Fort Point, the Customs House, the U.S. Mint, and other government buildings. Morris's claims seemed plausible because Sumner had arrived just days before Californians learned of the bombardment of Fort Sumter in 1861.

The story took on a life of its own in 1880 when the *San Francisco Bulletin* published an article, "How California Stands," alleging that Johnston had been disloyal and that Sumner had arrived unannounced. For the first time, although he did not use his own name, James McClatchy publicly explained why Sumner relieved Johnston and included his own role in saving California. As McClatchy explained it, a transplanted Virginia politician, Edmund Randolph, who was seeking a nomination to the U.S. Senate, had called McClatchy to his sickbed and warned him of Johnston's disloyalty and the possibility that he might seize nearly thirty-thousand arms in the arsenals at Benicia and Mare Island. Johnston's Southern sympathies were well known. McClatchy questioned Randolph closely to be sure he had heard the allegations clearly. James believed Randolph's allegation that a plot was afoot, and it so disturbed McClatchy that he went to his desk at the *Bee* and scratched out a warning to the government, which he dispatched dramatically on the fabled Pony Express to Edward D. Baker, the senator from Oregon who was a close personal friend of President Lincoln's.[26] Lincoln received McClatchy's warning from Baker, summoned the secretary of war, and had him quietly send Sumner to relieve Johnston in California. Sumner arrived unexpectedly and handed his orders to Johnston, who asked for time to implement them. Sumner abruptly refused and dashed whatever plans Johnston and Confederate partisans had for detaching California for the Confederacy. California was saved for the Union.

However, these assertions, even if James believed them to be true, did not withstand close scrutiny by others in a position to know. No less than the Civil War hero General William Tecumseh Sherman, in a letter to a Civil War remembrance group, credited the exposure of Johnston to a Colonel Stevenson. CK sprang to his father's defense, sending a clipping of a *Bee* reprint of the "McClatchy-Saved-California" article of 1880. CK bumptiously wrote to the aging Sherman, urging him to "correct any wrong impressions created in good faith by you" as "to whom the honor really belongs of saving this state to the Union." In 1894 the *Oakland Times* insisted that people in San Francisco knew of Johnston's transfer two months before Sumner's arrival.[27] To support a pro-Union candidate who was running for office, CK wrote an editorial in late June 1898 that repeated verbatim the story his father had shared in the *Bee* in 1880. Later that summer CK set out to verify his father's remarkable claims. In an August 3, 1898, letter to U.S. Representative Marion De Vries, a California Democrat, CK noted that "both Val and I are deeply concerned" about the questions surrounding their father's role in the Civil War. He asked De Vries to search among the War Department archives for "that letter from James McClatchy to E. D. Baker" or for other documents "to establish the truth of a statement which has been accepted by all the Pioneer Societies of the State of California."[28]

De Vries found nothing, as did other searchers for the documents. Nonetheless CK forged ahead—unwilling to admit his father was wrong. When C. C. Goodwin, editor of the popular *Goodwin's Weekly*, published an article in 1903 challenging McClatchy's story about the replacement of Johnston by Sumner, CK filled in the missing historical details, relating how his father warned the Lincoln government and claiming, "It was James McClatchy, the late veteran editor of the *Bee*, who saved California for the Union." The *Sacramento Bee* repeated this story frequently.[29] As with the "official" history of the *Bee*, CK kept an eagle eye out for any version contrary to his own and promptly corrected the record.

Indeed, many stories circulated about people who had supposedly saved California for the Union. In the 1940s the respected California historian Benjamin F. Gilbert examined the entire episode with some historical detachment and dismissed the Johnston conspiracy as "mythical." McClatchy's rendition was flawed at best and probably altogether wrong, but like any oft-repeated historical rumor, the California secessionist story contained elements of truth.[30]

It would take more than a hundred years for a *Bee* writer, Steve Wiegand, to demolish this myth as questionable at best and a complete fabrication at worst. To be fair, James himself seemed to give birth to this misrepresentation of events and of his role. But CK and the *Bee* kept repeating it even after it had been found to be without substance. As CK would learn with another of James's embellishments, memories could be faulty.

The Inspiration for the Henry George Myth

One of the greatest tracts penned by a reformer in the nineteenth century was Henry George's 1879 classic, *Progress and Poverty*. George had a career in California journalism and indeed knew James McClatchy. The two shared a common passion for economic justice based on land reform. George,

a native of Philadelphia, arrived in California in 1858 and became a part owner of the *San Francisco Evening Journal*. He eventually quit that paper, however, and moved to Sacramento in 1861 and worked as a printer for the *Daily
Union*. In 1862 George had come to know James McClatchy—attracted in
part by the land reform sentiment pouring from the editor's pen. The two met
again in San Francisco, where James had relocated in 1866 (temporarily as it
turned out) and was editor of the *San Francisco Daily Times,* where George had
worked as a typesetter.[31]

James confided to CK that it was he who plucked George out of the typesetting room and dispatched him to Oakland, where he produced a first-rate
article. As CK's mother also recalled, James was "astonished at the thought and
care and diction, and knowledge of good English shown in the article," and
transferred George from the composing room, making him a reporter and encouraging him to write editorials under James's direction. His formal sponsor-
ship of George ended when James quit the San Francisco paper and returned
to Sacramento for good; however, James maintained a lifelong friendship with
George and did him favors whenever he could—including nominating him for
secretary of the state of California and soliciting articles from him for the *Bee*.[32]

James and CK later insisted that McClatchy had inspired George's classic
Progress and Poverty. George had long been interested in the land question.
In 1871 he wrote a forty-eight-page pamphlet entitled "Our Land and Land
Policy," criticizing land monopoly in California and setting out his theories
on the relationship between land and labor—the kernel of what would be his
single-tax theory. He also began to hammer out editorials on this and other
subjects for the *San Francisco Evening Post*, whose staff he had joined in 1871.
In the aftermath of "Our Land and Land Policy," so the McClatchy version of
the story goes, George pressed McClatchy to write something more extensive
on the subject. McClatchy demurred, citing his age, but urged George to do
it—a task the nearly thirty-two-year-old writer could easily accomplish. The
work appeared in 1879, printed out of his own resources after the New York–
based firm of D. Appleton rejected it. CK insisted in one memorable editorial
that James was the mainspring of George's ideas, maintaining that the author
sat at the feet of James McClatchy and "drank in those ideas on the subject of
land reform, and the increase of wealth advancing steadily pace by pace with
a corresponding increase of poverty among the poorer classes . . . so graphi-
cally explained in 'Progress and Poverty.' In fact it was James McClatchy who
prevailed upon George to write that wonderful work."[33] The two men were

obviously simpatico and shared fears about land monopoly. Their conversations must have been stimulating and rich. However, the issue of inspiration was not as clear as CK believed.

McClatchy's role in these two major episodes of George's life—the deliverance from typesetting and the inspiration for his magnum opus—came under serious scrutiny when Henry George Jr. began working on a biography of his father. At first he accepted CK's rendition of events.[34] However, George Jr. soon encountered a rival claim about the discovery of George that had been advanced by Noah Brooks, the editor who succeeded McClatchy at the *San Francisco Daily Times.* Brooks insisted that it was he who first recognized George's talents while he was still in the composing room of the *Times,* brought to his attention by one O. B. Turrell at whose suggestion Brooks met George and invited him to begin writing occasional editorials. When one of the regular reporters died, Brooks made George a reporter and then a regular editorial writer.

When CK heard of Brooks's rendition of events through an article in *Century Magazine,* he became indignant. His father, not Noah Brooks, had discovered George's writing talents in San Francisco. When consulted, Brooks repeated his version and dismissed McClatchy's claim by pointing out that James had hardly lasted a month on the new newspaper before he quit in disgust. However, when George Jr. pressed CK for documentary evidence of James's role in advancing his father's career, CK once again had to throw up his hands because the seven letters between George and McClatchy, which his mother had preserved, gave no direct evidence. Finally, in April 1899 CK was forced to admit, as he had with the Civil War story, "I have no letters and no memorandum to substantiate the statement I gave you. All that I know is from my recollection of the story frequently told to me by my father."[35] Later the historian Charles Albro Barker's 1955 biography of George split the difference, suggesting that McClatchy had singled out George but that Brooks had given him the first opportunity to write.[36]

CK continued to privately maintain that his father was correct and Brooks was wrong. He publicly professed admiration for George and his ideas and offered qualified support for his bid to become mayor of New York City in 1886.[37] The *Bee* highlighted his single-tax ideas with a column devoted to the topic every week—edited by the attorney Albert M. Johnson (brother of Hiram).[38] CK also ardently defended the excommunicated Roman Catholic priest Edward McGlynn, who incurred this sanction because he was a vocal supporter of George's.[39]

The Editor and His Profession

Building on the legacy of his father, CK gave the position of newsman his own particular touch and created his own set of precedents and principles that his successors sought to emulate. He was clear about what it took to become credible. In 1887, commenting on a suggestion by Joseph Pulitzer that colleges have a chair of journalism peopled by brainy men of "elevated principles," CK scoffed that Pulitzer "himself never saw a college beyond viewing its architecture. . . . In his own person he controverts his opinion that journalists may be ground out of college or made to order by pedagogues." He insisted, "The place to learn journalism is in a newspaper office under practical journalists."[40] In 1894, at the annual appreciation dinner for *Bee* employees, he decried the faux hierarchy among newspaper writers that made the distinction between a newspaperman, which he was, and a journalist, which he was not:

> The newspaper men are the brain and brawn, heart and blood, the soul and life and genius of the newspaper world. The journalists are the lilies of the valley of idleness and the chrysanthemums of conceit. Thank God, we have very few 'journalists' in California, men who claim that they were born to the royal purple of intellect and have been baptized in the sacred waters of genius. . . . The newspaper men are the real workers of the profession; men to whom the papers are almost as their children; men who sink self and never think of what they have done or are doing, but simply keep on doing; men who take pride in their labors.

To those who decried the sensationalism of the press, he insisted,

> The crying evil of too many papers today is not licentiousness and not sensationalism, but hypocrisy. Hypocrisy is the idol and guiding star of a species of journalism that mistakes dullness for dignity, elevates cowardice into conservatism, and glorifies a shameful surrender of principle and a sycophantic truckling to power into a proper disregard for the opinions of others. Such journalism never starts on any crusade that it does not carry with it the white flag of truce, prepared to surrender at the first suspicion of opposition.[41]

In 1886, in the midst of a campaign against hydraulic mining, CK had put forward another manifesto: "It is not the duty of a newspaper to wait until half its readers know a fact before it thinks of publishing it, nor is it its duty to refrain from delving down into public crimes until the Courts have been made cognizant thereof. . . . Its first aim should be to tell the truth, no matter who is hurt."[42]

Although later generations would criticize his verbosity, he valued brevity in the *Bee*. "A real newspaper should give all the news, but should give it briefly and to the point. . . . No man wants to wade through twenty-eight pages to find that which he can find most easily and effectually in four."[43] He created the "Cardinal *Bee* Rules," thirteen exhortations governing the scope and content of reporting. Some of these reflected timeless values of accuracy, warnings against editorializing in articles, and opportunities for those of opposing viewpoints to offer their side of issues. Other rules reflected CK's Victorian morals when it came to women. For example, reporters were to "be extremely careful of the name and reputation of women"—so long as the women had committed no crime other than the "sin against" chastity, they were entitled "at least to pity." In a reversal of the type of reporting that led to guilty verdicts in two libel cases against the *Bee*, CK put out a stern memo in August 1910, placing restrictions on reporting rape cases:

> I wish it distinctly understood hereafter that the word 'outrage' when used in connection with sexual matters is not to be allowed in this paper under any circumstances; neither is the word 'rape'— neither is any word of that character. This may seem a strong order but I have come to the conclusion that it is necessary under the circumstances. . . . All writers on The *Bee* will hereafter kindly remember that although these things will have to be published, the less said about them the better the *Bee* will like it; it wants no details and it wants them made just as brief as possible.[44]

But his most famous injunction was against "sneers at race, religion or physical deformity." Words such as *Dago, Mick, Sheeny,* even *Chink* or *Jap*, were "absolutely forbidden."[45] For the most part, these rules were followed—with the exception of *Jap*, which appeared often in news articles and even headlines.

On racial matters CK appeared to be of two minds. The *Bee* frequently ran accounts of Negro "outrages" against women and children and stories of black lynchings.[46] However, CK at times approved of lynching both whites and blacks as an appropriate punishment for a malefactor who appeared to circumvent the law or who was plainly guilty of a crime against a woman or a child. He was also an ardent proponent of the death penalty. Yet, when his better angels governed his writing, he could be as articulate a proponent of racial justice as any civil libertarian. In the wake of the 1908 Springfield, Illinois, riots—set off when two black men, one accused of murder and another of having sexual improprieties with a white woman, were secretly transferred to an allegedly safer jail in nearby Bloomington and lynched—CK condemned the violence and noted, "Race feeling is by no means confined to the South, [and] . . . in the North it is likewise strong and dangerous. . . . Whatever may be thought as to the final solution of the race problem in the United States, there can be no question that the negroes are as much entitled to equal protection of the laws as any other class of citizens."[47] However, he generally treated African Americans paternalistically or sometimes with outright racism.

The McClatchy Brothers Take Over

The brothers wasted no time consolidating family control over the newspaper after their father's death. They quickly bought out James's partner, John F. Sheehan, taking over his share of the paper and the *Bee* building. On January 22, 1884, they announced: "As will be seen by an announcement in the *Bee* today, the proprietorship and management of this journal is in the hands of the family of the man who made the paper what it is. As the *Bee* has been in the past, so will it be in the future."[48] With this new arrangement Charlotte became the owner of three-quarters of the paper, while the two sons controlled one quarter. Charlotte owned half of the building, and the daughters (Fanny and Emily) owned the other half. They leased the building to the James McClatchy Company for a monthly rent. However, the widow McClatchy effectively turned over active control of the paper to her two sons in 1884. Her name appeared as owner, and lawsuits lodged against the paper cited her, but Charlotte and her daughters had little interest in the paper. Their names remained on the books until January 1901. Fanny did some work for the *Bee* as an artist, but after she married Scottish-born Bruce Richardson, she dropped out altogether.

The two brothers acknowledged they were deeply in debt and the recipients of much unsolicited advice—one elder suggesting they sell the paper "while it was still worth something." Perhaps to their own surprise, they paid off the debt within a year and began, with some bumps along the way, to transform it into Sacramento's most important daily paper (the *Bee* always had one rival and sometimes two).[49] In fact a new *Bee* was about to emerge; it would be on the cutting-edge technologically and unbeatable in the contest for advertising.

The main artificer of this was Valentine McClatchy, and his contributions to the health and economic viability of the newspaper were inestimable. However, a newspaper had to inform its subscribers of events near and far and help to shape public awareness of issues of common concern. This is what CK did.

Indeed Valentine respected his brother's ability to turn a phrase and his broad-ranging interest in local and national politics. Both men were devoted to their father's editorial legacy—although Valentine was more interested in James's efforts to promote the Sacramento Valley and increase the economic · prosperity of the region. Valentine often disdained his brother's seeming indifference to the practicalities of running a paper (or at least gave him the impression that he did so), but when Val's better angels were at work, he articulated the actual working relationship with his brother when he acknowledged to an employee: "I cannot write editorials like C. K., and I don't feel sore about it. There are some things I do better than C. K., and sensibly each does that for which he is best qualified, and The *Bee* is the gainer." CK publicly touted the separate but equal line and insisted on a firm separation between the editorial and financial departments. "There are only two personalities acknowledged in the *Bee* office—the managing editor in the conduct of the paper, and the business manager in all the details, small or large, of all business and financial matters. Each is distinct and separate from the other."[50] In fact this is what transpired for the most part during their partnership, although Valentine did participate in some editorial decisions. Valentine may have given CK a bully pulpit, but it was CK's voice that defined the *Bee* and his arguments that advanced whatever causes, candidates, or positions the papers stood for.

Fault Lines in Self-Perception

Valentine and CK made the *Bee* indispensable as a source of news and an effective medium of advertising. The paper regularly added new sections: literary, social, agricultural, and of course dramatic. The *Bee* also carried its share of the lurid and grisly, which captivated some and repelled others. The *Bee*'s dominance afforded CK free rein—within limits—to say what he wanted editorially. He could take unpopular stands—even bragging at times at a loss of advertising—and occasionally crusade against local, state, and national malefactors. He could even support doomed candidates out of principle.

CK cherished the belief that the *Bee* was independent in its thinking and its politics. In fact good reporting and punchy editorials lifted the paper out of relative obscurity.[51] However, since both CK and his brother were heavily involved in local business affairs—particularly land—their critics persistently questioned, and wondered about, the relationship of their advertising to their personal financial interests. Typical was the case of the local dredger and brewer W. E. Gerber, who charged the *Bee* with criticizing his interests in dredging while refusing to do the same to the rival Natomas Company, which advertised in the *Bee*. CK responded testily,

> When I first read your statement . . . that The *Bee* says nothing more against dredge-mining because the Natomas people buy advertising space—I became righteously and rightly angry. . . . A much bigger advertiser in The *Bee* than the Natomas Company is the Southern Pacific Company. Another is the Northern Electric. Another is the Sacramento Electric, Gas, and Railway Company, having or controlling the street franchises. Another is the local Telephone Company. You don't find any milk-and-water editorials in The *Bee* concerning these corporations. This paper lets them alone only when they are not infringing on the rights of the general public. . . . The *Bee*'s advertising columns are open to advertisers. But if any advertiser or advertisers or combination of advertisers think such advertising carries with it any obligation of favoritism in the editorial or news columns of The *Bee* . . . or . . . is to be immune from *Bee* criticism therefore,—if such scheme or interest infringe upon public rights or menace public welfare—then 'another guess is coming' to such advertiser.[52]

In fact the *Bee* had taken a strong stand against dredging, resurrecting old arguments of the impact of this process on the river bottoms. But even with this, enemies of the brothers accused the *Bee* of soliciting bribes from dredging companies and, when they did not receive them, of turning their editorial fire on the dredgers.[53]

As the McClatchy brothers placed their imprint on the *Bee*, sometimes their unsteady hands and managerial inexperience resulted in mistakes—at one point almost killing the newspaper. CK learned to temper himself, but sometimes heavy-handed and blunt editorials, as well as the imperious pose the paper struck with workers and members of the public, did not go down well. Indeed danger and controversy beset the first decade or so of the brothers' leadership.

Chapter Three
Defenders of the Valley
The Struggle with Hydraulic Mining

◆

PRESERVING, PROTECTING, AND ADVANCING the legacy of James McClatchy took CK into battle with the hydraulic mining companies of California. This had been his father's last crusade, begun toward the end of his life and brought to victory after he died.[1]

The source of the problem was the nation's increasing need for gold to meet the currency demands of an expanding population. Extricating the precious metal propelled the use of the environmentally destructive hydraulic mining process. Since the 1850s hydraulic miners had extracted gold from the mountainsides of the Sierra Nevada Mountains by shooting powerful streams of water that literally flushed out millions of dollars of the valuable metal. Hydraulic mining operations were located mostly in Nevada County, with San Francisco capitalists heavily financing the expensive equipment. To be sure these investments paid rich rewards to local investors but also to foreigners, mostly British.

All mining is environmentally destructive in some way, but hydraulic mining proved particularly problematic since it sent the debris, or slickens, from its power hosing into the major tributaries of the Sacramento River: the Feather, Yuba, Bear, and American rivers. Their fast-moving waters pushed the debris down to the flatlands of the valley, where they filled up the riverbeds. As the bottoms of the riverbeds rose, the areas near the shores began to shoal. This made river traffic more and more difficult and nearly impossible for low-draft vessels. During the rainy season the excess silt lifted the riverbeds, and the rivers overflowed their banks, flooding farmlands—row crops and orchards—and endangering river cities like Marysville. The overflow left behind a heavy layer of mud, gravel, and other debris, destroying whatever was in its path. Farmers lost valuable lands and trees. Marysville alone had to spend huge sums to build levees higher and higher.

Hydraulic miners noted the increasing damage their processes caused but insisted it was their right to dump whatever they wanted into the rivers. They loftily advised farmers to simply abandon their fields near the rivers. Farmers of course felt otherwise and in the early 1870s mobilized to do something about hydraulic mining. In 1876 a group of them asked the California legislature to petition Congress to step in and impose limits on the process. The petitioners argued that the basis for federal intervention involved the navigability of the rivers and therefore was the proper concern of the federal government. Private businesses did not have the right to destroy public waterways.

Both sides, miners and farmers, aggressively advanced their positions. Miners formed the Hydraulic Miners Association in 1876; it was headed by Lester L. Robinson, a forceful and resourceful advocate. Farmers formed the Anti-Debris Association in 1878 and relied on the leadership of the Sacramento attorney George Cadwalader and a Sutter County fruit grower, George Ohleyer, who "abandoned the plow and took up the pen" to wage "vigorous and unrelenting warfare against the foes of the Sacramento Valley" on the pages of the *Sutter County Farmer*.[2] Farmers and miners met each other in court.

Some hydraulic miners sought a compromise with the farmers, insisting on continuing the lucrative mining process but proposing the erection of holding dams that would capture most of the slickens. Opponents protested that the dams were useless. Often made of poor materials and too low, the traces allowed fine particles of slickens to escape and continue to foul the river bottoms and endanger the agricultural lands along the rivers. The failure to arrive at an acceptable solution led Secretary of War Robert Lincoln to withhold $250,000 that had been appropriated by Congress in 1883 to clear the Sacramento River channel. The potential loss of federal funds escalated the controversy, and both sides squared off for renewed battle.

The miners relied on the newspapers of the mining districts, especially the *Grass Valley Transcript*, edited by Leonard S. Calkins, later a McClatchy foe. The farmers and valley dwellers enjoyed the strong support of the *Sacramento Record-Union*, whose editor, W. H. Mills, frequently criticized the hydraulic process. The pro-railroad *Record-Union* had good reason to fight the effects of hydraulic mining. The paper had a vested interest in preserving the viability of valley farmers whose products the railroad shipped. Moreover, flooding not only wreaked havoc with farms and orchards but also wiped out expensive railroad bridges, halting rail traffic for days. Smaller newspapers from farming communities joined with the *Record-Union*. The *Bee* was a latecomer to the antihydraulic camp.

Although CK frequently lauded his father's as a "voice crying out in the wilderness," James McClatchy initially was not so sure that hydraulic mining was really destructive. In fact for a time he argued that the overflow of the silt-filled waters of the American River was a positive development, potentially increasing the fertility of Sacramento area farms just as the silt-filled overflow of the Nile River had done in Egypt. He wrote in 1875: "The land would never be exhausted—would never become poorer—but on the contrary would grow fat feeding on the rich waters of the American," making Sacramento "one of the best agricultural districts of the state" with "a population of half a million people." When torrential rains ended a drought in 1878, sending floodwaters hurtling into the valley, he urged that the silt and debris they carried "be poured into the tule lands of Yolo and Solano County," creating nearly 600,000 acres of "fine, warm, rich soil."[3] When a levee south of Sacramento at Sutterville broke, McClatchy again insisted the raging waters would fill up the low places, "fattening the soil generally."

However, as time went on he gradually tempered his enthusiasm. Commenting on a December 1875 antidebris meeting in Yuba City, James noted blandly the insufficiency of levees to hold back the floods and the need to keep the channels open: "It has long been apparent that legislative protection would have to be invoked sooner or later." He later followed the case of a Sacramento farmer named Atkinson, who in 1877 sued the Amador County Canal Company for damages done to his property. When the court issued a verdict in Atkinson's favor, awarding him $4,000, James noted the significance of the case, one of the first of its kind to compensate the loss of valley farmers for the practices of the miners.[4]

By 1878 James openly opposed hydraulic mining. "The rivers, filled up in their beds as they are with mining debris, have not sufficient capacity, even with their artificial banks in the shape of levees" to take the water crashing down from the mountains to the sea.[5] By 1880-81 James was appearing at public meetings to lobby against the practice. In 1881 the *Bee* gave a cost analysis of hydraulic mining, and in 1882 the paper proposed that the boards of supervisors from the affected counties form a state antidebris association to mobilize support.[6] The counties of Yuba, Sutter, Colusa, Yolo, San Joaquin, Butte, and Sacramento did form such a body in May 1882, and that summer they named James an honorary member of the board. After multiple lawsuits, injunctions, and rhetorical wars on the pages of newspapers, the issue came to a head in 1882, when Edwards Woodruff, a citizen of New York and a property owner in Marysville, asked the Ninth U.S. Circuit Court in San

Francisco to grant a perpetual injunction prohibiting hydraulic mining at the North Bloomfield and other hydraulic mines along the Yuba River. George Cadwalader of Sacramento argued the case before Judge Lorenzo Sawyer. Sawyer studied the matter thoroughly, taking trips up the river and into the mining areas, inspecting the debris dams and the mines. James McClatchy traveled with Sawyer in March 1883 when they toured the mines on the San Juan Ridge. Here they saw firsthand the destruction wrought by hydraulic mining and just how unsatisfactory slickens dams were. Many were already full and in some places breaking.

On January 7, 1884, Sawyer handed down his multiple-page decision in *Woodruff v. North Bloomfield Hydraulic Mining Company* and issued a perpetual injunction against many of the mines using hydraulic mining—unless some way could be found to impound the debris or solve the problem created in the river bottoms. James had died the previous October, and in tribute to his late father, CK noted the victory and gave credit to his father as "one who would have rejoiced" at the decision in *Woodruff.* Stretching the truth, as he would do with other episodes in his father's life, CK insisted, "He was a pioneer in this warfare upon hydraulic mining. He threw down the gauntlet long before others came to his assistance." In their inaugural column at the beginning of 1884, the McClatchy brothers invoked the memory of their father to "proclaim aloud the eternal truth that the land was made for the needy many and not for the greedy few."[7]

Vigilant Warriors: Keeping the Miners in Check

In reality CK and Valentine were more ardent opponents of hydraulic mining than their father, if for no other reason than that they owned land in the valley. In this endeavor they worked as a team, although CK did most of the writing. Their efforts made a genuine contribution to public knowledge about this complex issue, educating the public about the English common law theory of riparian rights—the rights of those who lived adjacent to rivers to have a steady and clear flow of water. Based on the principles of riparian rights, they argued against the dumping of debris into the waters of the Sacramento Valley. To their credit the brothers relentlessly reported and editorialized about the process, continually raising alarms that shifty "hydraulickers" would flout the ban and begin dumping slickens into the rivers. Again and again they insisted that hydraulic mining destroyed farms and property values and harmed the navigability of the Sacramento River.[8] The McClatchy brothers publicized any open flouting of the law, and CK took particular aim at the San Francisco capitalists who wanted to recoup their investments and looked for loopholes in the *Woodruff* ruling or proposed remedies that seemed designed to restart the destructive process.

They used any opportunity to advance the antihydraulic gospel. CK told the story of Jack Crum, an elderly pioneer of Butte County, who had a lovely ranch on the road between Chico and Oroville. Set near Dry Creek, which CK noted "was in early days a beautiful stream of sparkling water flowing down from the snow-capped mountains," and built on "rich, level acres of farming and fruit lands," Crum's ranch had an idyllic California setting. But "then commenced the terrible downpour of slickens from Cherokee hydraulic mine, and Crum's beautiful home was ruined. Nothing remains to mark the spot but an old wreck of a barn and a few cottonwood trees." Although the mining company reimbursed Crum for some of the damage, "he wandered away broken down in health and poor in purse."[9]

The *Woodruff* decision was not binding on all the hydraulic mines in the mountains, and miners continued to dump slickens where they could. The construction of retaining dams was proposed again, this time by James Budd, a member of Congress and future governor who had been an advocate of the dams even before the decision in *Woodruff*. When Budd urged passage of a $500,000 appropriation to build the dams, the *Bee* responded "that restraining dams are a delusion and a snare." Budd, CK contended, probably did not understand the issue well enough and added he was "not a fit man" to represent California in Congress.[10] The McClatchys forcefully responded to the "mountain press," particularly the Nevada County newspapers, and more specifically the pro-mining *Nevada Transcript*. On its pages ran lengthy discussions of the impact of the floods of yesteryear on valley towns like Marysville and Oroville and regular reports provided by informants—spies, the miners called them— told of slickens dumping.[11]

The McClatchys even used the issue to highlight a growing hostility to Asians, by reminding readers that low-cost Chinese labor did some of the illicit hydraulic mining. In the McClatchys' antipathy to hydraulic mining, the *Bee* worried that the *Woodruff* prohibitions extended to only a handful of mines, leaving other parts of the valley still exposed.[12] Hydraulic mining continued to pollute the waters around Stockton and even the headwaters of the Sacramento River around Yreka, as well as to affect the river's navigability and contribute to damaging floods. "The *Bee* advocates a thorough-going, uncompromising policy of aggression against hydraulic mining," CK declared in March 1884. "Let us kill this curse once and for all in California and be done with it. There should be no trifling with this evil. It continues to menace this city as it has in the past."[13]

On the Offense

The McClatchys insisted that mining companies not only stop their destructive processes but also repair the river bottoms to their full depth so river traffic could resume up the Sacramento River—and urged that the $500,000 federal appropriation Budd sought for the useless dams be diverted to repair the rivers. CK attacked the popular U.S. senator George Hearst (father of William Randolph) for weakening restrictions on hydraulic miners in a rivers and harbor bill.[14] When hydraulic miners complained they were being deprived of their livelihood, CK reminded them that Judge Sawyer had let them off relatively easily, since they did not have to pay farmers damages for the destruction wrought by their mines. However, the McClatchy brothers urged farmers and others to sue for monetary damages.[15]

When California's 1884 Republican Party platform seemed to waffle on a commitment to keeping hydraulic mining at bay, Valentine wrote a stern letter to Joseph McKenna, a Republican running for a seat in the House of Representatives, warning him that the denizens of Sacramento and Yolo counties, long afflicted by the evil effects of hydraulic mining, were "unalterably opposed to any trifling" with the ban on this form of mining.[16] Through the summer of 1884 the *Bee* goaded the Sacramento County Board of Supervisors to enforce the ban on hydraulic mining, accusing the board of "apathy and neglect" in making sure the mines had ceased operation. The paper further warned that an appropriation of $210,000 by the War Department for the cleanup of the Sacramento River could be permanently lost if the mining did not cease.[17] In late 1884 the *Bee* brought out a lengthy Christmas edition dedicated to the hydraulic mining issue.[18]

Tensions ratcheted up in 1885 when Lester L. Robinson, head of the Hydraulic Miners Association, urged state legislators to permit private parties to build high dams to restrain the debris. At his behest state senator Charles Cross of Nevada County introduced a bill to this effect, but with McClatchy opposition (among others) it was blocked.[19] CK kept an eagle eye on his fellow newsmen. When the *San Francisco Chronicle* doubted the effectiveness of litigation and challenged the findings of the Anti-Debris Association, the *Bee* retorted that the *Chronicle* represented the greedy San Francisco investors who had outlays in the mines. Although no fan of litigation, CK defended the sometimes tediously slow court process and urged persistence, noting "that much remains to be done on the American and Consumnes Rivers" and could be completed if the supervisors did their job. In July 1885 CK escalated the rhetoric: "The battle-cry of every man in this valley should be: 'No dams; no compromise! Every hydraulic mine must go!'" This also brought the McClatchys into conflict—and a moment of truth—with their friend and sometimes ally, William H. Mills at the *Record-Union*, who proposed federal intervention to help resolve the controversy. CK suggested that federal intervention—which might allow limited hydraulic mining—was tantamount to treason to the farmers. Even more the *Bee* accused its rival newspaper of accepting $5,000 from the Hydraulic Miners Association for its favorable reporting.[20]

Exasperated by the hardballs coming from CK, the *Record-Union* reminded him that the *Bee* had been a Johnny-come-lately to this issue, citing a series of James McClatchy's editorials from as late as February, March, and May 1878 that hinted at the benefits of the slickens for valley agriculture.[21] CK grumpily acknowledged the evolution of the *Bee*'s position but went forward nonetheless. CK pressed Zach Montgomery, an assistant U.S. attorney, to take whatever legal steps necessary to prevent the return of hydraulic mining. The Anti-Debris Association, a faithful ally, worked with the *Bee* to accumulate evidence of violations of the injunction in *Woodruff* and provided data for potential and actual lawsuits.[22]

Its harsh rhetoric took a toll on the *Bee*'s circulation in the mining counties. In fact the *Nevada Miner Transcript* suggested that a member of the legislature from a mining county should propose a bill entitled "An act to Forthwith Remove from the Confines of California the Messrs. McClatchy of Sacramento to Their Old Home in Ireland." CK replied tartly: "The home of the Messrs. McClatchy is in Sacramento where they were both born." But "when hydraulic mining shall have ceased . . . they will kindly take advantage of the invitation . . . to visit the hills and vales of their father's native land."[23]

The Revenge of the Miners: The Hobson Libel Trial

The hydraulic miners found an opportunity to make the McClatchys pay for their assault through a libel suit filed by one John Hobson. The case involved Milton McWhorter, editor of the *Marysville Democrat*, who had shot and killed Deputy U.S. Marshall T. G. Robinson in front of the State House

Hotel in Marysville on August 10, 1886. Robinson, an agent of the Anti-Debris Association, inspected hydraulic mining sites and occasionally cited mines that were using the banned processes. There was little sympathy for Robinson, who many suspected was also an informant for the McClatchys; some even tagged him a spy. The assault on Robinson became personal when McWhorter's pro-hydraulic *Marysville Democrat* published a story stating that Robinson had been caught fleeing a burning house of ill repute. After a copy of this story had been sent to Robinson's wife, Robinson became so infuriated that he publicly threatened to "stamp the guts" out of McWhorter and purchased a gun. McWhorter feared for his life and claimed he killed Robinson in self-defense. The hydraulic miners, who cheered Robinson's demise, strongly defended the editor.[24]

McWhorter went on trial for manslaughter, and his defense lawyers (including Grove L. Johnson, a bitter McClatchy foe) made the trial a referendum on hydraulic mining and the *Bee*. Johnson took delight in making the antihydraulic stand of the McClatchys an issue in jury selection and pointedly questioned potential jurors about whether they had read the *Bee* or were associated with the Anti-Debris Association.[25] During the nearly three-week trial Johnson insisted McWhorter had acted in self-defense. At one point a former miner, J. B. Hobson, one of the proprietors of the *Industrial and Mining Advocate*, a hydraulic miners' journal, and a miner himself in Iowa Hill, testified he had bribed Robinson to ignore tailings in the river with $200, a sum he shared with one Nathan Sexey of the Anti-Debris Association. Hobson asserted that when he stopped making the payments Robinson grew angry and vindictive. Hobson's story may have convinced jurors of Robinson's bad character, and after nine hours of deliberation they voted to acquit McWhorter. In a bitter editorial CK wrote, "As firmly as we believe anything, we believe that J. B. Hobson perjured himself in defense of McWhorter. . . . Dead or alive, there was more honor, more manhood, more true nobility, more truth in T. G. Robinson's little finger than in all the L. L. Robinsons [the well-known Miners Association representative], Hobsons, and McWhorters that ever lived. He is dead, and his vilified slayer walks the streets a free man. A just judge will judge between them."[26] CK later testified he did not believe Robinson had accepted a bribe and was suspicious of Hobson's testimony.

Less than a week after McWhorter's acquittal, Hobson sued the McClatchys for criminal libel. The trial was held in Placer County, home to many hydraulickers, before Judge B. F. Myres. Fearful that the jury and judge would be overwhelmingly anti-McClatchy, the brothers recruited Augustus Hart, former state attorney general, to defend them. Arrayed against them was Grove Johnson. The trial began in late October 1887.[27] Shortly before Thanksgiving the jury voted 8 to 4 for conviction; however, since it was a criminal rather than a civil case (therefore requiring a unanimous vote for conviction), this was tantamount to a hung jury, so nothing happened to the McClatchys. CK and Valentine were astounded by the fairness of the jury.[28]

The Aftermath of the Hydraulic Battle

By the end of the 1880s a downturn in the economy had led many to reconsider hydraulic mining and members of Congress to press for its legal restoration with appropriate safeguards. The need for gold bullion had increased, and expanding the national currency became a hot political question in the 1880s and 1890s. Although the condition of the river bottoms still required attention, and the Sacramento River remained muddy and unnavigable, a compromise between farmers and miners was reached with passage of the Caminetti Bill in 1893. The compromise had been spearheaded by Congressman Anthony Caminetti, whose district included the mining center of Amador County.[29] Caminetti's bill allowed hydraulic mining but only if with proper environmental safeguards—including the controversial retaining dams. To ensure that no one flouted the law, the bill empowered a California Debris Commission to regulate hydraulic mining and at the insistence of the antidebris activist George Ohleyer imposed heavy fines—$5,000 and jail time—for violations of the law. The law also made possible improvements in the navigability of the Sacramento, Yuba, and Feather rivers. It also made provisions for protecting Marysville from floods.[30] CK kept a wary eye on efforts to weaken the law and on miners who ignored it. He also wrote exasperated articles questioning why San Franciscans refused to take note of how the slickens were threatening the San Joaquin River delta and San Francisco Bay itself. However, by the early 1890s even CK had come around to the *Sacramento Record-Union*'s idea of seeking common ground through government intervention. The hydraulic mining controversy highlighted the need for rational policies that benefited all people, and national intervention was the key. In fact the *Bee*'s tone had shifted by June 1892, when farmers stalked out of a meeting with miners who were sent to negotiate with them over the fate of the Caminetti Bill. Valentine chided his usual allies for their unwillingness talk, and in an editorial on June 13, 1892, CK, while sympathetic to the skeptical farmers, criticized the behavior of the antidebris faction. Valentine wrote a letter of apology to W. C. Ralston of the State Miners' Association, regretting the actions of the valley folks and hoping for a new dialog "until the hotheads can see their error."[31]

One Last Gasp

The Caminetti Act allowed a limited resumption of hydraulic mining if retention dams were built and licensure sought from the California Debris Commission. In early 1898 the commission approved one such mining operation in Nevada County. But when its crib dam began to leak, Sutter County filed suit against the operation. At a meeting in 1900, the miner W. C. Ralston defended the dam and announced plans to test the constitutionality of the Caminetti Act. The Anti-Debris Association replied by citing the structural deficiencies of the dams and filing a number of petitions to enjoin hydraulic miners. Its members, too, sought to have the constitutionality of the law tested. CK jumped into the fray again, denouncing Ralston's speech and charging that the Miners' Association was only a "hydraulicker's clique." Ralston's defense of the leaky dams, CK wrote sarcastically, "is on a par with those of the Rebels who denounced the North for daring to try and save the country after the Flag had been fired upon."[32] However, the legal challenges never amounted to a serious threat and the Caminetti Act stood.

The antihydraulic cause brought out the crusading spirit of the brothers and was the first tribute they tendered to the memory of their deceased father. But they were also genuine boosters of the emerging valley economies of fruits and vegetables that could be processed and shipped in Sacramento. Valentine in particular strongly favored land reclamation and greater centralized control of irrigation policies in the Central Valley. Valentine himself (much to the consternation of his brother) became the chair of the State Irrigation Board during the administration of Governor Hiram W. Johnson. That this enhanced the scope of the *Bee*'s circulation and added to the brothers' personal fortunes was a happy coincidence.

Chapter Four
A World of Trouble
Boycotts and Libel Suits

◆

IN TAKING OVER the *Bee*, CK and Valentine believed they could continue along the path laid out by their father. But their sometimes combative ways also embroiled them in public controversy. Instead of reporting the news, they became the news. CK cherished journalistic independence and touted his courage in standing up to the "forces of evil." But occasionally he and Valentine took on too much. In a struggle with the typographical union, they experienced a backlash that nearly destroyed them and spawned their worst nightmare: a credible rival evening paper.

Antagonizing the Typographers

Typographers were the skilled workers who set the type (stereotyping) and produced the paper six times a week. They had a powerful union with chapters throughout the nation. The union had successfully waged a strike and boycott against two San Francisco papers, the *Call* and the *Bulletin*, demanding that the papers hire union men.[1] The typographers in Sacramento were also strong and had affiliated with the Federated Trades Union, an umbrella organization of skilled workers that had opened a chapter in Sacramento in 1889.

Valentine, in charge of personnel, did not approve of organized labor, and his was one of the voices raised against it at the annual convention of the American Newspaper Publishers Association (ANPA) in 1890. There Valentine called for a discussion of "the question of labor and the influence wielded by the Typographical Union—assisted by the federated trades—as one of the most serious in the newspaper business."[2] He lamented the growing strength of the union and claimed that fractious behavior by the typographers had all too often met with "cowardly servility" on the part of employers. He challenged the notion that workers were "entitled to a share of the profits." Although he thought it wise to admit "faithful employees of several years standing [be given] a division of a certain proportion of the year's profits"—he insisted they receive this largesse only if they were not union members or, if they were, that they be required to resign. He disingenuously declared that the goal of this conditional profit sharing was to remove "labor's chief cause for dissatisfaction that 'it does all the work and gets none of the profits.'"[3] It was union-busting discourse, worthy of another virulent California foe of unions, Harrison Gray Otis of the *Los Angeles Times*.

Rumors of a showdown between the *Bee* and typographers circulated in the late summer and fall of 1890. As the technology of printing evolved, the new techniques reduced the number of men needed in the composing room. As with all technology, this posed a threat to job security. These advances created pre-set forms and reduced the amount of work the typographer had to do. Typographers nonetheless insisted that their handling of this labor-saving technology should not mean any loss in pay. "The union was frightened that the new craft of stereotyping would destroy their trade and sought to insure that the *Bee* would never . . . import press-ready stereotype plates, or if the plates were brought in, the material would be reset in slack time for job printers." They maintained that these plates, received from the East, should be added to their work product (called strings), and since their pay was calculated by the amount of type set, this would mean no diminution of their wages. When *Bee* typographers made this demand on October 4, 1890, Valentine sternly rejected it. Even though the *Bee* would eventually discard the plate service (the plates were wider than the *Bee*'s own, and trimming diminished the quality of the paper), after his ANPA performance Valentine was not disposed to compromise. In a matter-of-fact way he asserted that since the typographers had not done the work, they should not claim pay for it. To William McKenna, foreman of the composing room, he offered what he thought were helpful analogies: "When Sacramento Teamsters are paid for hauling gravel taken in from the gravel pits by steam wagon; when employees in the Sacramento railroad shops are paid by the Southern Pacific Company for building locomotives constructed and paid for in New Jersey; then will the *Bee* consider the advisability of paying its compositors for work done by others." The typographers countered that the stereotypes were part of the larger newspaper work for which they required compensation. As the positions of both sides calcified, Valentine began placing ads in local papers for replacement typographers. Some papers, like the *Express* of Los Angeles, urged McClatchy to tread cautiously. Valentine replied, "I appreciate your motives in advising me to cave to the Union, and it is possible that I may regret not having adopted that policy, but you must remember that every one of us that yields, only weld the fetter more closely around his brethren."[4]

The Strike

Valentine at first tried to be conciliatory to the typographers. Even though he firmly insisted they be paid only "for the work they do and the time they are occupied—nothing more and nothing less," he nonetheless told the foreman William McKenna, "See that no man in our employ loses anything either in the amount of work or wages, by the use of these stereo-typed stores."[5]

But his conciliatory mood was only a veneer and belied by the number of scabs he had recruited from the Bay Area. He then picked a fight by alleging the typographers had damaged the *Bee*'s new Goss press, claiming the culprit was one Milton McMillin, a member of the union. When Valentine took steps to discharge him, McMillin protested his innocence, and the union asked for an independent evaluation of the press problem. On October 8, 1890, representatives of the W. T. Goss Company came to Sacramento to inspect the *Bee*'s equipment. They found some of the machinery damaged, but suggested the problems owed to poor maintenance and misuse rather than industrial sabotage. They even asserted that "McMillin can turn out good plates and is as good as the average stereotyper."[6] Ignoring Goss's report, Valentine contended that whatever was wrong with the press was McMillin's fault and fired him. McMillin contended the *Bee* had punished him because he was a union member, while Valentine declared it was because he had been insubordinate and harmed the machinery. McMillin was quickly replaced by a nonunion tradesman named William Milhan. Angered by McMillin's firing, the compositors walked off the job just before the deadline for setting the Saturday, October 11, 1890, edition of the paper. Within twenty-four hours Valentine managed to bring in the scabs he had been quietly recruiting, and the *Bee* did not miss an issue and was short only in telegraphed news items that were missed in the confusion. Since the paper did not have a Sunday edition in those days, production returned to normal by Monday evening. In fact so many typographers were willing to work on the *Bee* that the McClatchys shared the list with G. M. Brennan, manager of the American Newspaper Publishers Association, and even offered applicants from San Diego to their erstwhile enemy, Harrison Gray Otis of the *Los Angeles Times*.

The *Bee's* actions did not win universal approval. A blast of criticism came from William Randolph Hearst's *San Francisco Examiner*, which suggested the formation of a new paper in Sacramento since the McClatchys had locked the union printer out. Valentine dashed off an angry note to Hearst, claiming, "There has never been a lock-out on this paper. The compositors at 10 o'clock A.M. last Saturday deserted their cases and left the office because the *Bee* declined to comply with their demands in re-instating a discharged stereotyper." Valentine seemed to win the first round. Although he heard rumors of a boycott, he seemed sure that this would not materialize. He had worked hard to cultivate advertisers and subscribers and was bringing in more government business than ever. Reasoning that the advertisers needed the *Bee* more than the *Bee* needed them, he pompously declared, "We will hold the fort while the walls stand."[7]

However, talk of a boycott was more than an empty threat. Typographers and their allies in the Federated Trades Council began a boycott of the *Bee* that lasted from October to February and nearly killed the newspaper. Valentine kept a running account of the actions of the boycotters and included in one of his letter books a copy of a circular handed out by the Council of Federated Trades urging a boycott of Gus Lavenson, a local boot and shoe merchant who had originally pledged to uphold the boycott.[8] The McClatchys had sown the wind. They were about to reap the whirlwind.

The Boycott

Although the department store owner David Lubin and local clothier E. W. Hale—both important advertisers for the *Bee*—made desultory efforts to resolve the strike, the typographers' appeals to many of the city's merchants and the paper's chief advertisers succeeded. With the backing of the powerful Federated Trades Council, which also represented the workers at the railroad shops (Sacramento's largest employer), the typographers called for a general boycott against any and all who advertised in the *Bee* unless differences were resolved by January 1, 1891. Valentine nervously explained the situation to Brennan at the American Newspaper Association: "The boycotters are endeavoring to persuade the advertisers that their business will be ruined unless they cease advertising in the paper, and if they succeed in so persuading them we will have lost considerable of the business as the contracts expire."[9]

His early dismissal of the boycott now gave way to cold reality. Thirty-five Sacramento merchants, all of them advertisers in the *Bee*, including

Lubin's half-brother Harris Weinstock, drafted a resolution on October 21, 1890, expressing solidarity with the strike and urging the *Bee* to be concilia- tory. Weinstock's participation must have been somewhat surprising for the McClatchys. A respected Sacramentan, Weinstock had had a positive associ- ation with the McClatchys and advertised regularly in the *Bee*; he had even been a partner of Valentine McClatchy's in an Orangevale real estate venture. Weinstock had a reputation as a man of breadth, tolerance, and modest re- form instincts. But he set aside whatever friendship he felt for the McClatchys in sympathy for the typographers. On October 23, 1890, Weinstock con- vened a second meeting of the signers of the petition, asking what further action they could take; twelve of the advertisers present urged the *Bee* to re- spond to the workers' demands by the date stipulated by the Federated Trades Council, January 1, 1891.[10] The boycott was on, with some advertisers even thinking of pulling out of contracts that committed them to the end of the year.

The McClatchys now waged a public relations war against the union and the boycott. The McClatchys' attorney, the former Superior Court judge S. C. Denson, denounced the boycott as illegal, and the brothers reprinted his com- ments on the front page of the *Bee*, then circulated them throughout the state. One hundred copies were even sent to Harrison Gray Otis of the *Los Angeles Times* with Valentine's request they be distributed far and wide. McClatchy also sent the paper to every house in the city and by mail to everyone on the register of voters outside the city limits.[11]

On November 19, 1890, Judge John Wesley Armstrong issued a prelimi- nary injunction in favor of the paper—ruling that advertisers could not ab- rogate their contracts. Valentine made sure copies of Armstrong's injunction found their way to every businessman in Sacramento. Valentine also sent fliers to Woodland, San Jose, Stockton, Oakland, and Marysville editors, warning them about the demoralization of all business interests that comes in the wake of boycotts. He even proposed a "yellow dog" contract to the scab typographer Charles T. Kelly of San Jose, writing, "If you are capable of taking charge of a large job and are out of the Union and will stay out as long as you hold the position, we can possibly secure for you the position as foreman of a large es- tablishment." The McClatchys renewed their justification for firing McMillin, ignoring the report of the Goss investigation and accusing McMillin again of deliberately sabotaging their press. Valentine and CK defended the appoint- ment of the scab Milhan by asserting he was a member of the union's Chicago chapter. However, as it turned out, the Chicago union had expelled Milhan for nonpayment of dues.[12]

All these efforts were in vain. The boycott only grew stronger. Union men and their allied advertisers tightened their grip on the *Bee*, challenging the paper's assertions at every step. The strikers embarrassed the *Bee* with the same technique W. H. Mills of the *Sacramento Record-Union* had used in the hydraulic mining controversy: CK's own words. After the *Bee* had used gallons of ink to disparage the very idea of a boycott, the strikers found an editorial CK had run on March 13, 1886, arguing that working men had the right to unite and even boycott. CK had strongly condemned those who branded such actions as a conspiracy and un-American—exactly what CK had been doing. Unable to extricate himself from the hypocrisy, CK maintained that unions did have the right to exist and "withdraw their trade and custom from those who oppose their interests." But he somewhat illogically declared, "They have no right to threaten with bankruptcy and ruin all those who will not follow their lead."[13]

"We . . . are fighting the fight, not only of the *Bee,* but of the community in opposing the boycott," Valentine self-righteously declared in a letter to the Pacific Press Publishing Company. However, by late November the strike was taking its toll, as he acknowledged, "We . . . are really losing money now. . . . We may be forced to canvass for advertisers in San Francisco and Oakland in order that we may be able to carry on the suit to a final conclusion."[14]

The *Bee's* Worst Nightmare: A Rival Evening Daily

The worries of CK and Valentine took a quantum leap at the prospect of a rival evening paper. The *Daily Evening News*, established by the veteran editor Wells Drury, first hit the streets of Sacramento in late December 1890. Drury, a longtime Nevada newspaperman and politician, had run papers in Virginia City. In 1888 he moved to California and worked for the *San Francisco Call* and the *Examiner.* He knew Sacramento because he had served as news editor of the *Sacramento Union.* The *Daily Evening News* was a respectable and well-written newspaper, an acceptable evening alternative to the *Bee* and run by an experienced newsman with first-rate presses. It was also quite willing and able to attack "our evening contemporary" and capitalize on the discontent with the *Bee.* Truth be told, the *Evening News* was more legible, better written, and better illustrated than the *Bee.* With more than a hint of braggadocio, Drury noted his warm reception by the Sacramento community, repeating the comment of an anonymous K Street businessman that the *Evening News* printed more "good words for Sacramento in the first week of its existence than all the other papers of the city have printed for a year." When some newspapers asserted that Drury planned to supplant the *Bee,* the editor disingenuously replied he had no such plans and that Sacramento was big enough and literate enough to sustain two evening papers.[15]

Although Drury publicly foreswore any direct competition with the *Bee,* the *Evening News* quickly exploited any issue on which its opinion might differ from the *Bee's.* The *Evening News* gave sympathetic treatment to the strikers and denounced the McClatchy efforts to undermine the boycott. When he printed a letter from a self-described Pioneer, Drury expressed the feelings of some boycott supporters glad to see the *Bee* get what it deserved. "Pioneer" declared: "The *Bee* is being repaid in its own coin. Its chickens have come home to roost. I have lived in Sacramento for twenty years and in that time I have seen hundreds of men and scores of companies suffer on account of The *Bee's* boycotts."[16]

With troubles multiplying and money shrinking, Valentine was forced to travel to San Francisco to beg for advertising. Even there the opposition of the San Francisco Federated Trades intimidated some potential advertisers. This was the case for J. N. Knowles of the Arctic Oil Company of San Francisco, of whom Valentine reported: "Favorably disposed but feared that if he advertised oil, the engineers union might fight his oil."[17] Valentine replaced $1,500 of lost revenue with government printing contracts, delinquent tax lists that Sheriff George C. McMullen gave him without putting them out for bids. The Christmas of 1890 was bleak, with the *Bee's* future hanging in the balance. CK's wife, Ella, was pregnant with Carlos, and Valentine's young family was growing as well. Over Christmas dinner the McClatchys hatched a new strategy that would appear to make reasonable overtures to their adversaries, while they refused to admit the *Bee* had been wrong in its labor policy.

The first step was a public relations blitz, managed by CK, that asserted that the brothers were not "an enemy of labor" and "stood by the laboring men of this State against the encroachments of Monopoly and oppressions of capital."[18] The second phase, overseen by Valentine, attacked the boycott itself. Airbrushing away their earlier justifications for boycotts, they rejected the very idea of a boycott when it applied to them. The *Bee* also ran positive stories about the tremendous crowds that descended on stores like the Non Pareil and Lavenson's, which had defied the boycott and advertised in the *Bee.* Valentine pressed the legislature to outlaw boycotts as a form of conspiracy. He urged other newspaper moguls like Otis to travel to Sacramento to quietly push a bill Valentine had secretly formulated with state senators George J. Campbell of Solano and Solomon Solon Holl of Sacramento.[19] However, Valentine's efforts to remain behind the scenes were blown when Assemblyman Judson Brusie of Sacramento, who introduced an assembly version, blithely announced he had done so at the behest of Valentine McClatchy.[20] Although the bill never passed either house of the legislature, Valentine and CK consistently pressed the boycott's illegality, immorality, and demoralizing effect on the community.

A third prong of the strategy involved both brothers reaching out to the disgruntled typographers and pledging that they would pay union wages and in other ways make sure the *Bee* provided a cooperative and pleasant working atmosphere. However, CK and Valentine would not agree to the presence of the union. In the end these strategies failed. Although some local advertisers remained faithful to the *Bee,* a significant number of accounts pulled out after the first of the year, seriously affecting the paper's bottom line—as it was intended. Odd public relations stunts arranged by the *Bee,* like obtaining the signatures of 135 railroad workers to pledge a boycott of those who boycotted the *Bee* also faltered—never mind that the McClatchys believed boycotts were illegal when directed against them. The brothers eventually realized they could not exist for long solely with advertisers outside their circulation area nor could they survive the ill will of local workers. They realized the game was up. As the knowledge of their defeat settled in, CK took refuge in the theater, attending Shakespeare's *Henry VIII* with his favorite tragedian, Frederick Warde, in the role of Cardinal Wolsey. In his review CK lingered a bit on the fate of poor Catherine of Aragon, Henry's first wife, wondering whether the *Bee,* like Queen Catherine, might be "cast off without compunction and discarded without the quiver of an eyelash." Yet for CK she may have seemed a proxy for his own battles, as she held herself with dignity and "magnificently did she trample upon the traitorous hirelings" who persecuted her.[21]

Carpenters Union Local 341 provided the McClatchys' way out, offering to mediate at a tense meeting of the *Bee*'s owners and typographers on February 16, 1891. Although both sides had agreed to keep the negotiations under wraps, a labor supporter leaked details to the *Daily Evening News.* On February 27 they struck a bargain, bringing the boycott to an end. The McClatchys retained the right to dismiss a worker if they deemed it necessary. However, their attempts to end the role of the Typographical Union failed. Even Milton McMillin was invited to resume his job—an offer he turned down. The McClatchys took back eight of the sixteen who had walked out and let go those hired to break the strike. In a sour editorial on February 28, 1891, CK quietly announced the end of the strike, claiming it would have been settled long ago if it were not for "outside parties." He also noted the strike had unmasked those who make trouble of this kind. Two years later, when faced with another boycott, the *Bee* removed "any bar against the entrance into this office of any members of said [Typographical] Union."[22]

The typographers, the boycotting businesses, and the *Daily Evening News* cried victory. The *Evening News*'s support of the strikers was modest—the paper likely did not even pay its own compositors a union wage—but when the strike ended, the paper gleefully announced the capitulation of the *Bee*. Declaring the printers' victory a triumph for "every laboring man in the community," the paper proclaimed it was also "good for every business man in the city." Drury praised the conduct of the printers as exemplary and dignified and noted the victory was salutary for all working people. Thanks to the *News,* he wrote, "The *Bee*'s methods in regard to public and private affairs have been very much modified."[23] These comments were calculated to nettle the thin-skinned CK and Valentine, who even before the strike ended had begun a steady and unrelenting war against their "evening contemporary," accusing it of connections with unsavory speculators and using its influence with local and state government to deny the *Bee* lucrative printing jobs.[24] The typographers' strike permanently soured the McClatchys on organized labor, and they showed their disdain by supporting the railroad when workers went on strike in 1894.

Drury's management of the *Evening News* lasted until late 1892, when it was turned over to two local businessmen, General Thomas J. Clunie and Augustus Abbott. These men provided financial backing for the paper but handed over its day-to-day affairs to two competent newsmen, both of whom had formerly worked at the *Bee*—John A. Sheehan and Junius Brutus Harris.[25] The *Bee*'s circulation and advertising returned to normal levels, but the lessons learned from having to tolerate a rival in the face of a nearly successful boycott were seared on the minds of the McClatchys.

The boycott taught the McClatchys what was necessary to maintain peace with organized labor—paying good or comparable wages and being willing to compromise—but also how angry and resentful many Sacramentans were with the *Bee*'s reporting. Their clientele after all did not consist of just business relationships but acquaintances, neighbors, and associates, some of whom had been childhood companions of both Valentine and CK. They drank together, went to school together, married at the same time—shared the small social networks of Sacramento. While the McClatchys mended fences where they could, they also took notes about their friends and enemies.[26]

The McClatchys and Organized Labor

The typographers' strike and the disastrous boycott soured the brothers' relationship with organized labor. Being forced to make concessions to a union never went down well with Valentine. Yet CK insisted on maintaining sympathy for working-class people—part of his small *d* democracy. What evolved over the years in commenting on other labor issues was a somewhat schizophrenic policy of extolling the concept of organized labor—noting its contributions to economic stability and its role in alleviating grievances and asserting rights. However, whenever the unions asserted their right to bargain or compel management to pay attention to their grievances, the McClatchy reaction was nearly always negative, particularly when demands involved any kind of violence or threats of chaos.

For example CK warned continuously of the potential for violent overthrow of the government posed by the International Workers of the World. When IWW organizers turned up among agricultural workers in the Sacramento Valley and threatened to move into Sacramento, CK approved of heavy-handed methods to get rid of them, especially during World War I, when he favored jailing them as potential seditionists. He also worried that groups like the American Federation of Labor would be influenced by socialist propaganda and become injurious to the American economy. The only labor contract acceptable to the McClatchys mandated "compulsory arbitration." When strikes and other labor actions, such as boycotts, threatened economic and social stability and seemed heedless of public interest, the clause forced workers and management to sit down and hammer out an agreement. The strike and the boycott—the only weapons organized labor had to compel management to take workers seriously—were to be severely curtailed, if not actually banned. CK shared this with his prolabor friend James H. Barry, who seemed partially sympathetic to this approach. Barry wrote: "I have always been opposed to compulsory arbitration, but after reading your able articles on the subject recognize the force of your contention that something must be done to prevent strikes and lockouts at such time as this—particularly on Government work, which cannot be delayed or 'tied up' without peril to the country." But Barry could not wholly agree with his Sacramento friend's position, reminding CK that the reasons for labor unrest had something to do with the "vast profits being made by the 'Captains of Industry'" and the desire of workers to "share in this so-called 'general prosperity.'"[27]

Although the McClatchys' relationship with their workers was for the most part positive, for many years organized labor regarded the McClatchys warily. When a dust-up between the brothers and workers took place in 1912, Valentine wrote to Samuel Gompers, head of the American Federation of Labor, to refute the charges of unfairness leveled at him and his brother. CK appealed to Barry for help, asking him to intercede. Barry then sent a night letter to Gompers and to the labor leader Frank Morrison, insisting the McClatchys' attitude toward organized labor "has always been the friendliest."[28] Privately and sometimes publicly, CK disparaged labor leaders as power hungry or venal.[29] CK repeatedly claimed that he loved working men and strove to overcome the bad reputation the *Bee* had earned in the strike of the 1890s. At his funeral a flower-bedecked chair, marked "Friend of Workers," was among the tributes.

A Second Boycott: The "Thank God" Edition

Problems emerged again in 1893 when a second boycott was threatened after CK had directed some harsh words at the state legislature. Although the legislature was a social and economic boon to Sacramento, it was so dominated by the railroad that the California statehouse became something of a joke. The session that met in 1891, known as the Legislature of a Thousand Scandals, revealed "pay-off money wrappers"—bribes to avert hostile legislation—in trash cans in the library of the Assembly. The session, which ended on March 11, 1893, elicited special scorn from the *Bee* with an imaginative evening edition that day. The headline on its lead story said, "THANK GOD: The Legislature Is Soon to Adjourn." The headline on the third of the eight front-page columns was even worse: "THE SESSION: Is Nearing the Tick of Its Doom—And Sacramentans Should All Be Joyful." Other columns bore these headlines: "Now Is the Time When Churchyards Yawn," "Almost: a Counterpart of Boston's Former Fire," "Over Fifty Additional Laws Are Signed."

In fact some legislators believed Sacramento was willing to rid itself of the state capital when members from Sacramento voted against a constitutional amendment to prolong the legislative session. Even before the offending front page articles, Secretary of the Senate F. J. Brandon had floated a resolution to move the capital to San Jose, but no one stepped forward to formally introduce it. After the *Bee's* offending front page appeared, Brandon induced state senator E. C. Seymour of San Bernardino to introduce the resolution. In haste the senate passed it and sent it on to the assembly. Both chambers voiced a chorus of approval, some using frustration with the *Bee* as an excuse for the vote.

The proposal was never serious, but Sacramento hoteliers, publicans, and restaurant owners panicked. CK's big mouth now was threatening the economic stimulus provided by free-spending solons. City leaders also worried that the prestige of being the state capital—one of Sacramento's economic life-lines—was about to evaporate. Some melodramatically envisioned an empty state capitol building—a darkened hulk surrounded by weeds. This decaying building would symbolize Sacramento's future as citizens and businesses fled the community. What the fire, floods, and disease could not kill in the 1850s and 1860s, the bumptious McClatchys would accomplish with their grating words.

Anger at the McClatchys flowed freely at a hastily assembled meeting at the courthouse that was sponsored by the Board of Trade, a civic promotion committee formed in the 1870s. On March 13, 1893, prominent citizens and virtually every merchant on J and K streets jammed a room in the Superior Court buildings. Mayor William D. Comstock chaired a special committee to consider the response. This body consisted of Judge A. P. Catlin (who had brought the capital to Sacramento in 1854), E. G. Blessing, the lawyer and McClatchy foe Grove Johnson, and Harris Weinstock. A spirited discussion ensued, at once absolving state senator E. C. Hart of Sacramento from blame for not stopping the offensive resolution in its tracks but also accusing the *Bee* of libel. Grove Johnson in particular denounced the *Bee* and suggested that local businessmen "have the power to stop these libelous publications." The committee endorsed resolutions to "wait upon the legislature" and assured those in attendance that the McClatchys did not speak for the city. Former state attorney general Augustus L. Hart summed it up by imploring the legislators, "Don't get mad at Charlie and Val McClatchy and wreak vengeance on the rest of us."[30] The committee also passed resolutions disclaiming the actions of the *Bee* but stopped short of calling for a boycott. This action the committee left for the Board of Trade, whose members now took it upon themselves to address the situation.

The Board of Trade was populated by many of the same businessmen who had already boycotted the *Bee* in the typographers' strike. They were disposed to do it again. Urged on by Grove Johnson, Cyrus Hubbard (acting president of the board), and F. B. Adams, the board voted yet another boycott of the *Evening Bee*. This time, however, the McClatchys were ready with an active defense. Valentine appeared at the meeting and offered what sounded to some like an apology, regretting any loss to Sacramento because of anything published in the *Bee* but refusing to retract the criticism.[31] When two members of the board, David Lubin and J. O. Coleman, insisted legislators had demanded a boycott as the price Sacramento had to pay to keep the capital, Valentine again refused to retract the criticism of the legislature.[32] Hubbard and Adams began the boycott nonetheless and sought to dissuade advertisers from hawking their goods and services on the pages of the *Bee*. Although it dismissed the action as futile and the plans to move to San Jose as unrealistic, the *Record-Union* chastised its rival for its broad-brush assault on the legislature.[33]

Coming so soon after the first boycott, these threats at first rattled the McClatchys. In a self-pitying editorial CK complained that the McClatchy brothers had been among the city's most ardent boosters and had even turned down an offer to relocate their newspaper enterprise to Portland, Oregon. They had "a strong love for Sacramento," CK declared, then pouted, "Life is too short however and the reward too little to battle for a town whose citizens instead of standing shoulder to shoulder in advancing common interests waste time and energy in internal bickerings, petty jealousies and attempts to pull down men who by force of energy or ability have raised themselves little above their enemies."[34] But this was not 1890, and these opponents were not the well-organized and formidable typographers. In fact they were people the McClatchys had known since childhood. After a few uncomfortable days CK and Valentine were able to see the boycott resolutions for what they were: empty threats.[35] CK even admitted that the capital removal had been in the works even before the offending newspaper headline.[36]

That the *Bee* by this time was virtually boycott-proof was largely the result of Valentine's efforts to boost circulation. In fact the *Bee* was the single largest daily in California's interior—and its reach extended far beyond the city limits. Valentine made sure everyone who even toyed with the boycott idea knew that the *Bee*'s circulation was "four times the total circulation of any other evening paper in this part of the state." The McClatchys emerged unscathed, but they took note of their friends and enemies. The lawyer Grove Johnson already held a place of honor in the McClatchys' pantheon of the most despised.[37] Others who participated in this eruption (and the previous one) would one day feel the brothers' sting.

Striking Back with Wicked Claw: The Libel Cases

The McClatchys sought retribution against those who had endangered their livelihood and forced them to deal with the unions. Three targets came into view: Cyrus Hubbard, a local hardware retailer; Charles Gilman, owner of a clothing store called the Red House; and Harris Weinstock, head of Sacramento's best-known department store. Likewise, eliminating the *Daily Evening News* and its successor, the *Sunday News,* also became a key priority. Between 1893 and 1898 the *Bee* constantly warred with any and all of these people. The results were mixed.

Cyrus Hubbard, a supporter of the boycotts—in fact one of the prime movers in the Board of Trade's "Thank God" boycott—became the first target of CK's wrath.[38] Hubbard, a Civil War veteran who originally hailed from Ohio, had become a leading hardware salesman for Baker and Hamilton, a large San Francisco firm. A respected man of modest abilities, Hubbard nonetheless presented himself as a candidate of the Citizens Party for the mayoralty of Sacramento in the 1894 primary. When the McClatchy candidate, Benjamin Steinman, had declined to stand for reelection, this left only local businessman J. W. Wilson to run as an alternative to Hubbard. Hubbard's support of the boycott effort of 1893 gave the McClatchys reason enough to go after him, but when they learned of his affiliation with the anti-Catholic American Protective Association (APA), a group that had appeared in the city the year before, he offered an even richer target.

The APA, a nativist organization founded in Iowa in 1887, targeted the rising tide of Catholic power as a cause for public concern. Catholics, its members argued, were numerous enough to dominate public offices, including the ranks of schoolteachers and law enforcement. A bevy of anti-Catholic speakers hit Sacramento in the early 1890s, some purporting to be former priests and nuns, and they warned ominously of Catholic power.[39] The APA movement had made inroads in other urban communities like San Francisco and had even fielded candidates for state races—supposedly supported by the sugar millionaire John Spreckels, who exercised great clout in state senate elections in California and owned the *San Francisco Call.* Hubbard, who was not a vocal anti-Catholic, seemed content to allow others to define him as sympathetic to the APA cause. CK rushed to the defense of the church of his birth, decrying the bigotry of the APA and targeting local adherents by publishing the names of those who had affiliated with the local branch. The *Bee* highlighted Hubbard's links with the APA while also flailing him as a lackluster do-nothing with no record of achievement in public life or business. CK ridiculed him and published a cartoon of him as a glum loser with a padlock on his lips and carrying a scroll with the words "Don't ask me to talk."[40]

The 1894 contest came down to a showdown between Wilson, supported by the railroad, and Hubbard. This might have meant a victory for Wilson, but at the last moment Benjamin Steinman jumped into the race, and the *Bee* threw its support to him.

In the end Wilson and Steinman split the vote and Hubbard won the election. Angered by the turn of events, the *Bee* flayed Hubbard mercilessly, particularly for his APA links. He served only one troubled term.

The Charles Gilman Case

Cyrus Hubbard got off easy—by simply losing the race for mayor. Others who had crossed the McClatchys during the boycott era were dealt with more harshly. In a number of circumstances the *Bee*'s reporting was so harsh that several people filed libel suits against the paper. Since jurisprudence around the First Amendment had not yet been as finely articulated as it would be in the mid-twentieth century, the press was subject to lawsuits that today would be tossed out or never filed.

The libel suit brought by John Hobson (see chapter 3) was one of the most serious but had turned out in the McClatchys' favor. Others followed. In 1892 alone seven libel cases were filed against the *Bee*.[41] The most notorious was the Charles H. Gilman case. Gilman, the head of the Red House, a women's clothier, had been a faithful advertiser in the *Bee*, but during the boycott of 1890 he transferred his advertising to the *Daily Evening News*. When the boycott ended, Gilman apparently contemplated returning some of his advertising to the *Bee*. But in early April 1892 he received an anonymous letter congratulating him for supporting the workers and boycotters in the past, and it asked him to continue his boycott of the *Bee* and stick with the *Evening News*. The letter attacked the "venomous and dirty sheet, The *Bee*, which terrorized the good people of this city for so many years to gratify the growing desire of its treacherous and unprincipled managers to fill their purses through their hellish system of blackmail."[42] Troubled, Gilman took the letter—the language of which resembled that in *Evening News* editorials—to the *Bee*, which began an investigation of its origins and learned its author probably was George E. Harber, a compositor for the *Evening News* and a member of the executive committee of the Typographical Union and of the Federated Trades. The *Bee* speculated the letter had been sent with the concurrence of the managers of the *Evening News* and that Harber had been behind other defamatory mail directed at the *Bee*. Gilman, perhaps worried about the impact on his business, also visited the *Evening News*. The paper then issued "a disclaimer to any intention of joining with the McClatchys to hurt the *News* by giving that now famous anonymous letter to the *Bee* without letting us know what was going on."[43] Gilman kept going back and forth, between the *Evening News* and the *Bee*. But his continued attachment to the *Evening News* rankled the McClatchys, who soon found ample opportunity to get even.

The moment of truth arrived in August 1892 when Gilman was arrested in the rape of his housekeeper, Mrs. Lulu Estella Truitt, a widow. The *Bee* published at length all the lascivious details of Gilman's alleged assault on Truitt—including allegedly dislocating the woman's jaw. Gilman was twice divorced from women who had accused him of adultery, and people were willing to believe these allegations. Nonetheless he vigorously denied them, contending Truitt's accusations were payback for her dismissal from service and Gilman's refusal to give her free clothing from his store. The details of the alleged assault were so ambiguous that Judge W. C. Van Fleet of the Superior Court dismissed the case. Gilman sued the *Bee* for $50,000 in retaliation, insisting that after his denial the story should never have been circulated.[44] The McClatchys, believing themselves covered by the First Amendment for simply reporting what the police had told them, waived a jury trial.

The case came to trial in January 1894 before Judge A. P. Catlin but quickly fell apart because the alleged victim, Mrs. Truitt, who had given a deposition, was nowhere to be found.[45] In the absence of Gilman's key witness, his attorneys—Grove Johnson and Solomon Solon Holl—skillfully challenged the veracity of those brought forward to vouch for the sworn accusations of the elusive Mrs. Truitt. The *Bee* covered the trial for a while but stopped in early February, leaving the *Record-Union* to keep the story alive.[46] The trial ended in mid-February, but Catlin did not hand down his decision until nearly the end of March, when he shocked the brothers by deciding in favor of Gilman and awarding him $500 in damages. CK and Valentine privately raged against Catlin and publicly took issue with the decision, which seemed to suggest that the report of a crime could not be made public until the accused person was actually convicted. Meanwhile the unfavorable publicity killed Gilman's business, and he was forced to close the Red House.[47]

The McClatchys noted the implications of the decision for the freedom of the press, and sympathetic newspapers around the state rallied to their defense.[48] In a display of righteousness the brothers announced their intention to challenge the ruling "in the interest of what [the *Bee*] believes to be the rights of the press." To not do so would, they believed, "leave the press at the mercy of legal harpies who foment these suits against newspapers and enter into them for speculative purposes." The only contrary voice came from the *Record-Union,* which defended the Catlin decision, because the *Bee* did not claim press privilege under the First Amendment in its defense but rather tried to prove Gilman's guilt. In a follow-up editorial, the *Record-Union* became even blunter, claiming that simply reporting the allegations had not been enough for the *Bee:* "It lacked the 'sting' of the *Bee* and so it published a false, scandalous and sensational report—not of judicial proceedings, but of one private individual against another, charing [*sic*] the latter [Gilman] with all the nasty details of an infamous crime."[49]

The McClatchys appealed the case to the California Supreme Court in November 1895. In March 1896 the court allowed the earlier judgment to stand. Railing against the "arrogant and tyrannous outrage perpetrated against the most sacred rights of free speech and a free press," the *Bee* gave up the fight and paid the $745.35 judgment, with additional interest from March 12, 1894, for a total of $804.02. Valentine sent a check for that amount to his attorney A. J. Bruner, stating, "The blood of the martyr is the seed of the church, and in the interests of decent journalism we try to accept the result philosophically. To suffer injury from a skunk, is, however, a little galling."[50] However, in the wake of the Supreme Court decision, the *Bee* rehashed the episode, repeating the lurid details of the case, and Gilman filed yet another libel suit.[51] The second trial resulted in a $250 judgment against the McClatchys—no doubt a relief because it was so small.[52]

Held in Contempt

As the second round of the Gilman case moved forward, another lurid and sensational story hit the papers and landed in the court of Judge Catlin. This involved a wealthy Courtland farmer, advanced in years, named Charles V. Talmadge. He had met a young prostitute named Marta in a Second Street bordello in Sacramento, fell in love, and set her up in more respectable quarters. The lonely Talmadge married Marta and took her to his Courtland ranch.

He also moved in his daughter, Mary Jane. From the start the differences in age and temperament between the newlyweds soured their bliss. Young Marta was eager for life and frivolity while Talmadge could hardly keep up with her. Talmadge's daughter grew increasingly distrustful of Marta, whose penchant for shopping and demands for money became more insistent. Eventually the couple decided to divorce, and during the proceedings Marta accused Talmadge of being mean, suspicious, and abusive. Likewise, she asserted that the daughter treated her poorly. Talmadge suggested that Marta had not given up her whoring ways and that he had married her while in a drunken state—in fact the officer who married them in San Francisco was not even empowered to do so. The *Bee's* copious reports of the proceedings made for exciting reading, and the couple divorced; Marta was awarded $40 per month alimony, though she had requested $100.[53]

Talmadge's attorneys challenged the accuracy of a *Bee* reporter who laid out Marta Talmadge's allegations against her husband. Judge Catlin himself denounced portions of the *Bee's* May 28, 1896, account of the trial as "grossly false . . . a fabrication." In a stinging editorial of May 29, CK poured out his ire at the venerable Catlin, defending the reporter's accuracy and referring to Catlin as "a czar in the courts" and deriding him in an adjacent column, "Hail A. P. Catlin, Czar!"[54] CK scolded the judge, who had decided the proceedings should remain secret, and suggested that withholding the official court transcript implied that Catlin was fearful the reporter would be vindicated. In one last blast at Catlin, CK noted, "The *Bee* takes pride in being fair and truthful, in apologizing when it is wrong, but in refusing to budge one inch when it is right." CK also lambasted "the peculiar judicial proceeding by Judge A.P. Catlin." Catlin struck back. Charles T. Jones, Talmadge's attorney, swore out an affidavit accusing CK of contempt of court, and the editor was arrested on the morning of June 2, 1896. CK's friends, William J. Hassett and Al Johnston, posted his bail. In a swift hearing McClatchy was found guilty. Catlin intended to return him to jail and fine him $500 but refrained from pronouncing a jail sentence at the suggestion of some fellow jurists. The case was eventually appealed to the state Supreme Court, and both the *San Francisco Examiner* and the *San Francisco Call* backed the *Bee's* position. In the waning days of 1897, the Supreme Court overturned the contempt citation and decreed McClatchy had been denied his constitutional right to speak in his defense.[55]

In his editorials CK clearly presented the issues as good against evil, right against wrong, concentrations of arbitrary power, and dictatorial behavior versus democracy and accountable government. However, some of his statements were paybacks for the boycotts, reflecting the dark side of the McClatchys. The events, though, bore witness to the depth of negative feelings toward the McClatchy brothers that had developed since they took over the paper from James in 1883.[56] They did indeed dominate the newspaper market in their city and surrounding area, and controlling the competition was a nasty and brutish task—one the McClatchys did well.

Chapter Five
Creating a Press Monopoly

ESTABLISHING THE DOMINANCE of the *Bee* in Sacramento and its environs was not just the fruit of hard work and fair competition, but sometimes the result of good luck and a bit of sabotage by the McClatchys. The *Bee*'s main rival, the *Sacramento Union* (for a time the *Sacramento Record-Union),* was an older paper and at times provided an alternative slant on the news and public issues. However, it was a morning paper and had multiple owners. Although the papers sometimes exchanged harsh words, the *Union* was not considered a serious threat to the growing evening market in Sacramento. The McClatchys feared the *Union* only when a rival newspaper mogul or wealthy individual like Harrison Gray Otis, William Randolph Hearst, or Herbert Hoover made threats about taking it over. The McClatchys had one scare when a strong journalistic family, the Calkinses, ran the *Union* for a brief time. But none of the press giants of the day or big-name politicians ever bought or dominated the *Union.* Other independent papers tried to enter the Sacramento market, but they failed (sometimes with a shove from the *Bee*).

More feared was the short-lived *Daily Evening News,* which had the potential to become a worthy rival in terms of advertising, landing government printing contracts, and circulation. The *Evening News* threatened the McClatchys' economic security and presented a bitter reminder of the boycott that nearly killed them and forced a humiliating surrender to union labor. Although vehemently opposed to monopoly, the McClatchys did not apply this to the control of newspapers in Sacramento and did everything they could to destroy their evening rival.

Running Out the Evening Competition: The *Evening News*

The *Daily Evening News* had come into existence during the typographers' boycott and persisted even after the boycott was over. In 1892 its founder, Wells Drury, sold out to local businessmen, General Thomas J. Clunie and Augustus Abbott of the Capital National Bank. Clunie and Abbott hired John Sheehan, a tart-tongued former *Bee* employee, to edit the paper, and Junius Brutus Harris, also a refugee from the *Bee,* to work as an editor. Sheehan regularly heaped ridicule on the *Bee* and the *Record-Union*, writing condescendingly of its rivals: "Our sprightly little contemporary, the *Bee* entered upon a new volume. For so old a paper, it keeps up its pace remarkably well, but like the late San Francisco *Alta* it has many '49er' peculiarities that are more amusing than instructive." He took particular aim at the *Bee*'s lucrative county and state printing jobs, for example the printing of delinquent tax lists. These, the *News* suggested, had been obtained by working backdoor deals. Valentine tossed off Sheehan's complaints, replying that the *Bee* could produce these government jobs less expensively, run them more often, and circulate them more widely. But, more seriously, Sheehan gave a voice to those who felt that the *Bee* was a civic bully, insincere in its calls for reform and capable of "bull-dosing [*sic*]" people to do its will. Sheehan even suggested the two brothers had frittered away James's legacy: "They fell heir to a valuable newspaper property. It is now worth half as much as when it was dropped into their hands. . . . The present managers of the *Bee* have wrecked what was once a prosperous newspaper property."[1]

Sheehan accused his rivals of copying his reportorial and editorial innovations, such as reporting on organized labor and using quality pictures. In the manner of modern newspapers the *Evening News* stopped providing lengthy reprints of various government documents and instead offered helpful synopses of lengthy documents. It also opened its columns to more regular reporting from local labor groups and the Farmers Alliance, which was growing in political strength. But the most annoying trait of the *News* was that it sometimes scooped the *Bee.*

The *Bee* editors returned fire by reproaching the *Evening News* for being in the thrall of banks and local capitalists. When the *Evening News* took a moderate position vis-à-vis the efforts of miners in Iowa Hill to clean out bedrock with a promise to keep slickens from moving into the riverbeds, the *Bee* attacked the paper for being a tool of the hydraulic mining interests and prodded the county board of supervisors to block the proposed action. Later, when the supervisors approved a more moderate version of the plan, the *News* crowed it was "vindicated, and the untruthful statements published by Sacramento's antediluvian evening paper are shown to be as flimsy and worthless as its reputation for candor and honesty."[2] CK accused the paper of being "an obscure sheet" and ran an uncomplimentary cartoon of Augustus Abbott on the front page, depicting him as an organ grinder and as pretending to be a friend of labor, farmers, and the people when in reality he represented shady hidden interests.[3] The McClatchys also began a regular surveillance of Sheehan, documenting his every move and utterance through a private detective named "Rob." Rob faithfully recorded and provided to Valentine any lapse of judgment, association with local gamblers, bouts with alcohol, personal mishap, or words of anger directed at the McClatchys by Abbott.[4]

Unafraid of the abuse, Sheehan used the dirt—including CK's alcoholism—he had accumulated on the McClatchys during his years of employment at the *Bee*. On one occasion Sheehan managed to make fun of CK's penchant for scripture and his boozing by slyly quoting the Prophet Isaiah: "Woe unto them who are mighty to drink wine." Sheehan also accused the Sinophobic brothers of taking bribes from Foong Soon, "who runs brothels and opium dens and the gambling hells of Chinatown." Sheehan repeated accusations that Milton McWhorter, editor of the *Marysville Democrat,* and Lester L. Robinson, the well-known representative of the Miners Association, allegedly paid the McClatchys $500 in April 1880 to support hydraulic mining, and when they stopped payments the *Bee* switched positions on the issue.[5] Sheehan claimed credit for forcing the *Bee* to deal with the typographers and reminded working-class Sacramentans that even though the McClatchys were forced to accept the Typographical Union, the brothers did not want it. "If the *Bee* had been successful or if the *News* had not been started, there would not be so strong a printer's union in Sacramento as exists today." Sheehan summed up his attitude toward the *Bee*: "The *Bee* never praises, save for pay; it never criticizes when paid to desist. It lives solely on the tribute it can extort. Take from the *Bee* its subsidies it is now receiving from its victims and it would not last a month. . . . It has neither honor nor decency. It maligns the living and defames the dead with equal gusto. Its present managers are journalistic disreputes [*sic*] making merchandise of the sacred principle of educating public opinion."[6]

But Sheehan's journalistic pugnacity was not on secure ground. The circulation, although steady—about twelve hundred customers in 1893—came nowhere near the *Bee*'s more than four thousand. Eventually both Thomas Clunie and Augustus Abbott became tired of paying for the paper, which still could not land regular city contracts or even a steady flow of advertising. Abbott's interest waned as his business interests changed, and he turned his attention to monopolizing the city's water supply. Clunie was unwilling to underwrite it all, and the paper closed on September 12, 1893. Abbott allegedly agreed to shutter the paper in exchange for *Bee* support for his water project and supposedly even promised that the printing machinery would never be used to produce another newspaper. "The *News* is no more," CK crowed. "It gently folded its wings this afternoon, dropped its head upon its breast and lay down to a quiet and tranquil rest." CK suggested that ideological and financial differences between Clunie and Abbot sank the paper.[7]

But other papers offered an alternative view. The *Galt Weekly Gazette,* a feisty weekly edited by J. J. Campbell and owned by Sacramento lawyers and the California State Bank, related "a curious story . . . that bears the very semblance of truth." Dismissing rumors of the *Evening News's* financial collapse, the *Gazette* placed the blame indirectly on a scheme for a new water system that required the aid of the press to pass. Complicit in this were the city bond holders, "who have waxed fat on 55 percent of the revenue of the city waterworks." The head of this "bond holding gang," Augustus Abbott, turned traitor. In need of the *Bee's* support for the water project, Abbot went to the McClatchys, who allegedly asked for either $5,000 "cash down" or "the death of the *News*." Abbot chose the latter, and the *News* joined "the great throng of newspapers that have found a timely grave in the Potters' Field of Sacramento journalism," the *Gazette* claimed. Campbell further related that the McClatchy ally and then-mayor Benjamin Steinman, "the gas and electric light monopolist" who also "had a finger in the new water monopoly pie," also helped bribe the McClatchys with a promise to license gambling. However, this so stirred up the *Record-Union* that Steinman could not vote for his own resolution and earned the ire of the McClatchys. Campbell noted, "The Sacramento newspapers would not be prone to relate these little incidents," but their net result was that "the old newspaper cinch will be resumed and Sacramento [will] regain its reputation of publishing the most dreary newspapers on the globe."[8]

When the *Sutter Independent* reprinted Campbell's column, CK wrote the editor that it was "entirely wrong." CK declared that *Bee* support for the controversial water proposal had gone back seven years, and it was approved "despite the desperate silurian fight against it." He argued that the *News* "died because it had lost money to a very appreciable extent ever since its birth and its proprietors evidently grew tired of footing up the deficit." Still, accusations dogged the *Bee* and its favored mayoral candidate, Benjamin Steinman. Rumors persisted for so long that CK rebutted them on the *Bee's* front page and published a denial by Steinman, who declared that he had nothing to do with the demise of the rival paper.[9] In a darker version of events, Sheehan related that it was Valentine (to whom he referred derisively as "Whiskers") who had helped seal the fate of the *News* by conniving with the Southern Pacific to assure the election of a candidate they supported. Sheehan complained: "The *Bee* . . . [is] a damned monopoly—the Southern Pacific sheet is not worth a damn. . . . Whiskers owns more real estate in the city than any one man on it."[10]

By the fall of 1893 the *Bee* and the *Record-Union* once again controlled information in the city. John Sheehan and Junius Brutus Harris decided to publish a weekly called the *Sunday News,* issuing the first edition of the new paper on April 15, 1894. Without missing a beat, they resumed the verbal war on the *Bee.* Sheehan clearly nettled the McClatchys, and fears that the *Sunday News* would evolve into another evening daily drove the McClatchys to one of the more disastrous episodes of their joint ownership of the *Bee*—the tawdry Carl von Arnold affair. An unfortunate tendency of the brothers to use nefarious means to accomplish their ends backfired disastrously.

Seeking Revenge

Fears that an evening rival would appear were real. Rumors circulated sometime during 1896 that John Sheehan was making common cause with the McClatchys' nemeses—Grove Johnson, Amos P. Catlin, and others—to expand the *Sunday News* into a daily. Sheehan fed the McClatchys' anxiety by stating in one of his columns in January 1897, "In response to a very large number of anxious inquiries we announce there is the prospect of a new daily paper in Sacramento." Although he was somewhat vague, Sheehan dropped large hints that "certain persons of abundant means" were "canvassing the situation," but plans "were more or less definite, looking to the investment of a large amount in a new newspaper enterprise in Sacramento."[11]

At every opportunity Sheehan lashed "the scoundrelly McClatchys, thwarting their schemes to rob the city or county treasury, exposing their blackmailing operations and warning the people at every turn against the malevolent rascals." He took special aim at Valentine McClatchy, whose "nose has acquired an edge like a cimitar [*sic*] from sharp and incessant pursuit of the nimble dollar." In Sheehan's view "the scoundrel who edits and manages" the *Bee*, CK, was only the nominal editor, "who is permitted to assign details to reporters, write editorials when they do not interfere with [Valentine's] cunning calculations. . . . Val predominates over all." Sheehan even spread the rumor that Valentine suspected CK had taken graft and had him kidnapped in front of the Metropolitan Theater and held him in his home under guard until his friend "Lije" Hart could free him with a writ of habeas corpus.[12] While Valentine could indeed be domineering, the kidnapping was an obvious falsehood— or perhaps the embellishment of an episode in which Valentine punished his brother for another bout of public drunkenness. Sheehan's willingness to play fast and loose with the truth, and his sometimes unsavory personal life, riled the abstemious Valentine and the moralistic CK, who sought to expose Sheehan and drive him out of Sacramento permanently. CK, fed by continual reports by the detective, made clear his hatred of Sheehan, writing, "This vulture of the press; this vile blackmailer of defenseless women; this harpy who fattens on the failings of others; this professional, persistent and promiscuous guerilla of journalism . . . he is a man with the gratitude of a rattlesnake, the morals of a hog . . . a dangerous menace to the families of this community, a poisonous leech in more than one home."[13]

CK had written that description while formulating a plan to destroy Sheehan; it took shape in late 1895. The brothers needed no encouragement to take revenge on Sheehan, who had once worked for them and on whom they had been spying for months. When they heard from *Bee* informers that Sheehan was blackmailing certain prominent Sacramentans by threatening to release information about their love lives or their illegal activities—especially illicit gambling (which Sheehan hypocritically refused to cover because gamblers like Frank Daroux and Angus Ross paid him bribes)—the McClatchys decided to expose him. CK alluded to threats against socially prominent and religious figures when denouncing Sheehan's blackmailing ways. CK huffed that such revelations "would startle this community if they were published" but said that the *Bee* would not expose such indiscretions (even though the McClatchys had done so with people they considered enemies).[14] CK also believed that Sheehan was blackmailing members of the Sacramento city government who accepted bribes to protect illegal gambling. These included the city trustees James Devine, Charles Leonard, Eugene Wachorst, Robert Kent, and Timothy Pennish—as well as Mayor Cyrus Hubbard and Police Chief Warren F. Drew.[15]

The prospect of taking down the offensive Sheehan, killing the *Sunday News,* and going after urban corruption tied to gambling proved tempting to the McClatchys. Their desire for vengeance, poor information, and naïveté led the McClatchys to set up a sting operation that blew up in their faces.

The Von Arnold Sting

A complicated plot began in late 1896 when, at the suggestion of his friend Judge S. C. Denson, Valentine engaged the services of C. J. Stilwell, a hard-boiled San Francisco detective. To entrap both Sheehan and the suspected city officials into revealing themselves, Stilwell assigned an operative named Carl von Arnold to get the goods on Sheehan and any corrupt public figures who were doing business with him. Stilwell warned Valentine that the cost would be high, but the brothers felt it was worth it.[16]

Von Arnold arrived in Sacramento on December 18, 1896, posing as a well-heeled German American entrepreneur and all around bon vivant. He passed out his pink calling cards at every saloon and gaming establishment. To any who would listen, he spun an elaborate tale of his connections to Chicago millionaires, a rich inheritance from his mother, a promise of support from an equally wealthy brother, and his eagerness to invest in Sacramento. Von Arnold made it known that he and his brother ran a popular entertainment venue in Chicago called Over the Rhine—that also offered illicit gambling on the premises. His ribald sense of humor won him the hearing of many, and on Valentine's dime von Arnold threw parties with beer, silver, gold fizzes, and shots of whiskey. At these blowsy parties he declared his liking for Sacramento and promised to spend nearly $150,000 on a new entertainment hall similar to the one in Chicago—and he made quiet inquiries about getting in on local gambling. This did not get him anywhere at first, and Valentine grew anxious, complaining bitterly to Stilwell about the money this was costing the *Bee.*[17]

But just in the nick of time, the investment paid off. Von Arnold linked up with one Harry T. Schumann, who introduced him to Sheehan on December 29, 1896. Von Arnold again bragged at length about his fortune and his skills as a Teutonic Lothario. Impressed with the hard-drinking, womanizing von Arnold, Sheehan thought he might be a good benefactor for a new evening daily to replace the *Sunday News.* Von Arnold appeared interested in the project and asked if Sheehan could introduce him to members of the Sacramento City Board of Trustees, including its president, Charles Leonard; Mayor Cyrus Hubbard; and the chief of police. Since von Arnold planned to open an entertainment center, which was to include a gambling operation, he needed protection. Sheehan willingly made the introductions.

What happened next is a matter of speculation since we have no recording or transcription of what actually occurred. Von Arnold told the McClatchys that Sheehan approached von Arnold for money to purchase a portion of the *Sunday News* and to bankroll the re-creation of the *Daily Evening News*. Sheehan later insisted that von Arnold himself raised the issue and wanted to participate in the project with an investment of "five or ten thousand dollars." When Sheehan told his new friend start-up costs would be $50,000, von Arnold demurred but later came back and said he would put up $25,000 and would induce his brother (mockingly named Valentine) to put up another $25,000. Although Sheehan later suggested he had misgivings about von Arnold's identity, his doubts were stilled when he saw how much money von Arnold spent on liquor and women. Sheehan pressed von Arnold hard for money—and assured the free-spending stranger that other prominent figures—including David Lubin (now out of the city); John Weil, owner of Sacramento Glass and Crockery and a McClatchy foe; Grove Johnson; and, most important, Harris Weinstock—would agree on the need for a new evening paper. Von Arnold told the McClatchys that Sheehan believed that Weinstock was a potential mayoral candidate in 1897 and might be in an even better position to endorse the new paper. The possibility that the upstanding Weinstock might be somehow tied in with the disreputable Sheehan pricked up the ears of the McClatchys, who were still smarting from his support of the two boycotts of the *Bee*. But although Sheehan introduced von Arnold to the department store owner, he never directly implicated Weinstock. Indeed when von Arnold suggested Weinstock for the presidency of the newspaper's board of directors, Sheehan turned the idea down, noting Weinstock was busy enough with his own business.

Nonetheless, convinced that the promise of money from von Arnold was authentic, Sheehan began to draw up articles of incorporation and create a board of directors. Weil agreed to serve as president although he made no financial investment.[18] On the urban corruption front, von Arnold also told Stilwell and Valentine that he had indirectly asked if Sacramento board of trustee members were open to bribes to cover up gambling activities.[19]

All this was tantalizing but not sufficiently sourced to move it to print. No one contacted had done anything more than listen sympathetically to von Arnold's plans for a new entertainment hall. Valentine tried to confirm the story by having von Arnold leave the city on the pretext of tending to a sick child in San Jose. Von Arnold then drafted letters to each of his contacts outlining the details of the deal—and sent Valentine copies of each letter.[20] If the recipients did not write back indignantly, it would be a clear sign the allegations were true; if they did not respond at all, they were either innocent or cautious. The responses were inconclusive—city trustee Eugene Wachorst replied, virtually acknowledging his guilt; Hubbard was evasive, seeming confused by the letter he had received but later remembering he had met von Arnold. None of the others responded. The *Bee* would publish these letters on its front page in an effort to prove that those contacted by von Arnold were implicated in shady activities.[21] But the ruse was undone when Valentine sent a copy of von Arnold's letter, rather than the original, to Weinstock—a text that included Valentine's own handwriting. Weinstock in fact knew nothing of the plans for the new newspaper and had no interest in it nor was he even remotely considering running for mayor. His dealings with von Arnold were perfunctory and professional.[22] However, in relating these things to McClatchy, von Arnold made it appear that Weinstock and others were willing to participate in his scheme. At this point Valentine still did not have the definitive proof of the perfidy of those who spoke to von Arnold or received his letter. He would have been well advised to drop the whole thing and discharge von Arnold—but he didn't. Sheehan clearly was willing to take von Arnold's money, and for that he had to be punished and a rival paper stopped.

As time went on Sheehan grew impatient, as the money promised for the newspaper and the new hall was not forthcoming. Von Arnold parried Sheehan's requests with assurances the money would be on the way after he had arranged affairs with his brother in Chicago. Eventually von Arnold produced a telegram from his brother in Chicago who pledged $30,000 for the newspaper. Sheehan also hoped Weinstock would add $20,000 more. Von Arnold then placed a bank draft in the safe of the Western Hotel until it could be deposited in the California National Bank. Sheehan was overjoyed and had incorporation papers for the Capital Publishing Company drawn up by the attorney Albert Johnson; they listed von Arnold as contributing $16,666; his brother $16,666; and Sheehan $16,666. John Weil and Charles Leonard put in $100 apiece. The exultant Sheehan ordered new suits from a local clothier and bought a ticket to the East in order to shop for new printing plant equipment. CK and Valentine thought this was enough to spring the trap.

On March 3, 1897, the McClatchys printed von Arnold's allegations in the pages of the *Bee*. Even though they claimed disingenuously that they had first regarded these allegations "with grave suspicion" because they had included the names of "many officials and prominent citizens," the McClatchys gave them credence because these allegations had been corroborated by the discovery of a mysterious "red leather book"—perhaps Sheehan's red pocket book, which von Arnold pilfered—containing a number of incriminating documents.[23] The *Bee* accused von Arnold of corrupting city officials and exposed his plan to underwrite a new paper as a way of providing press support for this graft combine and purchasing cover for his new entertainment-gambling hall. The *Bee* demanded and received a grand jury investigation of all these allegations. Coming to von Arnold's defense was none other than Hiram W. Johnson, who offered his legal services to help von Arnold combat the *Bee*. Johnson did not know that the McClatchys were keeping von Arnold's true identity secret while accusing him of being a boodler and a thief. The grand jury looked into the accusations of urban corruption. CK and Valentine seemed less concerned about the cover-up of gambling than of the apparent collusion of their enemies, Weinstock and Grove Johnson, to give Sheehan's paper a boost.[24] Reporting was light as the grand jury deliberated.

Sheehan remained in the dark. In the March 7, 1897, edition of the *Sunday News* he praised von Arnold's generosity and denounced the *Bee* for impugning his motives—and besmirching the reputations of Harris Weinstock, Charles Leonard, and others accused in its front page stories. Sheehan coupled his denunciations of the McClatchys with a boast that a new evening daily would roll off the presses, and "no citizen of Sacramento will have need to fear the houndings of the notorious McClatchys." Sheehan and von Arnold were inseparable as the editor made sure to protect his asset.[25]

Finally, on March 13, 1897, the *Bee* revealed the sting, providing a lengthy account of von Arnold's true identity and how the ruse had successfully identified urban corruption and the activities of Sheehan. Explaining the earlier denunciation of von Arnold as a crook, CK explained, "In its handling of this case The *Bee* has been compelled in various ways to mystify the public in order that the guilty parties might offer the necessary corroborative evidence without which The *Bee* declined to publish the grave charges contained in Detective von Arnold's report." With delight the McClatchys taunted Sheehan: "What will [Sheehan] do with the new suits of clothes ordered by him for his eastern trip . . . and what disposition will he make of the railroad ticket?"[26] The revelation that von Arnold was a double agent blindsided Sheehan, and he poured out his anger on the pages of the *Sunday News,* denouncing the imposter. Detailing the detective's love of liquor and affection for women, Sheehan portrayed himself as a victim of the McClatchys' spite and declared everything he had done was legal and legitimate. He was not a blackmailer nor did he accept graft. He also insisted, erroneously, that the money for von Arnold's escapades had come from the real estate speculator and former mayor Benjamin Steinman, an enemy of Sheehan's since his *Daily Evening News* days.[27]

Admitting he had been taken, Sheehan dismissed the shenanigans of his bitter rivals and commented wistfully of von Arnold, "There was a chance he was genuine, and we took that chance." Sheehan seemed sure "the Grand Jury will not fail to do its duty undeterred by the manifest effort of the McClatchys to use it as the kite of the *Bogus Bee*. . . . All we ask is a square deal."[28] In the next issue of the paper Sheehan unearthed von Arnold's seedy past and some of the misconduct of C. J. Stilwell. Sheehan denied the accusations against the members of the city Board of Trustees and condemned the letters to and from von Arnold that had been part of the trap—insisting they had been altered and exculpatory material removed. Nonetheless, throughout March, even as the Grand Jury investigated, the *Bee* kept up a steady flow of damning articles with the material von Arnold had provided them.[29] In a response to a critical editorial in the *Oakland Enquirer* about the entire combine story, CK sniffed that Sheehan's blackmailing could have been avoided if the legislature had not forbidden local governments to license gambling.[30]

But all this sound and fury amounted to nothing. The grand jury returned no indictments because it could turn up no solid evidence or even a suggestion that the bribery scheme had been real. Indeed, apart from Wachorst, who may have taken money from the free-spending von Arnold, there was no evidence von Arnold had bribed anyone. What began to dawn on CK and Valentine was that von Arnold had lied to them. Even more galling was that, after wining and dining on McClatchy money, von Arnold himself disappeared into the mists—never to be heard of again. He not only fleeced the McClatchys but had embarrassed them and put them in legal jeopardy because they had publicly broadcast von Arnold's false claims.

The Weinstock Libel Case

Of all the misinformation von Arnold had passed on, the worst were his allegations of Weinstock's indirect complicity in Sheehan's schemes. In fact the department store mogul had met von Arnold only once and definitely had no interest in linking up with Sheehan in a newspaper enterprise or running for mayor.[31] Even worse, Valentine learned on March 5, only two days after the *Bee's* story ran, that Weinstock had proof of Valentine's part in this farce—the letter Weinstock had received from von Arnold that included Valentine's markings in the margin (von Arnold had sent the edited copy). Valentine nonetheless insisted, "It will doubtless please the gallant Major to have the assurance that neither of the *Bee's* proprietors, not anyone in their employ, has turned forger or conspirator against any citizen's good name."[32] But Weinstock believed he had been libeled by Valentine because of the markings on the letter. Through an emissary, Dr. Charles Van Norden of Auburn, Weinstock reached out to the McClatchys on March 8 in an effort to set the matter straight. Van Norden told Valentine:

> [Weinstock] had already evidence [von Arnold's letter] which made a very strong case against V.S. [Valentine] as having conspired with others to injure the good name of Mr. Weinstock, and that, if by proper publication, Mr. Weinstock would be set right here before the community as not having been in any way implicated in the matter of recent publication in The *Bee*, Dr. Van Norden thought there would be no occasion for any trouble. Otherwise, Mr. Weinstock was determined to commence suit for damages to set himself right before the public.

McClatchy replied that "he was not convinced of Weinstock's innocence"; only if Weinstock could convince the *Bee* that he was without guilt would the *Bee* "very gladly state that fact without solicitation." Valentine, writing an aide memoire in the third person, said he "regretted that Van Norden, whom he had known for some time, should believe that McClatchy was directly interested in a conspiracy to blacken Mr. Weinstock's reputation before the community." Van Norden even tried to help Valentine explain away how Weinstock received a letter from von Arnold with Valentine's markings on it (maybe the letter had been stolen from von Arnold's "secretary," a Mr. Schuman, and given to Valentine, who merely wanted to investigate the truth of the matter).

Valentine thanked Van Norden but would say no more. Van Norden left, telling Valentine that he believed in Weinstock's innocence and that the *Bee* should expect a lawsuit.[33]

Then Weinstock filed a $50,000 libel suit against the McClatchys on March 20, 1897, with Hiram Johnson as his lead attorney.[34] In a statement to the *Record-Union* Weinstock insisted that the actions of the *Bee* were deliberate and harmful: "I believe one of the most contemptible and despicable among God's creatures is the libeler and slanderer, the destroyer of other men's characters and reputations, and I believe that to transmit slander is to be as guilty as to invent slander." Weinstock spoke of *Bee* detectives dogging his every step and even violating the privacy of his household. He lamented that his advertising contract with the *Bee* had many months to go. Although advised against going after the McClatchys, he felt it his civic duty to do so. The *Record-Union* permitted Valentine and CK a partial response; it took issue with every one of Weinstock's assertions. Stoutly defending the actions of their reporters, the brothers asserted that they did not believe "that Weinstock was engaged in corrupt matters of the combine." In the *Bee* the McClatchys disputed Weinstock's allegations and declared they had intended only to expose boodlers such as Sheehan.[35] However, the strong implication of the reporting on Weinstock was guilt by association. He had been contacted by von Arnold; hence some of the taint of the sting splashed onto him.

Realizing that their elaborate plans were now a disaster, CK and Valentine pursued a dual policy. On the one hand, they presented their questionable "evidence" as though it were unassailable, even if the public might reject it. "The public knows the facts," CK sniffed. "If the people desire to maintain guilty men in office, The *Bee* will perhaps suffer no more than other taxpayers."[36] On the other hand, they tried damage control. Of particular concern was the revelation that they had impugned the reputation of Weinstock out of pure spite and vengeance. Smaller papers repeated the sensational charges against Weinstock, reinforcing his accusation of libel. At the same time, CK attempted to stanch the damage. In a letter to the editor of a Modesto paper he wrote: "I notice in commenting upon the Weinstock-*Bee* libel suit that you have made a mistake as to the tenor of the articles in The *Bee*. The *Bee* has never claimed in any of its articles that Mr. H. Weinstock was a member of any boodling combine, or of any blackmailers, or of any corrupt and corrupting politicians, who are looting the City Treasury." Instead, CK insisted, the "gang of scoundrels" who was corrupting city government "had endeavored to bring a reputable merchant into their newspaper combine in order to give it some respectability before the general public."[37] The McClatchys' efforts to absolve themselves of guilt in accusing Weinstock, however, proved to be impossible to pull off. CK vigorously attacked his future friend and confidant Hiram Johnson, who was demanding from the *Bee* all the documentation it had accumulated in "proving" the guilt of Charles Leonard, chair of the Sacramento Board of Trustees, and suggesting that Weinstock was involved in the scheming.[38]

It finally hit the McClatchys in mid-April that von Arnold was a fraud. To their great embarrassment, however, another of von Arnold's scams hit the front pages of the *San Francisco Examiner*. Apparently, while he was passing himself off as a jovial German tavern owner and benefactor in Sacramento, he was also posing as Count von Turkheim and wooing one Jeanne Young, whom he married in mid-April 1897. When the *Examiner* revealed that von Arnold was a bigamist (his first wife, Emma Long of Louisville, was named in the paper), it also discussed his escapades in Sacramento, particularly the suggested misconduct by Weinstock. [39] This distressing news must have given CK and Valentine a few sleepless nights, and it elicited notes of sympathy from colleagues. However, CK put on a brave front and urged readers, "Don't worry about us," assuring them that no matter where von Arnold had gone, the paper still had evidence that could sink the careers of many in Sacramento.[40] Weinstock was intrigued by the reports of von Arnold's antics and traveled to San Francisco to meet with Police Chief Isaiah Lees to inquire about von Arnold. During their brief conversation, Lees claimed he knew little or nothing about what had happened in Sacramento. Later, in an effort to derail Weinstock's libel case, the McClatchys had Lees and the *Examiner* reporter Edward Moran deposed. Both Moran and Lees claimed they really did not know Weinstock and had not consulted him about von Arnold's deceptions. The McClatchys derided Lees as a victim of von Arnold's, much as they had been.[41]

The libel trial took place in the early months of 1898 with all the principals appearing on the docket.[42] Although Weinstock produced the von Arnold letter with Valentine's markings on it as evidence of McClatchy perfidy and intent to defame, Valentine and CK contended they had been scrupulous in their reporting. They insisted they had in no way linked Weinstock to the combine scandal. In a remarkable defense (given that they had planned the sting against their enemies), they instead claimed to be the real victims, asserting that because of Weinstock's support of the boycotts, he had plotted the destruction of the McClatchys' reputations and livelihood. Several witnesses came forward to attest to Sheehan's blackmailing and to tag Charles Leonard with being in on a plot to create a new newspaper and otherwise use his office as president of the Sacramento City Board of Trustees in an inappropriate way. The jury deliberated for the better part of Saturday, February 26, and was strongly divided, 5–7, in favor of Weinstock. The jury announced its decision on February 28 in favor of Weinstock but substantially reduced the award from $50,000 to $400. CK and Valentine framed the outcome as "a great victory for this paper" and ridiculed the effusive public praise given to the injured Weinstock: "Mr. Weinstock soars very high. In his own estimation, his reputation is irreproachable and unapproachable, the spotlessly white Taj Mahal of character architecture of this community . . . the best citizen of Sacramento." CK became cocky, even warning other participants in the graft investigation that if they had ideas of attacking the *Bee* and winning, "it would give us the greatest pleasure on earth to undeceive them. Don't be bashful gentlemen!"[43] The McClatchys appealed the decision but were unsuccessful. They steadfastly refused to pay the damages until a lien on their properties made it impossible for Valentine to conduct his real estate affairs. The great von Arnold sting had cost them not only the price of the failed investigation but also $400 more in the judgment. They were fortunate that the judge was so lenient.

The McClatchys never gave up trying to topple Weinstock and continually rummaged for information that would cast him in a bad light. In late 1899 Weinstock was arrested for advertising a forbidden object (probably some women's apparel) through his company's catalog, which was against U.S. postal regulations. John Sexton of Diamond Springs filed the complaint, and an El Dorado County sheriff arrested Weinstock.[44] When the *Sunday News* defended Weinstock and decried the *Bee's* vendetta against him in an article headlined "An Infamous Assault," CK replied loftily, "The *Bee* knows but one rule and that is to treat all men alike. The rich and the poor; the employer and the clerk; the capitalist and the laborer . . . the merchant prince, who stands well in the community . . . all are treated . . . with the same impartiality."[45] But such elevated sentiments notwithstanding, the brothers' hatred for Weinstock overwhelmed their good judgment, and they unabashedly libeled an innocent man. Moreover, their use of the shady von Arnold did not reflect well on either their judgment or their morality. Sheehan continued to conduct the *Sunday News* until his death.

An Attempt at Reconciliation

Because the McClatchys and Weinstock were prominent in the community, the split between them was a public issue. Valentine, flush with other advertisers, hoped to punish Weinstock by refusing his advertising and even threatened the immediate discharge of any employee who approached the company for an ad. As time passed, Weinstock's half-brother and business partner, David Lubin, sought to mend fences and wrote to the McClatchys to see if he could bring healing to the still bitter relationship. Lubin, who was one of the most beloved figures in the city and even internationally, was not someone who could be easily ignored. Moreover both CK and Valentine considered him a good friend. Valentine responded graciously and urged Lubin to contact CK, promising, "I will abide by any conclusion which you and he agree upon in this matter."[46] Valentine nonetheless insisted Weinstock had to make amends for his attempts to ruin the *Bee*. Valentine knew Weinstock would never do this and so managed to finesse the gentle Lubin's call for peace.

Weinstock indeed vigorously defended himself against the charge he had attempted to hurt the *Bee* during the printers' boycott. He reiterated the indignities of the von Arnold episode: "Their [the McClatchys'] conduct in this matter was absolutely without warrant and in the eyes of all disinterested parties familiar with the facts, malicious and unpardonable. . . . I do not believe in, and never will consent to be a victim to public insult, with a private apology." Weinstock declared he had evidence Valentine actively plotted to trap him by revealing the existence of "a skillful and incriminating decoy letter [which] through a blunder on his part, bore on its margin the initials of and notation made by Mr. McClatchy and which he later acknowledged." CK also rejected Lubin's appeal for arbitration. He drafted a multipage report "to put down in black and white so that Mr. Lubin could hereafter refer to it as he wished to know the McClatchy side of a great many things."[47] The report said in part:

> Mr. Weinstock cannot remember where and when he has helped to boycott The *Bee*.
> I can.
> Mr. Weinstock cannot call to mind any occasion where he assaulted the McClatchys in public.
> I can.

Mr. Weinstock does not know that he ever tried to keep public news away from The *Bee*.

I do.

It is remarkable how forgetful Mr. Weinstock can be on some things which are not to his advantage, and how imaginatively reminiscent he is on some things that might be advantageous—like the "deliberate malice" of V.S. McClatchy, "proved to the satisfaction of two separate juries" for instance.

If Mr. Weinstock had succeeded, The *Bee* would not have been in existence under the McClatchys to stand the libel suits in 1897 and 1898.

Mr. Weinstock denies the "assumption" by V.S. McClatchy that what he did "in those instances"—meaning the two *Bee* boycotts—"was meant to ruin his paper in order to save my interests."

Then, what in hell was it done for?

Mr. Weinstock joined and was in the lead in two boycotts against The *Bee* which, had they succeeded, would have bankrupted this paper and its proprietors. If he did not for policy, did he do it for principle? And for what principle. The *Bee* had then no quarrel with Mr. Weinstock. He said he was its friend. And yet he did the Brutus act, and did all he could to mortally stab his friend! Is that the "Abraham Lincoln spirit" which you find in Mr. Weinstock?[48]

A mutual friend, Judge Peter Shields, also attempted a reconciliation in 1908. Although Shields acknowledged the McClatchys had used von Arnold's false information to damage Weinstock's reputation, Shields argued the McClatchys did it only because they thought Weinstock was out to destroy their business with the boycott. Even more, Shields insisted, in print and in the court cases the *Bee* expressed no desire to harm Weinstock personally. Weinstock rejected these conclusions and steamed off to Europe. Weinstock remained resolute in his hatred for the McClatchys until his accidental death in 1922.[49]

In the end, despite the embarrassment of the von Arnold sting, the McClatchys did put an end to Sheehan's plans for a rival evening daily. The *Sunday News* continued for some time as a pesky fly but was never again a serious threat to the *Bee*. The tale of this sordid scheming attached to demolishing the *News* had no comparison when dealing with other rivals. Relations with the morning paper, the *Sacramento Union*, were difficult at times, but nothing compared with the evening rivalry.

Dealing with the *Union*

The *Union*, established in 1850, had survived the bitter competition among newspapers in early Sacramento—a rivalry so intense that Sacramento was known as a newspaper graveyard. An independent and feisty paper, the *Union* claimed fame as the former employer of the legendary Mark Twain. The *Union* was one of the first journals in the state to raise a concern about the increasing power of the railroads and actually opposed railroad expansion in Sacramento. In retaliation the railroad, which controlled a rival paper, the *Sacramento Record,* bought the *Union* in 1875, and for many years the paper was called the *Record-Union.* William H. Mills, the proprietor and editor of the *Record*—and later a land officer of the railroad—became the editor. Under Mills the paper prospered, and while it maintained a strong prorailroad stance, it also took advantage of Mills's exceptional knowledge of California's terrain and advanced the preservation of the natural beauty of the state. Mills, as I have discussed, was one of the first to take up the perils of hydraulic mining. When Mills was promoted within the railroad, he turned over administrative duties to other editors—but kept his eye on the content and scope of the newspaper until it was sold.

Valentine worked hard to secure loyal advertisers and subscribers to the *Bee*, but he was blessed that the *Record-Union* was not an energetic competitor. Likewise, like their father, both brothers had cordial relations with Mills and his staff even after Mills left Sacramento. So amiable were the relations between the two rivals that when a new *Bee* building was erected in 1902–1903, the papers shared printing facilities. They also agreed not to hire each other's employees or accept the other's rejects. All this did not preclude occasional bouts of editorial waspishness, especially if CK's facts or opinions were challenged. But for most of its existence the *Record-Union* (or the *Union*) did not present serious competition. At one point the McClatchys derisively called it the "old woman across the street."[50] The *Union* would ultimately prove about as annoying as a mosquito at a picnic. In the end it stayed alive thanks to secret loans made by CK, who wanted the appearance of a newspaper rival.

Both papers supported the railroad until Collis P. Huntington died in 1901. E. H. Harriman replaced Huntington, and he relieved Mills of his responsibilities (and oversight of the *Record-Union*) on May 1, 1901. Valentine and CK genuinely lamented the departure of Mills. Valentine wrote:

The *Bee*'s relations with you have been so pleasant that from a self-ish standpoint I might feel regret at any change in the department. But because of personal friendliness, inspired by association in various matters of concern, I am impelled to congratulate you on relief from an excess of duties demanding close attention to the office and precluding the recreation and rest which the man of affairs deserves as much, and needs more, than the day laborer. I should be gratified indeed if our relations leaves in your memory nearly as pleasant an impression as in mine.[51]

In late May 1901 the *Record-Union* went up for sale, and the McClatchys actively considered purchasing it, but the projected expenses of a new *Bee* building held them back.[52] The *Union* then passed into the hands of Colonel Epaminondas Ahasuerus Forbes. This grandiloquently named editor had been publisher of the *Marysville Appeal.* He attempted to liven up the Sacramento newspaper, first by returning it to its original name, the *Union,* and trying to strike out on a new editorial path after its years of bondage to the Southern Pacific. He also tried to beef up circulation so as to attract more advertising revenue. The subscription crusade begun in 1906 must have worried Valentine enough to press the *Bee* business manager H. J. F. Berkeley to inaugurate a rival contest. "There are several reasons why it seems to me it would be well for us to inaugurate a contest at this time if we can do so successfully. One reason, of course, is to offset any possible gain which might accrue to the Union from their efforts." But he also wanted to teach the *Union* a lesson about becoming seriously competitive with the *Bee.*[53]

Forbes and his top editor, Alfred Holman, strongly supported the cause of Progressive reform. In fact Holman was present at the beginning of the California Progressive crusade and active in the formation of the Lincoln-Roosevelt League. In early January 1907, when L. E. Bontz, a new *Union* business manager, came on board, Valentine renewed "the former understanding between the two papers to the effect that neither will attempt to secure the services of an employee of the other without consent of the other first obtained." Valentine told Bontz: "This is a continuation of the arrangement which existed between the two papers while the Union was under the management of Mr. Alfred Holman."[54] But Forbes found himself overextended, and when his finances deteriorated, he sold the *Union* in February 1908 to a newspaper syndicate headed by the Calkins family, a prominent journalistic clan.

The Calkins Brothers

Under any other circumstances the McClatchys and the Calkinses would have been friends. Both families had printer's ink in their veins. The family patriarch, Major E. A. Calkins, a veteran of the Civil War, served as an editor for papers in Wisconsin and then moved on to edit the *St. Paul Pioneer Democrat* and the *Chicago Evening Journal.* In 1852–53 his son, Malcolm Dunn Calkins, and his wife, Elizabeth Sayler Calkins, arrived in California. The family moved back and forth between the West and the Midwest, but the couple and their seven sons went into newspaper work. The Calkinses eventually returned west for good in the late 1870s and began to buy up small papers in the mining districts, first taking over the *Amador Record* in 1878. Malcolm was a strong advocate for mining interests throughout his career. Willard Peck Calkins, one of the younger sons, bought the *Colfax Sentinel* and the *Grass Valley Daily Union.* Thomas Calkins began with the *Amador Record* and owned a number of newspapers and periodicals in California during his forty-two-year career.[55] CK noted of Willard Calkins, "He springs from a newspaper race extending back for at least two generations, each one of whose members seem to have taken to that business as naturally as a duck takes to water."[56] The Calkins brothers formed a newspaper syndicate to coordinate and expand their rapidly growing Northern California newspaper empire. They even won a bid to print the Southern Pacific's famous *Sunset Magazine.*[57] Willard's desire for expansion took him into the highly competitive San Francisco market, where he formed the *San Francisco Globe,* which he intended as a rival to the *San Francisco Bulletin.* Then he moved back to the Central Valley and purchased the *Fresno Herald* and the Sacramento *Union.* After learning the printer's trade in a variety of places in the Midwest, Leonard Calkins made his home in Nevada City, where he edited and later bought a portion of the *Nevada City Miner-Transcript.* Leonard was a respected citizen who had served as a postmaster for his community. He was also a sought-after public speaker, an accomplished pianist, and a journalist of no mean reputation. Willard made Leonard Calkins the *Union's* publisher and Edward Insley its editor.[58]

The Calkinses' takeover disturbed the McClatchys. These were not fly-by-night rich boys like Hearst who collected newspapers like children's marbles but skilled journalists with a long family history in the newspaper business. They had made a success of California's mountain press. Moreover because of the hydraulic mining issues they had every reason to dislike the McClatchys.

No strangers to good management, the Calkinses knew how to contest the *Bee* for circulation and advertising. However, when they purchased the Sacramento morning paper, they moved into a new league that far surpassed the rather modest operations they ran in communities like Grass Valley or Colfax. Their Achilles heel, as CK and Valentine quickly surmised, was a lack of capital. They acquired their publishing empire—including the *Union*—on a pyramid of credit that seemed precarious and aroused wonderment among the press fraternity. Valentine, who knew something about financing a newspaper, wondered how they could sustain such rapid expansion.[59]

CK blamed the Calkinses for the hatred engendered by the Calkins-run *Nevada City Miner-Transcript* over the issue of hydraulic mining. Even before the purchase of the *Union,* CK had lashed out at Leonard Calkins: "Will anyone kindly tell this paper at what period in his life Leonard S. Calkins was ever anything else than he is today, the sycophantic and serviceable tool of corrupting corporations?" Nor did CK spare Willard Calkins a verbal thwack, denouncing him as "Janus faced"—appearing to oppose government corruption while promoting the agendas of corporations like the Southern Pacific. Even more, CK tagged Calkins as aiding and abetting those who wanted to move the state capital to Berkeley.[60] CK reprinted from the *Nevada City Miner-Transcript* Willard Calkins's reply, a denunciation of the "unchecked insolence" of the "Sacramento yellow journal."[61] Willard Calkins also fired back on February 23, 1908, from the editorial page of the newly purchased *Union:* "Our coming to Sacramento has already been heralded not by acts of obeisance . . . but by the howling of an excited band of newspaper dervishes and medicine men who pursuing the methods of witch doctors, have sought to frighten strangers from invading the territory which they have so long posed as squaw men and outlaws from Bitter Creek." Willard Calkins swore allegiance to the greater good of Sacramento and attempted to exploit what he hoped was a still festering mass of discontent with the McClatchys. Willard Calkins righteously insisted that his purchase of the paper was "proof of the failure of the Chinese stink pot methods of the newspaper that has so long taxed the patience of the law-abiding citizens of Sacramento and Northern California." He noted that the opposition "feared a strong business rival" and manifested "the narrowness and provincialism of villagers of limited experience and resources." He took particular offense at the charge of being owned by the "higher ups": "We are absolutely free from the collars of grafters, railroad companies and other corporations and individuals."[62]

But CK was determined to stop the Calkinses before they had a chance to settle in. Already a master of what would later be called opposition research, CK gathered damaging information from informants, private detectives, and gossip from other colleagues in journalism. At an opportune time he uncovered a telegram from Willard Calkins to Assemblyman George W. Root of Nevada County, urging a yes vote for the 1903 bill that would have moved the capital to San Jose. CK also linked Willard to the odious political agent of the Southern Pacific, William F. Herrin. CK called the paper a "vapid and evasive sheet" and insisted it was a mere mouthpiece of the Southern Pacific, derisively referring to the paper as the "Morning Herrin."[63] Calkins claimed the McClatchys were guilty of libel and blackmail and of taking bribes to support certain legislation.[64]

Under its new editor, Edward Insley, the *Union* publicly broadcast embarrassing details of CK's struggle with alcohol and suggested that the *Bee* operated primarily to shore up Valentine's extensive real estate holdings. But the *Union* blunted the impact of its attacks by taking unpopular stands on city politics. During a convention held in Sacramento by Christian Endeavor, an evangelical society, Insley opened a blistering attack on Mayor Clinton F. White for allegedly permitting underage drinking in city saloons (called deadfalls), which led to debauchery. What this meant was that the saloons served liquor to "children" who were eighteen to twenty years old. This of course led to sexual promiscuity—and child prostitution.[65] Angry local officials worried about the impact of such reports on future convention trade. In a now common practice in Sacramento, local merchants met at the Chamber of Commerce to plot a boycott against the *Union*. Insley refused to back down and continued the assault on White. Leonard Calkins brushed aside accusations that he was a carpetbagger and supported Insley while publishing pictures of innocent children in white gowns to underscore his point about their jeopardized innocence.[66]

Encouraged by CK, a committee of angry Sacramentans descended on Leonard Calkins to demand an apology and a cessation of the negative publicity.[67] Calkins insisted that the *Union* was an enemy of cheap saloons—also a *Bee* position—but one that Calkins had recently connected with allegations that Sacramento had a problem with child prostitution. Nevertheless the anger shook Calkins and Insley, who nonetheless pressed forward, urging the creation of "a responsible non-partisan organization to hold in check the notoriously abusive and malignant newspapers that have flourished practically unchallenged in the past."[68] This of course meant the *Bee*.

The war of words continued well into the fall of 1908. CK's response to the scurrilous Insley revealed that he had published pornographic literature, which a postmaster in Chicago had seized, resulting in his imprisonment for six months. A bout of public drunkenness by Insley also found its way to the front page of the *Bee* just ten days before Christmas.[69] In October 1908 CK gave front page coverage to a critical letter by the editor of the Calkins-owned *Fresno Herald*, Colonel Edwin Emerson. The open letter was addressed to Chester Rowell, a reformer and editor of the *Fresno Morning Republican*. In it Emerson revealed that Willard Calkins had directed him to write negatively of President Theodore Roosevelt—with whom Emerson had served in the famous Rough Riders regiment during the Spanish American War. Emerson said Calkins also tried to coerce Emerson into supporting the major defendants in the San Francisco graft prosecution (a major San Francisco bribery scandal). When Emerson refused and instead wrote a piece decrying the vacating of the indictment of the corrupt San Francisco mayor, Calkins fired him.[70] Rowell also publicly attacked Calkins and drew his share of abuse from the *Union* owner.[71] Willard Calkins denied pressing Emerson on Roosevelt but declared he fired Emerson because "he wrote and published contrary to the desires of his employers a vituperative editorial" by suggesting strong measures in the San Francisco case.[72]

Maintaining a Competitive Edge

These public brickbats were just part of the story. The *Union* under Leonard Calkins's management appeared to be in Sacramento for the long haul. The paper could always rely on a strong base of supporters who preferred a morning paper or who just hated the *Bee*. But, skilled journalists that they were, the Calkinses knew how to improve it and make it more attractive to subscribers and advertisers—and set out to do so.

In July 1908, when the *Union* purchased a new press and began to put out an improved edition, Valentine worried the paper might lunge ahead of the *Bee*. Since the *Union* was making the liquor traffic the cause célèbre of Sacramento life, Valentine urged CK to meet the competition head-on by essentially scooping them. "It seems to me," Valentine wrote CK, "that while the Union is making its fight for place, we had better clean up all the news that we can in order that the people will not be forced into its columns the next morning for information." Valentine further urged that *Bee* reporters handle "every story of crime and misdemeanor so as to connect it if possible with the liquor which probably led up to the crime. . . . Almost invariably liquor is at the bottom of such items if the connection can be ascertained."[73]

But once again mere competition was not enough. The McClatchys continued to troll for unsavory information about their opponents. Shortly after the Calkinses had taken over the *Union,* CK uncovered confidential information about the shaky finances of the Calkinses' interests. H. A. French of the *Call* told CK that there were definite connections between the Southern Pacific railroad, particularly the Harriman interests, and the Calkinses' enterprise. French also maintained that Willard Calkins received money from the Sacramento banker Alden Anderson and the Southern Pacific. CK also relied on tips from Chester Rowell, editor of the *Fresno Morning Republican,* and Franklin Hichborn, who covered the legislature for both the *Sacramento Bee* and the *San Francisco Examiner* and reported on the Calkinses' financial dealings.

Valentine managed to procure a confidential copy of a Dunn and Bradstreet audit of the Calkinses' holdings, confirming their precarious finances. The report noted $90,000 in liabilities, including money still owed to the former owners of the *Union,* American Type Founders, and Zellerbach for paper. Warnings of dire financial troubles were already appearing in the San Francisco press, noting that the Calkins brothers were behind in paying the bills for a substantial remodeling of the *Sacramento Union*—and in arrears to a number of suppliers and vendors in Sacramento.[74] By January 1909 the Calkinses' financing began to collapse. On March 27, 1909, Valentine wrote CK at Del Monte, California: "The Calkins explosion has occurred. We published the story today although in San Francisco and here they are strenuously denying it. The apparent intention of the creditors is to secure such a temporary reorganization as will enable them to get the property in shape for sale. They will perhaps offer the various plants to the highest bidder as soon as the details have been adjusted."[75] To add to the Calkinses' troubles, *Bee* articles highlighted the plight of teachers in Yuba County who lost their life savings because they had invested in the Calkinses' holdings. In May the McClatchys published on the front page the particulars of Mary Alice Calkins's divorce proceeding against her husband, Willard, detailing the physical and verbal abuse she had suffered from the earliest days of their marriage.[76]

The *Union* went into receivership to pay creditors. L. E. Bontz, a former business manager of the *Union,* served as receiver and after lengthy negotiations purchased the paper outright in November 1910 from Sidney Ehrman, a prominent San Francisco attorney. Bontz was joined by Lynn Simpson, a San Francisco newsman who also bought an interest in the paper. In August 1918

Bontz sold the paper to C. M. Wooster, a former editor of the *San Jose Mercury*. CK wrote to his brother about the transaction: "Of course it is too early to prognosticate; but I believe the *Union* under Wooster will be absolutely colorless. He has a cracker-jack in [John] McNaught [editor]; but I don't believe he will allow him to do any punching. And I know McNaught's disposition aright he will chafe and chafe and then quit."[77] Subsequent owners did their best to keep up with innovations in newspaper layout, printing, and features, but the *Union* struggled financially every step of the way.

In 1924 CK picked up rumors that his archnemesis, William Randolph Hearst, was about to purchase the *Union*. CK, who had just bought his brother out of his share of the *Bee,* now worried that he might have a real fight on his hands with a Hearst-run operation vying for subscribers. He reached out to John Francis Neylan, who worked for Hearst, and gently suggested that the publisher should "avoid a row" and resist the temptation to come to Sacramento. Neylan reassured CK that it was not likely that Hearst would purchase the struggling *Union*. However, Neylan later revealed that Hearst was offered the paper and refused it on Neylan's advice.[78] Rumors floated for a time that Herbert Hoover was going to buy the *Union*—but they amounted to nothing. In 1929 yet another fiscal crisis threatened the survival of the *Union*. CK and his son Carlos pondered allowing their longtime rival to fold but believed that "the capital of the State . . . the metropolis of Superior California should have a strong, independent morning paper" and "loaned sufficient money to Mr. [William H.] Dodge to buy the morning paper."[79] The loan was reported to be $350,000.[80]

CK never really worried too much about the *Union*. In September 1931, when that paper sought Hiram Johnson's endorsement for an eightieth anniversary issue, CK told his friend to go ahead and write something, but he noted, "The *Union* is not 80 years of age at all. The *Union* is not alive. . . . The *Union* died in 1872—59 years ago—when it was swallowed up by the Southern Pacific's Organ known as the *Sacramento Record*. It changed its name then to the *Record-Union*. The *Record* didn't die, but the *Union* did."[81] Nonetheless the paper survived. The powerful Copley chain eventually purchased the *Union* in 1966, but the paper died in 1994.

The *Sacramento Star*

In 1904 the Scripps chain of newspapers introduced an evening daily, the *Sacramento Star*. The *Star* brought some pizzazz to Sacramento journalism, including the city's first comics page. Although CK and Valentine feared it might cut into their business, it became clear that potential advertisers were not about to throw over the *Bee* for the new paper. In a note to a local merchant, Valentine reassured an anxious advertiser about the *Star*, saying that the *Bee* covered five-sevenths of the city's population and the *Union* two–sevenths. Moreover, the number of *Bee* subscriptions continued to increase, even after the *Star* began publishing on November 21, 1904, and *Bee* subscription sellers were "bringing in each day from three to seven new subscribers." He assured his skittish customer that "under our system of long-term contracts, under which we have tied up almost the entire city circulation, old and new" for the next eighteen months, a material decrease in city paper routes "is impossible."[82]

Valentine tried the gentle approach with the *Star*, helping to keep its wage scales down and befriending its manager, W. H. Porterfield. However, Porterfield began snooping into the tax records of the *Bee* property—he no doubt smelled reduced assessments and taxes and suspected discrimination in the *Bee's* printing rates, that is, that it charged more to government entities and less to lawyers. Valentine lashed out at Porterfield, reminding him higher rates came with higher circulation. Porterfield especially spooked the *Bee* when he offered two-thirds the rate the *Bee* charged for publishing county business. Valentine reminded Porterfield: "You doubtless do not know that the wage scale in the Star pressroom would have been raised to the *Bee's* standard but for my personal opposition." He concluded coldly, "In organizations of which we both happen to be members I shall continue to treat you on necessary business as I should other members. At other times and places it would please me if you would forget that there has been a speaking acquaintance between us."[83]

The *Star* occasionally jabbed back at the imperious Valentine. One incident involved a private report Valentine had drafted about the precarious finances of the McNeill Club, a local singing fraternity. The club had used an old Congregational church for its concerts. But the building seated only 816 people, and the club needed a larger venue (and more ticket revenue). However, Valentine observed, "The Clunie Theater, the only available auditorium of greater capacity, is objectionable because many of the seats in the gallery are undesirable; because the theater is not clean and women object to wearing good dresses therein." Someone passed this report to the *Star*, which reprinted it in its September 26, 1906, edition, and included McClatchy's unfavorable comments about the cleanliness of the Clunie. Embarrassed, because the theater had been a generous benefactor for the choir and an advertiser in the *Bee*, McClatchy dashed off a note of apology to the treasurer of the Clunie, claiming he had been misrepresented; he asserted his comments about dirt in the theater pertained only to the gallery. In a terse note to the *Star's* editor, Valentine distanced himself from his own words, decried the addition of the word *disreputable,* and declared he meant the word *dirty* to apply only to the gallery. He insisted the *Star* run this correction.[84] From that point relations between the *Bee* and the *Star* remained chilly, with the rival paper never coming close to the *Bee* in terms of total circulation.

After Valentine had left the company in 1923, Carlos McClatchy opened up discussions with Roy T. Howard of Scripps-Howard Newspapers, suggesting the *Bee* purchase the struggling *Star.* In an October 11, 1923, letter to Howard, Carlos laid out the practicalities of the deal, including the absorption of the wire services and its staff of two. Negotiations took two years, and in early 1925 the *Bee* absorbed the *Star.*[85] The *Star* brought comics to the pages of the *Bee,* as well as a fresh young reporter, Walter Jones, who would be CK's editorial successor. The *Bee* ruled triumphant over the information circuit in Sacramento—and its support was needed to advertise everything from soap powder to candidates.

Chapter Six
A Tribune of Reform

---◆---

CK LIVED AND DIED as a son of Sacramento. He loved the city and he supported many important improvements in the city's quality of life. His hometown pride was sincere. However, there was also a mutuality of interest in the advancement of the community and the fortunes of the *Sacramento Bee*—and the McClatchy family. Long before the famous dictum by Dwight Eisenhower's defense secretary about General Motors, the McClatchys operated on the principle that what was good for the *Bee* was good for Sacramento and vice versa. Valentine summed it up best in a letter to a Minneapolis-based land developer who inquired about "the measure of confidence" he had in the city: "The most conclusive evidence which can be offered in this matter is the fact that the Sacramento *Bee*, of which I am half-owner, has recently put in an expensive plant which would be absolutely valueless were the city and the valley to be retarded in development. Beyond that, all the personal investments which my brother and myself have are in this city and in this valley. They have been made because we believe that the opportunities for enhanced values and for speedy development are greater here than elsewhere in the State."[1]

Enhancing Sacramento's Economic Viability

Nowhere was the partnership between CK and Valentine more effective than in their common concern for the advancement of Sacramento. Valentine represented the paper in local booster organizations, joining with other Sacramento businessmen like Joseph Steffens, Benjamin Steinman, and David Lubin to move the city along the path of economic and social progress. CK and Valentine closely monitored transportation franchises, water contracts, street paving, sidewalks, tree planting, and other urban amenities that contributed to the common good. CK reported on these efforts in detail.[2] Those who stood in the way of needed urban improvement he labeled "Silurians:" "Fossilized creatures who firmly persist in setting themselves against every public improvement that might help to beautify the city and thus promote its progress and development." At times the *Bee* published the names of opponents of public improvements on its front page.[3] The McClatchy brothers also had a regional vision—of linking the great Central Valley (their coverage area) to national markets by its railroad connections. CK touted the superiority of local products and urged city participation in expositions, fairs, and other venues that would show off the products and possibilities of the Sacramento Valley.

In November 1885 CK and Valentine put together a special edition of the *Bee* to be circulated in the eastern states; it touted the glories of Northern California. Valentine pressed land settlement by urging the railroad to sell its unused parcels. When Val asked the railroad land agent William Mills for "details concerning the various pieces of railroad land for sale in the district [north of San Francisco]," McClatchy noted that this information "will prove valuable to immigrants and possibly induce some to think of California who had not done so before."[4] In 1911, while orienting a new Washington, D.C., correspondent for the *Bee,* Valentine reported in glowing terms the beauty of what the *Bee* called Superior California:

> In Superior California, within say three hours' ride, 100 miles by railroad, we have all kinds of climate, all kinds of soil, all kinds of products, all sort of conditions; we drop from the Sierras, covered with snow, through the foothills with deciduous orchards in blossom, the orange crop partly gathered, partly hanging to the trees, on down to the alluvial valley where we have all sorts of garden truck, all kinds of fruit and dairy products. You have within that same territory also interests as diversified as gold dredging, quartz mining, placer mining, irrigation projects, water power, electric energy, reclamation projects, and all on a large scale. You have raisins, wines, asparagus, and hops, all kinds of fruits; you have a development that is really only commencing and resources which are wonderful.[5]

The McClatchys were keen on the conservation of water resources, including centrally planned irrigation, and the end of hydraulic mining and dredging. Valentine McClatchy became an expert on water policy, recognizing its potential for the development of the valley (and his various land holdings throughout Northern California). The McClatchys fought to make sure there was "a broad view of all the interests involved in the subject of water rights."[6]

Beautifying and improving the city of Sacramento was a key priority. The *Bee* supported various groups like the South Side Development Association and emphasized the civic significance of new building projects. Both brothers inherited their father's dislike of land monopoly and advocated breaking up the huge Haggin Grant, one of the last of the old Spanish land grants in the Sacramento area. The forty-four-thousand-acre grant—at one time the home of Lloyd Tevis and James Ben Ali Haggin's important Thoroughbred-breeding operation—had few settlers.

From time to time people noted the conflict of interest in *Bee* positions and the enrichment of the McClatchys' personal holdings. Valentine joined a group of speculators, including the furniture store mogul Louis Breuner, who bought the Rancho del Rio, another land grant property, in 1907—1,059 acres in Sacramento County. Their hope was that the local government would purchase the property for a much-needed park—a position of the *Bee* and one that would financially benefit Valentine and the other investors.[7]

A Moment of Urban Improvement

Economic development stimulated interest in responsive, business-friendly, and efficient city government. Since the 1860s the city had been governed by a board of trustees, with each trustee assuming some responsibility for an area of urban life—roads, police force, fire protection, and the like. By the late 1880s, however, this system could not keep up with the increasing demands of city life. Because the city groaned under huge bonded indebtedness accrued to pay for the expensive street raising, the board held to a conservative economic policy, which slowed development of important infrastructure. The *Bee* supported the impaneling of fifteen freeholders, who rewrote the city charter in 1891. This new instrument, approved on May 17, 1892, instituted a more effective central government led by a mayor with executive powers, including the management of nearly forty city employees who oversaw important city services. The charter also divided the city into nine wards, creating a new political dynamic as both mayoral and city council elections became hotly contested and often fought out on the pages of the *Bee*.

The updated city government roused civic energies. Citizens now became enthused about confronting Sacramento's dowdy appearance and poor public services. In 1895 a new Chamber of Commerce formed, and it, too, became an important ally of city government for urban improvements and expansion. These efforts gradually remade the face of the city. On the dirty and rutted K Street cement sidewalks replaced the decrepit wooden walks, and even the ugly awnings on storefronts began to come down. Local organizers put on midwinter fairs and marketed the advantages of Sacramento to the Midwest and the East. Private enterprise built new hotels and improved theatrical and other entertainment venues. Architects took their cue from the elegant capitol and Catholic cathedral, producing respectable new public buildings, including a central library and a city hall. Eventually, after many bond-issue failures, Sacramentans improved their water system. Tired at last of drinking dark water that the locals called "Sacramento Straight," city voters approved a water purification plant. In the 1920s, with CK's endorsement, the city approved the Silver Creek Project, which tapped Sacramento into fresh mountain springs.

CK unabashedly claimed credit for these changes. For example, he argued that his sassy attack on the outgoing legislature in March 1893 had stimulated a season of reform in Sacramento. In a retrospective written shortly after the spectacular Electric Carnival to celebrate electrification of the city on September 9, 1895, a smug CK wrote: "Last night's magnificent tribute to the resources of the New Sacramento—a Sacramento made new largely through the sturdy efforts of this paper, and a tribute rendered possible because of the improved conditions of things in which The *Bee* was so potent an instrument—could not fail to evoke memories of the night of March 12, 1893, when the merchants of this city desired to boycott this paper out of existence." CK told of long-deferred sidewalk construction, new streets laid "according to the latest approved models," the taking down of unsightly awnings (the construction of which had led to the destruction of shade trees), improvement of business blocks, and the building up of residential blocks. Congratulating himself for his role in this great explosion of urban uplift, CK modestly noted, "The Thank-God edition [the March 1893 front-page attack on the state legislature] of the *Bee* was the greatest blessing that was ever vouchsafed to Sacramento."[8] (This March 11 edition of the *Bee* criticized the legislature and provoked a move to relocate the state capital.)

In their lengthy booster publication, *Where the California Fruits Grow,* the McClatchys further burnished their "Thank God" mythology. "The newspaper stood by its guns," they reported. Noting the city was becoming the object of unbecoming remarks in the press around the country, "The wrath of Sacramentans, which was boundless, under the spur of such remarks, took practical shape. . . . The officials and the newspaper united in pushing a number of public improvements simply to demonstrate the stuff that was in the city."[9]

Urban Governance

The strong executive leadership proposed by the new charter held great promise. A strong mayor could not only tackle the need for improved infrastructure but could also lead the fight against urban vice, which also blighted Sacramento's reputation. CK always found city politics exciting, and the new powers of the mayor and the city council offered enticing opportunities for investigative journalism. The mayor's patronage appointments, especially to the ranks of police and firefighters, came under close scrutiny, but so also did the appointments of other government officials. CK wrote extensively about city politics and advanced his candidates and issues with great candor. But here he experienced some limitations. The indeterminate party structure of the city in the late nineteenth and early twentieth centuries often produced multiple candidates who split the vote. Eight mayoral elections were held under the new charter, and politicking in each of the city's nine wards were intense. In only two of these elections, in 1893 and 1907, were clear McClatchy favorites the winners—Benjamin Steinman (1893–95) and Clinton White (1907–10). The charter was reformed again in 1914, when the city embraced a commission system, and again in 1921, when the city put in place a city manager system, with a weak mayor and city council.

C. K. McClatchy took all the mayors to task. He reserved his worst treatment for Cyrus Hubbard, who had come into office as the result of a tight three-way election in 1896. Hubbard had received the endorsement of the anti-Catholic American Protective Association (APA), which had arrived in Sacramento in 1893 and been welcomed and endorsed by several of the city's Protestant ministers. Hubbard, although not an APA member, nonetheless seemed willing to accept its support. The APA's backing of Hubbard was all CK needed to attack him relentlessly on the pages of the *Bee*.[10] In fact Hubbard offered a perfect combination of everything CK disliked: religious bigotry, support from a hated newspaper rival John Spreckles, who owned the *San Francisco Call*, and above all a chance to strike a blow at one of his boycott tormentors.

How the mayor handled such issues as the bonded debt and urban improvements, as well as the railroad, was important to CK. When he disliked a mayor (as he often did), CK often called him a boss or made allegations of incompetence and even corruption. A favorite target was city vice—especially prostitution and gambling, which required protection from law enforcement and in turn required graft, thereby undermining of democratic governance. Pay-offs to city officials and police made Sacramento a bad place to live. Likewise, cheap saloons, gambling houses, and houses of prostitution gave the city an unsavory reputation. CK believed to his dying day that the solution to city vice and the graft it required was legalization. Unless local government became realistic about human weakness and abandoned efforts to eliminate certain vices, reformers would be forever frustrated and the city caught in cycles of corruption. The proclivity to gamble and whore, as well as drink, he believed, could never be eliminated but should be regulated and controlled.[11] Regulation, not eradication, would contribute to a cleaner political culture primarily by eliminating the graft that protected these forbidden pleasures. Drinking—which was his particular vice—he considered a right that could be exercised responsibly, and he opposed state and national efforts at prohibition. However, CK made a couple of exceptions to this philosophy: poolrooms and homosexual activity. The coercive power of the state, he believed, should curb both.

Regulating Poolroom Gambling

Gambling was in Sacramento's DNA. From its very beginnings various games of chance were an integral part of the city's entertainment venues. Control of these lucrative games attracted the usual mix of seedy characters and respectable citizens. The counterforces to gambling were, of course, the dynamics of collective morality: churches, women's groups, and social reformers who lamented the effect of these games on the quality of urban life. Ethnic issues also often floated to the top: In Sacramento the Chinese were among those who ran games of chance.

By calling for the regulation of these games rather than abolishing them, CK kept faith with his father. Toward the end of his life James had realized that gambling could not be stopped but should be controlled. During the administration of Democratic mayor John Quincy Brown (1882–87), the city actually did briefly legalize and regulate gambling in 1884. But Brown soon became the object of "abuse from pulpit and from pew," as Sacramento's clergy attacked gambling and linked it to general social corruption. CK tried to defend Brown and showered harsh words on the clerics.[12] Nonetheless by the end of 1884 the law was on its way out. Assemblyman C. T. Jones of Sacramento introduced a bill making it a felony to license gambling in the state. When the city overwhelmingly elected an antigambling candidate as a trustee, the legislature handily passed the Jones bill, which the governor signed in March 1885. Brown's work was undone despite CK's vigorous defense of regulation over eradication.[13] When the *Record-Union* bragged that gambling had been "wholly, completely suppressed in Sacramento as it will be we believe for all the future" without formal licensing or regulation, and instead had been "conquered without a blow or the corruption of any of the law's forces," CK snorted, "Conquered, forsooth!" He continued in another piece the same day: "The people will soon learn that the 'tiger' [gambling] in Sacramento is the liveliest, conquered animal they ever saw." Six years later CK insisted, "Gambling cannot be stopped. . . . It can only be driven from one avenue into another . . . the only way to deal with this evil . . . is to have the licensing of it made permissible under the Statutes and then elect Trustees who will license it."[14]

In 1891 the legislature approved yet another bill to allow regulation of gambling, and CK and Valentine implored Governor H. H. Markham to sign it into law. They argued that bringing gambling out into the open would advance the cause of civic honesty. With illegal gaming "the city is degraded, the Police Department corrupted—it is everybody's loss and nobody's gain." Markham did not sign the bill, however, and gambling continued to flourish in Sacramento in various venues—especially William Land's Western Hotel. CK begged again in 1894: "The sensible plan is to treat evils as they exist. . . . Gambling always was and always will be. . . . Is it not a hundred times better that it be under the watchful eye of the law?"[15]

The poolroom issue became especially tense in Sacramento because its poolrooms were not billiard halls but betting parlors—bookmaking operations—that took bets on horse races at different tracks. CK found poolrooms distasteful because they attracted young boys and even women, and corrupt politicians shielded the establishments. One of Sacramento's most notorious political bosses, Bartley Cavanaugh, epitomized this unholy marriage of gambling interests and corrupt politics. Born in Sacramento in 1865, Cavanaugh had been a bookmaker and was well known at a number of prominent racetracks. After a stint in the East, he returned to Sacramento and became involved in politics, a protégé of Andrew Jackson Rhoads, a legendary political boss in the Sacramento area. Although Cavanaugh and Rhoads had a falling out, Cavanaugh continued to work in local government and became the collector of the city waterworks. Together with one James Davis, Cavanaugh operated a poolroom that fielded bets on horse racing in California (Tanforan in San Mateo and Ingleside in Los Angeles) as well as at major East Coast tracks. Because he could easily obtain results of so many races, his pool hall became one of the most frequented in the city. This made Cavanaugh fantastically rich. When he died at the age of forty in 1905, he had acquired a number of properties in the city, including a lucrative hops ranch on Riverside Road.[16]

In 1896 city officials began to crack down on these operations. In March of that year Mayor Cyrus Hubbard signed a bill banning poolrooms; after some skirmishing city police finally closed them down in November. Cavanaugh, however, simply moved his betting parlor across the river to Yolo County. He also kept his pool hall behind the city post office. To the frustration of many, the city's ordinance was eventually declared invalid. Later Yolo County invalidated a similar antipoolroom ordinance.

The hotelier William Land succeeded Hubbard as mayor, and the *Bee* joined his efforts to close the city's poolrooms. But CK had few illusions about Land, whom McClatchy privately tagged as a miser; CK also knew Land ran one of the largest gambling operations in his Western Hotel. Land, too, signed an antigambling measure but exempted the betting that went on during the state fair held at Sacramento's Agricultural Park. Superior Court Judge E. C. Hart struck down the ordinance as unconstitutional in late 1899.[17]

Soon after Hart's decision the city trustees began searching for a legal formula to curtail poolrooms and pass constitutional muster. They discussed various measures and decided to wait until after George Clark, who had defeated Land in 1899, took office. As far as CK was concerned, Clark came in under a cloud because he had violated the Purity of Elections Act of 1893, which limited to $300 the amount of money that could be spent on a campaign. Clark, it was alleged, had spent nearly $3,000 and had collaborated with the gamblers Bartley Cavanaugh and Frank Daroux, as well as a McClatchy foe from the *Sacramento Evening News*, George Royster (to whom Clark promised a city job).[18]

Clark proved to be an even more vigorous foe of the poolrooms than his predecessor, and his efforts won strong support even from CK, even though he distrusted him. The poolrooms, which were located in the block bounded by Sixth and J and Seventh and K streets, were a true source of moral depravity, especially for young men. CK lamented, "At the noon hour will be found rushing to these poolrooms merchants neglecting their business; city and county officials losing money they can ill afford to squander; employees living beyond their means . . . young men who are putting into these pool-rooms every cent that should go to their needy mothers; lads from the High School . . . and even little boys—children, one might say, who put their nickels into a pool and have some tout place their bets." On January 22, 1900, Clark sent a strong message to the city trustees explaining his plan to eliminate the poolrooms. The *Bee* strongly endorsed the move and helped to round up support for a proposed ordinance.[19]

Clark skillfully formed an ad hoc committee of clergy, including the reverends John Quinn of the Catholic cathedral, Charles Miel of the Episcopal church, and A. P. Banks of First Baptist. They mobilized other clergy to preach against the poolrooms and stir up the support of their congregations.[20] The ministers also drew the business community into the crusade, and Mayor Clark became so confident that he issued an order to close all gambling houses in the city. However, even with CK's help and the active efforts of this antipoolroom lobby, the bill failed. Undaunted, Clark, local ministers, and the *Bee* agitated for it again, and in February Clark presented another bill to the trustees. Large mass meetings then ensued to pressure reluctant trustees. On February 12, 1900, a tumultuous meeting of the city trustees took place. Ed Kripp, one of the city's leading poolroom owners, attacked Clark, accusing the mayor of taking bribes from Kripp's poolroom. So contentious did the meeting become that the two nearly came to blows. Poolroom owners and their friends in government fought back. The trustees approved the measure, but supporters of the poolroom owners had slipped a poison pill into the law; it banned poolroom betting even during racing at the state fair—a tremendous money maker for the city and an important part of the annual event. Aware poolroom owners had done this to weaken the law and to bring about its eventual repeal, CK worried about its fate, but he willingly accepted the law for the sake of ending the blight. Subsequent prosecutions of the poolroom kingpin Frank Daroux and others took place; the only effect was to once again send poolrooms across the river into Yolo County.[21]

In July the poolroom victory seemed to be compromised when city trustees proposed a plan to simply license the practice rather than abolish it outright—a position favored by the *Bee* on most vice issues. Clark vetoed the bill, but the city council overrode his veto. Clark then seemed to change his mind—now seeing good in the regulatory scheme.[22] All was quiet for a time.

Then on November 12, 1900, a dispatch from the *San Francisco Examiner* revealed poolrooms were again operating in Sacramento. CK sent a reporter to query Clark, who denied the report—although Police Chief John Sullivan confirmed some informal pool selling (bookmaking) probably was going on. The next day the *Bee* publicly questioned Clark's denial and listed three locations in the city doing a brisk business in pool selling. The *Bee* then mocked Clark and Sullivan.[23] Finally a grand jury investigated the allegations. After this poolrooms vanished and Clark took credit for it—much to CK's everlasting consternation. From that point on Clark could do nothing right, according to the *Bee*. Even though Clark was a personal friend (and had lent CK $4,500 for a mortgage), CK challenged him at every turn, calling him the "hot-air" mayor and mocking his Christian Science faith by calling him a "faith-cure fakir." At one point he accused Clark of dealing with the poolrooms in a manner similar to the faith healing of Mary Baker Eddy—that is, by simply wishing it away.[24]

Segregation and Scatteration

CK believed regulation was also the best policy for dealing with urban prostitution. His late nineteenth-century Victorian ideals about women made the very subject of prostitution difficult. CK detested the idea of women working in public or in any way appearing at places where their virtue would be besmirched. Yet in approaching the "social evil" of prostitution he had the same view he had of gambling: it could not be stopped, only contained. Likewise, after reading a great deal on the subject he again worried about the impact of prostitution on local governance. As with poolrooms and other gambling establishments, protecting houses of ill repute often required bribes to police and city officials. CK may also have been sympathetic to the plight of the women involved. His wife, Ella, often went to seedy bars and dives as well as to local madams to collect money for charitable activities. One of these madams, Fanny Brown, was quite generous and left the bulk of her rather large fortune to charities and the local sheriff, William Gormley. Ella McClatchy's interaction with the women may have softened CK's often peremptory treatment of social ills. CK believed that the solution to prostitution was the formation of a "cordon sanitaire" to localize the evil. In an 1893 editorial he noted: "A great many good people will doubtless be shocked to hear that The *Bee* thoroughly endorses that proposition. It is the only method of treating an evil that has existed since God ordered light to shine on the globe, and that will exist until the world dissolves. License, strict medical surveillance, and regulation are the only means by which the evil can be kept in proper bounds."[25]

He was not alone in this position, then called segregationist. A municipal clinic in San Francisco, created in March 1913 to check prostitutes for venereal disease, helped those who wanted to exit this life and to dissuade youngsters from entering. One of its supporters was the socially prominent Dr. Julius Rosenstirn, a respected San Francisco physician who endorsed the work of the clinic, which had to close in September of that year. As the years went on, CK became an expert on the topic and assumed a pose of intellectual superiority when it came to the issue of arresting the spread of vice. He simply knew more than anyone else. In late 1912, while spending time in Milwaukee with his daughter Eleanor, he studied that city's efforts to suppress prostitution by closing down houses of ill repute. He interviewed police and local journalists and quickly determined the attempt had been ineffective, noting, "I find there is a notorious house under cover, within less than a block and a half where I live with my wife and daughter, in the residential portion of Milwaukee."[26] He wrote to a Long Beach reporter, "I have spent five weeks in Milwaukee and have never seen a more quiet, sober, respectable place to live. . . . And yet the abolition of the segregation plan in Milwaukee and the suppression or alleged 'suppression' there has done infinite damage to morality, the health and the womankind of Milwaukee."[27]

The California legislature took up this issue and in 1913 considered a bill that was based on a law drafted in Iowa (the Iowa Injunction). This law not only cracked down on houses of prostitution but held owners of such places open to prosecution. CK disliked this law and became unhappy that California women, who now had the vote, would exercise their clout on the issue. CK was especially annoyed when he heard the women of the Women's Christian Temperance Union were behind the legislation. "I have had experience, in my journalistic life with these W.C.T.U. women. They are impractical, given to hysteria; and in a goodly number of cases they do not know what they are talking about. . . . These unfortunately, will be the majority of women who will appear before the legislature of 1913 shrieking hysterically upon the subject of the social evil and demanding its total extermination."[28]

To counter the meddling ministers and the "hysterical sisterhood," CK wrote to Robert Davis, the manager of *Munsey's Magazine*, asking for statistics and expert testimony on the issue. He confided to Davis, "Now you know Bob, as well as I do . . . that there never has been an attempt yet to drive out this social evil that has resulted in anything less than in multiplying that evil and scattering it in lodging houses, rather than keeping it in one place." CK made similar requests to John Chambers, his assistant editor, and to the *Bee's* Washington-based correspondent, Ernest G. Walker, and CK recommended that Frank Havenner, the *Bee's* San Francisco correspondent dig up information on the issue in the Bay City.[29]

Valentine shared these sentiments and warned about the influence of women's groups. "We are equally sincere in desiring to find a remedy for what is conceded to be a dreadful evil," he wrote to Mrs. Mary Hawley of Lodi, superintendent of purity for the W.C.T.U. of California, "but we differ in our views. . . . The graft and abuse which comes from the present system of concentration exist because there is an attempt to permit under police protection something which the laws forbid." He met Hawley head on, saying, "This cannot be accomplished as long as good women like yourself create a public sentiment which is opposed to any official recognition of the evil." When an article by the local lawyer L. T. Hatfield ran in the *Bee* in 1913, calling for stamping out prostitution and insisting that there be one moral code for men and women, Valentine refuted it.[30]

Both brothers worked tirelessly. Valentine in Sacramento sent an array of literature on the subject to legislators. CK contributed from Milwaukee, writing to the leaders of other cities to learn of their experiences. He reached out to Progressive mayors such as Brand Whitlock of Toledo, Ohio, and Newton D. Baker of Cleveland. In fact Toledo had a program of segregation, which was also used in Cleveland.[31] Each mayor replied with letters detailing their experiences and policies. As the 1913 legislative session began, a flurry of bills were introduced into both the Assembly and the Senate to restrict and abate prostitution. One, the Bohnett Bill, adapted from a similar law enacted in Iowa in 1909, introduced a new element to the elimination of prostitution: removing its economic incentives.[32] In contrast to other antiprostitution legislation, which cracked down on women, pimps, or johns, this bill permitted the law to go after the owners of the houses where prostitution flourished. Edwin Grant, a representative from Vallejo who would become a bitter foe of the McClatchys, became a cosponsor of this bill.

When CK returned from Milwaukee in February 1913, he urged a frank discussion based on the best scientific and sociological knowledge. In a series of editorials he challenged the common wisdom that Milwaukee had effectively ended prostitution. "I desire now to record this in the most emphatic language. Prostitution has been suppressed in Milwaukee in about the same way the average street sweeper suppresses dust—by scattering it all over the community and into the very Homes [*sic*]."[33] Of Sacramento's expanding vice zone he noted to Frank Havenner, a political progressive and ally from San Francisco: "There is scarcely a lodging house on J and K Streets that is not tainted."[34] In a letter to state senator Ernest Birdsall of Auburn, who disputed the need for segregation in a small town like Auburn, CK wrote,

> I think if the houses of ill fame were all put on a hill near Auburn and all painted red so that they could be seen for miles around, that notoreity [*sic*] would not be half as bad as the danger there would be in having women of this character scattered around the place generally. . . . I notice, for example, in Colfax, Washington, where places of this character were very prominent across the river on the side of a hill, that men were very, very chary in crossing the little bridge across the stream and going there before the eyes of the whole community.

He concluded sardonically, "However, this is merely my view formed after nearly a whole life spent in the newspaper business."[35]

CK kept up the editorial barrage. To his friend state senator A. E. Boynton of Butte CK complained that even though physicians, police, and newspapermen knew about the issue and the importance of segregation to public health, few raised their voices in support of CK's position: "The trouble is that they do not want to talk." Ultimately, however, the Assembly passed the Red Light Injunction and Abatement Law (the Bohnett Bill).[36]

While the state Senate deliberated on the bill, CK came out against it, because it failed to deal with regulation. Valentine and Carlos also weighed in, urging regulation instead of suppression.[37] Despite their opposition and with the strong support of women's organizations, the bill passed and Governor Hiram Johnson signed it on April 7, 1913. A referendum was held on the law in 1914 (one of the first in California's long history of these ballot measures). In deference to his friend Governor Johnson, CK urged his reporters to treat approval of the law as an accomplished fact, and voters handily upheld the measure.[38]

CK resented what he regarded as the interference of newly enfranchised women and once again wrapped himself in self-righteousness for having backed a losing cause. In a lengthy letter written in 1916 to Franklin Hichborn, the *Bee's* state legislature reporter, CK lamented the work of women's groups on prohibition (and scolded him for favoring this policy) adding a snort of resentment about the earlier campaign to demolish prostitution: "As long as I am Editor of The *Bee*, The *Bee* will not follow along with the mob simply because the mob is running one way. I know what some of the church people think about me, but I do not care a cent. There is not one of them—ministers or laymen—that know one-tenth as much about the social evil conditions in Sacramento and about whether 'exterminating the prostitutes' would result in more good or ill, as does the messenger boy in The *Bee*'s news room."[39]

The campaign for segregation also revealed a fault line in the relationship of the brothers. Valentine did not buy all of CK's arguments, and the issue soon regressed to what the *Bee* always believed. Valentine insisted the *Bee* had not always stood for segregation, to which his brother retorted:

> The *Bee*, through James McClatchy, favored segregation, to my positive knowledge when I returned from college and was employed as a reporter on the papers. It never deviated from that position at any time nor under any circumstances. In fact the two owners of the paper—you and I—went so far at one time as to go with Frank Snook and make a personal investigation of the Concentration Camp at the northwest corner of 2nd and L St. And editorials were written and published. . . . That was in 1904. And so the thing has continued straight along.[40]

Cleaning Up Sacramento

Prostitution in Sacramento became an issue again in 1917 when the federal government proposed the location of a new aviation field in eastern Sacramento County. West Coast military installations attracted temporary populations of wives and families and with them a quickening of the local economy. CK and other Northern Californians wanted these outposts, not only for patriotic reasons but also for the economic stimulus military procurement and salaries would bring. CK did his part on the pages of the *Bee*, accentuating the positive about Superior California, especially the sunny skies, which were perfect for training aviators. In February 1918 the site selected was Sacramento. Construction began on a proposed $1 million, fifty-two-building site just south of Mills Station and east of the city, to be called Mather Field.[41] Federal officials wanted to make sure that Sacramento was also morally fit for the young men who would be stationed there. They were particularly concerned about the incidence of venereal disease among servicemen and had heard rumors about Sacramento's thriving prostitution industry as well as the number of taverns.

In December 1917 Lieutenant Allison French of the Department of War's division of training camps appeared in Sacramento with Dr. H. G. Irvine, director of the U.S. Bureau of Venereal Diseases, to confer with Dr. Wilbur Sawyer, secretary of the state board of health, and later with Dr. Gustavus C. Simmons, Sacramento city commissioner of public health and safety. The federal officials explained how they anticipated and planned to isolate and care for every case of venereal disease contracted by servicemen in the city. At this meeting city and county officials devised a joint plan for action. In another unofficial meeting with a group of citizens, French made suggestions about curtailing prostitution but maintained he was at the meeting unofficially at the request of the state board of health and not under any instructions from Washington. The city commission that was overseeing the community reception's for the new base pledged its efforts to protect soldiers from both alcoholism and prostitution.

CK telegraphed his *Bee* correspondent in Washington, Ernest Walker, informing him that "Prohibitionists [are] evidently trying to bone dry Sacramento because of [the plans for the] aviation camp, although it is about eleven miles from here. Threat made that Government can take the school away from Sacramento if she doesn't clean up." Federal officials had heard "disquieting reports" about moral conditions in Sacramento from Simon J. Lubin, California state commissioner of immigration. These were reported to Major [Bascom] Johnson, director of the Law Enforcement Division of the War Department, who sent a stern message to city officials: "We ask for Sacramento the same that we asked in other towns and cities in the vicinity of the training camps, the closing of open houses and that street walking be reduced to an absolute minimum. Cafes and dance halls that cater to prostitutes must be either closed or cleaned up. Taxi cab drivers who act as pimps or go-betweens or bellhops and others of like character must be weeded out. Landladies of rooming houses used for improper purposes must either close their places or conduct them in a proper manner." CK criticized the Redlight Abatement Act as he leaped to the defense of his native city, informing Major Johnson: "As a citizen of Sacramento who was born here; as a citizen who, without any vanity, has the right to say he has always fought for the public honor, for public integrity, for public morality, for communal decency— permit me to state that I entirely disagree with the statements of Mr. Simon J. Lubin that conditions are 'rotten and vile' in Sacramento." CK acknowledged:

"There is prostitution in Sacramento, as there is [in] every other city on God's footstool. And if conditions in Sacramento are worse than they were before, it is the fault of radical enthusiasts who have lashed the women of the underworld from pillar to post; have driven them out from the secluded portion of the city until they have forced them to infest the apartment houses and invade some of the residence districts." He insisted that Sacramento was "willing and ready to do all the Government may ask her to do in the line of a clean-up" but lambasted "local fanatics who are translating progressivism into a kind of Frankenstein of blind Puritanism."[42]

Despite some precarious moments, Mather Field opened in 1918 and for just a few months served its purpose as a training facility for new aviators. CK wrote to his friend Newton D. Baker, former mayor of Cleveland and now secretary of war, assuring him that Sacramento would comply with any "clean-up" orders but warned him the image of the city given by "shriekers" and even by the respectable Lubin was false.[43] To U.S. Representative Charles Curry, CK privately blamed the ongoing existence of prostitution on the misguided policy adopted by the legislature in 1914:

> Time was when a woman of the tenderloin was a woman of the tenderloin. She was scarcely ever seen outside the limits of the tenderloin. Her evil did not spread. Hundreds of young men never went that far down town; and most of the visitors never saw the tenderloin. But take it today, there is scarcely an apartment or lodging house on J or K Streets from Front to Twelfth that isn't an assignation house, or worse. And these women, driven out of their holes . . . by these shrieking moral reformers are today invading the best residence districts of this community.[44]

Prohibition

Congress passed the Eighteenth Amendment and submitted it to the states for ratification of Prohibition in late 1917. The requisite number of states—including California—approved it by January 1919, and it took effect on January 17, 1920. CK took the law as an affront to American freedom and also as a personal insult. No California editor was as adamantly opposed to the law as he was.

CK's views on alcohol could be confusing. Although he vigorously opposed the Eighteenth Amendment (and earlier efforts to turn California dry), he also bitterly opposed saloons and dives, which he felt should be restricted to certain areas of the city and regulated. He was insistent that such establishments be kept out of the city's residential (or Homes) district, favored midnight and Sunday closings, and the abolition of side entrances to saloons and nooks for women and underage youth. However, he drew the line at outright prohibition in Sacramento—ideas advanced by his old bête noir, the W.C.T.U. He made this clear to W. E. Gerber of the California National Bank: "The *Bee* is not a prohibition organ. It believes prohibition to be an un-American interference with the rights of persons."[45]

CK's struggle against prohibition was of long duration.[46] When a campaign had begun in 1914, he wrote his friend the journalist Karl von Wiegand in Germany, "A constitutional amendment is before the people calling for state-wide and drastic prohibition, which would close up all the wineries and breweries, etc., etc. and would ruin the great wine industry of this state. . . . Now The *Bee* is not in favor of prohibition. It never was. It does not believe that the drinking of light wine or beer makes for drunkenness in the end or in the majority of cases, but rather the reverse." CK constantly urged the California Grape Protective Association to organize and rebut these accusations and gave it column space. He told the association: "Why would it not be a good idea for the wine growers and wine makers of California, through you, to get reputable physicians in the large cities and even in the country districts to combat this new fad that [claims] everyone is ruining himself and the unborn children by even taking a little wine." He also related his efforts to his old friend David Lubin, by then living in Rome. Recalling his overseas travel experiences, CK noted: "It might be a good idea if we followed the example of southern Europe and had places where papa and mama and the children could congregate together in the evenings and eat their little repast and drink their light wines and beers."[47] The 1914 prohibition initiative went down in defeat—but the issue would not go away.

In 1916 prohibition returned as a ballot initiative in two forms: the first, a proposal for total prohibition, the other for partial. CK considered both bad. "The *Bee* has ever held that prohibition does not prohibit; there is more drunkenness in the prohibition state of Kansas than there is in all Italy. My wife and I spent several months in Rome, Florence and Naples some four or five years ago, and we never saw a drunken man anywhere." He urged interest groups like the California Wine Growers Association not to overreact to the occasional stories that extolled the virtues and social benefits of prohibition in states like Oregon and Washington, which had only recently adopted the law.[48] He passed on the names of friendly newspaper people to the group, including William Devlin, publisher of the *Santa Cruz Surf*:

> Some of your people should go to Joe Knowland of the *Oakland Tribune*, and to Pardee or Daniels of the *Oakland Enquirer* and get them to go to the bat. The same thing should be done with Fremont Older of the *San Francisco Bulletin*; with the proprietors of the *Call, Chronicle, Examiner* and the *News*. . . . An appeal should also be made to the *San Jose Mercury*, which is owned by the Hayes brothers. . . . Down in Los Angeles, too, somebody that has some influence with them should go to the manager of the Hearst papers and also to Harrison Gray Otis, or his representative at the *Times*.[49]

In fighting the prohibition amendments in 1916, CK used his usual rhetorical devices of ridicule and accusations of inconsistency and hypocrisy but also waged war against "scientific" evidence that alcohol seriously impaired health and the ability to function. "What I think is about as necessary as anything right now," he wrote the head of the Rainier Brewing Company in San Francisco, "is [to gather] definite statements from doctors, scientists, and statisticians completely refuting the declarations of faddists that the lightest drinking of light wines and beer materially decreases the lifetime of any person."[50]

Given the growing sentiment nationwide in favor of prohibition, CK nervously monitored the fate of the two prohibition amendments throughout the fall of 1916. He contacted two sympathetic state legislators, Walter McDonald and Robert Baines, and even reached out to his usual foe, Southern Pacific's political chief, William F. Herrin, through an intermediary. Herrin believed there would be a heavy dry vote in Southern California for total prohibition but that it would be offset by an equally heavy vote against it in Northern California. However, he predicted that partial prohibition would be passed. Checking with sympathetic local politicians in San Francisco districts, Herrin had found that they also predicted the passage of partial prohibition based on a desire to stamp out saloons because of the social costs of alcohol-related problems. CK related this possibility again to the vintners:

> I send this thing to you with a second admonition that your men ought to get busy with the newspapers of San Francisco. There is not one of them that has told The People what Amendment No. 2 will do. . . . Prohibition Amendment No. 2 in California does

not permit a man to get wine except on an order from the winery, and it has to be shipped to him and shipped only to his permanent home. . . . The papers of San Francisco, and Oakland, and of Napa, Sonoma, and Santa Clara Valleys and any paper in Los Angeles that you can get, ought to go to the front now and educate the people on this subject.[51]

CK received support from Archbishop Edward Hanna of San Francisco, Cardinal James Gibbons of Baltimore, and former U.S. representative Marion De Vries, all of whom defended the moderate use of drink. To the bitter end CK fought the amendments and flayed anyone who differed with him. When Alison Ware, head of the California State Normal School at Chico, signaled his support for Prohibition, CK laid out in even greater clarity the reasons for his staunch opposition to it: "I cannot rejoice at any time, under any circumstances, in any place where intolerance reigns; and when any man, or set of men, declare that I shall not drink or are afraid to drink, they are attempting to force upon others that which is nothing more nor less than slavery." He reinforced his position on a more personal note, saying, "My wife practically never touched a drop of liquor in her life. But she is even more indignant upon this subject than I am. . . . My good mother-in-law died only a few years ago, aged 90. She was never ashamed to take wine or beer with her meals. I was never ashamed to see her do it; and I think she lived considerable more years than she would have lived had she been a total abstainer. My good mother only died only a few days ago, aged 88. During all the years of her life she liked her wine or her beer with her meals."[52]

To CK's consternation, even his investigative reporter Franklin Hichborn (who had also differed with him on the Redlight Abatement law) defended the prohibitionists. CK rebutted what he called Hichborn's unbalanced view and portrayed himself as the victim of hyperzealous prohibitionists. He recalled the story of a minister who wanted to place a prohibition advertisement in the *Bee* in 1916. When CK refused to run the ad, "He [the minister] went all over this community . . . declaring that The *Bee* refused to permit his side to be heard and that The *Bee* was in the pay of the liquor men."[53]

To CK's delight California voters defeated both initiatives in 1916. When proponents pushed prohibition as a food conservation measure during World War I, CK exploded with anger. He replied brusquely to a gentleman who asked him to sign a petition to prohibit the manufacture and sale of intoxicating liquors for the duration of the war: "I must decline. I have no use for men who make their patriotism a cover and an ambush for jamming down the throats of other people their own ideas—and cramming them down unnecessarily." He then asked: "How is it that the French and the Germans fight along so magnificently, each being supplied with his daily rations of wine and beer." In light of the new war-based prohibition campaign, CK tried to round up specialists who could provide an objective tone to his views. But he often failed to convince doctors to sign on to his antiprohibition position—even when they privately expressed agreement. This especially disturbed him since the prohibitionists often invoked the testimony of physicians to either curtail or end drinking altogether. To one Los Angeles physician who had privately dissented from a negative view of the use of alcohol but refused to allow his ideas to be published, CK chided, "Really, my dear doctor, I would like to understand why you medical men who are on the sensible side of this question don't want to be quoted."[54]

In late 1917 Congress passed the resolution to submit to the states for ratification an amendment to the Constitution prohibiting the manufacture, sale, or transportation of "intoxicating liquors" within the United States. The requisite number of states ratified it by early 1919, and Prohibition took effect in early 1920. But CK never accommodated himself to the law. He evaded it in both letter and spirit, by traveling abroad where he could drink without question and by frequenting a favorite San Francisco restaurant, which kept a private stash of wines for his dining pleasure. No doubt he also hid bottles in his den and even in the *Bee* office, to take the edge off a difficult or cold day.

Homosexuality

CK made a critical exception to his preference for regulating social vice: homosexuality. Revolted by the very thought of same-sex relations, he wanted to publicly expose gays and lesbians and proscribe their behavior by law. The historian Sharon R. Ullman notes some early cases of gay sex made the pages of the *Bee*. Sacramentans learned from the *Bee* of incidents of gay sex at a local livery stable, among professional boxers, and others. These accounts also revealed the uneven prosecution of "crimes against nature." Some resulted in long sentences for those who came to the city for gay sex, but men who were city residents often were granted leniency.[55]

CK used euphemisms to refer to homosexuality. Just as CK described heterosexual rape as "an outrage against women," he labeled homosexuality as either a "crime against nature," or using the legal term of the day, *social vagrancy*. Typical of his era CK referred to the unspeakable degeneracy of those who did such things. He also worried that youth enticed to try gay sex would become gay themselves. When he heard that police had raided a homosexual ring in the city of Long Beach, California, in November 1914, he dispatched a reporter, Eugene Fisher, to dig out the details in Los Angeles and other municipalities nearby. Both Fisher and CK approached the topic with great personal distaste—almost as though they were holding a stinky fish or a filthy rag. Fisher reported his findings in a lengthy and graphic report, painstakingly assembled from interviews, police reports, and fragments of gossip. As he described the sexual behavior of these subjects, he pointed out something that surprised and offended CK: "There is no law under which this crime against nature is punishable directly, hence they are arrested and prosecuted as 'social vagrants' and lewd and dissolute persons." CK applauded Fisher's diligence "with a great deal of interest, mingled with disgust."[56]

Fisher's squeamishness about the project led him to petition CK to withhold his byline: "Owing to the nature of the subject, I do not care to have my name attached to the articles." CK allowed him to take the pseudonym Clayton Campbell and ran Fisher's reporting just before Christmas 1914. These articles laid out the lurid details of the activities of "queers," as Fisher referred to these men, and described efforts to entrap them in public bathrooms. Fisher pointed out the high prevalence of these "disgusting practices among men" in Los Angeles, Long Beach, Pasadena, and Venice, California, tantalizingly implicating "men prominent in the financial, social, club and civic life" of these communities. In one article he revealed the names of thirty-one men who had been caught in homosexual acts of various types and named those who tried to bribe their way out of public exposure. When this list appeared, one of these men, a Long Beach druggist, committed suicide by swallowing cyanide. Meanwhile CK followed the trials of those picked up for social vagrancy. Of one who was acquitted, he observed, "It strikes me that the juries there do not want to convict anybody on any testimony." He wrote a lurid exposé of a Long Beach florist, Herbert N. Lowe, whose "Love Cottage" was a notorious trysting spot for homosexuals—most of whom had been lured into this way of life by molestation as young men. The point of these articles was to increase penalties for homosexual behavior, which was a $500 fine and 180 days in jail. Indeed such crimes could be punished only by using statutes that applied to vagrancy.[57]

CK sent copies of these articles to Cleveland's mayor, Newton D. Baker:

> I enclose you clippings from The *Bee* of recent dates concerning an evil which is spreading in California and undoubtedly is elsewhere, and which is infinitely worse than prostitution. It is a strange but a true thing that this particular form of homosexualism is not mentioned in our codes; and that therefore the beasts guilty of it can be punished only under stretching the vagrancy act—and then punished only by a short imprisonment in a County Jail and by a limited fine. The *Bee* will endeavor to have the next Legislature specifically penalize this nasty thing to see if something cannot be done to check it.[58]

Baker replied, "I am told that the practice is much more common in the larger cities of Europe than it is anywhere else in the world." He concluded, however, "I doubt very much, however, whether law of a repressive sort will do very much in dealing with a thing which is so obviously a manifestation of degeneracy. Indeed, I feel more or less hopeless about this sort of sexual vice except that its victims are midway in the process of biological elimination which is automatic and irresistible."[59] In January 1914 the Sacramento assemblyman Lee Gebhart introduced a bill making the acts of fellatio for men and cunnilingus for women felonies punishable by "not less than 20 years" of imprisonment. The amended bill banned the practice for both men and women and reduced the penalty to "not less than 15 years." It was passed in June 1914. Sodomy had already been outlawed, but the penalties were increased.

Given CK's Victorian manners and formality, that he would care to even discuss, much less press for laws and regulations regarding, these behaviors is amazing. Like all Progressives, his streak of moralism generally confined itself to larger public issues such as government corruption and monopoly. In this however, he seems to have lost the libertarian views he had about ordinary gambling, prostitution, and drinking. Gays and lesbians were simply too repugnant to countenance even for a moment.

Chapter Seven
Railroad Politics and Populist Upheaval

◆

THE GREAT TRANSCONTINENTAL RAILROAD transformed the American West in the 1860s. The artificers of the Central Pacific were a handful of Sacramento businessmen—Leland Stanford, Colis P. Huntington, Mark Hopkins, and Charles Crocker (the Big Four)—who implemented the risky ideas of an engineer named Theodore Judah. The imaginative Judah pressed hard for a route that began in Sacramento and moved east over the daunting heights of the Sierra Nevadas. Despite a host of challenges, the entrepreneurs connected their eastward line with the westward Union Pacific in 1869. These same Central Pacific moguls bought up routes all over California, assembling a powerful transportation juggernaut called the Southern Pacific. The Southern Pacific's tracks stretched from the Pacific Northwest through California, Arizona, Texas, and into Louisiana. Administratively reorganized in the 1880s, this huge rail system became the most important force in the social and economic life of California, creating jobs and regional progress.[1] James McClatchy knew the Big Four and considered Leland Stanford a personal friend. James and his sons were strong supporters of the railroad.

The railroad brought prosperity to Sacramento. However, its sometimes peremptory behavior produced a backlash in California as elsewhere in the nation. Nationally the railroads charged excessively high shipping rates and monopolized grain elevators. In the Golden State the Southern Pacific demanded and received concessions of land and rights-of-way along its route. When a community resisted, the railroad at times retaliated against small towns by building depots and repair facilities elsewhere. Sacramento was on the receiving end of those threats as the company occasionally pledged to withdraw the huge repair and construction shops it had built just north of the downtown. The powerful railroad not only manipulated the commercial life of the state, it also penetrated

California's state and local governments. Efforts to curtail the railroad's power were already in play during the 1870s, and antirailroad animus had been written into the state constitution of 1879, which created the regulatory Railroad Commission. However, this body proved to be weak and ineffective.

The McClatchys supported the railroad because it was integral to the life of Sacramento and the Central Valley. Valentine put it succinctly to the local Southern Pacific agent and "press handler," William H. Mills: "Sacramento's interests to a great extent are identical with those of the company."[2] When the Southern Pacific incorporated, its central offices were moved to San Francisco from Sacramento, but Sacramento retained the rail workshops. The Southern Pacific also built a hospital in the city and offered medical care to workers. James and his sons celebrated the railroad as the literal engine of Sacramento's progress and were intensely grateful for the jobs and economic vitality the railroad provided. The extent of their fealty was already evident in the 1870s when the Southern Pacific demanded a prime parcel of land that city fathers were reluctant to grant. When company officials dropped wide hints they move the repair yards from Sacramento, the *Sacramento Daily Union* blasted the company for its endless demands. However, worried city leaders and merchants formed a delegation to visit the railroad's San Francisco headquarters to willingly offer up the land—and apologize for the opposition of the *Daily Union*. One of those delegates was James McClatchy, who returned to Sacramento and praised the deal when he addressed a rally. James's surrender to the railroad then was considered an act of civic prudence. He and his sons for a long time thought such concessions were the price Sacramento and California had to pay for progress.

William H. Mills

The chief intermediary for the Southern Pacific and the *Bee* was William H. Mills, who had purchased the *Sacramento Record* in 1872 and transformed it into a railroad mouthpiece. In 1875, after a dust-up between the *Daily Union* and the Southern Pacific, he purchased the obstreperous *Daily Union* and merged it with the *Record*, creating the long-lasting *Record-Union*. In 1882 he became the land agent of the Southern Pacific and turned over the day-to-day editorial duties at the *Record-Union* to others but continued to write editorials for the paper through 1903. Mills kept a close watch not only on the policy of the *Record-Union* but on much of the California press, making sure that Southern Pacific's policies were presented in a good light.

From 1883 until his resignation in 1901, the erudite Mills exercised extensive oversight of the land, water, agricultural, wilderness, and resource conservation policies of the far-flung railroad. Mills was quite friendly with James McClatchy (and even served as a pallbearer at his funeral). When U.S. Senator Leland Stanford of California died unexpectedly in 1893, CK endorsed Mills as Stanford's replacement in Washington. CK noted admiringly: "He is not only a tireless thinker, he is an indefatigable doer. . . . He is a persuasive rather than a demonstrative reasoner and it is difficult to resist his pleas." Mills knew everything about California, "soil and climate . . . its flora and its fauna, its viticulture, horticulture and agriculture." Mills and the McClatchys both detested hydraulic mining and shared a belief that California's future lay in specialty crops. Mills may have had a closer affinity with Valentine since both were interested in land development; however, his dealings with CK, who wrote most of the *Bee's* editorials, were also strong. To show his appreciation for the *Bee's* support, Mills regularly provided free rail passes to the brothers and their families, a standard Southern Pacific bribe.[3]

One of the key links in the McClatchys' railroad connection was their friendship with Stanford. The boundaries between business and government were never very clear during Stanford's years in politics (he was governor from 1862 to 1863 and served in the U.S. Senate from 1885 to 1893). However, when Collis P. Huntington ejected Stanford from the company's presidency in 1890, the new president abandoned Stanford's style of mixing politics and business, saying, "Don't you think it is a queer sight to see politicians continually hanging around a railroad office? It is to me . . . and if I have to stay around 365 days in a year I'll see that there is no more of it. Things have got to such a state that if a man wants to be a constable, he thinks he has first got to come down to Fourth and Townsend streets [Southern Pacific headquarters in San Francisco] to get permission. . . . The Southern Pacific is out of politics and will attend to its business like any other private company or individual should do." CK lamented Stanford's abrupt departure, calling it "a great public calamity" and insisting, "There is not a working-man on the great railroads of the Pacific Coast today who would not take off his coat to do Leland Stanford a service."[4]

CK never warmed up to the distant Huntington, who lived in New York and had little interest in California.[5] Nor did Huntington really foreswear attempts to affect public policy. He worked Congress tirelessly to approve a refinancing of the huge loans the railroads had taken from the federal government.

Likewise, the Southern Pacific still controlled the vote of the railroad shops in Sacramento (a crucial feature in local elections), and its local political operatives continued their grip on state politics.

Yet even during Huntington's tenure the McClatchys supported the railroad. Most important, they were fortunate and perhaps secretly glad to have a nominal rival like the *Record-Union*. Although the editorials of the *Record-Union* occasionally angered CK, the railroad-dominated paper had little ambition to excel or even compete seriously for advertising. Its agenda was focused on preserving railroad control of state and local politics rather than appealing to a wider public.[6] Like their father, CK and Valentine acknowledged that the benefits of the railroad outweighed the company's liabilities—at least for a time.

Mills kept tabs on the local press and reported dutifully to Huntington. He never related a single problem with the *Bee,* except to note the paper's long-standing position regarding government ownership of the railroads: "James McClatchy was in favor of this long ago and his boys have imbibed the idea that the Government ought to own everything. They are natural communists." Huntington did have problems with some California papers, especially some in the San Francisco—Oakland area—in particular the *Examiner* owned by William Randolph Hearst. However, Mills always counseled tolerance when a newspaper diverged from the railroad's official line. "We wanted friends, not slaves," he explained to Huntington. "A paper absolutely subservient to us in every particular . . . acquire[d] the reputation of being an organ and lost influence with the public." In all likelihood the McClatchys typified Mills's policy of tolerance.[7] Hence they could indulge the notion of public ownership since Mills knew such an expropriation of property was utterly impossible at that time. However, in truly important matters Mills leaned on the McClatchys, and they fell into line. Not only did he convince the brothers to initially support a congressional effort to reduce the amount of interest the railroads had to pay on their government loans to build the railroad, but Mills did so knowing the effort had the backing of the McClatchys' archenemy, Grove Johnson.[8] The brothers further proved their good will by strongly supporting the railroad during the 1894 strike in Sacramento.

The Railroad Strike: Taking a Stand Against Anarchy

Support of the railroad reflected CK's antipathy to organized labor born of the struggle with the typographers' union. Labor unrest also had a radical air when added to the complaints of the wandering groups of homeless men, tagged as "industrial armies," that appeared in the 1890s. These were mostly unemployed workers caught up in the nationwide depression that began in 1893. In 1894, at about the same time that Jacob Coxey (the originator of the march strategy for the unemployed) was leading his so-called army from Ohio to Washington, groups of unemployed men began marching in the Sacramento Valley, gradually coming closer and closer to the state capital.

When 250 of them appeared in Sacramento in April 1894 they were at first warmly received as they camped at the city's Agricultural Park. However, when they asked for transportation out of the city and began to beg from citizens, the welcome mat was taken in. Mayor Steinman and the city trustees ordered them to break camp and leave. CK had at first been sympathetic, but in the end he lectured them: "No matter what the wrongs of these men, they cannot expect Sacramento to be their Mecca."[9] Still, CK realized they could not simply be turned away. While Sacramento "has more than her hands full of paupers from other counties and states," the city could not become a "dumping ground for so-called Industrials. . . . Clearly it would be an act of barbarism, of inhumanity to allow them to starve." Tough economic times, he explained, had broken "the backbone of private charity." Speculating that as many as twelve hundred could come to Sacramento, he urged that "it might become necessary to provide work for them . . . upon county roads, each man to work a certain time, receiving a meal ticket." As much as he disliked the unemployed (calling them bummers and moochers), he could see that their cause had appeal. "Laugh at [Jacob] Coxey as you will . . . but when he declared that the Government should provide work for the idle people, he struck a popular chord that was encored from one end of the country to the other." CK warned that if the economic distress that gave rise to these movements was ignored and politicians moved to other issues, "the Industrial Armies of 1894 will be but child's play compared to the revolution which the near future is destined to bring forth."[10] Yet there were limits to what a city could take. The Industrials were soon sent packing—a move McClatchy endorsed.

As the depression of the 1890s deepened, labor unrest erupted. The most famous flare-up began in May 1894 when railway workers went on strike at Chicago's Pullman Yards. Eugene V. Debs, America's most famous socialist, rallied the Pullman workers and pledged the support of the American Railway Union. In solidarity with the workers in Chicago, railway workers in Oakland and Sacramento refused to let trains leave or enter their depots.[11] This could not have happened at a worse time in California as the first harvests of certain fruits and vegetables were being prepared for shipment. The economic disruption threatened California agriculture and Sacramento's canning and packing economy as well.

CK immediately backed the railroad, insisting the company and the city had treated the workers well. He lectured: "They should reflect that a tie-up of the roads at this time will mean not only disaster for the railroads and ruin this year to the fruit interests, but trouble and calamity to their loved home of Sacramento, grievous loss to the merchants who have been their friends and a very, very, serious loss to themselves."[12] Merchants raised the loudest outcry as the halt in transportation affected their businesses and supplies. A meeting of the Sacramento Industrial Improvement Association, an ad hoc organization of the city's most prominent business leaders, drafted a harsh resolution condemning "the present strike" as "unlawful, un-American, subversive of all Constitutional and personal rights and absolutely destructive of the commerce of this country." Among the signers was V. S. McClatchy. CK endorsed the resolution, and the *Bee* gave it wide circulation. As tensions rose, CK warned the workers against any sort of violence. But tensions escalated when strikers tied up the Sacramento depot on the Fourth of July 1894, and a local national guard unit led by the merchant Harris Weinstock arrived to reopen the facility. This proved to be a fiasco. In the sweltering Sacramento heat the young and inexperienced soldiers—many of them relatives and friends of the strikers—literally wilted and were unable to disperse the crowd. Ultimately a detachment of the regular army had to be dispatched from San Francisco. The soldiers easily drove off the strikers and reopened the depot. William Mills acknowledged how helpful the local press had been in bringing an end to the strike: "But for the *[San Francisco] Post*, the *Record-Union*, the *Bee*, the *Los Angeles Times* and the interior press, the strike would have lasted ten and possibly twenty days longer than it did."[13]

However, angry rail workers retaliated by damaging a trestle in Yolo County, thereby causing the departing train to crash, killing some workers and soldiers. CK bellowed his outrage, denouncing the violence as "Anarchy, the devil's own viper and spawn from hell. Anarchy, nursed in Erebus and spewed out of Pandemonium; Anarchy that breathes arson and preaches murder; Anarchy that answers argument with dynamite." Any plea to consider workers' rights or issues of wage and working conditions met with instantaneous condemnation from CK. Labor violence, even if provoked by management or for "just cause," was never justified.[14]

But the crushing of the strike was not enough for the vengeful Southern Pacific. At the direction of company chieftains, virtually every worker who had anything to do with the strike was blackballed and unable to obtain work on the railroad. Colonel Weinstock and his troops were hauled up on court-martial charges—and only barely acquitted. The workers would strike again but never with the vehemence of these days. Yet the harshness of Southern Pacific vengeance severed the bonds of cooperation between the city and the company. The railroad's image as a beneficent creator of wealth and civic prosperity gave way to one of a bully and a source of urban corruption. Even Southern Pacific's William Mills acknowledged it had made the company unpopular in many localities.[15] Still, even as antirailroad sentiment grew in the Capital City, the McClatchys would be followers, not leaders.

A New Mood

As time went on CK became more ambiguous about the positive effects of the railroad. In 1897, when a bill refinancing the railroad's enormous debts advanced in Congress, CK supported it. In the original legislation the government had required that the credit and loans the United States extended be paid back thirty years after the railroad was completed. The railroad moguls insisted that their improvement of the land merited them either a cancellation of the debt or a renegotiation of the terms (6 percent annual interest). When Congress dismissed the claim and created a sinking fund into which the Central Pacific had to pay 25 percent of its net earnings each year, Huntington denounced them as communists. Of the many proposals before Congress, Huntington supported the Reilly Bill, which generously offered the Central Pacific a seventy-year extension at 3 percent annual interest. Southern Pacific's political officer, William Mills, worked diligently to build public support for this controversial legislation and at first found a welcome response from CK, who argued it was in the public's best interest.[16] However, as the fight raged CK wanted to switch his position on the bill—especially when he learned that its strongest proponent was none other than his tormentor Grove Johnson. But even Johnson changed his mind and voted against the bill. Mills had to labor long and hard to convince McClatchy to stay with the measure. Nonetheless, on January 3, 1897, the House defeated the Reilly bill, 168 to 103—although Congress later would give the railroads all they wanted.

Mills kept McClatchy's loyalty because of close personal ties. However, this changed dramatically once William F. Herrin, the Oregon-born lawyer, replaced Mills and helped the Southern Pacific swat away the challenges that came from its political and journalistic enemies. Herrin worked through local bosses up and down California, especially Republicans Dan Burns of San Francisco and Francis Xavier Parker of Los Angeles. In Sacramento Herrin's mail came to the home of Bartley Cavanaugh, the well-known poolroom gambler and local Democratic boss, who associated with such unsavory characters as the gambler Angus Ross and the local political boss Andrew Jackson "Frank" Rhoades. Herrin's links to these mavens of vice changed CK's long-held belief that the railroad was an agent of local prosperity to a view that it was a purveyor of urban decay that thwarted urban progress. When Edward Harriman replaced Huntington in 1901, the McClatchys became more critical of the railroad and increasingly vocal in their opposition to it.

Edging Toward a Break

Other factors contributed to the *Bee's* antirailroad sentiment. CK's animus was also fueled by his embrace of the principles of populism, with its democratic rhetoric and hatred of monopoly. But as with so many other crusades, there was a personal twist. Hating the railroad gave him an excuse to publicly excoriate his archenemy and relentless antagonist, Grove L. Johnson—father of his future friend, Hiram W. Johnson. The McClatchys detested the sharp-tongued and vindictive senior Johnson, who participated in virtually every libel suit directed at the *Bee*.[17] Wreaking vengeance on this abrasive lawyer who cost the McClatchys thousands in legal fees became a source of great pleasure to the brothers.[18]

Johnson returned the loathing, considering CK and Valentine to be bullies. He also gave voice to the "protest of the people against sensational newspapers, personal journalism, the revolt of the people against the tyranny of the newspapers, which has become more insupportable in this city and State than was the reign of the thirty tyrants in the history of Athens."[19] This quarrel was deeply personal at times. According to another version of an apocryphal story, it was Johnson, not Charles Curry, who assaulted CK with a spittoon at the block-long bar of Sacramento's Golden Eagle Hotel. The McClatchys spread malicious rumors about Johnson's unsavory personal life (he was a notorious womanizer)—all of which seemed to have little effect on his public reputation.

Huntington and Mills, however, came to count on Johnson as a strong protector of their interests. A rock-ribbed McKinley Republican, Johnson had served in Sacramento city government and was one of the freeholders who rewrote the city charter. He later served several terms in the state legislature. To the dismay of the McClatchys he was elected to Congress in 1894. CK did everything in his power to undermine him, and with the *Bee*'s help the Populist-Democrat Marion De Vries defeated Johnson in 1896.[20]

The loss of Johnson's congressional seat ruffled the normally good relations the McClatchys had with Mills, who privately conveyed Huntington's displeasure at the loss of Johnson. Valentine sought to soothe the neuralgic railroad mogul. In a letter to Huntington, he pointed out Johnson's unfitness for office, manifested in "his unfortunate methods of treating associates, friends, and the public." However, Valentine assured Huntington the *Bee*'s opposition had little to do with Johnson's stout defense of the Southern Pacific. Citing a number of Johnson's actions, which had been recorded in the *Bee,* Valentine dryly noted, "Of course, if Mr. Johnson insists on making history, we must, as public journalists, transcribe it." Huntington seemed mollified by the McClatchy protestations, replying, "We do not ask special favors from the *Bee* or from any other paper; we do ask fair and honest criticism, and I believe we shall get it from the *Bee*. I knew your father thoroughly well, and for a long period of years, and always liked him, I believe he did me. It would be a great gratification to me if my relations with those who have continued his interests could be cordial, and I believe in time they will be."[21]

Valentine quietly reassured the railroad of the paper's good intentions and suggested the Southern Pacific improve its public image by removing the impression it was manipulating local politics. But in 1898, when Mills requested "a well-tempered editorial on the right of railroad employees to act together politically the same as any other profession," even Valentine balked. Seeking to deflect the pressure by suggesting it was a joke, Valentine wrote, "If you have inadvertently included in your letter to me instruction intended for someone else, the joke is on you. But if, in our friendly discussion of railroad policy in organizing its employees to aid its political interests, I failed to make clear my meaning that The *Bee* could not endorse such a policy, and that particularly in Sacramento County did we regard it as uncalled for, then the joke is on me."[22]

The relationship continued to deteriorate. As late as 1900, the year before he stepped down from his post, Mills chided the *Bee* for publicly insisting the company install automatic gates at various street crossings in Sacramento—especially at a particularly dangerous crossing at Twenty-first and R, where speeding trains had killed several people. Once again the more conciliatory Valentine issued a gentle warning to his longtime friend and ally: "It seemed particularly unwise to treat Sacramento—the one place in the State where the Southern Pacific Company, partly from sentiment and partly from local interest, has the general good will of the community—with a neglect in this regard which would not be deemed good policy in a less friendly community." He characterized the *Bee's* criticisms as "a friendly act" calculated to make friends for a company whose public image was daily battered.[23]

After Edward Harriman became the railroad's president in 1900, the *Bee's* criticisms of the railroad became more open and vitriolic. There was less and less patience with the railroad's ham-handed tactics and periodic threats to make Sacramento one of the "spite towns" of the valley by threatening to close the railworks and transfer operations to a friendlier political climate.

The ultimate rupture, however, occurred several years later, when the brothers played an active role in organizing a consortium to attract the Western Pacific Railroad to Sacramento and even offered the company two of their lots.[24] In addition to the land, Valentine provided cash incentives, collected from local businessmen. The Western Pacific even promised to build shops in Sacramento "if the necessary site be provided." Valentine explained to M. E. Hornlein, a real estate business contact in Sacramento and San Francisco:

> The location of the shops here . . . means of course immediately a force of one thousand men and upwards at work which will steadily increase until the present standing of the Southern Pacific will be reached, since in the years to come, the Western Pacific will have at least as much mileage in this State to look after. This means an almost immediate access to the population of five to ten thousand people and a monthly disbursement of say $100,000 running up ultimately to some such figure as the Southern Pacific disburses.[25]

In the end the Western Pacific submitted to a general vote of the people and won resoundingly. Although it never brought the kind of economic boost Valentine and his fellow advocates predicted, it did break the long-standing rail monopoly of the Southern Pacific and its aura of dominance over the city.

A New Political Awakening

The growing opposition to the railroad took place against the backdrop of major political changes in California and the entire nation. By the late 1890s the Southern Pacific railroad loomed large as the source of California's corruption, and the *Bee* supported politicians like James J. Maguire, Franklin

Lane, Theodore Bell, and Hiram Johnson, who publicly attacked the railroad. These new politicians mirrored the sweeping political discontent in America of the 1890s that made the railroads and laissez-faire politics their flashpoint. Farmers took the lead in protesting perceived injustices imposed upon them by railroads, eastern bankers, and international trade policy. Political mobilization channeled this discontent into a viable third party in the 1890s, the People's, or Populist, Party. CK embraced the movement tentatively at first and later with great enthusiasm. The change was quite dramatic for a man devoted to perpetuating his father's memory. James had been a traditional Lincoln Republican, and his editorials and reporting reflected this stance up to the time of his death. CK believed he was remaining faithful to his father's legacy, even as he became critical of the Republican Party of his time, and later he and the *Bee* endorsed the Populist message. In 1896 CK supported William Jennings Bryan and would continue to support him for each of his three tries at the presidency. The *Bee* thus became not just an extension of James but developed its own distinct voice.

Populism was a multifaceted political uprising that harnessed a number of issues, many of them dealing with agriculture and monetary policy. Populist heroes decried the plight of the sturdy yeoman farmer. Silver miners protested the government's insistence on maintaining the deflationary gold standard. These interests coalesced in electoral politics, and in both agricultural and silver-mining states, with Populist candidates winning offices at the local, state, and national levels.

The California Populist Party emerged from an amalgam of Farmers Alliances, assorted reformers taken with Edward Bellamy's utopian ideas (called Nationalists—sort of soft-shell socialists), opponents of railroad monopoly, and some urban reformers.[26] Animus toward the Southern Pacific in California fueled the rise of political unrest in the 1880s and 1890s. Anger, directed at the company's huge land holdings, and above all its open and persistent meddling in local and state governments, sometimes met with a violent response from Southern Pacific.

California's Populist Party was born at a convention in Los Angeles in 1891. The delegates drafted a program calling for government ownership of communications and transportation, women's suffrage, and the outlawing of saloons. Planks also sought to enlist the support of organized labor—and included advocacy of an eight-hour workday. Sacramento's local Populist organization, headed by J. E. Manlove, met in February 1892, and pulled together delegates from Farmers and Citizens alliances, the Grange, Knights of Labor, and Federated Trades—sixty-nine people in all.[27] Among the positions they advanced were women's suffrage and prohibition. Also that year, similar movements in various midwestern and southern states came together to form a national political party. In July 1892 the People's Party, as it called itself, met in Omaha and nominated James Weaver for president. Weaver had come up through the ranks of Iowa's politics, serving as a local mayor. After a run as the presidential candidate of the proinflation Greenback Party in 1880, he migrated to the Iowa Populist Party and took strong stands in favor of monetary inflation and was elected to Congress for several terms. He was a forceful critic of monopoly, opposed a national bank, and advocated the use of even more silver in the national currency. His campaign of 1892 did respectably well, given the uneven appeal of third parties in American politics.

In California populism's appeal spread to local county organizations. In Sacramento, Populists gathered in August 1892 to nominate candidates for local offices—including Hiram Johnson for sheriff—and to endorse Weaver and the national Populist ticket. Populists picked up recruits in both parties but especially among Republican silverites in the western states who were interested in the currency question and felt shut out of both political parties, because the proponents of the gold standard—known as gold bugs—dominated them.

CK was slow to appreciate populism. He dutifully perpetuated the *Bee's* Republican leanings and even admired the mugwump Republican James G. Blaine. A bitter critic of Democrat Grover Cleveland, CK joined the Republican chorus of denunciation when the president offered modest tariff reductions in 1887.[28] However, CK's positions began to change in 1892. When the Populist candidate Weaver campaigned in Sacramento that August, the *Bee* covered his visit extensively and provided important information about the party and its leading figures. CK praised Weaver's gifts as a stump speaker but believed that Populist ideas, while good in theory, were "utopian and inexpedient in their practical workings." He worried that a vote for Weaver would be a vote for the Democrat Grover Cleveland. When Weaver lost and Cleveland won, CK admitted the new movement had an appeal. Populism was a force that stood for values always embraced by the *Bee.* In a December 1892 letter to a subscriber, CK wrote: "For a great number of years, The *Bee* has advocated principles, which, have lately been taken up by this new political organization. . . . The *Bee* is an old line Republican journal. It believes that the captains of that party decoyed the organization far-way from those principles mapped out by Lincoln, by Grant, by Sumner, by Stevens, by Garfield, and by Blaine." Still unwilling to give up on the Grand Old Party, CK concluded, "but it [the GOP] believes that the bone and sinew of the party are in the right; that its brains, and heart and conscience will re-assert themselves . . . it will again rise to the dignity of its mission."[29]

However, when the economy collapsed in 1893 and labor strife and unemployment stalked the land, McClatchy took a fresh look at the Populist agenda and liked what he saw. At the heart of the new movement-party was an abiding belief in democracy and a healthy opposition to concentrations of power. The energy and idealism of the movement appealed to McClatchy's dramatic worldview: arrayed against each other here were the armies of darkness and light. His disaffection with the Republican Party grew exponentially. When U.S. Supreme Court Justice Stephen A. Field, an old Grass Valley Republican, died in 1899, CK referred to the deceased jurist as "one of the greatest scoundrels who ever disgraced the Bench in any age or in any Nation." Taking to task the jurisprudence that always elevated corporations over people—now a cardinal principle of the Republican Party—CK insisted, "He has raped Justice even in her own sanctuary," twisting the law "to serve oppressive and corrupt purposes." CK compared him to Benedict Arnold, Aaron Burr, and even Judas Iscariot.[30]

The Panic of 1893 further radicalized CK. Never kindly disposed to Grover Cleveland, McClatchy took aim not only at his "inept policies" but at his weight and marriage to a younger woman. Still, CK did not make the jump to populism. In the gubernatorial election of 1894, he supported the Republican Party's candidate—the former Sacramento resident Morris M. Estee, a perennial candidate for statewide office—against the Democrat James H. Budd and the Populist candidate, A. H. Webster. Budd squeaked through to election, and although he had advanced some good ideas (such as a state highway system), McClatchy detested him and repeated terrible stories about his personal life. His invectives against the governor continued even after Budd had left office.

Concerns about the monetary supply reached a flashpoint during Cleveland's second term. The debate about American currency had raged all through the 1870s and 1880s. Many advocated for silver, especially those in the western states, but farmers and debtors also were demanding a robust silver currency to create inflation and spread prosperity. Industrialists, workers, and longtime proponents of a "sound dollar"—much influenced by British economists and others—maintained that the gold standard presented the only plausible choice for a stable and solvent country. Cleveland, an advocate for the gold standard, was highly suspicious of even the limited amounts of silver Congress permitted in the national economy.

When the 1893 panic hit, Cleveland contended the Sherman Silver Purchase Act of 1890 had caused it. Faced with an unprecedented drain on the nation's gold reserves, he turned to the financier J. P. Morgan to coordinate a bond sale to a coterie of wealthy speculators. This stopped the flow of gold from the U.S. Treasury, but when it became known the already wealthy Morgan had not only received interest on his loan but had even finagled a hefty commission for his bond sales, outrage fanned across the country. CK attacked the deal, lacerating "Wall-Street wolves" who depreciated greenbacks, demonetized silver, and otherwise rigged the monetary system to the detriment of working-class Americans. "The leading lights among them were the authors of that most infamous bond transaction of February 8, 1895, by which people were deliberately swindled out of $8,000,000 and in which President Grover Cleveland proved himself to be either a scoundrel or a fool."[31]

In 1896 CK became an ardent proponent of bimetallism and urged the free and unlimited coinage of silver. Silverite politics came easily as California produced large quantities of the precious metal—and some of those in mining districts were within the circulation area of the *Bee*. As national conditions became increasingly distressed, CK embraced free silver even more stridently. In a March 7, 1896, double-spaced editorial headlined "Listen Silver Men!" the editor cautioned Republicans not to pick a man until they knew his stand on the silver question. McClatchy forwarded copies of this article to Republican leaders in California and declared: "The *Bee* believes that the cause of silver is the cause of the people." In anticipation of the state and national Republican conventions, CK kept up a drumbeat of support for the silverite position.[32] The Republican state convention, held in May 1896, witnessed vigorous debate about the currency issue and a vote on a silver plank in the party platform, but local delegates were not eager to sign on because national party leaders and the putative Republican nominee, William McKinley, favored the gold standard. However, McClatchy and his silverite allies brought heavy pressure on the state's Republican Party to adopt the silver plank.[33] Editorials kept the heat on Republicans who embraced McKinley. The state Democratic convention, held in Sacramento, embraced the prosilver position.[34]

Sprung from jail on the contempt charge stemming from the Talmadge libel case (see chapter 4), CK traveled to the Republican convention in St. Louis and witnessed the takeover of Lincoln's party by the forces of big business.[35] CK heaped scorn on the tactics of Marcus A. Hanna, a Cleveland industrialist and political Svengali who had engineered the nomination of William McKinley. The failure of the Republican convention to include a silver plank in its St. Louis platform was the last straw for CK.

In an editorial headlined "The Parting of the Ways," McClatchy declared he could not support William McKinley, refusing to follow the GOP "into its house of bondage, into its land of captivity, into its slavery to the Kings of Wall Street." His paper, he insisted, "will not sacrifice its manhood and degrade its honor—it will not bastardize its Republicanism—by bowing the knee to Mammon and accepting as an article of faith a declaration of principle antagonistic to every interest of the people, destructive to the welfare and corroding to the progress of the nation and beneficial only to those who fatten and thrive upon the very life blood of the masses."[36]

CK returned from the convention in time to take his young family on a summer break to Upper Soda Springs in Siskiyou County. But even there he could barely rest. He no doubt regretted having missed the Democratic convention held in Chicago in early July. At this momentous gathering the Democratic Party split between the conservative backers of outgoing President Cleveland and the voices of reform coming from the South and the West. California's delegation had already come on strong for the free silver policy, and its votes helped propel the youthful William Jennings Bryan to the nomination. Bryan's memorable "Cross of Gold" speech, with its poetic cadences and biblical imagery, transfixed CK as he read it. He not only embraced the candidacy of Bryan but became his lifelong friend (Bryan's teetotaling notwithstanding). The Populist Party also embraced Bryan's candidacy—creating a fusion of the two parties. CK announced that the paper would endorse Bryan, explaining, "It [the *Bee*] cannot stultify itself. It will not swallow its honest principles. It will earnestly, faithfully, unswervingly, in its humble field, do what it can do to promote the election of William J. Bryan of Nebraska."[37]

CK made sure other papers understood his new position. To the editor of the *Atlanta Constitution*, he wrote, "The *Bee* a Republican paper for 40 years has felt compelled to leave the party this campaign because of the silver issue. . . . The *Bee* is now the only prominent Republican silver paper in this state, and so far as we know at the present time, the only one west of Salt Lake."[38]

Valentine concurred: "The Democratic party is giving us in strong and almost unmistakable language, one: Free Silver, two: liberty of conscience [the anti-Catholic practices of the American Protective Association], and three: liberty of press. These are enunciated both in the State and National platform. On each of these issues, the Republican Party is either silent, or is opposed to our views." From this point on Bryan could rely on the McClatchys to be strong backers and faithful friends.[39] They remained true even when they parted company on such issues as prohibition and religion.

The 1896 election brought Silver Democrat Marion De Vries of Stockton into the McClatchy circle. De Vries was born August 15, 1865, in Woodbridge, California. He studied in California schools and received a bachelor of philosophy degree from San Joaquin Valley College, where he was valedictorian. He then attended law school at the University of Michigan and received his law degree in 1888. The year before, however, he passed the Michigan bar. He returned to California and soon immersed himself in the practice of law and local politics. He married Mary Snead, a McClatchy family friend, in 1892 and owned a big ranch near Stockton. When CK met De Vries is unclear, but CK had held little Mary Snead in his lap when she was a toddler and was always fond of her. In 1893 De Vries was assistant district attorney in San Joaquin County; he became "a liberal Democrat of anti-railroad reputation" and was chosen as a congressional candidate precisely to combat the staunchly prorailroad Grove Johnson.[40] De Vries was one of the first politicians whom CK actively cultivated not only as a source but as an advocate of his reformist positions.

CK waged a vigorous battle for Bryan and De Vries in the pages of the *Bee,* giving careful attention to all their public utterances and speeches and doing what he could to influence opinion in heavily Republican Sacramento County. The results were impressive: Bryan narrowly edged out McKinley, 4,854 to 4,600. For the first time since the Stephen Douglas–Lincoln election of 1860, a Democrat had carried the county. The election of 1896 was tight in California, with McKinley beating Bryan by a mere 1,922 votes. Bryan took 48 percent of the total vote and captured thirty-one counties. However, Republicans dominated state government, including the governor's mansion and the statehouse, until the end of the 1930s.

Populism, always an unstable coalition in national and California politics, began to fall apart by the end of the 1890s. However, the 1896 campaign was the turning point for CK and the *Bee*. From this point on CK maintained a rare independence when it came to national elections, supporting alternately Democrats and Republicans who reflected his values. This independence was, to be sure, a principled position—at least in CK's mind. But the personal warmth he felt for Bryan, who was an occasional houseguest, and his friendship with De Vries drove his independence. Principle and passion always meshed.

Chapter Eight
California Lion

◆

CK'S CONVERSION TO REFORM in 1896 came into full flower with the 1898 gubernatorial election. On August 18 the Democrats nominated the reformist James G. Maguire—a former judge from San Francisco and a U.S. representative. Maguire was a rising star in the Democratic Party, and his platform encompassed everything CK wished for in a candidate. He was an advocate of the single-tax system, a bitter foe of the railroad, a critic of land and water monopolies, and a supporter of the direct election of U.S. senators. The California Democratic platform even waded into foreign policy, endorsing the recently concluded Spanish American War but rejecting the lands acquired from Spain. Maguire's fusion of Democratic, Populist, and single-tax issues won him many supporters, especially in urban areas. Maguire was also a Catholic, but this gave him no leverage with heavily Catholic parts of the state (such as San Francisco), because he had written a controversial tract accusing the pope of selling the Irish out to the English.[1] This also would be a major challenge to his electoral prospects. Maguire was not perfect—he had an off-putting personality, and some of the positions of the party factions endorsing him were inconsistent. Still, he was better than what the Republicans offered.

The Republican nomination went to Henry T. Gage, a Los Angeles lawyer who had actively worked for the Southern Pacific in the legislature. Gage's loyalty to the company and his bella figura as a candidate ("a handsome man of splendid physique") made him the pick of the Southern Pacific political boss William Herrin. Herrin's approval sounded Gage's death knell as far as CK was concerned. He also took a disliking to Gage's running mate, Jacob H. Neff, "a popular old warhorse from Placer County and idol of the miners."[2]

To Valentine, CK wrote, "I do not see how The *Bee* can possibly support Gage for Governor and be consistent with its declarations of principle . . . granted that he may stand on two or three conflicting platforms, Gage stands on one which is just as inconsistent as all the three of Maguire put together." Adding a dose of personal invective, he confided to his brother: "Mr. Gage was arrested for stealing sheep not many years ago, and the indictment was squashed on a technicality." In a postscript he included, "It might also be stated that Gage is the sworn thrall of M. H. de Young [owner of the *San Francisco Chronicle*], and Colonel Harrison Gray Otis [owner of the *Los Angeles Times*], but more particularly Harrison Gray Otis. If Gage is governor, Otis will be the Warwick with a vengeance."[3]

Once the state fair ended in September, the *Bee* went all out for Maguire and the Democratic ticket. CK bitterly attacked Gage as a railroad lackey. As the election approached, CK believed that the rising tide of reformist sentiment, coupled with a growing anti–Southern Pacific backlash, augured well for a Democratic victory. However, the opposition made maximum use of Maguire's weaknesses, especially his authorship of his controversial text, *Ireland and the Pope* (1888). This treatise shined a light on his fallen-away status as a Catholic (similar to CK's) and earned him the scorn of one of the most popular and powerful Roman Catholic clergymen in the state, the Reverend Peter C. Yorke. Yorke was an Irish nationalist who wielded powerful influence with Irish Roman Catholics all over the state but especially in San Francisco and Sacramento. Yorke had no fear of personally attacking fallen-away Irish Catholics—including Maguire, San Francisco mayor James Duval Phelan, and McClatchy himself. To Yorke, Maguire was not only an apostate to his church but also a disgrace to his nationality. CK defended Maguire's controversial book, insisting in 1892 that Maguire "told the square truth when he arraigned the Popes as enemies of the Irish people in their contention with England. . . . The Church has always been arrayed on the side of might."[4] Yorke denounced the tract as a slander on the papacy and on the Catholicism of the Irish. That fallen-away McClatchy had endorsed it further confirmed the book's perfidy. Maguire lived to regret stirring up the eloquent, popular, and fearless Yorke.

Yorke and McClatchy

Peter C. Yorke (1864–1925), a native of Galway, Ireland, studied for the priesthood in Ireland and the United States. Ordained in 1887, he became a priest of the Archdiocese of San Francisco and a confidant of San Francisco's archbishop, Patrick Riordan, who made Yorke his chancellor and editor of the archdiocesan paper, the *Monitor.* Riordan even tried to appoint Yorke a bishop. Yorke was forceful on matters of Irish nationalism and union rights and fierce in his defense of attacks on the Catholic Church. Yorke soared into public view when he took on the rise of the American Protective Association (APA) during the 1890s.[5] He fervently defended organized labor, insisting that Pope Leo XIII's 1891 encyclical, *Rerum Novarum,* had validated the right to organize and bargain collectively. Yorke was a popular preacher and a natural leader of San Francisco's large Irish American community, and his sphere of influence spread throughout Northern California. He eventually became pastor of St. Peter's Church in San Francisco.

His tangles with CK began when CK publicly criticized Pope Leo XIII in regard to the excommunication of a popular priest, Rev. Edward McGlynn (a supporter of Henry George's in New York). Yorke sprang to the defense of the pope and poked back at McClatchy, whom Yorke considered an apostate and a disgrace to his Irish heritage. Unlike others who resented McClatchy but had no public forum (except the courts), Yorke was able to use the pages of the *Monitor* and later his own independent newspaper, the *Leader,* to hurl colorful language back at the Sacramento editor. Yorke had other beefs with McClatchy. When CK denounced the 1894 railway strike in Sacramento and called for a larger standing army to combat violent unionists, the staunchly prolabor Yorke ridiculed "the principles of the apian philosopher" and wondered "if such unmitigated trash is ever read or if read its tendency understood. . . . A free people cannot be persuaded into peace by bayonet." Yorke concluded, "The servile fear of riots is responsible for this Sacramento theory."[6]

On rare occasions, however, the men agreed and even made common cause. One mutual enemy was the APA, whose efforts to stir antipathy toward Catholics met with contempt from both men. Yorke provided CK with the damning information that the Reverend Donald Ross, chief spokesman for the APA, was of Canadian birth. This incensed CK, who snorted: "The loyal citizens of this country do not need aliens and particularly British subjects to teach them the duties of citizenship."[7] Yorke also enlisted McClatchy's aid in exposing efforts of the sugar millionaire and owner of the *San Francisco Call,* John D. Spreckels, to purchase the support of the APA for his senatorial campaign. Both men took delight in accusing Spreckels of bribery.[8]

In the 1896 presidential campaign, Yorke praised the *Bee* as "about the only paper west of the Rockies that rises above the dead level of mediocrity. It is now engaged in a free fight for free silver. And it is right."[9] McClatchy also supported Yorke in his quarrel with the Oakland Library Board regarding the exclusion of the *Monitor* from the library's subscriptions.

While Yorke and CK by turns sparred or united over various issues, the 1898 gubernatorial campaign created a permanent rift between the two men and started a harsh verbal feud that lasted nearly three decades. James Maguire's controversial book offended Yorke, and Maguire refused to criticize a San Francisco supervisor (also a Catholic) who had voted against a Catholic ministry to the city-owned Sailors' Home. Yorke denounced the supervisor, Dr. Henry Clinton, as a traitor to his faith, and Maguire, who kept Clinton as a member of his campaign committee, shared the opprobrium.

At the height of the 1898 gubernatorial campaign, Yorke struck back at Maguire during a charity event at St. Francis de Sales Church in Oakland. There he publically denounced Maguire as a "traitor to the faith of his mother" for writing the derogatory book. Yorke also attacked the San Francisco mayoral candidate James Duval Phelan, referring to him derisively as "Jimmy the Rag," and urged a vote for Gage. The wide publicity Yorke's comments received in the San Francisco press enraged McClatchy, who quickly fired off a telegram to Yorke's superior, Archbishop Patrick Riordan, demanding to know, "Does the Catholic Church endorse the attack of Father Yorke on James G. Maguire?" Unsure of how to deal with his brilliant but sometimes headstrong cleric, Riordan demurred, noting that Yorke's positions were his own.[10] McClatchy understood something about the power of the Catholic hierarchy: if it had been anyone other than the popular Yorke, the hammer of clerical discipline would have come down immediately.

McClatchy railed,

> Father Peter C. Yorke, no longer editor of the *Monitor*, voicing his own personal bitterness, took advantage of a Catholic Fair in Oakland to become a political haranguer. . . . He used his holy office to bitterly denounce supervisor Clinton, [as well as] Phelan and Maguire. Under the guise of a champion of civil and religious liberty, he vented his personal spleen and attacked honest, manly, God-fearing noble American citizens—two of them stalwart followers of the Catholic faith—because they would not do his arrogant bidding.[11]

In the end Gage defeated Maguire by a vote of 148,334 to 129,255. Republicans swept all major offices and achieved majorities in both houses of the legislature. They also captured the populous counties of San Francisco and Alameda. Even Sacramento County went for Gage with a vote of 5,317 to 3,036 for Maguire.[12] It's not clear whether Yorke's insult fatally damaged Maguire, whose poor campaign skills did not help his cause. Moreover Phelan, whom Yorke had also attacked, won the mayoralty. CK wrote bitterly about Maguire's defeat, criticizing the candidate's "idiotic campaign," which focused too much on the railroad and the heavy hand of C. P. Huntington.[13] Nonetheless a disappointed CK also blamed Yorke's meddling and never forgave the priest.

CK became utterly convinced of the unholy alliance between the priest and the new governor when Gage appointed Yorke to the Board of Regents of the University of California. Nothing Yorke did escaped CK's attention and censure. So, too, with Governor Gage.

Living with Gage

CK was already contemptuous of Gage when he appointed Yorke to the board of regents, but the governor had enraged McClatchy even more by scheduling his press releases from three to four o'clock in the afternoon—thereby releasing news only after the *Evening Bee* had been put to bed. Valentine objected: "To confine your interviews with newspaper reporters to the hour named would practically bar the afternoon papers from securing, in time for publication, any matter requiring submission to yourself. . . . Aside from the desire and duty of the press to present news as accurately and as speedily as possible, it would be a hardship on the public to be forced to wait until next morning for correct information as to matters of general importance that might be authoritatively covered in the afternoon paper." Valentine concluded, "I speak in this matter not only for The *Bee*, but for the afternoon papers of this state and of the nation, since they are served through the Associated Press, which depends on The *Bee* for day service in Sacramento." To mollify the *Bee* Gage grudgingly set the press hour back one hour.[14]

Because of the way Gage received the nomination and won the election, CK always suspected the governor of some sort of chicanery. CK went after Gage regarding the nomination of U.S. senators. Gage had apparently promised that he would support Michael de Young, publisher of the *San Francisco Chronicle*, for the post when the Democrat Stephen M. White retired in 1900. Instead the nod went to Gage's operative Daniel Burns, a San Francisco saloon keeper, politician, owner of Mexican mines, and one of William Herrin's chief lieutenants. Gage's betrayal of de Young drew scorn from former supporters like John Spreckels and Harrison Gray Otis. But Burns's quest went forward in the state legislature, which at that time still chose U.S. senators. For a year the state legislature was unable to choose either Burns or his opponent, Ulysses S. Grant Jr. Despite numerous votes and deals, the senate seat remained vacant. Finally Thomas R. Bard of Ventura emerged as a compromise candidate. Bard, a successful farmer and oil company executive (one of the founders of Union Oil), had amassed a large personal fortune and a reputation for probity. Despite Gage's efforts to secure the seat for Burns, Bard's cause gathered momentum, and Burns finally withdrew in early February 1901. Thus the legislature elected Bard to the Senate.[15] Bard's victory spelled the end of Gage's hopes for a second term as the candidate of the railroad, which had withdrawn its support for Burns and for the governor as well.

CK contributed to Burns's defeat with a steady flow of negative reporting. In retaliation Gage's supporters in the legislature passed a series of antipress bills that were at odds with the First Amendment. One of the most controversial measures, the Morehouse "signature bill" of March 21, 1899, demanded the byline of the author appear on all newspaper articles that questioned the integrity, honesty, or reputation of any individual.[16] CK and Valentine mobilized opposition to the law. CK laid out strategy in a letter to a local press agency chief:

> I have no doubt that the only course for the papers to do is to fight the foolish act. Probably the best [*sic*] of the two plans suggested is for some paper to be selected to ignore the law and have a friendly test suit brought against it; and pending the decision upon that test suit by the higher court, the other papers in the State should obey the law. If, however, the papers should all continue to ignore the acts as unconstitutional, while the first violation of the act was still on trial, there is no doubt that papers would be put to an immense amount of annoyance by a lot of legal harpies looking for pigeons to pluck.[17]

Ultimately, instead of a direct challenge to the law, CK decided to follow it literally and mocked it by signing virtually every sentence of his editorial column of April 19, 1899:

Ah, there! Henry Theophilus Gage! CHARLES KENNY McCLATCHY. To you, Grove Lachrymose Johnson, the Veepin' Villam of the Valley, a royal salaam! CHARLES KENNY McCLATCHY. . . . And thou likewise, Heleorus Elephantine Wright, do we turn our eyes unto you and give the Morituri Salutamus act! . . . And well are thou entitled Elephantine, for sooth to say, none but one possessing the face of an elephant would have daily occupied your position in the Forum in Sacramento when the health-giving air of San Quentin invited. CHARLES KENNY McCLATCHY.[18]

The unwieldy and even ridiculous aspects of the law made it impossible to enforce. Gage only inflamed press sentiment against him, especially from the *Bee.*

The Battle with Peter Yorke Resumes

The feud with Yorke resumed with a vengeance in the summer of 1901, when teamsters and longshoremen in San Francisco went on strike. The newly formed Employers' Association—a loose confederation of management in the Bay City—refused to deal with the strikers. The situation became increasingly more volatile, and the positions of both sides hardened.[19] Yorke sided with the union members, and at an August 8, 1901, meeting at Metropolitan Hall, he reminded listeners that Pope Leo XIII himself supported unionism and fair wages.[20] CK, wary of any kind of labor unrest, roundly condemned Yorke's invocation of papal social teaching in support of unionism. It also offended the editor that a cleric should be participating in these affairs. When the escalating unrest provoked a general strike, CK worried as Sacramento canneries began to experience delivery shortages. True to previous practice the *Bee* denounced the strike participants as anarchists.[21] Yorke endorsed the strike and publicly embraced its two main leaders, Andrew Furuseth and Michael Casey.

Yorke's involvement took a more forceful turn when, at a fateful meeting of union leaders, San Francisco mayor James Duval Phelan allegedly threatened the workers to return to work "if they do not want to be clubbed." Yorke seized on this remark and repeated it in an interview with the labor-friendly *Examiner.* Phelan denied having made the threat, but Furuseth pledged to provide an affidavit that the mayor had said words to that effect. This inflamed the situation. At a critical point Gage met with Yorke and the union leader Michael Casey and negotiated an end to the strike in the latter part of

September.[22] Yorke and Casey helped sell it to the workers. By October 2 it was announced that the Employers' Association had struck a bargain with the teamsters, preserving their union rights and sending the men back to work.[23]

Hearst gave Yorke free rein to discuss his views on the strike on the editorial page of the *Examiner.* Yorke took aim at the "misrepresentations of the *San Francisco Chronicle,*" which, he quipped, some San Franciscans read "for penance and others through habit, no sane man ever perused it for pleasure." Yorke pronounced a particularly scathing indictment of Police Chief William Sullivan Jr., in which the cleric attacked the chief's shoot-to-kill order against strikers who attempted to board seagoing vessels.[24]

McClatchy poured editorial scorn on Yorke, but the popular priest had no fear of CK and traveled to Sacramento whenever invited. On January 28, 1902, at the invitation of local clergy, Yorke gave a lecture, "The Rights of Labor," to hundreds who packed Sacramento's Clunie Theater.[25] In the spring of 1902 the priests of the cathedral (where CK's wife, Ella, attended Sunday Mass) invited Yorke to speak at a fund-raiser for a new Catholic school being started on Sacramento's West End.

McClatchy took these visits as a personal affront and was convinced the real reason for them was to promote a second term for Governor Gage. The *Bee,* which covered the school fund-raiser depicted it as a political event and noted that Gage appointees, including lieutenant Daniel Burns and his closest political allies, were assembled on the stage as vice presidents of the event. During his speech Yorke did not endorse Gage but rather addressed the rights of labor from a Catholic perspective, citing papal documents. McClatchy, the Catholic school dropout, again disputed Yorke's interpretation of Pope Leo XIII's landmark encyclical, *Rerum Novarum,* arguing Yorke had distorted its meaning and intent.[26]

Yorke replied to McClatchy's charges on the pages of his newly founded *San Francisco Leader,* and the *San Francisco Star,* run by CK's friend James Henry Barry, reprinted them. "The agency responsible for the appearance of the *Bee* (and by the way it is published in Sacramento) is an illiterate person named Charlie McClatchy," Yorke wrote. "We say illiterate advisedly because, though the Jesuits taught him to read and write, even they, one of the most successful bodies in Christendom, could not educate him. It passes the powers of nature to make a silk purse out of a sow's ear." Alluding to the bestowal of an honorary degree on CK by Santa Clara College in 1901, Yorke remarked: "People remember with disgust his last public appearance when some Catholics in their holy simplicity asked him to a banquet on the principle that a surly cur is best quieted with a bone. They did not realize that currishness is not in McClatchy's stomach alone, but in the very fibre [*sic*] of his soul."[27]

McClatchy reprinted Yorke's piece in the February 18, 1902, edition of the *Evening Bee.* The next day CK issued a sarcastic response to the San Francisco priest: "The trouble with Peter C. Yorke is that he is swelled with an exalted idea of his own importance. He considers himself a Liebig's Extract of the Pope, the College of Cardinals and the Catholic priesthood. . . . He is not the Church of Rome. He is not even a commendable nor admirable priest therein. He is a tool of Henry T. Gage, working among the Catholics of this state in the interest of that individual for Governor, and not at all particular as to the truth of his statements in championship."[28]

Less than a month later Yorke blasted McClatchy in response to another wave of the editor's taunting.[29] The exchange of invective continued for a few more salvos and then tapered off as McClatchy and Yorke turned to other matters until the summer of 1903. As he had done with newspaper rivals (Sheehan and later Calkins), CK employed a private investigator to dig for unsavory information about the cleric. One of his sources was James Barry, the head of a small printing company that put out the weekly *San Francisco Star*. Barry, like McClatchy, was the son of a California newspaperman. A hardworking printer, Barry had an important contract with the Archdiocese of San Francisco to print its widely circulated newspaper, the *Monitor*. He had also printed Maguire's controversial pamphlet. A staunch Democrat, courageous journalist, and often in trouble with church authorities, Barry, too, was a fallen-away Catholic and a hard drinker but maintained friendships with some important clerics. McClatchy loved Barry's progressive politics and fed him bits of news and gossip for the *Star,* and Barry cordially reciprocated.

As the McClatchy-Yorke antagonism persisted, they developed a shorthand for one another—with McClatchy regularly referring to Yorke as the "Jack Cade" of the priesthood, evoking the image of a fifteenth-century English rebel who was the villain in Shakespeare's *Henry VI*, while Yorke continually referred to McClatchy as "Civet McClatchy," a reference to a skunk that inhabited the local region. They would continue to carry on like two scorpions in a bottle until their next full-blown battle about San Francisco's political future.

Chapter Nine
Public Health and Urban
Corruption in San Francisco

———————————◆———————————

THE BATTLE WITH YORKE focused CK's love-hate relationship with San Francisco. He traveled there regularly, often to see his mother and sister Emily, who had taken up permanent residence there after 1900. His dentists were in the Bay City, and one of his closest friends, James Barry, editor of the *San Francisco Star,* was a supporter throughout the years. So also was Rev. Denis Crowley, the director of the Youth Directory—a home for "friendless" and poor boys aged seven to fourteen (a charity CK privately and generously supported). CK had a favorite restaurant that knew his tastes and kept a special wine cellar for him, even during Prohibition. He frequently attended the theater in San Francisco.

Yet at the same time CK regarded "the Metropolis" with suspicion, in part because it seemed to dominate the culture and financial resources of Northern California. He detested the city's politics and most of his newspaper rivals there. It was also the home of his archenemy, Peter C. Yorke, so when an outbreak of the dreaded bubonic plague in San Francisco threatened to spread contagion and disease all over Northern California, CK made it his duty to make sure the whole world knew San Francisco was literally a toxic place to visit—because he believed its establishment (press and politicians) deliberately withheld information about the gravity of the public health crisis. Even though his perceptions of events in San Francisco were filtered through his penchant for the dramatic, his distaste for the Gage administration, and his Sinophobia, this was McClatchy at his finest: a crusader against secrecy and public corruption, not only against the usual suspects (urban and state governments) but also against his press rivals who voluntarily censored themselves to the detriment of the people.

CK and the First Plague Crisis

The California plague crisis occurred in two phases. The first extended from 1900 to 1903, the second during 1907 and 1908. Bubonic plague, the scourge of late medieval Europe, publicly surfaced in San Francisco on March 6, 1900, when Chick Gin (Wong Chut Gin, or Wong Chut King), a Chinese man, succumbed to the disease. The determination of the cause of his death set off a quiet frenzy in San Francisco.[1] Chick Gin's decomposing body was found with the classic signs of plague infection: enlarged lymphatic nodules in the groin. William H. Kellogg, the city bacteriologist, confirmed the disease. Kellogg then submitted his evidence to Dr. Joseph J. Kinyoun, the chief quarantine officer at San Francisco's Marine Hospital on Angel Island; Kinyoun corroborated Kellogg's findings. The city's board of health then promptly placed a quarantine on Chinatown. The presence of the plague raised several issues that would preoccupy CK, city and state officials, and members of the San Francisco press.

The fear surrounding the discovery of plague was real. This highly contagious disease brought about a speedy and painful death. Because of the squalid living conditions in some parts of Chinatown, its appearance also contributed to stereotypes about the Chinese as bearers of illness. CK's reporting on the crisis and its cover-up in San Francisco had an undertone of racism. When the poet Oscar Wilde visited California in 1884 and gently praised San Francisco's Chinatown, CK dismissed Wilde's words, noting, "The rottenness of that locality is sufficient to sicken the average white man at close quarters." The *Bee* had actively campaigned for restrictions of Chinese immigration and detested low-wage Chinese labor. CK had even urged ministers to preach against the Chinese in 1886, writing, "The Chinese question is merely whether the labor of this country shall be given up to heathen coolies from Asia or whether it shall be preserved for the American laborer. . . . Every Joss-worshiping Chinaman who comes to California shuts out a God-fearing white man, with wife and children brought up under the influences of the Christian religion."[2] However, the nexus of the Chinese and the plague was secondary to CK's pique at the denial of the plague's existence by a cabal of local merchants as well as city and state representatives. CK believed, with good reason, that officials downplayed the seriousness of the public health crisis in order to maintain the city's attractiveness as a commercial center and tourist destination. Even worse, his colleagues in the press voluntarily censored themselves on the issue—depriving citizens of their right to know about a potential threat to their lives. For a time CK was the only California journalist who acknowledged the existence of this dreadful disease and exposed the cover-up—especially the role of Governor Gage. Once CK determined to speak out, he never shut up.

The Story Unfolds

The reaction of the San Francisco press to the potential outbreak was indeed curious. The *San Francisco Call* had noted the existence of the plague in a freighter docked in Seattle, as well as an outbreak in Honolulu and unhealthy hygienic conditions in San Francisco's Chinatown.[3] With the discovery of Chick Gin's body the board of health imposed a quarantine on Chinatown. City papers such as the evening *San Francisco Bulletin* reported the plague as front page news but tamped down alarm by calling the quarantine a "precautionary measure." The editors of the morning papers, the *Chronicle* and the *Call,* met the very night the body was discovered and reported the quarantine but did not extensively publicize the possibility of wider infection. Only the *Examiner* promised to report on the spread of the plague. However, as doctors waited anxiously to see what would happen to animals injected with samples from the dead man's body, citizens and merchants grew more critical of the inconveniences of sequestering part of the city.[4]

Only two days after Chick Gin's body was found and the quarantine imposed, some newspapers began to tag it a con job. The *San Francisco Call,* owned by the sugar shipping magnate John D. Spreckels, who had a vested interest in keeping the port open, denounced the quarantine as a ploy by the board of health to "get snout and forelegs in the public trough."[5] Michael de Young's *San Francisco Chronicle* declared it a scare, and Fremont Older's *Bulletin* lambasted it as a scam perpetrated by a money-hungry board of health that was "threatening the very life of the city." Only William Randolph Hearst and the *Examiner* expressed concern about the potential for contagion. Nonetheless, with the pressure from the press, city officials, and merchants, the board of health lifted the quarantine, prematurely as it turned out, on March 9, 1900. Everybody rejoiced except the *Examiner,* which caustically suggested that the demand to lift it came from those who missed their Chinese cooks and bakers.[6]

The *Examiner* Tries to Report the Story

Hearst continued to spotlight the issue as the board of health went forward with its investigation of Chinatown. At first it seemed the city could relax when the first test animals inoculated with the bacillus from the dead man's body did not show any symptoms. However, on March 11 all the test animals died of the plague. Seeking to keep the lid on the issue, the *Bulletin* reported this but noted the board of health had not reinstated the quarantine—hence all was well. The *Examiner,* quoting Kinyoun's authoritative statement and invoking his reputation as one of the leading bacteriologists in the United States, stated baldly that plague had caused the death of Chick Gin. Mayor Phelan supported the board of health and took action with the help of ten doughty physicians (he had asked for one hundred) who went door to door in the twelve-block Chinatown area and reported on the unsanitary conditions.[7] When some Chinese residents refused to allow autopsies of their dead relatives, confusion and fear grew. Chinatown, it was feared, might be host to other contagious and dangerous illnesses, including leprosy, tuberculosis, and syphilis.

Hearst's *San Francisco Examiner* asserted that the situation offered an opportunity to clean up the city and defended Mayor Phelan's health board against attacks. As cases multiplied, the *Examiner* became more forceful in its reporting and insistent that the city take positive steps to acknowledge and deal with the plague in its midst.[8] But this commonsense campaign on behalf of public health met with howls of outrage from local business and commercial leaders when on March 18 Hearst's *New York Journal* ran a huge "Plague Edition" warning that the Black Death might be creeping from the Bay City across America. Hearst was attacked as an enemy of the city's economy, and his sensational reporting, San Francisco leaders claimed, had single-handedly caused a thirty-thousand-person decline in tourism and a steep drop-off in ocean cargoes. The *Bulletin* denounced Hearst on its front page.[9] The *Call,* which later admitted that the papers' silence on the plague was deliberate, derisively referred to it as the "Yellow Plague" and excoriated Hearst and Phelan for the "bubonic buncomb."[10] Faced with public outrage and a potential loss of advertising revenue, the *Examiner* moved the stories off the front page and buried them inside the paper.[11] The *Examiner* then backed off altogether on April 1 and said little or nothing further about the matter. The *Bulletin* reported sporadically about the ongoing efforts in Chinatown and noted on March 24 that local merchants wished to band together to "counteract reports of plague."[12]

But denial of the plague did not make it less real and lethal. Plague-related deaths mounted in March, April, and May. Kinyoun wired U.S. Surgeon General Walter Wyman in Washington that the plague had now become an epidemic. Wyman issued an order on May 21, 1900, forbidding transportation on common carriers of any Asiatics or people of other races susceptible to the disease. A second quarantine was imposed, and Wyman transferred four additional officers to San Francisco, at the same time ordering Kinyoun to bring on other physicians to investigate. President McKinley invoked an 1890 law quarantining Asiatics in California—permitting none to come in and none to leave, while armed patrol boats trolled the California coast. The board of health, with the concurrence of the board of supervisors, once again quarantined Chinatown—this time with boards and barbed wire, a move that was quickly challenged in the courts.[13] Kinyoun and his team began to vaccinate Chinese with an antiplague vaccine that had only recently been developed by a Russian bacteriologist named Waldemar Haffkine. However, terrified by reports the drug was dangerous (and it did have serious side-effects), Chinese San Franciscans refused to accept the inoculations.[14] When a local court overturned the quarantine, Kinyoun appealed to the federal government to enforce a quarantine of the entire city of San Francisco. An active campaign to vilify Kinyoun now began, and on June 19 all quarantine orders were suspended.[15]

Enter CK and the *Bee*

The *Bee* took note of the plague issue on March 8, 1900, at first reporting it as a scare and suggesting that while medical reports were incomplete, there was no cause for alarm. But as the other Northern California papers went silent on the issue, CK grew more distressed—especially when rumors of similar plague-related deaths began to be reported in the Central Valley and even in Sacramento.[16] CK suspected a cover-up, abetted by journalists working in collusion with government and San Francisco business officials. As he often lamented, these corrupt politicians and profits-at-all-cost businesspeople thought nothing of putting the lives of innocent Californians in jeopardy. He no doubt read the *Call's* admission that the newspapers had voluntarily suppressed news of the plague and lashed out at what he called the "ostrich press" of San Francisco. He sardonically noted that many of those keeping silent were the very publishers who often lauded themselves for their fearless reporting. If they would do nothing, CK would report the story.

As the weeks passed and plague cases multiplied, CK wrote to a former employee now working on the *Call*, John Cosgrave, to say, "Your newspapers in San Francisco do not seem to know that there is any Bubonic Plague. The Federal authorities, however, know it, and the San Francisco Board of Health, after three months of continuous lying, have at last been brought to see the enormity of their sins and have confessed the truth. . . . This is a matter that

I believe ought to be published; the truth, the whole truth; and nothing but the truth. The Bay papers are injuring San Francisco enormously, because their absolute silence in that matter causes everybody else in the state to believe that the plague is 100 times worse than it probably is."[17] He implored Cosgrave "to write a very readable article" on the topic, but Cosgrave referred CK to J. M. Williamson, the president of the San Francisco Board of Health. Williamson was also alarmed by the plague and distressed that the work of the board of health had now become a political nightmare. On May 24 McClatchy wrote directly to Williamson:

> In view of the fact that the San Francisco newspapers will not pub-lish anything that your Board of Health does except in abuse, and will publish none of the facts concerning the recent deaths from Bubonic plague during the last three months in San Francisco— and considering also the fact that the people of the interior of the State of California think the Board of Health has been right and the newspapers wrong all through this business—The *Bee* extends to you the use of its columns for the publication of whatever you may desire to write in connection with this matter and for the dis-semination of whatever additional facts you may be pleased to give to the public.[18]

With Williamson as his mole, CK exposed the mounting number of cases of the plague in San Francisco.[19] CK also railed against the Bay City's news estab-lishment: "The San Francisco press has been pursuing a narrow, short-sighted head-in-the-sand policy which will inflict not only temporary injury upon the State, but will attach to it a stigma from which it will not recover."[20]

In August the *Bee* escalated the controversy by contacting the secretary of the state board of health in Colorado; CK had heard the Colorado secretary had written to the secretary of the California State Board of Health about the plague. CK asked for reasons why California officials had neglected to "notify you [Colorado] of cases of the plague in addition to those referred to in [your] original statement." CK observed sarcastically that even U.S. Surgeon General Wyman, who had first reported the outbreaks, was censoring himself under pressure not only from the business interests in San Francisco but also from the Gage administration.[21] Hearing that the despised Henry Gage was behind the cover-up provided CK with a reason to pursue the issue.

To be sure, CK was not shocked that the governor was in on the cover-up. McClatchy had always distrusted and even hated the governor and anyone who supported him. CK seized every opportunity to attack Gage on this issue, and the governor provided a lot of ammunition. One such episode came when the state board of health commissioned reports on the plague by two bacteriologists: Dr. Silas Mouser and Dr. H. A. L. Ryfkogel. By the end of July 1900 these reports further confused the situation. Mouser denied the outbreak of plague while Ryfkogel affirmed it. CK demanded to see copies of both reports, insisting they were public documents. When Gage refused, CK petitioned Superior Court Judge E. C. Hart for a writ of mandamus to release the records—especially the Rykfogel report. At the same time the *San Francisco Chronicle*, a skeptic of the plague scare, demanded the Mouser report. Hart found in favor of the newspapers and on August 8 instructed Secretary of State W. F. Matthews to release the documents. The state board of health quickly appealed Hart's decision, and the reports remained in limbo for at least another year.[22]

In the absence of hard evidence, the *Chronicle* suggested the Mouser report (which the paper had not seen) was correct and attacked the *Bee* for "reviving the plague fake" and harming San Francisco. CK retorted, "The *Bee*, so far from making an effort to damage the interests of the State, has been endeavoring to repair the damage done the State by the *Chronicle* and the other San Francisco papers in their failure to look beyond the mere commercial side of the case and in their endeavor to suppress all news relative to the matter." Nonetheless the *Bee* continued to run stories about additional cases, highlighting one in which the victim was Caucasian. These reports and persistent complaints about the cover-up continued throughout the summer.[23] Even though CK turned his attention to the various state and national political campaigns of 1900, he never let up on the plague issue and had the *Bee* reporter H. A. French continue to investigate in San Francisco. In October CK wrote to the embattled Kinyoun, eliciting a summary of events regarding the plague.[24]

In the fall of 1900 Gage emphatically denied the existence of the plague in California. CK forcefully refuted the governor's assertion and attacked the self-imposed news blackout by the leading papers in San Francisco. CK also sent the Associated Press the names of those infected and expressed a hope that it would send his article to all the members of the national wire service. To his consternation the AP superintendent in San Francisco, Paul Cowles, rejected

CK's report. CK angrily wrote to Cowles and contrasted the handling of the crisis in San Francisco with that of Glasgow, Scotland, where bubonic plague had also been discovered and dealt with openly.[25]

Cowles countered CK's arguments by downplaying the outbreaks and comparing the number of plague deaths to those caused by consumption or pneumonia. McClatchy retorted, "The question of how many deaths occur in San Francisco from consumption or pneumonia is of no general interest. But it is of vital interest and of vital importance to know whether or not the bubonic plague has been stamped out in San Francisco." In November CK released yet another summary of the twenty-one confirmed cases of the plague in San Francisco and also reported that the Medical Society of Northern California had in fact confirmed the existence of the plague in San Francisco.[26]

As 1901 approached, CK persisted in his coverage with bulldog tenacity. Those who denied the plague then took aim at Kinyoun and worked to remove him as the government health officer in San Francisco. CK came to Kinyoun's assistance, calling in friends in Washington, including U.S. Representative Marion De Vries. CK also wrote to the former *Bee* reporter Colvin Brown, now editor of the *Stockton Record*, urging him to bring the plague situation to the attention of U.S. Representative Samuel D. Woods in order to save Kinyoun. However, Gage stubbornly stuck to his denials, using a portion of his annual governor's message in January 1901 to attack "plague fakers" and singled out Kinyoun as one of the primary culprits. Gage cited the testimony of sympathetic San Francisco physicians and noted that local businessmen like Levi Strauss, Joseph Tobin of the Hibernia Bank, William Alvord of the California Bank, and even former governor James Budd agreed with him. Remarkably Gage even suggested that plague bacilli may have been injected into the Chinese after they had died. Gage was not afraid to cripple the workings of a free press (First Amendment jurisprudence was not what it is today) and proposed a law making it a felony for anyone to publish allegations concerning the existence of the plague unless the state board of health had first made a determination of fact.[27]

CK condemned Gage's attack on Kinyoun as "shameless, unwarranted and cowardly."[28] Shortly after Gage's speech, CK revealed that a new victim, Chang Wey Lung, had been found in San Francisco just days after the governor announced there was no plague. CK derided the governor's false assertion, the ongoing cover-up by local papers, and their "pathetic efforts" to attack Kinyoun.[29]

Central Valley Fears and Renewed Federal Intervention

CK stoked fears the plague may have traveled to the Central Valley, especially Bakersfield. "There have been I learn on good authority," he wrote to Alfred Harrell of the *Californian Bakersfield*, "some twenty-eight deaths which are traceable to two Chinese. There is a pneumonic form of bubonic plague which is frequently diagnosed as pneumonia by those unfamiliar with the plague itself." The editor also wondered "from what place the two Chinese, supposed to have started the epidemic, came—if from San Francisco or if they have long been residents of Bakersfield." McClatchy sent inquiries to medical people in the San Joaquin Valley towns of Delano, Visalia, Fresno, and Bakersfield; he wanted to know whether the disease had been carried to the coast from the inland regions and promised them confidentiality in their replies.[30]

On February 14, 1901, three more cases of plague appeared in San Francisco, and the next day the *Bee* published a map of the areas of the city most affected by the disease. The *Bee* again listed the known cases, including a Chinese man who had traveled from San Francisco to Sacramento—with the implication that he may have introduced the fearful disease in the state capital. The *Bee* also began a campaign to solicit reports of plague outbreaks in other parts of the West.[31]

CK's press offensive, and concerns raised by others, pressured federal authorities to investigate. U.S. Secretary of the Treasury Lyman Gage appointed a California plague commission consisting of three university professors— Simon Flexner of the University of Pennsylvania, Frederick Novy of the University of Michigan, and Lewellyn Barker of Johns Hopkins University— and charged them with determining authoritatively whether the plague existed in California. They first established an office at the University of California, Berkeley, but were unceremoniously evicted by a skittish university administration fearful of losing its annual appropriation from a vengeful state legislature and governor. Mayor Phelan of San Francisco provided space in a room in city hall. By February 18, 1901, the commission had verified additional new cases. Its full report, completed on February 26, 1901, vindicated both Chief Quarantine Officer Kinyoun and the San Francisco Board of Health. The federal commission made recommendations for the eradication of the illness. Rumor had it that among the commission's suggestions was the destruction of Chinatown or that all Chinese should be moved to Mission Rock, an outcropping in San Francisco Bay. This report was to be kept quiet, but someone leaked it to CK, who then published portions of it in a story that alarmed Governor Gage and San Francisco merchants and politicians.[32]

Governor Gage at first tried to cajole the commissioners into downplaying the report but they refused. Gage then fought back by assembling a group of journalists, business types, and politicians to go to Washington, D.C., to urge federal officials to suppress the report of the three medical experts. On the day Gage and the delegation left, CK ran a story saying that the plague crisis was real and that "responsible" parties were covering it up.[33] To CK's disgust, Gage managed to stave off publication of the report (in this he was aided by California's senators, George Perkins and Thomas Bard). Wyman and other McKinley administration officials were swayed by the potential economic fall-out for California if this became known. Instead the McKinley administration settled for a quiet plan to eradicate the disease in Chinatown while at the same time planning a series of events for the president's visit to the Pacific coast later that year. CK erupted in anger at the cover-up and denounced it on March 16, 1901, in bold headlines as an "infamous compact."[34] In March 1901 Kinyoun was unceremoniously transferred from San Francisco to Detroit. He resigned from the Marine Hospital Service several months later. To his dying day he was deeply hurt and bitter about what had been done to him. The cover-up did not last long. CK managed to get a copy of the suppressed report and printed it in the *Bee* by mid-April.[35]

A Frustrating Effort to Publicize the Plague

CK continued to do all he could to make the plague a bigger story. Even though the Associated Press had agreed to censor plague reports or suggest that the type of plague found in California was not contagious, CK hotly contested the AP action and repeatedly warned that the plague would not remain contained in San Francisco.[36] Indeed, he took every opportunity to publicize cases that appeared elsewhere—especially in Sacramento.[37]

Frustrated at the cover-up, the *Bee* began a campaign to alert other parts of the country. The *Bee* reporter H. A. French wrote a lengthy letter that circulated to several eastern press outlets and noted the willingness of Surgeon General Wyman to suppress the damning report of the three professors at the behest of Gage. French warned: "The dangerous character of this agreement and the interest which the people of New York and other people in the East have in it will be seen when it is remembered that of all the tourists who visit San Francisco, 99 out of every 100 visit Chinatown. They are taken into the very worst quarters and darkest holes in that section. It is in these quarters that the infection exists. These tourists, by the acts of Governor Gage and Surgeon General Wyman, absolutely have no protection." French insisted: "The action of Surgeon General Wyman and of Governor Gage is little short of criminal."[38]

In another letter French asserted that it was "established fact that the plague exists in Bakersfield in a perhaps more dangerous form than in San Francisco, as the cases there seem to have been of the bubonic form and are largely among whites."[39] In an addendum to a copy of the same letter sent to the *Star* in Washington, D.C., French wrote, "I have just been informed from reliable authority that the Governor of Texas has demanded of the government that unless the most stringent, complete, and strenuous efforts are made by the authorities to suppress and prevent the spread of bubonic plague, he will impose a most complete, severe, and drastic quarantine against California." Indeed Governor Joseph D. Sayers of the Lone Star State had sent a telegram to Wyman in which Sayers threatened to quarantine Californians and California goods if the report was not released, and he expressed his shock that California authorities were denying the existence of plague. The *Bee* immediately communicated to W. F. Blund, state health officer of Texas, its information about both Wyman and the possible Bakersfield case.[40] These public officials in turn began to demand answers from federal officials and copies of the report by the three professors that had been suppressed.

CK turned to his usually outspoken friend James Barry, who had also kept silent on the story. Handing him an Associated Press report that acknowledged ten fatal cases of the plague since the beginning of 1901, CK noted that the *San Francisco Evening Post* and the *Bulletin* refused to publish them and stated, "We are now just about beginning to do the work that ought to have been done at least ten months ago and would have been done, had it not been for the idiotic action of the Governor and the press of San Francisco." Barry never followed through. Meanwhile CK unleashed a major investigation of the cover-up—which seemed worse than the plague itself. As noted earlier, on April 15, 1901, the *Bee* published a copy of the report obtained through its sources in Washington. This in turn was picked up by other newspapers with which the *Bee* had correspondence. The California Medical Society also verified that plague existed in San Francisco.[41]

The public attention now embarrassed Surgeon General Wyman, and he began to back away from the deal he had reached with Gage and his cronies.

Wyman communicated the Texas governor's statement to Assistant Surgeon General Joseph. H. White in San Francisco, who in turn passed it on to an angry Gage. Stung by this, Gage reluctantly began a small-scale cleanup of Chinatown under the direction of the Marine Hospital Service. Gage had always promised this in the past, but the effort was halfhearted and public relations conscious. The clean-up, Gage and San Francisco officials insisted, was for purposes of urban improvement rather than disease eradication. Inspectors were instructed to avoid the word *plague* or any of its synonyms. Any reports of illness were to be first reported to the Chinese Six Companies, a consortium of Chinese businessmen who had also worked hard to deny the plague's existence. These obstacles slowed White and eventually limited him to only surface cleaning of the area. The Chinese Six Companies further thwarted investigations by again insisting there was no plague, and indeed White's team found no new outbreaks. In all likelihood, however, this was because the Chinese had hidden the bodies of their sick and dying. But after sixty consecutive days of no new cases, California officials attempted to call off the Marine Hospital Service, which was overseeing these flaccid attempts at cleanup. The formal cleanup operation ended on June 1, 1901.

In fact, the operation was mostly cosmetic. It had come up short, ending with inspections of only 50 percent of the city's twenty-five thousand Chinese homes. Moreover, even though it was clear that the plague was being transmitted by rats that roamed freely around portions of the city, nothing of substance was done about rat abatement. Of course the plague was not stopped. When a Chinese man who had been in the Sacramento River region died in San Francisco on July 5, 1901, Kinyoun's successor, Dr. Rupert Blue of Angel Island, determined the cause was the plague. CK reported this in the *Bee* on July 9. State officials once again went into a defensive posture and contended it was *not* the plague. They even trotted out Gage's absurd conspiracy theory that the marine hospital had planted plague bacteria on the bodies of the deceased. The Chinese Six Companies continued to pressure the Chinese to keep silent and to secretly dispose of the corpses of people who had died of the plague. When the city's Japanese began to be affected by the disease, they, too, found themselves under pressure to shut up.[42]

In early September 1901 CK became even more resolute in exposing the plague (although the assassination of President McKinley in that month drove everything else off the front pages). CK released the long-hidden report Ryfkogel had submitted the previous summer but that had been suppressed by the state. Ryfkogel's findings affirming the existence and danger of the plague seemed more relevant than ever. In late September McClatchy published yet another front-page article reporting the discovery of more plague victims in the Bay City.[43] In 1902 CK was dismayed and angry when the newly elected San Francisco mayor, Eugene Schmitz, and the political boss Abe Ruef dealt with the issue by simply removing members of the city's board of health who acknowledged the plague problem. And while plague cases continued to be reported throughout the rest of 1902, Gage remained frozen in denial. At every possible opportunity McClatchy tied Gage to the cover-up.[44] The battle ended in a draw.

Temporary Truce

Serious engagement with the dangers of the plague came only after Gage was replaced in 1902 by George Pardee, an Oakland physician. Hoping for a more sympathetic ear in Sacramento, CK renewed the battle for full exposure of the plague threat. In a statewide letter-writing campaign to physicians, merchants, judges, and legislators, CK circulated facts about the plague, some of which came from the nearly suppressed Ryfkogel report and some from Dr. Louis Kengla, an editor of the *Occidental Medical Times* who had written a concise and damning article in the September 1902 edition of his periodical..

Closer to home CK wanted to make sure that local officials in Sacramento were not going to play ostrich. He pressed the Sacramento clothier and mayoral candidate E. W. Hale to call upon Kengla, who "knows from beginning to end the methods taken by the San Francisco authorities and by Governor Gage to suppress information, and to do nothing while the plague was on its way. He [Kengla] can also give your firm much valued information concerning the danger in which San Francisco at present lies if she and the state . . . [do] not awaken to the necessity of the hour." CK also urged Kengla to share information with W. E. Gerber, cashier of the California State Bank and a leading fruit grower and shipper.[45] Finally, on December 6, 1902, CK wrote governor-elect Pardee, enclosing two clippings from the *Bee*—one a copy of a recent editorial "proving beyond the possibility of doubt the presence of the plague in San Francisco"—and mentioning Kengla's diagnoses of four cases of "pneumonic bubonic plague, which [is] the most virulent and deadly type." The editor emphasized to the incoming governor "that the State and San Francisco must take proper precautions."[46]

Finally, resistance began to crumble. Other officials who had publicly denied the presence of the plague began to speak up. Some disclosed what CK had known all along, that in fact a cover-up had taken place. CK informed a friendly San Francisco priest that "ex-senator S. C. Smith from Kern County, publicly stated in his Bakersfield paper the other day that Governor Henry T. Gage acknowledged on more than one occasion privately, that he knew that plague existed in San Francisco." McClatchy added what to him had been the most outrageous aspect of the entire matter: "There is not a manager of a newspaper in San Francisco that has not privately admitted the same thing, and yet they and the merchants of that place are making fools of themselves by continuing to lie to the world."[47]

Finally, in early 1903 health authorities from twenty-one states gathered in Washington, D.C., where they roundly condemned the California Board of Health and the "obstructive influence" of Gage and threatened that if something were not done, they would endorse a massive quarantine of traffic from California to the other forty-seven states, along with an embargo on all railroads leading out of the state.[48] Fearing a national boycott, San Francisco civic groups finally did an about-face and organized a massive campaign to eradicate the plague, including the systematic extermination of disease-bearing rats, the demolition of unsanitary housing in a twenty-two-block area, the cementing of basements that trapped disease-bearing rats, and the exposure of subterranean tunnels filled with excrement and broken sewer pipes. Governor George Pardee quietly promoted this campaign. The last plague case, for a time, was reported on March 1, 1904. No newspaper ever acknowledged its efforts to whitewash the city's disastrous health hazard. The plague receded into the background until 1907.

The Second Plague Scare: Listening to CK This Time

San Francisco suffered its disastrous earthquake and fire in April 1906. In the midst of rebuilding Franklin Hichborn, who covered the legislature for both the *Bee* and the *San Francisco Examiner*, informed CK of another plague case in mid-1907. CK gave Hichborn complete authority to "cover [the story] fully."[49] Hichborn's first article appeared in the *Bee* on September 4, 1907, and "created a riot in San Francisco," where officials once again worried that such publicity would cause panic and hinder the city's rebuilding efforts. Hichborn continued to investigate and found more cases of the horrific disease. This time people may have listened when the *Bee* urged that "a systematic campaign against rats should be made in this city. . . . The fewer the rats, the less possibility of the distribution of the disease."[50] Dr. Rupert Blue, whose efforts focused on exterminating the rats that carried the disease-bearing fleas, fully agreed.

Opposition from the top was virtually nonexistent. Thanks to a graft prosecution in San Francisco, Mayor Eugene Schmitz and his plague-denying regime were gone or in retreat. A new mayor, Edward Taylor, reconstituted the formerly corrupt board of health and began to investigate the issue. The new board backed Blue's rat extermination campaign. Indeed, rather than denying the plague, the new governor, James Gillett, and Taylor discussed the problem openly, and the state appropriated $1,500 from the contagious disease fund to help San Francisco battle the scourge.[51]

The plague killed forty-two San Franciscans by the fall of 1907, and threats of another quarantine loomed. Once again the press lords began to condemn the bearers of bad news: the *Bee* and Hichborn. This time, however, business interests did not shirk their civic responsibility. At a key meeting of civic and commercial groups on January 28, 1908, Hichborn recalled, "They did not pull their punches. In no uncertain terms each insisted that the conditions in San Francisco were most serious; not one of them hesitated to warn that unless the plague were crushed out before the return of warm weather, a serious outbreak threatened San Francisco; and not one of them hesitated at pronunciation of the dread word, quarantine."[52]

With the veil of silence lifted, the same groups that had fought CK so intensely now echoed his cautions and solutions. The *Examiner* once again took a lead in facing up to the problem and calling for health-care measures. CK took pleasure in the newfound openness of his press rivals (and decried the continually obtuse reactions of the *Chronicle*). Praising the *Examiner's* support for honesty, he could not resist giving himself a pat on the back: "The course of events with respect to the plague has not only vindicated the position taken by The *Bee* from the beginning, but also placed it in the lead of the press of California in the prompt recognition of a great danger to the State and in the publication of the fullest information regarding the disease in order that the public might be warned and take the requisite steps to guard against the peril."[53]

Blue's rat abatement program achieved the desired results. Thousands of yards of Portland cement were poured into the city's underground chambers, where rats and fleas could breed. Steadily the plague infection diminished. Some later questioned whether rats were the carriers, others wondered if the whole episode was nothing more than veiled Sinophobia. Perhaps the most credible concern was that other diseases, such as diphtheria, scarlatina, and measles, killed more people than the plague. Nonetheless CK's crusading journalism, and the publisher's intense dislike of his San Francisco press competitors, came together to make things better and advance the cause of public health. Had the Pulitzer Prizes existed at the time, the *Bee* might have been a nominee.

Chapter Ten
The Graft Trials and the Cause of Righteousness

◆────────────────────◆

THE BUBONIC PLAGUE CONTROVERSY was a window into the unsavory world of San Francisco's political culture. The Bay City had always had a freewheeling civic life. It was as resistant to reform crusades—especially the control of urban vices—as Sacramento was, in part because San Francisco's government considered its gambling and prostitution sectors to be an integral part of the city's appeal to visitors. San Francisco was also a working-class community where organized labor played an important role. The tensions between capital and labor, which erupted in the longshoremen's strike of 1901, laid bare the wide divide between the city's capitalists and workers. San Francisco's early twentieth-century political controversies became an important hotbed for urban reform.

Even before the turn of the century there had been a growing sentiment for reform in the Bay City. Mayor James Duval Phelan had helped rewrite the city's charter in the 1890s. Elected mayor in 1898, Phelan ushered in some modest reforms before retiring from office in 1902. His efforts had won the support of at least a portion of the local press. His two most prominent supporters were Fremont Older's *San Francisco Bulletin* and William Randolph Hearst's *Examiner*. CK also kept a keen eye on San Francisco's efforts at reform.[1] When its famous graft trials rocked the Bay City, CK stood on the sidelines, cheering those who attacked the nexus of corruption that existed between city leaders and local industrialists.[2]

Setting the Stage

In the aftermath of the labor unrest of 1901, workers walked away from the Democratic Party and formed the Union-Labor Party. This was done with the help of a wily lawyer named Abraham Ruef, a graduate of the University of

California and Hastings School of Law. Ruef, a successful real estate speculator, entered politics not as candidate himself (being Jewish was a liability), but
through the Union-Labor Party. In 1901 he pushed forward the mayoral candidacy of his longtime friend and client, the affable Eugene Schmitz. The tall
and handsome Schmitz was a theater musician who had composed some memorable melodies and headed up the local Musicians Union. A good-natured,
happily married Catholic of Irish and German descent, Schmitz relied heavily
on Ruef for guidance and won a three-way race in 1901. Schmitz and Ruef
enjoyed a good run for a time, as Schmitz was reelected in 1903 and again in
1905—each time further consolidating and expanding Union-Labor's control
of San Francisco's governance and cementing Ruef's power.

Ruef soon became Schmitz's link to some of the city's most powerful business moguls, including William F. Herrin of the Southern Pacific Railway
and Patrick Calhoun, president of United Railroads, a San Francisco streetcar company. Ruef was known as a fixer—and made it clear that anyone
conducting important business with the city, its police powers, and its public
works had to go through him. Even before the disastrous earthquake and fire
of April 1906, plans were afoot to remake the cable car system by transforming it into an electrical network with overhead power lines. After the earthquake public works were more important than ever, given the devastation
and chaos. United Railroads, headed by Andrew Pickens Calhoun, was eager
to claim a lion's share of the lucrative public transit routes in the rebuilt city
and willingly worked with Ruef. The treasurer of United Railroads, Tirey L.
Ford, a former legislator and attorney general, was one of the intermediaries
between the company and city officials, especially Ruef.

Calhoun had purchased a patchwork of San Francisco's city transit and
sought franchises from the city government to upgrade and unify the system. Calhoun argued for putting in overhead electric lines, which some parts
of the city already had. Others, including the former mayors James Phelan
and Rudolph Spreckels, wanted an underground conduit system. Working
closely with Ruef, and through his two assistants, Ford and William Abbott,
Calhoun delivered more than $200,000 in bribes to Ruef, Schmitz, and the
city supervisors in exchange for the franchise. Calhoun then installed overhead wires down Market Street so public transportation would be running
again. Then in mid-May 1906, the board of supervisors gave permission for
the entire United Railroad system to run on overhead wires and later that

month awarded a twenty-five-year franchise to United Railroads for the entire city.

Even before Calhoun's coup, urban reformers and other contenders for the labor vote had developed suspicions about Schmitz's attachment to Ruef. Already in 1904 the duo had attracted the attention of Fremont Older at the *Bulletin*, who suspected Ruef was the power behind city government and had extorted graft from a variety of sources—in particular the owners of "French restaurants," which many knew to be fronts for houses of prostitution.[3] Older's concerns were ignored for a time, since he had taken free railroad travel from Southern Pacific. Meanwhile the likeable Schmitz enjoyed strong support from Hearst's *Examiner* and other San Francisco papers, as well as among the working class and from their putative leader, Father Yorke. This made Schmitz relatively impervious to Older's attacks.

But after Schmitz's reelection in 1905, Older traveled to Washington, D.C., where he met with President Theodore Roosevelt, who knew of San Francisco's unsavory political reputation. With Roosevelt's blessing Older laid the foundation for an investigation that would rock San Francisco. He recruited the dynamic U.S. attorney and prosecutor Francis J. Heney and his associate, the investigator William J. Burns. Heney, a San Franciscan, had the reputation of being a fearless and scrappy prosecutor and had won kudos for his prosecution of timberland fraud in Oregon. Heney felt a deep loyalty to San Francisco, and while he did not want a salary, he demanded enough money to support a thorough investigation of Ruef. Roosevelt allowed the Justice Department to transfer Heney to San Francisco. The mustachioed Burns, owner of a successful detective agency, was tough and fearless; his methods of "getting his man" would likely raise hackles from civil libertarians today. The sugar millionaire Rudolph Spreckels and former mayor James Phelan stepped up with money to underwrite Burns's probes.[4]

Heney was appointed assistant to District Attorney William A. Langdon in October 1906. Burns and his agents began digging up information about Ruef and Schmitz (Burns even sent his son to tail Schmitz on a trip to Europe). Burns learned that millions of dollars had flowed through Ruef's hands to most of the city supervisors and of course to Schmitz. Ruef himself, meanwhile, had quietly piled up a small fortune and always delivered votes when they were needed. He would insist that these payments were simply fees for legal consultation.

Ruef and State Politics

Ruef, who hoped that Schmitz could become governor of California, had an eye on a seat in the U.S. Senate. His clout in state politics was on display at the Republican state convention in Santa Cruz in September 1906. At the behest of the Southern Pacific political operative William Herrin, Ruef stopped the renomination of the incumbent governor, George Pardee, and replaced him with the prorailroad candidate James Gillett. Gillett, CK lamented, "stands today in his triumph upon the dead bodies of a betrayed people."[5] A famous picture of Gillett, snapped by a photographer for the *San Francisco Bulletin*, shows the nominee surrounded by the figures who procured the nomination for him, including Ruef. Captioned "The Shame of California," the photo was a brazen acknowledgment of boss rule. CK printed the picture in the *Bee*.[6] CK enthusiastically endorsed the candidacy of his friend the Napa County Democrat Theodore Bell. But for CK this was no routine gubernatorial election. "The issue is not between Theodore A. Bell and James N. Gillett. The battle is to determine whether or not one corporation shall dominate in the Executive, Legislative and Judicial departments of the Government of this state or whether the People themselves shall rule."[7] Gillett won the election.

The Beginning of the Graft Trials

The rebuilding of San Francisco after the earthquake, and the huge amount of money flowing into the city, heightened fears of graft and misappropriation of funds. The rebuilding process was slow, police protection against crime was erratic, landlords charged exorbitant prices for humble quarters, and fear and indecision seemed to paralyze city life. In a classic display of tone deafness, Mayor Schmitz decided to take a lengthy vacation to Europe to calm his nerves. Angry citizens met to address the city's lack of progress, and when Ruef appeared, people voiced their disapproval and began to pay attention to the long-disregarded reporting of Fremont Older. When the city supervisors approved the United Railroads franchise for the streetcar system, popular discontent exploded. By late October a grand jury armed with information procured by the investigator Burns and his operatives was ready to indict Ruef and his associates on charges of graft and malfeasance. Ruef brazenly tried to fire District Attorney Langdon and appoint himself to that position. He then hoped to fire Heney and end the investigation. But Langdon refused to accept his dismissal, and chaos erupted in the streets of San Francisco as citizens openly protested Ruef's blatant effort to subvert justice. In the end a court injunction prohibited Ruef from taking over.

CK announced these developments in bold headlines and watched with satisfaction. His experiences battling the plague had brought home the rottenness of the San Francisco city regime, and the high-handed seizure of the Republican nomination at Santa Cruz had outraged him. When he again ran the famous "Shame of California" picture on the *Bee's* front page, CK taunted Governor Gillett, writing: "Your attitude toward Abraham Ruef—reproduced on the first page of The *Bee* today—most accurately represents your feelings toward the man who handed you the votes necessary for your nomination."[8]

On November 15, 1906, Langdon announced that the grand jury had indicted Mayor Eugene Schmitz and Abraham Ruef on five counts of bribery and extortion by French restaurants. In a relatively restrained editorial CK noted this was only "a good beginning." CK wanted a full airing of the complete scope of the official perfidy—especially Ruef's demanding bribes under the guise of "attorney's fees." CK pleaded that the grand jury should have "the courage to follow wherever the trail of graft may lead, even to the doors of the greatest corporations." However, even at this early date CK worried that there would be a lack of nerve. He warned, "Too often Grand Juries are like the man who followed a grizzly bear for days through the mountains but finally left the trail because it was becoming 'too fresh.' They are willing to indict bribe-takers, but not the rich, 'respectable' and influential givers of bribes." In fact the prosecution would stop short of rounding up all the malefactors. CK followed the details of the prosecution avidly. He seethed when Schmitz, arrested on a train at Truckee while returning from Europe in November, received a hero's welcome at a rally organized by Peter Yorke.[9]

Both Ruef and Schmitz used legal maneuvers to delay their trials, but when Burns obtained evidence that one of the supervisors had taken a bribe, Heney pried from the official damning information about the questionable activities of the rest of the supervisors. Heney leveraged the information to offer immunity to eighteen supervisors if they would testify against Ruef. Sixteen accepted the offer, allowing Heney to present sixty-five indictments against Ruef and Schmitz for bribery on four separate occasions. The grand jury heard from the sixteen supervisors how various city businesses had greased their palms: $9,000 from prizefighters, $13,350 from Pacific Gas and Electric, $62,000 from the Home Telephone Company, and a whopping $85,000 from United Railroads— payment for the board's approval of the controversial trolley franchise.

CK wanted to be in on this action and turned to Franklin Hichborn for additional coverage of the graft trials. Hichborn was already in the Bay City working on the second phase of the bubonic plague outbreaks. A native of Eureka, California, and a graduate of Santa Clara College, Hichborn had first been introduced to McClatchy by Judge James Maguire in 1891 and as a free-lance reporter had produced three solid and critical sets of reports on three sessions of the state legislature.[10] CK liked Hichborn's well-written and timely work, and the two shared a moralistic detestation of government corruption and business domination of government, especially by the Southern Pacific. They viewed the press as an agent of public good. Hichborn's reporting appeared regularly in the *Bee* throughout the graft trials.[11] CK's volcanic editorials played off Hichborn's revelations.

The Graft Trials Resume

The graft trials moved along slowly—until a bombshell fell in May 1907. Under intense pressure from Burns (who had interrogated him 150 times), Ruef broke and in exchange for immunity agreed to turn state's evidence against his colleagues and those who had bribed him. Although dismayed that Ruef might be saved "from the punishments he deserves," CK saw Ruef's treachery as an opportunity "to bring to justice the officials of the great corporations who have employed this master grafter and scheming political boss to accomplish their greedy and unscrupulous designs." After all, CK observed, "Ruef has been merely their tool, and they are the men who most deserve punishment." Yet shortly thereafter CK rejected any notion of pity or forgiveness for Ruef, telling readers, "He is not entitled to any sympathy whatsoever. His whine today has in it not one single element of genuine remorse; it is simply the squeal of a trapped rat."[12] Based on Ruef's testimony, Schmitz was convicted of taking bribes from French restaurants.

Giddy with delight that Schmitz and Ruef had been toppled, Heney, Spreckels, Older, and other reformers believed that they now had the bribers in their crosshairs. Patrick Calhoun, William Herrin, and even E. H. Harriman—indeed the entire Southern Pacific political machine, which had so brazenly manipulated the governorship just the year before—would be headed to the penitentiary. CK in particular salivated at the prospect of snaring the oily Herrin. For years the Southern Pacific overlord had dictated local Sacramento politics, thwarted city development, and even threatened to relocate the state capital. In 1907 Herrin's henchman George Hatton had narrowly escaped indictment by a Sacramento grand jury after the *Bee* reported at length accusations that he had attempted to bribe the state legislature to pass the capital removal bill.

However, to the dismay of the reformers, a backlash against the prosecution set in among San Francisco's rich and powerful, some of whom had done business with Ruef. Others (including Older) argued that an aggressive attack on the city's financial elites would disrupt San Francisco's economy, dry up the flow of eastern capital necessary to rebuild the city, and desolate its business climate. The pugnacious Heney also proved a target for the increasingly unfriendly city newspapers. CK watched this turnaround with disbelief and cynicism, warning: "Unless the bribers be made to suffer the consequences of their crimes, corruption will be more strongly intrenched [*sic*] than ever and public sentiment become hopelessly calloused and depraved." He once again denounced San Francisco's "Ostrich Press," "journals which delivered long moral platitudes over the fall of Ruef" but were now silent or even sympathetic to the millionaire bribers. Some San Francisco elites argued that prosecuting these bribers would endanger the city's economic life.[13]

But San Francisco ignored the spouting of the far-off CK. The Bay City wanted to be done with the prosecution, and when a violent public transportation strike erupted, a bitter standoff between labor and management actually awakened sympathies for the masters of capital, especially Calhoun, who had refused to give in to the demands of his striking car men. CK kept up a barrage against the "higher-ups," as Fremont Older termed them, who provided the bribes and thought themselves above the law.[14] CK was heartened in November 1907 when San Franciscans elected the scholarly Edward A. Taylor to serve the remainder of Schmitz's mayoral term and reelected Langdon as district attorney—which meant Heney would remain as special prosecutor. CK praised Taylor as "a good man struggling with adversity," given his ambiguous support among the city's unionists and also big business.[15]

CK watched as Heney went after various malefactors and paid close attention to the trial of Tirey Ford, once a close friend of CK's. Ford was accused of being Calhoun's agent in offering Ruef bribes from United Railroads. However, Heney could make only a weak circumstantial case, and after three trials Ford was acquitted.[16] Although passionate on the subject of convicting higher-ups, CK felt a twinge of sympathy and relief for Ford, who had represented Sierra County in the legislature and had helped punish the hydraulic miners.[17] Indeed CK eventually granted Ford a pardon of sorts—something he rarely did with those he was sure had committed crimes. Besides, Ford was a small fish. CK believed Calhoun had "directed and procured the bribery of the Board of Supervisors in the trolley franchise matter and the 'best people' of the city thoroughly understand the fact."[18]

Indeed by 1908 the prosecution had begun to experience serious setbacks. In early January an appellate court threw out the convictions of Schmitz and left Ruef's future up in the air. CK bitterly attacked the decision, accusing the judges of having "gone out of [their] way to help free Schmitz and thus make him a precedent for freeing the others. . . . It is a decision at which Satan laughs and Hell chortles."[19] In March the California Supreme Court validated the appellate decision and threw out the original indictments of Schmitz and Ruef, drawing a howl of protest from CK. He fired off an open letter to Chief Justice William H. Beatty (a former Sacramentan) demanding to know how the court had arrived at this decision. In late April Beatty responded with a thoughtfully worded letter pointing out flaws in the indictment procedure—and insisting that due process of law required these procedures be properly followed—a serious slap at prosecutors Langdon and Heney and the grand jury. In response Francis Heney revoked Ruef's immunity and tried him for bribery. CK came out strongly in defense of Heney's plans to put Ruef, Schmitz, and Patrick Calhoun behind bars. In a letter to District Attorney Heney several weeks later, CK urged a pushback against the Supreme Court, which had voided the convictions in the Schmitz extortion case.[20]

The remaining graft prosecutions were a dead end for CK. Other cases seemed to slip through Heney's fingers. However, the prosecution against Ruef went forward. On November 13, 1908, one Morris Haas, who had been falsely accused by Heney, returned to the courtroom and shot Heney in the head, nearly killing him. Heney survived the almost point-blank gunshot, and Haas later committed suicide in jail. An appalled CK jumped on the attempted assassination as an opportunity to skewer the enemies of the prosecution: "Who shall not say that back of that man's pistol was not the voice of Peter C. Yorke. . . . Who shall say that when the bullet entered the head of Francis J. Heney, it did not receive some of its propulsive force from certain Jewish rabbis?" CK indicted the *Chronicle, Examiner,* and *Argonaut* (all published in San Francisco) as "kept sisters of harem journalism," and he reserved harsh words for the Calkins syndicate, whose "constant assaults . . . press upon everything decent in public life in San Francisco."[21]

Hiram Johnson replaced Heney, hammering away at Ruef and warning the jurors they needed to convict. Johnson opened up a channel of communication with CK, writing and phoning him, and expressing gratitude for the *Bee's* support. Johnson also occasionally used CK as a sounding board.[22]

After a day and a half of deliberation, Ruef was convicted on December 10, 1908, and received fourteen years in prison for his crimes. "No intelligent and well-informed person in California can have the slightest doubt of the guilt of Ruef in the case just closed," crowed CK. He worried only that, as in the previous convictions, "technical or other exceptions" might overturn the verdict.[23]

The Ruef conviction was the high-water mark of the prosecution; by 1909 San Franciscans had had enough of the graft trials. Nonetheless CK trained his fire on Patrick Calhoun, the United Railroads chief whose trial began in earnest in April 1909. As jury selection was underway, CK noted that many of Calhoun's class brazenly proclaimed that even if he were found to have done wrong, he should not be prosecuted. Contrasting the wealthy businessmen with the "gutter public enemies" like Schmitz and Ruef, of whom "nothing better is expected," CK lacerated the "pompous business, society and club men—these self-elected Atlases who . . . are so vulgarly frank and so disgustingly open in their shame that they repel." When the jury was unable to render a verdict, CK lamented, "Any sane, betting man would have wagered 10 to 1—with probably no takers—that had the jury convicted Calhoun, the higher courts would never have sustained the verdict."[24]

Political winds changed. William Langdon did not want to run for another term as district attorney, and the irrepressible Heney lost his bid for district attorney to Charles Fickert, a former football star and well-known legal advocate for corporations. Mayor Taylor also agreed to step down, replaced by Patrick Henry "Pin Head" McCarthy, a Union-Labor candidate. CK commented sourly on the election of Fickert and "Pin Head": "With McCarthy mayor and Fickert District Attorney, bribery and graft may be expected to hold high carnival in San Francisco."[25] Under Fickert the prosecution of Calhoun ended with a whimper in 1911.

CK and the Churches: Working Out the Frustrations

Frustrated by the collapse of the prosecution and the seeming triumph of everyone (except Ruef) associated with San Francisco's shame, CK embarked on a crusade against local religious leaders whom he believed had been opponents of the prosecution. This led to some of CK's worst journalistic excesses.

Religious institutions were indeed caught up in the vortex of the city's struggle.[26] Because a Catholic, Schmitz, and a Jew, Ruef, were involved, adherents of both religions had opinions about who should have been prosecuted, and their positions were usually, but not always, partisan. Jewish support for Abe Ruef came from two San Francisco rabbis, Jacob Nieto of Temple Emmanuel, the largest synagogue in San Francisco, and Bernard Kaplan of the Bush Street Temple who had helped broker Ruef's immunity offer. In late 1906 McClatchy had taken exception to a statement by Jacob Voorsanger, the well-known rabbi of Temple Emmanuel who had released some flattering comments about Schmitz's home life and noted that Ruef was a graduate of the University of California—an institution where Voorsanger himself lectured in Semitic languages. CK dismissed the rabbi's praise as irrelevant and accused the venerable Voorsanger of "not doing his honest duty as a man of God" by not saying anything negative about either man.[27] Protestants generally hailed the first phase of the prosecutions but reacted adversely as the cases turned against corporate leaders—the "higher-ups"—some of whom were quite prominent and generous members of their congregations.

In 1907, after a long *Bee* litany excoriating everyone and anyone who wanted to stop the prosecutions, CK blasted the churches. "You remember how the pulpits rang with praise of Heney and Spreckels and denunciation of public crime when Ruef and Schmitz were cornered?" He nudged his readers, "Have you heard from any of the Churches any word of commendation of this prosecution now that it has bagged the biggest pillars of some of these Churches? Have you?"[28] His attack included San Francisco's largest religious group, Roman Catholics, many of whom were supporters of the Union-Labor Party and partisans of Schmitz. Although they were divided in their feelings, most— not all—Catholic leaders trod carefully on the subject of the prosecution.

More Bitterness Toward Yorke

CK's first target was his archfoe, Peter Yorke. From the start the priest had suspected the graft prosecution was a way of getting at labor—revenge for the strike by teamsters and longshoremen in 1901. CK noted with disdain that when Mayor Schmitz arrived home from Europe in 1906, Yorke had staged a huge welcome rally and promised him support. The priest defended those under indictment and heaped opprobrium on the prosecutor, Francis Heney, and his benefactor, Rudolph Spreckels. CK opened fire on Yorke, especially as the graft battles heated up. In August 1908 Yorke wrote a smirking article ridiculing "the young and beautiful patriot Rudolph Spreckels," the financier of the investigation, insisting and repeating often: "The graft prosecution was a political move we have always believed and have always said." The result was political impasse in San Francisco: two parties, one beholden to the Southern Pacific and the other to Rudolph Spreckels. Yorke meanwhile rejoiced in prosecution setbacks and made it clear that the graft prosecution was really an attack on working people dressed up as civic virtue.[29]

But the Catholic Church in general came under assault from McClatchy. After the attempted assassination of Heney in November 1908, the Catholic *San Francisco Monitor* expressed gratitude that Heney was on the road to recovery. However, Archbishop Patrick Riordan, speaking through his representative, Monsignor Charles Ramm, resisted pressure to approve of the graft prosecution. "Here is her [the Church's] answer to those who have found fault with her for not having 'Come out for the prosecution,'" Ramm wrote. "She does not conceive it her duty to do so. She teaches the principles of morality, she does not feel called upon to support parties." McClatchy railed against the "milk and water" statement. When the antigraft organs—the *Examiner* and the *Oakland Tribune*—ran Ramm's statement, CK understood it as a cowardly defense of "that notorious and shameless disgrace to the Catholic Church or any other religion—Peter C. Yorke."[30] McClatchy even implied that Yorke's continual criticisms of the prosecution had led to Heney's near death.

Yorke replied with his usual overblown accusations and false claims:

> There is no record in the annals of human depravity of a person so universally despised and so universally detested in his own town as Charlie McClatchy. His paper has done more to hurt the Capital City than the ten plagues of Egypt could and it can be shown to a demonstration that Sacramento has prospered in spite of the *Bee*. The McClatchys have been false to everyone who ever befriended them. They have betrayed every cause they undertook to champion, and today Charlie McClatchy is recognized throughout California as the indelible shame and abiding disgrace of the journalistic profession of the State.[31]

Copies of the *Leader*, a weekly carrying this screed, were sold on the steps of San Francisco churches, and Yorke made sure that his paper was distributed in Sacramento—on the steps of both the cathedral and St. Francis of Assisi Church. CK was apoplectic.

Once Yorke had taken the battle to CK's hometown, McClatchy hit back and dumped the contents of a grudge file he had compiled over the years into an article called "The Plain Truth About Peter C. Yorke" that ran in the *Bee* on December 10, 1908. The contents of this file, which CK later published as a pamphlet, had come from private investigators whom CK had unleashed on Yorke (as he would do with other people he regarded as enemies), seeking information to discredit the priest—and his causes. The investigators were unable to come up with the kind of accusation CK would have relished, namely evidence of sexual impropriety. To CK's consternation Yorke lived his celibate commitment without stain. Upon learning this, CK then loosed his gumshoes against Yorke's brother, F. M. Yorke, a building contractor, and learned he had been convicted of attempted rape in British Columbia. CK also revisited his still-smoldering ire over Yorke's last-minute support of gubernatorial candidate Gage over Maguire in 1898; CK denounced Yorke for stirring up the strikers in San Francisco in 1901 and for spreading his radical union ideas in a famous Sacramento "labor talk." CK even suggested that Yorke used the proceeds from charity events for his own political agenda. Revving up his colorful invective, CK fired off: "He [Yorke] has ever been the friend and champion of the Fagins, the Bill Sykeses and the Black Barts of municipal thievery. . . . A blackguard of the cloth, a boodling Bedouin of the priesthood, a pirate in the pulpit, he stands today the degradation and the shame of the Catholic Church in California, a travesty upon manhood, a slur upon common honesty, a scandalous blasphemy against Christ whose religion he uses to exalt the public boodler and to provide a sanctuary for the public thief."[32]

Yorke retaliated, releasing similarly disconcerting revelations about McClatchy in the *Leader.* Yorke did not need investigators, as he found many people willing to tag CK's personal weaknesses, making strong (and true) statements about McClatchy's public drunkenness and even alleging—less credibly—that he indulged in gambling activities. Yorke recruited the former *Sacramento Union* editor Edward Insley to repeat well-known accusations that the McClatchys were susceptible to bribes to change their principled editorial opinions. Insley noted that the Natomas Dredging Company had silenced the *Bee* on the issue of dredge mining by purchasing 261 acres of swampland worth at best $10 an acre for an undisclosed price. Likewise, he pointed to the use of X Street as a railroad corridor rather than the more central H Street, where, Insley claimed, CK owned two blocks. Insley also noted Valentine's ultimately futile efforts to market his Rancho del Rio holdings for the new city park.[33] Even the good cheer of Christmastide did not dim the battle. On Christmas Day 1908 the *Leader* ran a cartoon depicting a beaten dog retiring to a dog house called the *Bee*. These were the papers Yorke dispatched to Sacramento churches, where they were sold and even handed out to morning worshippers.

It may have been the church-going Ella who brought the *Leader* to her husband's notice when he picked her up after Sunday Mass. Far from calling a truce to the mean-spirited exchange, this only escalated it. To his friend James Barry, CK ranted:

> He has used in covering me, nothing but filthy language; I have proved him to be a contemptible scoundrel, blackguard and boodler and I propose to continue to prove him. But what I have said of and concerning him and which he dared not deny, has only been read in this section of the state. A few here and there of course, have read it in San Francisco and some have sent for extra copies. But the great mass of people to whom this fellow Yorke appeals and has appealed from the steps of the churches are utterly ignorant of what can be said on the other side. And so I intend to reach them with a printed copy of my 'Few Remarks.'[34]

CK then asked Barry, who printed the *Monitor* for the Archdiocese of San Francisco, to contact Rev. Denis O. Crowley, who "thinks a great deal of me," to show him how the *Monitor's* subscription list might be obtained. Barry wrote back just before Christmas and encouraged CK's attack: "Why should you lie supinely on your back and permit this blackguard of blackguards, Peter C. Yorke, to traduce you as he has done" However, Barry told CK, "I know I cannot use the Monitor [subscription] list as such, but if you will send me 5000 copies of [your] pamphlets [on Yorke] I will see that they are circulated where they will do the most good." True to his word, the feisty Barry had the pamphlets distributed at his own expense. So enthusiastic was Barry to pass them around that he planned to give them out to members of Irish Societies on St. Patrick's Day 1909. Fearing this might precipitate a row, CK urged Barry to be cautious: "I leave the whole matter to your own judgment Jim, but I honestly think you won't get the pamphlet read that way and that little by little you can get rid of it easily in other more quiet ways which will produce a great deal more good."[35]

In the end the effort was a costly dud as McClatchy convinced few. In fact he galvanized others to the priest's defense, including the Reverend William F. Ellis of Eureka (who would soon move to Sacramento to open a new parish in Oak Park). The pamphlet also elicited formal condemnations from the Oakland Council No. 784 of the Knights of Columbus and the state officers of the Yorke-controlled Ancient Order of Hibernians.[36]

In fact Yorke proved to be a formidable foe—unafraid to fight fire with fire and capable of the same level of abuse and invective as the Sacramento editor. Imitating his enemy, Yorke also engaged a private detective, R. S. Lake, in 1911. Lake pretended to be a bitter foe of Yorke, who sent him to interview his enemies in San Francisco and Sacramento. Lake had the temerity to approach all of CK's friends and even his aging mother, Charlotte. Lake then submitted what he had found to Joseph T. Harrington, manager of Yorke's paper, the *Leader*, and Harrington produced an eighty-page pamphlet that he sent to priests in California and Rome. Harrington insisted that the pamphlet was supposed to refute Barry's boasts "in the saloons which he frequented" that CK's pamphlet "had the sanction and encouragement of men holding the highest ecclesiastical office." CK managed to obtain a partial copy from a source who had worked his way into the good graces of Lake. A few days later CK had the full account compiled by the wily and brazen Lake. CK sent it to several sympathetic friends and wrote to James Barry: "I send you today a full and complete accurate copy of the report of that scoundrel R. S. Lake hired by that other scoundrel Father Peter C. Yorke. . . . The whole thing is such a mass of lies from the beginning to the end."[37] CK then dashed off a letter to Archbishop Patrick Riordan of San Francisco protesting the lies in the pamphlet and Lake's audacious approaches to CK, his mother, and Rev. Robert Kenna of Santa Clara. In retaliation CK produced yet another pamphlet that exposed Lake. The controversy between the two men faded after Archbishop Riordan died in 1914 and the more irenic and liberal-minded Edward Hanna succeeded him. Yorke was assigned to the pastorate of St. Peter's Church in San Francisco and continued to attract a loyal following among his fellow Irish Catholics and among Catholic educators. When he died in April 1925, the *Bee* buried his obituary deep in the paper.[38]

Time never seemed to dull CK's hatreds. In the case of Yorke CK had a mirror image of himself: principled, passionate, articulate, and with barrels of printer's ink.

Other Ecclesiastical Villains

But Yorke was not the only religious figure involved in the prosecution imbroglio. Others also seemed amenable to curtailing the prosecution. Unlike Yorke, however, few were powerful enough or commanded enough print to counter the *Bee's* attacks. So McClatchy began to bully and harass them relentlessly. He had help from one cleric, the Paulist Michael Otis. Otis had requested ten copies of McClatchy's pamphlet on Yorke, declaring, "The prosecution has had my support from the start and I only regret that I can't help it more." The Paulist priests of San Francisco, of which Otis was a member, ran Old St. Mary's Church in San Francisco and also the Catholic ministry for students at the University of California. At some point Hiram Johnson passed on a rumor that a dispute had arisen among the Paulists in San Francisco about the graft prosecution.[39] The internal dispute may have been ignored, except that one of the figures involved, Henry Wyman, had been elected the first Roman Catholic chaplain of the California State Senate in early 1909.[40] In addition, Henry I. Stark, a Bay Area native, had been at Old St. Mary's for years and was indirectly involved with jury tampering in the Ruef trial.[41]

Wyman had been at Old St. Mary's since 1895 and was well known and loved throughout the city. The senate welcomed him warmly, and during his time of residency he enjoyed cordial relations with the local clergy, including McClatchy's close friend Monsignor Thomas J. Capel. Wyman even socialized with CK himself—although the editor was against the whole idea of chaplains to the senate.[42] In trying to rebuild Old St. Mary's Church after the 1906 earthquake and fire, however, Wyman had received the promise of a new pulpit from the attorney Frank Murphy two days after his acquittal in December 1908. Murphy had been accused of jury tampering in the Ruef trial, and two Paulists, Wyman and Henry Stark, had been supportive of Murphy and his family during the stress of the trial. The pulpit arrived in ample time for the June 1909 rededication of the refurbished church. Wyman did as he had done with other gifts and affixed a donor's plate on it that bore Murphy's name.

Wyman and Stark's support for Murphy during his trials and the acceptance of the nameplate offended two of their Paulist confreres, Michael Otis and a young university chaplain from Berkeley, Thomas Verner Moore. In what Moore years later described as a prank, the two men ripped the Murphy nameplate off the pulpit and threw it into the bay. Its disappearance was noted and promptly reported to the police. An innocuous report about the incident appeared in the *San Francisco Globe*, an anti-antiprosecution paper that passed it off as an act of vandalism or petty thievery rather than evidence of a serious disagreement within the church community about the prosecution. The putative affinity of Stark and Wyman for the disreputable Murphy no doubt perked up CK's ears. Allowing his penchant for melodramatic conspiracy to run free, CK believed some connection existed between the gift of the pulpit and the softness of the church toward the prosecution. CK was also convinced that the support of Murphy resulted in Wyman's election to the chaplain's position. CK summoned Franklin Hichborn and directed the reporter to get to the bottom of the story.

Hichborn accepted the task with relish and secretly contacted Otis in early July 1909 seeking to uncover evidence of the Paulist perfidy. However, all he uncovered was an internal spat among the local Paulist community, and the graft prosecution was incidental to the rift. The Paulists differed on a number of issues. Regarding the prosecution, some, like Stark, followed the lead of Yorke and thoroughly disapproved of the whole affair. Others, like Otis, took a strong position on the other side. Wyman apparently had no strong feelings about the issue but did have compassion for his parishioner Murphy, who was caught up in the mess. If Wyman had any objection to the prosecution, it was one shared by many San Franciscans, to the methods used by Burns and Heney. Wyman was a compassionate man. "The older I grow and the longer I meditate on the divine law," he wrote to McClatchy, "the more lenient I become in regard to men's motives. . . . I am ready to do favors for saints and sinners alike and am equally pleased if they make offerings to St. Mary's Church." He pointed out that both sides of the controversy donated to the church: "Hon. James D. Phelan is one of our greatest benefactors [including the donation of a window] and Frank J. Murphy has donated a pulpit for both of which we are most grateful and always shall be."[43] None of this washed with CK.

To the editor's great unhappiness, when the moment of truth arrived, Hichborn reversed his earlier observations and told his boss, "I am convinced that the majority of both Catholic and Episcopal clergy favor the graft prosecutions." In the end Hichborn's case against the Paulists—and the Catholic Church in San Francisco—rested on unsubstantiated community gossip. CK would have none of this. Sweeping aside Hichborn's counsel, he arrogantly informed his investigator: "You say it will cause a storm. Well, let it. Storms are good things in the world in general. They are excellent for clearing the moral atmosphere; besides, I like a storm."[44] The Page One article and accompanying editorial detailed the activities of Stark and Wyman, spinning the pastoral work of the priests in the most unfavorable light. Wyman's election to the chaplaincy of the state senate was, in CK's mind, a payoff for services rendered to antiprosecution forces. The gentle Wyman, saddened by the article, wrote a short letter to McClatchy: "I can only say that my life is an open book to the Superior General and members of my order and has been for the last fifteen years. . . . Tomorrow morning I shall offer Mass for you, the writer of the article and all those who helped him make it up. May God in His great mercy, forgive you." McClatchy erupted in anger.[45]

Repercussions in the aftermath of the article were quick in coming. Archbishop Riordan used it as an excuse to slap the Paulists with whom he had other difficulties. He supposedly summoned Wyman and informed him that he had handled the affairs of the Paulists poorly. Hichborn told CK, "I am told that when he [Wyman] issued from the conference, his face was like that of a dead man." Riordan demanded the removal of Stark from St. Mary's. Wyman took this hard and urged Stark to take it in stride.[46]

But if the intent had been to injure Wyman and Stark, the effort failed. Wyman came out virtually unscathed and was reelected senate chaplain during the next session. Stark's exile from his native San Francisco was short, and he too had the exquisite delight of being elected chaplain to the senate in 1914; and in 1925 he was named pastor of the American Church of Santa Susanna in Rome, a popular American tourist site. In June 1940 Stark was elected superior general of the Paulist Community. The only support CK received was from the garrulous Father Otis, who somehow believed his petty internal grievances were part of some larger plot. He requested two hundred copies of the paper and wrote to CK: "I wish to congratulate you for your fearlessness in standing up for principle. . . . I think you ought to publish the article in pamphlet form. If you do this I'll donate $20 to help pay for it."[47] Like his holy war against Yorke, this latest assault on the character of clergy did CK no good. His efforts to be a paladin for righteousness in San Francisco once again fell flat and came off as bullying.

The Aftermath

CK also tried to indict the Jewish community for unwarranted sympathy for Ruef. These attacks met with indifference. CK could find no tiny bit of sympathy in his heart for Ruef and adamantly opposed any leniency for the once powerful "Curly Boss." When even his boon friend James Barry supported efforts to win parole for Ruef, CK wrote a terse note expressing his displeasure. Even more infuriating was Fremont Older of the *San Francisco Bulletin,* who had actually kicked off the graft prosecution: he reversed course and called for leniency for Ruef twelve months after his conviction.[48]

Ruef served eight years and ten months in San Quentin before being paroled in August 1915. CK wrote an uncharacteristically gentle editorial about Ruef's parole, assuring readers that his release met the criteria of the state. CK once again lamented that the "prime movers" of the corruption never spent a day in jail. "It is hoped," he wrote of Ruef, "that this man of great ability, insight and mental energy—a man of genius in his way—may profit by his painful experience and henceforth devote his talents to honorable and useful ends."[49] After his release Ruef worked until his death on an array of projects, including the creation of San Francisco's now iconic Fisherman's Wharf. Ruef died at the end of February 1936—less than one month before CK died.

Chapter Eleven
The Progressive McClatchy

◆

THE SAN FRANCISCO GRAFT TRIALS provided a catalyst for social and political reform in California in the early 1900s. During these Progressive years CK flourished as never before—and hit full stride in his journalism career. The accomplishments of the California state government, and especially of Governor Hiram Johnson, seemed to be the culmination and vindication of the public policy positions CK had advanced for nearly a generation. The forces of Progressive reform in California had no greater cheerleader than CK and the *Sacramento Bee*.

California progressivism, like the larger national movement, was diverse.[1] Its spectrum of personalities included politicians, philanthropists, and journalists—all of whom labored to remake California government and society. Some proponents embraced new democratic impulses: referendum, recall, direct primaries, women's suffrage, and direct election of U.S. senators. Others emphasized greater efficiency, scientific methodology, and regulatory bureaucracies to rein in inhumane or monopolistic features of social and economic life. CK embraced all the agendas and editorialized incessantly about them while supporting politicians who advanced them. In a state as large and geographically and socially diverse as California, region provided another prism for understanding Progressive reform. Southern and Northern California Progressives differed on issues such as prohibition, the suppression of social vice, and the vote for women. However, all embraced social safety net legislation. And nothing unified California Progressives like their belief that the power of the Southern Pacific over state government had to be broken.

CK shared a Progressive belief in the power of government action for the common good. When he urged the City of Sacramento to assume ownership of a municipal theater in 1887, he wrote: "The care which a government [has] for its people should be fostered not cramped. Its aim should be to see how much it can do, not how little." CK also shared the Progressive concern for the troubling economic inequalities of modern America. At least theoretically he believed government ought to help the poor and downtrodden and equalize the skewed distribution of wealth under the existing capitalist system: "One of the duties of . . . government will be to see that the necessities of life no longer are permitted to be monopolized by millionaire gamblers; that corn and wheat and meat and fish and vegetables and ice and fuel, which all mankind must have shall not be in desperate times at almost prohibitory prices over the poor—held by men whose hearts are as a glacier as they pile wealth upon wealth while others starve." During World War I, he applauded government control of food and railroads, as well as its coordination of industrial production. He regularly heaped obloquy on "malefactors of great wealth." When J. P. "Jupiter" Morgan died in 1913, CK discarded the maxim "Speak no ill of the dead" and wrote a sarcastic editorial: "No Loss to Humanity in This Man's Death." He wrote, "Now that he is pulse less, can it be said that the world lost anything it could not well afford to lose when it lost him? . . . Mankind has no reason to mourn."[2] Although by no means a socialist, McClatchy understood the limits of capitalism and embraced progressivism's distrust of concentrated wealth (even though his newspaper business was a virtual monopoly). He remained a firm believer in nationalizing certain kinds of property (such as utilities and communications industries) for the common good.

McClatchy approved of government action to curtail monopolies, attack crime and corruption in high places, make urban politics more honest and efficient, and advance the democratic participation of citizens through the direct election of U.S. senators. He also wanted to abolish the Electoral College. He hated Prohibition as an affront to personal liberty, and he found ways of circumventing it. At the same time he could be heedless of the civil liberties of those who dissented from government policies. He barely concealed his contempt for unions, was prejudiced against Asians and other people of color, and inveighed against people accused of disloyalty, although some were falsely accused. He occasionally cast doubt on the integrity and patriotism of those who differed with him. Although he supported women's suffrage in theory, he raged privately against the influence of women in public life. Sometimes he was an outright misogynist. He treasured learning and was a cultured and sophisticated man but clung to outmoded historical thinking and entertained no challenges to his schoolboy depictions of the past. This medley was not unlike the contradictory mix of ideas resting in the bosom of the so-called typical Progressive.

Sacramento's Progressive Dawn

In the state capital the 1901 election of Mayor George Clark stirred reforming energies to life. Even though CK disliked and mistrusted Clark, his administration did do battle with the city's poolrooms—and especially the grafters who paid city officials to look the other way at their illegal activities. Political tides in the city had shifted decisively by 1907 when the railroad-dominated city administration approved Western Pacific Railway's plan to build a freight and passenger depot within city limits. That same year the city faced yet another effort to move the state capital. This cynical ploy was proffered to the legislature by solons who disingenuously wanted to move the legislature to Berkeley so that—in the style of Robert La Follette of Wisconsin—it could draw on university professors for legislative ideas. Among the journalistic voices raised in favor of the move was that of Alfred Holman, whom CK mockingly referred to as "Weary Willie." Holman had at one time been the general editor of the *Sacramento Union* and had clashed often with the McClatchys about local issues. Holman later moved to San Francisco, where he edited the sassy *Argonaut.* His argument in favor of moving the capital attacked the *Bee,* which he described as "imbued with the narrowest spirit, confirmed in an obsolete provincial habit, fixed in the character of the rustic smart-aleck, devoid of integrity and decency." He was sympathetic to legislators who "suffered under the jabs of this journalistic mosquito."[3] CK replied sarcastically to Holman, whom he tagged a railroad lackey.

Although Governor Gillett signed the bill that called for moving the capital, voters roundly defeated it in November 1908—largely with the help of CK and the *Bee,* who mobilized scores of voters who considered the scheme costly and dangerous. This second capital removal crisis, however, issued in another burst of civic energy in Sacramento—supported and endorsed by the *Bee* and for which CK again took credit. City residents approved a bond measure to construct a new city hall in March 1907. Designed by the local architect Rudolph Herold (who would also design CK's home), the structure rose majestically along I Street. CK pointed out the need for new hotels, an improved water supply, additional parks and playgrounds, and a new sewerage system, declaring, "Sacramento should rear her head proudly among the cities of the coast; she should shake off the garments of the '49 era. It should assert itself as a Class A city, with a Class A people doing business in Class A buildings and living in Class A homes." Through gritted teeth CK even praised the "hysterical shriekers" (as he called them in private) of the city's Women's Christian Temperance Movement who promised to "purify the moral atmosphere" of Sacramento by closing some of the saloons "that derive great revenue from some of these legislators."[4]

CK's divorce from the railroad was now complete. He exposed the nefarious activity of Southern Pacific and its political agents Jere Burke, Walter Parker, and George F. Hatton, who were pressing friendly legislators to pass the capital removal bill in retaliation for Sacramento's support in the 1906 gubernatorial election for Theodore Bell rather than the railroad-anointed candidate, James Gillett. Finally, public pressure built to investigate how the railroad was manipulating state and local politics. Railroad operative George Hatton was hauled before the Sacramento grand jury investigating criminal lobbying. CK pressed hard for his indictment, but when the grand jury found no evidence, CK denounced its dereliction of duty.[5]

The long-festering issue of gambling drew attention again when *Bee* reporters found the clandestine activities of thriving gambling establishments, including one run by Angus Ross in a building at Sixth and K owned by the city trustee Edward J. Carragher and his partner, George A. Buckman. Other gambling dens included one owned by Ed Kripp on Sixth and J, and a "resort" atop the Bank Exchange Building at Second and K, as well as numerous gaming parlors in Sacramento's Chinatown. A prostitution racket was also uncovered involving two former policemen-turned-saloon-keepers, Jack Duhain and George Radonich, who were accused of extorting payment from women selling sexual services. When one of the principals in the case produced a cache of more than a hundred letters written by former officer Radonich regarding the funds, CK printed them.[6]

The onus for this perceived dereliction of duty fell on Sacramento mayor Marshall Beard, a close personal friend of CK's. Friendship notwithstanding, CK denounced Beard as a boss in the thrall of the Southern Pacific.[7] In reality Beard was a supporter of city reform, but this did not seem to matter to CK. At the 1907 city Republican convention, the *Bee* supported delegates of the Sacramento branch of the Lincoln-Roosevelt League, a breakaway group of Progressive Republicans who proposed a reform ticket. "Sacramento has reached a stage where prosperity is knocking loudly at her doors," CK declared, urging voters to free the capital from those "now engaged in throttling the progress and growth of the city." Progressive forces banded together to nominate Clinton White, a lawyer, to run on the Republican ticket against Beard in October 1907. CK praised White as a tower of strength and predicted that as mayor he would strictly enforce laws on public vice, drinking, and other aspects of public morality.[8]

As a candidate White indeed brought stellar credentials. He was a prominent local attorney who had also been one of the freeholders who had rewritten the city charter in 1892. Over the years he had been active in other city reform efforts. He promised to create a new spirit in city government, and the *Bee* praised him as though he were the Messiah.[9] His support for the Western Pacific Railway also buoyed White's candidacy. For years the Western Pacific had been purchasing property and making plans to establish a rail yard in Sacramento—aided in part by Valentine McClatchy, who personally solicited from Sacramento citizens a portion of the $90,000 needed to pay for property for the new railroad. Under the lash of the Southern Pacific, Beard and city trustees denied the Western Pacific the rights-of-way it needed, as well as the cost-saving benefits of a station to serve both lines. Western Pacific's proponents forced a special election to decide the issue in October 1907. When the plebiscite produced a resounding victory for the Western Pacific, CK made sure that White benefited from the passions stirred by the issue. CK characterized White as the living embodiment of a new Sacramento.[10] Yet, despite CK's enthusiastic support, White only squeaked by "Boss" Beard with a margin of a mere 115 votes. The tight election notwithstanding, a golden era seemed to have arrived with the new mayor.

But the new mayor did not entirely meet the McClatchys' expectations. White offended the *Bee* early on by offering some city advertising to the rival *Sacramento Star*. City trustees had approved the *Star* contract—even though the *Bee*'s bid was lower.[11] The new mayor also occasionally gave scoops to the *Bee*'s rivals and was not politically skilled enough to advance the Progressive agenda he had advocated in the 1907 campaign. When White abruptly announced in 1911 that he would not stand for reelection, CK was surprised but not totally unhappy. The Republicans nominated Frank Sutliff to replace White, and CK chose to support Sutliff over Marshall Beard, who ran again. By this time, however, the electorate had approved a new city charter, reconfiguring Sacramento's city government into the popular commission system. The new charter eliminated city wards, which seemed prone to manipulation by outside forces, and created a commission of five members elected at large. These members would have control of vital city functions (unlike the patronage appointments of the previous regimes); the commissioners could appoint officials to subordinate positions and could remove them as well. The commission could also grant franchises—a hotly contested area of city governance under the old charter, which had made city officials susceptible to bribery. The new charter also provided for the recall of city officials.

CK strongly endorsed the new charter with its provision for stripping power from the mayor.[12] Urban issues would never be far from CK's concerns, but from 1910 on, his attentions and energies turned to state, national, and international issues. As he entered his fifties, CK began to enjoy greater challenges and satisfactions in both personal and political realms.

Stirrings of Progressive Reform in California

Progressive currents greatly affected California state politics. The first casualty was Governor Henry T. Gage, who served only one term in Sacramento. The gubernatorial campaign of 1902 pitted two relatively progressive politicians, Franklin Lane, a Democrat, against the physician George Pardee, a Republican. Pardee had been Oakland's mayor in 1893. Like CK, he took a firm stand against Southern Pacific railroad strikers in 1894, and in 1898 he became an active candidate for governor but was passed over by party bosses for Gage.

Distrustful—but not disdainful—of Pardee, who appeared to have links to the Southern Pacific, CK threw his support to Franklin Lane.[13] In a tight election Pardee emerged victorious—by only 2,539 votes—and those only after 5,000 votes were disallowed in Los Angeles and Oakland. Prefiguring the presidential election of 2000, the Supreme Court of California designated Pardee the winner.

Although Pardee was tainted by Southern Pacific's support, CK held back from attacking him with his customary vigor. Pardee endeared himself to CK by addressing the plague crisis in San Francisco and managing its resolution.[14] In 1903 Pardee was also the first governor to move into the stately Victorian mansion on Sixteenth and H streets that served as the governor's official residence until 1967. But as governor Pardee soon lost favor with the Southern Pacific, when he removed the railroad's control of the Port of Oakland. He further compounded his heresy by encouraging the Western Pacific Railway to come into Sacramento. In retaliation the railroad barons unceremoniously dumped Pardee in 1906. In his place they selected the pliable James Gillett, a member of Congress from Humboldt County, as their gubernatorial candidate. At the conclusion of the Santa Cruz convention, a *San Francisco Call* photographer snapped a shot of candidate Gillett surrounded by the politicians and political operatives who had strong-armed the nomination for him. As noted earlier, the photo epitomized the cozy corruption afoot in California politics. The group included the San Francisco boss Abe Ruef, who was the focus of extensive investigation into bribery deals in San Francisco. The *Call* captioned it "The Shame of California." These political shenanigans triggered a reformist uprising in the state.

CK threw his support to Theodore Bell, a native of Napa. Bell had defeated an incumbent Republican, Samuel D. Woods, for a seat in Congress in 1902.[15] Bell had been a schoolteacher before being admitted to the California bar at the age of twenty-one and later was elected district attorney for Napa County. He also became counsel for the California Grape Growers Protective League and strongly opposed Prohibition. Bell and McClatchy became close personally and even shared rooms at party conventions.

In 1904, however, Duncan McKinlay, a Republican who rode the vigorous coattails of a victorious Teddy Roosevelt, defeated Bell in his bid for re-election to Congress[16] In 1906 California Democrats nominated Bell to run against Gillett. Despite Bell's strong Progressive views and verbal assaults on the Southern Pacific, as well as CK's vigorous support, Bell lost that election as well. Revolted by Republican machine politics, several previously unaligned reform groups and journalists came together in 1906 to take back the state from Southern Pacific dominance. John Randolph Haynes, a wealthy physician from Los Angeles—a Christian Socialist and a Fabian—led the group.

In Los Angeles, Haynes had drafted a new city charter in 1903 and assembled the Non Partisan Committee of One Hundred in 1906; it included such prominent figures as Edward A. Dickson, a correspondent for the *Los Angeles Express*, and the attorneys Meyer Lissner, Russell Avery, and Marshall Stimson. This small but focused group intended to change the politics of Los Angeles. They persuaded Lee C. Gates, a vice president of the Title Insurance and Trust Company, to become their nominee for mayor, along with twenty-two hand-picked Non Partisan candidates for municipal offices. Gates lost the mayoral election, but seventeen of the twenty-two Non Partisan candidates won. It was encouragement to press on.

At a dinner given by Haynes for those who worked on the Non Partisan campaign, the muckraker Lincoln Steffens urged the audience to finally overthrow bossism and political corruption in California. Journalists in California were inspired to take the lead in pressing for state reform. California newspapers like the *Stockton Record, Sacramento Union, San Francisco Examiner, San Francisco Bulletin,* and *Los Angeles Express* called for statewide political reform. CK's strong endorsement of Franklin Lane in 1902 and of Theodore Bell in 1906 earned him a niche in the emerging reform coalition. Sometime after the dinner at Haynes's home, Edward Dickson met with another reform-minded journalist, Chester H. Rowell of the *Fresno Republican* in Sacramento, where both were covering the legislative session of 1907. Appalled by the buying and selling of votes they witnessed, both reporters made common cause for reform. In a move that warmed CK's heart Rowell's article condemning the legislative session began with these words: "The Sacramento *Bee*'s famous caption 'Thank God: The Legislature Has Adjourned!' will be repeated in many newspapers and echoed in thousands of hearts this morning."[17]

Rowell and Dickson formed a statewide organization known as the Lincoln-Roosevelt League at Levy's Café in Los Angeles on May 21, 1907. About fifteen people adopted "Lincoln-Republicans" as their provisional political affiliation. CK had been invited, but with his customary aversion to groups, he did not accept. Yet he did pay attention as the league demanded the elimination of railroad dominance of state politics and pushed for reforms long advocated by McClatchy.[18] The league identified candidates for the legislature and enlisted the backing of more than thirty California newspapers—including the *Sacramento Bee*. In 1908 Rowell returned to Sacramento and gave a rousing speech at the Clunie Theater, urging Sacramentans to embrace the agenda of the Lincoln-Roosevelt League and reminding them that "the League was born right here in Sacramento."[19]

CK was always skeptical of the league; he was suspicious of anything that came from Southern California and also disliked and distrusted some of his fellow journalists, especially Hearst.[20] CK's rogue's gallery came to include Edward Dickson, whom the editor later considered a traitor to the Progressive cause. CK also developed a special loathing for Chester Rowell.

Chester the Chameleon

Chester Rowell, a native of Bloomington, Illinois, was the son of a lawyer who served four terms as a Republican member of the House of Representatives.[21] The son was well educated, having studied at the University of Michigan and at the University of Halle in Germany. A gifted linguist and speaker, he had been inspired by his father to embrace a life of public service. Rowell's study of philosophy and his belief in evolutionary development provided the underpinnings of his ideology of positive change. He had served for a time as clerk in Congress but hoped for a career in academe. However, financial distress and new opportunity brought him to California in 1898. He settled in Fresno, where his uncle Chester (for whom he was named) was a prominent physician, a regent of the University of California, and the owner of the *Fresno Republican*.

Fresno had been founded only in 1872 as a Central Pacific Railroad town. Irrigation transformed the surrounding lands into a rich agricultural heartland—producing valuable grain crops, alfalfa, and fruit. The community grew much the same way as Sacramento, with steady expansion of its infrastructure and its "civilizing" institutions (local government, education, houses of worship). The elder Dr. Chester Rowell helped organize the local Republican Party and founded the *Fresno Republican* in 1876.

The younger Chester Rowell began editing the *Republican* and pressed for municipal and county reforms. These early efforts focused on gambling, prostitution, and opium use in Fresno's Chinese district. Rowell also channeled growing local anger at the Southern Pacific Railroad, which had absorbed the Central Pacific; its rates and demands riled Fresnans as much as they did Sacramentans.

In 1902 Rowell attacked Henry T. Gage, insisting that he was unelectable because of his unsavory association with William F. Herrin. Indeed Rowell's condemnation of Gage was similar to the abuse CK heaped on him. In 1900 Rowell went back to Washington to serve as a secretary to the newly elected senator from California, Thomas Bard (whose nomination had been made by Uncle Chester). When the Southern Pacific's choice, Frank Flint, displaced Bard in 1906, Rowell returned to California and to the *Republican.* In 1907, after his fateful meeting in Sacramento with Edward Dickson, Rowell published his famous *Fresno Republican* editorial on March 13 under the headline "Adjourned—Thank God." Rowell's scathing summary of that legislative session denounced it for its "exhibition of personal graft, of shameless servility, of blatant indecency, and of total unfitness to be the representatives of a self-governing people." Assailing the legislature as "boss ridden," Rowell challenged Californians to rise up against such corruption. CK proudly reprinted the *Republican* article in the March 14, 1907, edition of the *Bee*.[22] Chester Rowell took over the leadership of the Northern California phase of the California

Progressive movement, and Hiram Johnson quickly admitted him into his inner circle—which probably made McClatchy jealous. CK never trusted Rowell and considered him to be someone willing to tailor his beliefs in order to advance his own interests.

CK knew from his regular reading of the *Republican* that Rowell had initially opposed Progressive reforms. Even when Rowell took CK's trademark "Thank God" as the opening of his attack on the dysfunctional state legislature of 1907, CK wondered querulously what took him so long—insisting that the corruption of state government had been well known before 1907. "Like Saul of Tarsus the Fresno Republican at last sees the light," CK editorialized sarcastically.[23] Over time CK's suspicions about Rowell's Progressive purity increased. Rowell's picking and choosing of Progressive policies suggested a lack of principle and a willingness to tack with the wind—causing CK to refer to him as "Chester the Chameleon" and to frequently warn his friend Hiram Johnson about Rowell's mendacity and infidelity. By the mid-1920s Johnson shared CK's attitude.

When the *Bee* expanded into Fresno in 1923 and displaced the *Fresno Republican*, CK wanted to erase Rowell from the city's memory. (Rowell had sold his share in the *Fresno Republican* two years earlier.) However, Fresnans loved him, and, ironically, when CK's son, Carlos McClatchy, expanded the appeal of the newly created *Fresno Bee*, he recruited Rowell—over the painful objections of his father—to provide occasional editorial columns. CK's dealings with other Progressives in California had the same level of mistrust, ideological scrutiny, and even jealousy.

National Progressivism: The Presidential Campaign of 1912

Theodore Roosevelt's accession to the presidency in 1901 allowed Progressive issues to go national. CK had followed the rise of Teddy Roosevelt with great interest and noted the disappearance of the energetic young Rough Rider into the vice presidency in 1900. In May 1901 CK ran a picture of the young TR with the caption "Vice-President Roosevelt has lapsed into obscurity."[24] Five months later, however, after an assassin's bullet cut down President William McKinley, TR suddenly became president of the United States.

CK cautiously endorsed the new Republican president, predicting that Roosevelt's administration "will be virile and energetic. Independence and force of character have always been among his marked attributes." CK also noted approvingly that the new president was "a bold foe of every form of political corruption." Regarding foreign affairs, however, McClatchy warned that Roosevelt might be "if anything . . . too aggressive."[25]

McClatchy admired the president's domestic agenda, especially his antitrust suit against J. P. Morgan's Northern Securities Company in 1902. The *Bee* strongly endorsed Roosevelt's bid for another term in 1904, rejecting the bland corporate attorney, the Democrat Alton B. Parker. As time went on, however, CK kept a respectful distance from the ebullient president, whom he considered an egomaniac.[26]

Even with his misgivings about the president's activist foreign policy and his penchant for seizing the limelight, CK continued to support him and circulated a petition calling for TR to run for a third term in 1908.[27] Despite vigorous efforts to draft him, the popular Roosevelt easily delivered the presidency to his handpicked successor, William Howard Taft.

Because Taft ran against the beloved William Jennings Bryan, CK dutifully gave "the Commoner" his support. CK had misgivings about Taft (and poked relentlessly at his huge size, calling him "Fatty" on any number of occasions), but he did support the president's Progressive agenda. However, Taft's inept handling of key Progressive legislation soon soured CK and many other Progressives. As Taft's term continued, Progressive discontent escalated and fostered Progressive insurgency. CK mirrored the general unhappiness with Taft's missteps. He was especially angry at Taft's secretary of the interior, Richard Ballinger, whom CK believed had scaled back Roosevelt's support for land reclamation and conservation (an important issue in the Sacramento Valley and a particular cause of the *Bee*).

Progressives opposed to Taft pushed Senator Robert M. La Follette to challenge the president for the Republican nomination in 1912. But Roosevelt, who had become increasingly disturbed by Taft's decisions, eventually broke with his former friend and entered the contest for the Republican nomination. When TR went head to head with Taft in twelve presidential primaries, he won nine—eight of them by a landslide.

Although CK preferred La Follette, in the end McClatchy swallowed his misgivings about TR and urged *Bee* subscribers to vote for him in the May 14, 1912, primary. Roosevelt handily swept the California Republican primary, claiming a plurality of 2,000 votes in Sacramento County alone, although La Follette made a respectable showing. Democrats cast their ballots for the Missouri Democrat Beauchamp "Champ" Clark, Speaker of the House. Hiram Johnson, who supported Roosevelt, declared it a "great and glorious victory" and a confirmation of the Progressive trend established by his own election as governor in 1910.[28]

After Roosevelt won the California Republican primary, CK and his son Carlos traveled to the national convention in Chicago and sent breathless articles back to the paper describing the bitter struggle between Roosevelt and Taft for the nomination and soul of the Republican Party.[29] Taft's steamroller denied many Roosevelt delegates their seats (including two in the California delegation). CK sardonically portrayed the Republican convention as a scene of "contending sets of professional bosses, each backed by complacent delegates, bickering, trading and fighting to obtain the largest share of the spoils." This assured a walkout of the Roosevelt delegates—Progressive Republicans, including Hiram Johnson, who regrouped to retain Theodore Roosevelt as an independent candidate. CK supported the walkout and hailed the formation of a new Progressive party with Roosevelt as the nominee. The move was nearly unprecedented in American politics.[30]

Following the shocker in Chicago, CK and Carlos took a train to Baltimore for the Democratic convention. When the McClatchys arrived, Speaker of the House "Champ" Clark was the odds-on favorite. His opponent was the reformist governor of New Jersey, Woodrow Wilson, a respected former president of Princeton University. Bryan, now the senior statesman of the Democratic Party, also attended. CK, ever loyal to Bryan, kept him at the center of the party struggle, reporting to California that Bryan really held the balance of power in the party.[31] In the end Bryan's public support shifted enough votes to secure the nomination for Wilson on the forty-sixth ballot of the convention. "The nomination of Woodrow Wilson," CK opined, "may be regarded as a popular no less than a Progressive Democratic triumph, and as showing the irresistable [*sic*] force of public opinion when fully roused and enlightened."[32]

Through Bryan's intercession, Carlos traveled to New Jersey to snare one of the first one-on-one interviews with the new Democratic nominee—and Wilson, for reasons still unknown, subsequently asked that it not be published.[33] At the same time CK was making his way to Oyster Bay, Long Island, to visit with Teddy Roosevelt. After a short stay in Washington, D.C., Carlos and CK went to Chicago in August and witnessed the birth of a new political party—the insurgent Progressive, or Bull Moose, Party. At this convention Theodore Roosevelt was nominated for the presidency and Hiram Johnson selected as his running mate. Although CK genuinely admired Wilson, there was no soul searching here—he would support Roosevelt and Johnson without qualification.

"The *Bee* has been for some time in the ranks of the Progressives—in fact for years and years advocated the course for which Roosevelt stands—and is in the battle this year for Roosevelt and Johnson," CK announced to the *Progressive News* of New Haven, Connecticut.[34] After the turmoil of the three conventions, father and son steamed home from New York, returning in mid-August. On August 23 CK warmly endorsed Roosevelt.[35] The three-way election threw a narrow victory to Woodrow Wilson, with Wilson taking the largest number of popular and electoral votes and poor Taft coming in last. CK rejoiced in the triumph of Progressive ideals and praised the work of Hiram Johnson on the Bull Moose ticket. The Progressive defeat was not, in CK's view, "any more a Waterloo than the Battle of Bunker Hill or the first Battle of Bull Run" but was "simply an engagement foreshadowing the success of the principles for which the Progressive Party was battling."[36]

After the 1912 election the Progressive Party wanted to create a more stable political apparatus. A December 1912 conference at Chicago brought together the major elements of the Progressive coalition of politicians, journalists, and professionals who had formed the Bull Moose Party. Johnson chose not to attend but invited CK to participate and report to him. McClatchy agreed but insisted he would go only if he were under no obligation to support all measures adopted. He reserved the right to chide publicly or to disagree with "future doctrines or acts" of the Progressives if such principles clashed with those of the *Bee*.[37] In a rare exception to his nonattendance policy, CK did go to the Chicago meeting but did not join the League of Progressive newspapers proposed at this summit.

From Chicago he wrote to Johnson that "it was a really splendid meeting" with "intense enthusiasm present. Of course there were the usual jealousies, and bickering, and here and there an occasional petty spirit; but on the whole, it was a very harmonious meeting . . . with the thorough determination to go ahead." One disappointing aspect of the conference was the poor representation of California. "Nobody at all was present . . . at the meeting of the National Committee, neither Meyer Lissner, nor [Chester] Rowell showed up." He also told Hiram that "there was very intense disappointment prevalent throughout the meetings and at the banquet that you were not present."[38]

To Valentine CK was more troubled about Johnson's absence: "There was a very strong feeling of disappointment, if not worse, over the fact that Hiram never sent any message of any character to the conference; and that he never responded even to the telegram which the conference sent him from the banquet chamber. . . . Even his best friends felt hurt over the matter."[39]

The disappointment even with the beloved Johnson typified CK's relations with other prominent figures in the loose Progressive coalition. He felt free to disagree with aspects of the Progressive agenda and embraced the "dark side" of some Progressive policies—taking an increasingly dim view of immigrants while emphasizing personal respect for individual freedoms and choice. But he viewed the recipients of such tolerance selectively.

The Assault on Academic Freedom

CK valued his reputation as a muckraking or crusading journalist. Ferreting out graft and corruption in Sacramento and turning a spotlight on the cover-up of the plague and the political evils of San Francisco were the kinds of press crusades he truly loved. But as I have shown, CK's journalistic wrath was not always altruistic. Evening scores and wreaking vengeance on those who plotted against the *Bee* led to scathing attacks on people who may have been innocent. He could write rhapsodically about American freedoms and liberties, become tearful over the Declaration of Independence and the Constitution, and wave the flag in the cause of American exploits abroad (even if he disagreed with them). Nonetheless, when faced with a conflict between order and liberty, he chose order. However much he paid lip service to freedom of speech, it had limits.

Free speech that led to violence and social disruption was to be punished. Three years after taking over as editor of the *Bee,* CK wrote: "Let the anarchists talk as they have a right to do, but the moment they lift a finger in violation of law, against life or property, clap them into jail."[40] During World War I he supported provisions of a national sedition act that would have used military tribunals to try critics of the government. When violent acts occurred, seemingly spurred by radicals, he grew volcanic. He was one of the most vigorous critics of the McNamara brothers, who bombed the *Los Angeles Times* building in 1910, killing twenty-one during an antiunion bombing campaign.[41] He insisted on swift punishment for another accused bomber, Thomas Mooney, who allegedly set off an explosive at a 1916 Preparedness Day event in San Francisco—even after exculpatory evidence cast serious doubt on his conviction. This did not sway CK, who insisted to his dying day that Mooney was guilty and deserved the death penalty. Destruction and bloodshed that came from a radical fringe were one thing, but CK's intolerance came to the fore if anyone challenged his ideas on American history or attempted to bring different insights to California schoolchildren.

Adrianism

CK venerated certain figures in American history. On Lincoln's birthday in 1906 he addressed the children of the Sacramento Grade School on the importance of the sixteenth president and occasionally reprinted his speech in the *Bee*. "I want you to consider the man as thoroughly human. I want you to put away from your minds any idea that he was a gilded statue or a steel engraving. He was plain, modest, God-fearing, God-trusting, all mankind-loving man. He never walked on stilts, traveled in an airship or talked above the clouds. His habits were as simple as his own soul and his daily life as open and frank as the meadows in springtime. He was honest, he was brave; he was gentle, he was forgiving—'with malice toward none, with charity for all.'" He then wove Lincoln into the biblical past, comparing him with Moses, St. Paul, and even Jesus. Old Abe, CK declaimed, "walked with God"—through "the stormy Galilee of his war career" and spoke "with more touching eloquence than any man since the Sermon on the Mount capped with the Sinai of simplicity."[42] This speech epitomized McClatchy's understanding of U.S. history: romantic, heroic, democratic, exceptional—indeed nearly scriptural. When others offered revisionist views or seemed to contradict the heroic narrative CK had laid out, he attacked them relentlessly.

One poor soul, Henry A. Adrian, found himself in McClatchy's crosshairs for violating his views of the American past. Adrian, a former superintendent of schools in Santa Barbara, spoke at a Sacramento Teachers Institute on November 29, 1911. His address suggested some new directions in the study of the American Revolution and proposed that the British were not entirely to blame for the rupture with the American colonies. When Carlos, who covered Adrian's speech, relayed its message to his father, CK boiled with anger. What Adrian suggested was nearly treasonous.[43] CK then waged a holy war against Adrian and the principal, H. O. Williams, who had invited him, accusing them of disloyalty and tagging these heretical ideas as "Adrianism." CK insisted that the school's duty was to teach patriotism.[44] In response Williams drafted a public letter of support for most of Adrian's contentions.[45] Accusations of disloyalty and outrageous extrapolations from Adrian's rather mild revisionism dominated *Bee* coverage.

CK became so obsessed with his crusade that at Christmas 1911, instead of urging parents to read St. Luke's account of the Nativity or Dickens's *A Christmas Carol*, he urged them to share the Declaration of Independence with their children.[46] Urged on by CK, the legislature took up the matter. State senators A. E. Boynton and Edward Wolfe introduced a resolution calling on Governor Johnson to begin a probe of the teaching of history in California's public schools.[47] A joint resolution of the legislature passed just before Christmas incited the ire of academics, journalists, and others who took it as a threat to academic freedom. This resolution, probably penned by CK, urged that any caught teaching the "subversive" version of U.S. history "should be weeded out forever" and that "such traitors" should be banned from the school system of California.[48]

But the heresy was not restricted to California. CK found a similar interpretation, "Peculiar History," written by an army officer for *Collier's Weekly*, and McClatchy directed his Washington correspondent to interview senators Robert La Follette and Francis Newlands, and representatives William Kent and John Raker, and "all others you can think of as to what they think of such un-Americanism written in the alleged American history by an officer of the United States." CK learned from Anna Weeks, a Sacramento school principal, that she had heard H. Morse Stephens, a professor of history at UC Berkeley, utter the very same unpatriotic sentiments in a talk in Sacramento three years earlier. Finding that Stephens was behind this further inflamed CK. Looking for someone with similar credentials to take on Stephens, he dispatched Alva Johnston, a family friend, to interview Woodrow Wilson, then governor of New Jersey and former president of Princeton, who had written a history of the American people.[49]

CK accused Stephens and his "disciples," of being the "fountain head" of this treasonous teaching. When asked by the editor of the *Herald* in Livermore why CK made such a big fuss about Adrian, CK turned his fire on the man whose notions had inspired Adrian, H. Morse Stephens. Stephens, CK said, "is a British subject and not an American citizen; and . . . from the University [of California], graduates go out to teach history in our public schools who have no reverence for America, or American institutions, and worship everything British. . . . In other words, we are paying teachers to undermine the government. For patriotism is the only bulwark we can present in years to come to the on-moving waves of rabid socialism."[50]

The Case Against Adrianism Dissolves

Reactions to McClatchy's bleating about Adrianism were largely negative. Chester Rowell of the *Fresno Republican* openly accused the *Bee* of "frothing hysteria" and "daily spasms." The younger Rowell, also a member of the Board of Regents of the University of California, as had been his uncle, firmly rejected CK's basic premise about a patriotic version of history and insisted that CK's naïveté made "the standard of history . . . not truth but national vindication."[51] CK rejected Rowell's arguments with quotes from legislators and local teachers that affirmed CK's concerns. Irving Martin of the *Stockton Record* downplayed the whole business as the "vaporings of a sensation hungry country school master." When Martin pressed CK again to tone down, McClatchy hurled all his ammunition at Adrian in the *Bee* a couple of days before Christmas Day 1911.[52]

Since few of his journalism counterparts took up his cause, the issue gradually faded away, leaving CK resentful toward highbrow academics and especially the University of California—including its president, Benjamin Ide Wheeler, whom CK derisively called "Old Banjo Eyes" Wheeler.

He reserved choice invective for H. Morse Stephens, a specialist in the French Revolution who had indeed influenced the teaching of history in high schools and colleges through his work on a committee to draw up guidelines for instructors. Stephens himself tried to insist he meant no disrespect for the Revolution or the American cause by his mild revisionism but did not get into the mud with McClatchy. Academics in the American Historical Association closed ranks around Stephens, eventually electing him president of the prestigious organization in 1915. Alumni and other professors meanwhile condemned state senator Boynton and the meddling legislature.[53] Stephens died unexpectedly in 1919, and pursuing the issue became moot.

Ultimately nothing came of it. Yet the episode itself, like CK's other constructions of the past, was significant. This view of the American past, characterized by some as American exceptionalism, provides critical insight into his worldview and offers an important perspective on his views of America's foreign policies, a topic on which he would hold forth on many occasions. Although he reserved for himself the right to be highly critical of the actions of local, state, and national governments, there were limits when it came to criticizing the nation itself. Because he tolerated no analytical hermeneutic for the history of the nation as he had learned it as a young child, he deliberately adopted a "facts-be-damned" attitude toward perspectives or people he felt were critical of national ideals. He was driven by his passions, rather than his principles.

(Right) James McClatchy, longtime editor and part owner of the *Bee*.

(Left) A childhood photo of CK.

(Above) CK as a young editor.

(*Right*) Valentine Stuart McClatchy, CK's brother and longtime partner.

(*Below*) CK at his ranch, Casa Robles, Carmichael

(Above) Ella Kelly McClatchy

(Right) Sketch of Carlos Kelly McClatchy.

(Below) Eleanor Grace McClatchy on her wedding day in 1924.

(Above) CK with his friend Hiram Johnson.

(Above) CK with William Jennings Bryan, an occasional houseguest.

(Left) Floral funeral tribute to CK lauding him as "labor's friend."

(Below) Liberty ship named for C. K. McClatchy.

Chapter Twelve
Hiram

———————◆———————

COMMON POLITICAL PRINCIPLES accounted for a bond that linked C. K. McClatchy to Hiram Johnson. But this thirty-year friendship went even deeper. CK came to regard Hiram as a brother—closer than even his own blood brother. Understanding the chemistry between the two men is not easy. The mercurial Johnson often struck a pugnacious, even belligerent, pose in public but at times quavered inwardly. CK was an introvert with few close personal relationships and a shy public personality. However, his strong opinions and sage advice often shored up the sometimes depressed and indecisive Johnson. Though older, CK treated the prickly Johnson with a deference he accorded to few others.

CK's nearly unilateral surrender of the columns and editorial positions of the *Bee* to the California politician demonstrated the measure of his loyalty and trust—indeed love. CK jealously guarded the *Bee* from any and all who sought to dictate its policy—including his own brother. No one could raise his ire quicker than those who told him what he ought to be writing in the *Bee*. However, Johnson had virtual carte blanche. The two men wrote to each other frequently throughout their lives—sometimes twice a day. "There are very few people to whom I like to write intimately," Johnson confided to CK, "and I think you know that you are the very first of these. There is a double pleasure to me in thus writing—I feel that I am talking intimately to a very dear friend, in the first place, and, in the second place, it is a vent for pent up feelings which cannot be publicly expressed." On one occasion when Johnson fell sick, CK sent him flowers. Johnson wrote, "I follow you in the *Bee* and each night have a sort of lop-sided conversation with you in which you speak in trumpet tones to me and sometimes I respond with applause and very rarely with muttered profanity."[1]

Since both men had streaks of pettiness that often drove away some of their staunchest allies, it seems miraculous they sustained any kind of friendship—or even began one. In the relatively small Sacramento environment, CK and Hiram had known each other since they were boys, as their fathers were both active professionally and politically in the city.[2] CK was nearly eight years older than Johnson (who was born September 2, 1866), and their families were not friends. As I have discussed, Hiram's father, Grove Johnson, detested both Valentine and CK, considered them bullies, and managed to be part of virtually every legal action against them. When Valentine and CK took over the *Bee,* they attacked Grove on every occasion, not only disagreeing with his politics but spreading scurrilous rumors about his financial dealings and womanizing (Grove was a widower for many years). They did everything they could to see him removed from public office and had a hand in getting him ejected from Congress in 1896.

Grove's two sons, Albert and Hiram, had a love-hate relationship with their father, and both moved out of Sacramento to get away from his overbearing ways. In his early years Hiram shared his father's distaste for the McClatchys. After college he studied law and opened a practice in Sacramento with his father. He became known as a passionate and sometimes even hysterical litigation attorney. Hiram also became tangentially involved in the famous von Arnold affair that tarred Harris Weinstock with accusations of bribery. For some reason Hiram escaped the fate of other men who opposed the McClatchys on matters of substance. Even after they were friends, CK overlooked Hiram's divergences and heresies—including a vote in favor of Prohibition. Hiram Johnson was the "Great Exception" to CK's periodic personal vendettas.

In 1897 Hiram dissolved his relationship with the family law firm, and in 1899 he and Albert enthusiastically supported the reform mayoral candidacy of George Clark. Clark's victory over William Land was nearly negated when it was found Clark had not filed a statement of his election expenses. Hiram and Albert vigorously defended Clark, who was then seated. After Clark won, he appointed Hiram as city attorney and set him after two of Sacramento's most notorious gamblers, Frank Daroux and Bartley Cavanaugh. This immediately impressed CK, who remembered that Hiram had been a proponent of reform during the Populist heyday. Even when *Bee* investigators learned that gambling still went on in the city—including in the supposedly banned poolrooms—CK blamed Mayor Clark, not Johnson.[3]

The *Bee's* relentless hectoring of the affable Clark amused and even secretly pleased Hiram, who sometimes found Clark a bit flamboyant.[4] Still, Hiram was loyal to Clark, and when he ran for reelection in 1901 both Hiram and his brother campaigned for him. At a large pro-Clark rally attended by more than fifteen hundred people, Johnson decried the negative reporting about his candidate by the *Sacramento Record-Union* but took pains to single out *Bee* coverage for its fairness.[5] Nothing could have pleased CK more—for even when he was at his most hyperbolic he cherished the illusion that his positions were fair. Johnson did become mildly irritated with caustic *Bee* coverage by the end of the campaign, but when the mayor was handily reelected, all was forgiven. Johnson continued to serve ably in the second Clark term, and even challenged Henry T. Gage for the Republican nomination for governor. Clark's defeat, brought about by the machinations of William F. Herrin, hit Hiram and his brother hard. Clark lost the mayoralty to William Hassett in 1902, and with that the Johnson brothers departed Sacramento to open a new law practice in San Francisco.

In San Francisco Hiram's dramatic flair in the courtroom made him a local luminary, and his reputation as an aggressive litigator won him numerous clients and great financial success. As noted earlier, in 1906 District Attorney William Langdon tapped him to assist Francis Heney in conducting the San Francisco graft prosecutions of Mayor Eugene Schmitz and "Curly Boss" Abraham Ruef. After Heney was shot in November 1908, Johnson stepped forward to complete the prosecution. Together with his friend Matthew Sullivan, Johnson made the case against Abe Ruef—for what turned out to be the single successful prosecution of the graft trials. Johnson stepped aside and was not on hand to press further against those who had offered the bribes—a deft move since the remaining prosecutions fell flat. CK nonetheless heaped praise on Johnson for his role in the graft prosecution. The compliment went a long way with the often insecure attorney.

By the early years of the twentieth century, the Progressive impulse was rippling across the nation—especially in states like Wisconsin, Iowa, Indiana, and New York. President Theodore Roosevelt spearheaded important reforms—tackling trusts, imposing regulations on food and drugs, and moving aggressively to conserve lands and resources. In California the Progressives in the 1909 session of the legislature attempted to more effectively regulate railroad rates and services. These efforts fell short, but the legislators did manage to push through a modified popular primary law that went into effect in 1910. Johnson seemed to some to be the best Progressive candidate to run for governor that year. However, he claimed he did not aspire to political office—even though he spoke frequently on behalf of various candidates. Even more, he liked the money he was making in private practice. This would change.

Contending for Governor: Hiram Johnson and the 1910 California Primary

Throughout 1909 and into early 1910 the Lincoln-Roosevelt League, the cadre of diverse California Progressives, pressed Johnson hard to become the Republican candidate for governor. Johnson held out, and in early 1910 several leading California newspapers, including the *Bee*, carried the announcement of his refusal.[6] When Hiram shared his thoughts about not running with CK, the editor had mixed feelings but could hardly gainsay a man who did not want to leave a good job and domestic arrangements for the perils of politics.

But the lure of power and the eventual agreement of his wife (to whom Hiram referred as "the Boss") made Johnson reconsider, and he announced his candidacy on February 19, 1910. In a handwritten letter he explained to McClatchy that he had "yielded against my better judgment to appeals to duty, principle, etc." His petitioners, he explained, had put the request this way: "If the selection of a candidate were left only with [Charles] Belshaw, Matt [Sullivan], or [Harris] Weinstock, there'd be no League, no opportunity this year and perhaps not for another decade to make the fight against the Southern Pacific . . . and to make a stand in California for the awakening, etc." Admitting "I wouldn't give a tinker's damn to be governor. . . . I would like to die feeling that I'd done my part." He concluded with words that must have touched CK's vanity: "Write me what you think of matters and what you hear. It's impossible to trust our idealists—they mean well and think they know, but their political acumen is in inverse ratio to their patriotism."[7]

CK praised Johnson's decision in a long series of adulatory editorials and articles. CK also noted with some delight that Johnson's candidacy, as well as Theodore Bell's (he was the eventual Democratic nominee), was likely to create anxiety among the Southern Pacific interests and especially the boss William Herrin. CK was elated that California now had the prospect of a genuinely Progressive regime.[8] Johnson's opponents for the Republican nomination were Charles Curry, secretary of state, and the Sacramento banker Alden Anderson.

CK had a sentimental attachment to Bell, the Napa Democrat, even though Bell irritated CK by accepting the support of William Randolph Hearst. In advice offered to Bell, which really described CK's dilemma, McClatchy wrote: "I still think as I have thought right along, that Hiram Johnson will be the strongest man the Republicans could nominate against you. However, I may be mistaken. Between you and me, I do not believe Hiram is going to be nominated. I would like to see it because I would like to see both parties put up men in whom the people could have confidence."[9]

He also freely dispensed advice to Hiram and strongly urged him to keep the panjandrums of the Lincoln-Roosevelt League at bay. When Johnson himself complained of his discomfort with the league, which he described as a yoke, CK readily agreed. "You are packing a good deal of dead weight around with you when you take with you on your stumping tours some of the men with whom the Lincoln-Roosevelt League has inflicted [upon] you."[10] CK also warned Hiram against consorting with those who might damage his chances with the wider electorate.[11] All through the primary campaign CK fed Johnson bits of gossip, including the musings of CK's African American barber, Frank Butler, who had overheard U.S. Attorney William H. Devlin's law clerks chatting at lunch that Johnson would win the Republican nomination. McClatchy wrote friendly editorials and shaped news coverage to favor Johnson, and CK disparaged Curry and Anderson. Johnson won the nomination handily in mid-August 1910, and Theodore Bell again became the Democratic Party's standard-bearer, as he had been in 1906. The battle between these two reformers, enemies of Herrin and the Southern Pacific, was at once a dream come true and a nightmare for McClatchy.

CK's Dilemma: Choosing the Right Progressive

CK tried at first to walk a narrow line. In the weeks before the primary election he wrote a memorable editorial that ran on April 8 directed at those who seemed confused by the *Bee*'s positive coverage of both candidates. Headlined "You're Right—the *Bee* Is for Hiram W. Johnson and Theodore A. Bell," CK acknowledged he was supporting both. "This is true. And this paper has no apology to make for its continuous consistency in the battle for principle, for the rights of The People and the overthrow of corporate domination." In typical McClatchy prose he noted: "Either is a valiant, militant leader in the fight for The People. . . . Either is a righteous manly soldier battling to wrest sovereignty of the State from the brigandish clutch of the Captain Kidds of public piracy. Either is a Richard Coeur de Lion in a modern-day crusade to drive from the holy of holies of Justice such Saracenic blasphemers as the William F. Herrins and the Patrick Calhouns of public sacrilege and public dishonor. . . . The days of party thralldom are over."

But he had trouble maintaining an evenhanded approach. Loyalty kept him tied to Bell, with whom he had already become close and whose cause he had endorsed in 1902 when Bell ran for Congress and again in 1906 when he ran for governor. CK had written encouragingly to Bell about his prospects in May 1910.[12] But he also kept up an active correspondence with Johnson, who relied on CK to spread the Johnson message to the northern valley and to refute the negative stories in the *Sacramento Union*.[13] CK appears to have supported Johnson in the exchange of letters. However, as the election grew tight and the scramble for ballots became more intense, both sides grew impatient with the *Bee*'s approach. CK worried that Bell would backpedal on his earlier condemnations of the Southern Pacific Railway to set himself apart from Johnson's blunt attacks on it. Bell reassured CK he would not change his stance but asked CK for an outright endorsement from the *Bee*. CK was sympathetic but declined. He rationalized his choice of neutrality. "From one point of view it is unfortunate that Hiram W. Johnson was nominated. It spoils a mighty good fight which this paper could have made. From another point of view it is for the best—for I feel that the State will be honored, no matter which man is elected." Nonetheless he reassured Bell that "the columns of the *Bee* will be open to you at all times." In a confidential note to a colleague, Hensley Davis, however, CK confessed, "The Bells can say positively that Charley McClatchy will vote for Bell."[14]

CK counseled the volcanic Johnson to curtail his temper. "Just received your letter in which you ask whether it would be good policy to attack the *Examiner, Call,* and *Chronicle* simultaneously . . . my advice to you Hiram is the advice which Punch gave to the woman about to be married: don't." CK believed Hiram was "making a winning fight" and had "nothing to gain by doing any more than you are doing at present. Hearst may be against you and probably is not giving you a fair shake. But there are numbers of people who work for Hearst in various ways who are for you and who would be very angry at an attack on Hearst. The same way with John D. Spreckels of the *Call*. Therefore my advice to you is not to go any farther than you have gone. Suffer these things in silence."[15]

The campaign, however, was not destined to remain civil. Johnson's attacks on Bell became increasingly vituperative, and CK expressed sympathy to Bell. CK likewise warned Bell that "the negative attacks made by his own campaign would do him no good and that he ought to stick to the high road."[16] In the end Johnson won a relatively narrow but decisive victory, trouncing Bell 177,191 to 154,835.

An Interlude of Discontent

As Johnson and his staff examined the reasons for their victory, some felt the last days of the election would have gone better had CK been more supportive. The bitterness of the campaign staff became evident when CK's congratulatory letters to Johnson went unanswered. At first confused, CK quickly became defensive and then angry at Johnson's ingratitude. He groused to Hichborn, "I think you will find that Mr. Johnson will go into office with a big case of the swelled head; that he will forget everything that ever was done for him; and that he will recognize only those who are willing to do whatever he wants without criticism. . . . I will continue to ignore the Governor-elect until such time as he sees fit to answer a decent letter." Hichborn attempted to calm CK by assuring him that it had been Johnson's associates, H. A. French (a former *Bee* reporter) and Al McCabe, who apparently spread the rumors of McClatchy's supposed disloyalty, and they were not worth becoming upset over. Hichborn noted that the cause of reform was more important than personal issues. And, Johnson "is going to need you far more than you can ever need him." CK agreed, but in the final triumph of the Progressive cause for which he had labored for many years, CK felt left out.[17]

In December 1910 Francis Heney explained the reason for Johnson's chilly treatment of McClatchy, informing the Sacramento editor that Frank Hering, a stringer for the *Bee* who supported Bell, had written uncomplimentary articles about Johnson that ran in the *Tulare Register*. CK replied defensively, noting that the Johnson supporter Fremont Older had run negative editorials about Bell in the *San Francisco Bulletin*. However, CK hoped to use Heney as an emissary to Johnson and suggested that neither candidate should be held accountable for the overexuberant opining of independent newspapermen.[18] But this did not move Johnson or his transition team staffers, who were also preparing for what would be an action-packed session of the legislature in 1911.

Travel was always a respite from stress, and CK and Ella made the first of many trips to Europe. They sailed from New York in late 1910 and remained abroad until the middle of 1911. As he heard of the exciting events unfolding in Sacramento, he must have been chafing to get home. Also, even before he left, problems had erupted once again with his brother Valentine, a harbinger of difficulties to come in the partnership. When he returned home, CK was anything but relaxed or at peace.

The ice finally broke when CK sent Johnson a lengthy memo on the "Adrianism" issue.[19] Johnson did not seem too concerned about Adrianism, but CK's overture provided an excuse for the two men to reconcile. Hiram invited CK to his office for a discussion of political affairs in October, and CK used the visit as an opportunity to clear the air. Johnson expressed his disappointment about the mixed signals from the *Bee* (and CK) during the election. The story Heney had shared about Frank Hering never came up, but the case of a former *Bee* reporter, Will Wayne, did. Johnson claimed that Wayne, who had covered a Bell campaign event in Exeter, California, had suggested that even though the *Bee* supported Johnson in the primary, it supported Bell in the general election. CK assured Johnson this was not the case. "If such a thing ever occurred, it was contrary to my orders," CK assured the new governor.[20] CK produced quotes from his letter book, to underscore that he had maintained strict neutrality for the *Bee*. He did not inform the governor, however, that he had personally voted for Bell. This two-hour talk, and CK's eagerness to make the *Bee* a mouthpiece for Johnson, restored friendly relations, never to be broken again. CK stuck with Johnson, although the *Bee* sometimes was the only paper in California to endorse what he did as governor and senator. Johnson's friends were CK's friends, Johnson's enemies CK's enemies. McClatchy dutifully funneled news of events in state government to Johnson—and was often the recipient of information from statehouse or Washington, D.C., that could be used in the *Bee*.

The End of the McClatchy-Bell Friendship

CK's long-term relationship with Theodore Bell was the casualty of the October meeting with Johnson. After the election CK genuinely tried to help reposition Bell, who wanted to keep his hand in state and national Democratic politics. CK encouraged him to remain faithful to the Progressive cause. When it appeared Republicans would renominate Taft, CK urged Bell to get behind New Jersey governor Woodrow Wilson. CK lauded the Progressive governor as a stalwart for Progressive principles. "He is the stuff of which great men are made," CK told Bell. "He is what he is, not from policy, but because of principle."[21]

But Bell ignored his advice and created a casus belli at the Democratic Party convention of 1912, causing CK to dump Bell. At the convention Bell blocked Williams Jennings Bryan from becoming the honorary chairman and threw his support to Bryan's foe, the Tammany-backed Speaker of the House Beauchamp "Champ" Clark of Missouri.[22] Bell also ignored CK's advice and worked against the nomination of Wilson. This insult to the venerated Bryan and disloyalty to the Progressive cause severed whatever ties Bell still had with CK, who thereafter criticized him periodically on the pages of the newspaper.

When Bell jumped into the 1918 California governor's race as an independent, CK assured Hiram Johnson, who was now a U.S. senator, "This paper will never support Theodore A. Bell again for any office unless it may happen to be—which is very unlikely—that somebody even more distasteful than Bell shall be his opponent; also upon an obnoxious platform." To make sure Bell would not win the governorship, CK organized and opened a successful and party-splitting write-in campaign for James J. Rolph Jr., a San Francisco Democrat—thereby assuring a victory for the incumbent, Republican governor William Stephens. Bell eventually switched parties in 1921. He died the following year in a tragic automobile accident near San Rafael.[23]

Friends for Life

CK's friendship with Hiram made the *Bee* the politician's mouthpiece. When press rivals twitted him about this, CK maintained the fiction this was not true and reacted sharply when others pointed it out. When V. L. Ricketts of the *Goldfield (Nevada) News* attacked the California governor for some failing, noting "the odor of this scandal has become so great that it has forced Johnson's own newspaper organ, The Sacramento *Bee*, into the open," CK accused Ricketts of misusing a *Bee* quote and blustered, "As to the *Bee* being 'the newspaper organ' of Governor Johnson, The *Bee* upholds Governor Johnson only insofar as it believes him to be right. It has criticized his administration on more than one occasion, and may have occasion to criticize it more than once before his term is over."[24] But CK defended Johnson at every turn and frequently opened the columns of the newspaper to him to rebut accusations or to argue points.

In turn, Johnson often asked CK's advice on legislation or local politics. CK always approached this task with great delicacy and a hint of obsequiousness. Johnson had an enormous ego and was hypersensitive to criticism. CK always offered difficult advice with a heavy dose of flattery. He continually reassured

Johnson of his loyalty by responding to any attack on the governor's public image. As time went on, the two men became deeply dependent on each other—with CK providing moral support and a steadying hand on Johnson's sometimes roller-coaster personality and turning to Johnson for ideas about California, national politics, and international affairs. In turn Johnson provided a regular stream of behind-the-scenes information from Washington that proved far more reliable and enduring than the whisperings of any other political operatives CK had cultivated over the years.

CK would not entrust Johnson to any mere reporter but insisted that he (and later Carlos) be the sole conduit between the *Bee* and Johnson. Typical of this was an incident that occurred during Johnson's second inaugural in January 1915. To capture the event the *Bee* contracted local photographer H. J. McCurry to take shots of the inauguration for the *Bee*. On his own McCurry sent the governor a framed picture of Johnson taking the oath of office. CK exploded, "The negative from which that picture was taken was the personal property of The Sacramento *Bee*. You were paid, or you will be paid for your work on that negative. The *Bee* intended to have one of these pictures made and presented to Governor Johnson with its compliments; and you had no right to use our property for the purpose of making such presentation to the Governor with your compliments."[25]

Covering Johnson as Governor

While CK was away in Europe for much of the 1911 legislative season, he and Valentine dispatched Franklin Hichborn to cover the proceedings in Sacramento. The *Bee* stalwartly supported the various initiatives of the Johnson administration.

Johnson had the backing of Progressives—and a compliant legislature that shared his views on reform. He tackled a number of issues, including railroad reform, efficiencies in state finances, and democratizing reforms such as initiative, referendum, and recall. He gave attention to state water reclamation efforts and rationalized the state's burgeoning agricultural sector. Home rule was accorded to cities, freeing them to make laws without interference from the rural-dominated legislature. He pressed passage of the Seventeenth Amendment, providing for the direct election of U.S. senators, and of laws expanding the use of the primary for the selection of senatorial and presidential candidates. Civil service reforms, cross-filing for seeking the nomination of both parties, and above all women's suffrage were hallmarks of the busiest legislative session of California history.[26]

Valentine proudly wrote to his vacationing brother: "Mr. Hichborn tells me that he heard Governor Johnson say some days before the close of the session that in his fight for good government during this administration he relies on three papers only: The *Express* of Los Angeles; the *Republican* of Fresno; and The *Bee* of Sacramento." Hichborn did not come cheap. He had charged $650 plus expenses for his work on the legislature. CK wanted Hichborn to investigate the California Supreme Court, which he felt was still under the thrall of Herrin of the Southern Pacific. But Hichborn's fees and his sometimes quirky behavior gave CK pause. He wrote to Valentine, "I do not know whether we can afford to put out that much money. In my mind the Supreme Court of California needs showing up as much as the Legislature did." When Valentine balked at Hichborn's high fees, CK abandoned the idea.[27]

Johnson himself reached into the *Bee* staff in August 1913 and selected John S. Chambers, the newspaper's business director, for the new job of state controller. CK explained to an irritated Valentine, "The idea came to him as a flash that Chambers would be an ideal man for the place, and that his appointment would not get the Governor into the difficulties and embarrassments into which the appointment of probably any other man would drive him." After some agonizing, Chambers accepted. Valentine insisted that, like other *Bee* employees who took jobs elsewhere, there would be no "return rights" for Chambers, but CK assured his brother that he had made no such promise to Chambers, who would have to stand for election in 1914.[28] CK also reminded his brother that other employees had been allowed to come back. CK was pleased to give Chambers to Johnson, further cementing his good relations with the governor and gaining a source within the administration as well.

Reelecting Hiram

The electoral cycle in California began when the Democrats nominated John D. Fredericks of Los Angeles to run against Hiram Johnson in 1914. CK did his best to keep a clear Republican field for Johnson and warned away potential rivals who shared the governor's Progressive ideology. Never again did CK want to find himself caught between competing Progressives as he had in 1910. Young Carlos covered the Johnson campaign and provided a steady stream of positive articles, which he signed "C. K. McClatchy Jr."[29] CK used the *Bee* to run a virtual propaganda operation for Johnson, soliciting numerous Progressive endorsements for his friend.

CK sought national exposure for Johnson—and the *Bee*. He wrote to Robert Davis of *Munsey's Magazine*: "Of course you know me personally but probably because of your long absence from California you are not aware of the position which The *Bee* holds in this state and on this coast. I have never looked for publicity and have never written for outside publications and subsequently my name may be unknown in comparison with other California editors." CK noted that "the idea of breaking into print on my part is far from being a personal matter. I do not care a cent for it." But he wanted "to let the people in the East know there is a paper of high repute in California known as the Sacramento *Bee*."[30]

Hiram Johnson set to work on an equally ambitious agenda of more liberal legislation for the legislature of 1913. This time CK saw it firsthand. A raft of laws concerning fair wages and working hours for women, reform of conditions in penitentiaries, and controversial measures dealing with foreign land ownership were enacted. This legislature also dealt with the issue of prostitution. For Johnson's benefit CK abandoned the unending carping he had directed at other administrations. In 1913 he wrote,

> Never before in the history of California has there been a State administration which promised so much and which has kept so many of its promises. Never before in the history of the State has there been a time when the throat of California has been so free from the corporate clutch. Never before in the history of California has there been a Governor who has honestly, earnestly and faithfully and conscientiously and pugnaciously endeavored to do so much for The People. And never before in the annals of this Golden State has there been a Governor who has succeeded in accomplishing so much.[31]

To his contemporaries in the press CK praised Johnson far and wide. He wrote to the editor of the *New York Independent* in 1914, acknowledging the seachange in California politics that had taken place under Johnson. In particular he singled out the appointment of James L. Gillis as state librarian as an example of the governor's ability to rise above partisanship to appoint the right people to positions of leadership:

> The history of these two men has been remarkably dissimilar. Hiram W. Johnson always was a Progressive, long before a Progressive party was conceived. James L. Gillis always was on the other side of the

fence. In fact, he was a Southern Pacific lieutenant at the time he was chosen, through the influence of that organization, to be State Librarian. The work he has done has surprised everybody. Up to the time of his appointment, the State Library was slovenly conducted, and managed as a political alms house in which to shelter, at the public's expense, some favorite of the bosses. Mr. Gillis started in at once to change all that. He inaugurated the civil service system. Gradually, he weeded out the old worthless superannuated timber.[32]

Going to the Senate

Johnson was only two years into his second term in 1916 when he pondered running for the U.S. Senate seat left vacant by the retirement of John Works. After going through his customary gyrations and bouts of anxiety, Johnson eventually decided to run. CK gushed, "There isn't a Californian here—friend or enemy with whom I have talked, who does not privately express his belief you can beat any man before the people for United States Senator."[33]

CK stood on the sidelines offering advice to steady his sometimes impulsive friend. During the primary campaign Johnson determined to "read De Young and Otis out of the Republican party." However, a level-headed CK, who also had no love for either publisher, urged calm: "I would not, were I in your place . . . would it not have to some extent at least, an opposite effect to that intended? Hearst was not injured by being read out of the Democratic Party years ago. On the contrary, it was the best advertisement he could have had."[34] Johnson heeded his advice.

However, there was a shadow on Johnson's reputation stemming from his alleged snub of the Republican presidential candidate Charles Evans Hughes during the 1916 presidential campaign. Republican loyalists always blamed Johnson for the narrow loss of California, which deprived Hughes of the presidency.[35] In a memorable incident at the Virginia Hotel in Long Beach, where both Hughes and Johnson were guests, Hughes did not pay a courtesy call on the California governor, nor did Johnson reach out to him. This snub was ignored by the *Los Angeles Times* but picked up by other papers—including the *Bee*—and it angered Progressive Californians. In the tight election of 1916, Hughes narrowly lost the presidency to Woodrow Wilson when he lost California's electoral votes by a mere 4,000 popular votes. This Republican loss also would dog Johnson in later years.

Johnson handily defeated his primary opponent in the Senate race, Willis Booth, a lawyer from Southern California, and just as easily dispatched his

Democratic opponent, George S. Patton (father of the famous World War II general) in the general election. Grateful to CK, who had encouraged him and run a continuous series of popular articles about him, Johnson wrote tenderly, "I know between you and me, with the intimacy that exists and which I so highly prize, letters of appreciation or thanks are wholly unnecessary; but, nevertheless, I wish you to know how very grateful I am to you and to the '*BEE*' for your constant and able and most valuable advocacy. . . . When days have been dark with me, I have ever felt that I could turn to you and the '*BEE*' for comfort and for solace . . . none has contributed more to the success of what we prize governmentally and to my personal success than you."[36]

CK's relationship with Johnson matured over the years, largely because CK was willing to set aside certain principles—even strongly held ones like Prohibition and control of social vices. Even when he would go through a charade of telling Johnson he disagreed, CK always followed up with affirmations of friendship and respect. These two men were more than ideological soul mates; they were what the Italians call simpatico. They understood each other at a deep level and shared a common bond of friendship that transcended their occasionally clashing ideas or temperaments. CK helped Johnson keep a watchful eye on California issues and politics. Occasionally CK reined in Johnson's behavior with various politicians who shared Progressive ideas but did not care for Johnson's personality.

As Johnson left California to take his Senate seat, the Progressive tide had crested in California. Within a year the United States would be at war. New and sobering issues crowded onto CK's desk—issues that he cared about deeply. Without Johnson, though, he was never again able to exercise the influence or clout in state government he had enjoyed since 1911. These years had seen the peak of CK's powers and influence.

Chapter Thirteen
A New Era
Preparing the Heir

———————————◆———————————

ON TOP OF the uncertain relationship with Hiram Johnson at the end of the 1910 gubernatorial campaign, an embarrassing public relations fiasco engulfed CK and Ella when they tried to sell their Tenth and O Street residence to the county for a juvenile detention home. Ella, who had an interest in juvenile justice, had been selected to sit on a county commission on juvenile crime chaired by Judge Joseph W. Hughes in 1909. Acting on the commission's recommendation, the legislature created a new juvenile court for Sacramento, and with it came the need for a separate detention facility for youthful offenders. At the same time the McClatchys had put their house on the market and moved to temporary quarters at 1906 Twenty-first Street. The first prospective buyer of their old home, Sacramento's Episcopal bishop, wanted to use it for a recreation and shelter facility to be called the Sunshine Home. He planned to offer $8,000 for it—with furnishings. But when the county also expressed an interest in the property, CK changed real estate agents and hiked the selling price to $10,000.[1]

Judge Hughes had recommended its use to the county board of supervisors and young offenders immediately moved in. At that point all hell broke loose. Robert Callahan, a county supervisor always at odds with the McClatchys, did everything he could to stop the sale of the house to the county, claiming the county did not have enough money (while proposing a ranch he owned as an alternative site). Neighbors complained about the noise and unpleasant characters who disrupted the neighborhood. The issue dragged on for many months, compelling the McClatchys to wait for their money.[2] CK wrote imploring letters to local politicians to try to move disposition of the house along—all to no avail. Eventually the McClatchys withdrew the offer to sell and rented it to the county until 1917, when it became a multiunit rental property. Ella eventually sold it to the State of California in the 1930s, and today the state archives is located on the site.[3] The McClatchys eventually built a new house at Twenty-first and U streets (today a branch of the city library). Designed by the local architect Rudolph Herold (the architect of Sacramento's city hall), the house was a comparatively modest structure but had a lovely wood-paneled library. CK employed a Japanese cook and housekeeper, and a chauffeur, who drove CK's limousine-sized automobiles around the area every day.

Ella's concern for youth did not diminish with the house fiasco. In 1915 she was appointed to do fieldwork for the juvenile court commission, advising on cases of youthful law violators. She helped with the creation of the first kindergarten in Sacramento and was a director at the Home of the Merciful Savior, founded for disabled children by local Protestant churches.[4]

Going Abroad

The house imbroglio and the strain of work, whetted CK's need for escape. The first of several long stints abroad began in early 1911 and coincided with son Carlos's graduation from Columbia University and his return to Sacramento. Although Valentine would be overseeing the newspaper, having Carlos as his eyes and ears would reassure CK that all would remain in place. The trip took the McClatchys to some of the most popular sites of Europe, including Rome. CK drew on all his friends to write letters of introduction to various dignitaries, including colleagues in the foreign press. To please Ella he even had the local Catholic bishop write a letter of introduction to the pope.

CK always traveled as a tourist, carrying his cocoon of American identity and cultural standards wherever he went. For example, speaking of the habits of the Romans, he complained, "If you make an engagement with a business man for 8 o'clock and he turns up at 8:59 don't be surprised. Make no comment. He will be insulted if you see anything peculiar in his distinctly Roman action." Of Algiers, Morocco, he wrote, "On the surface, Algiers is all the eye could ask. But a little investigation will show that her magnificence and her charm conceal indescribable filth that would not be tolerated in an American city for an hour; that her moral condition is a stench in the nostrils."[5]

CK's rhapsodic articles about Florence, Venice, and Milan emphasized the architecture and artwork. In Paris he was swept away by the sycamore trees that lined the broad commercial streets Napoleon III and Baron Georges

Haussmann had constructed. "Fancy proposing lining J and K Streets with generous shade trees! I can hear the Voice of Business saying: 'What nonsense! Too many trees in Sacramento.'. . . If Mr. Wise Business Man would come to Paris and look around him, he would probably change his tune." In London CK sought out the haunts of "the world's greatest novelist, the evergreen, the immortal Charles Dickens." He made a beeline for the Old Curiosity Shop and then to Samuel Johnson's Ye Olde Cheshire Cheese, also "a favorite resort for Charles Dickens," where CK sought "the particular bench where the Master sat and thought, and studied human nature and wove plots and built the greatest character gallery the world has ever known." A trip to Ireland included a search for the ancestors of his late and venerated father but also an opportunity to ponder the state of Irish political and domestic affairs. One of his last columns from Dublin criticized the growing sentiment for prohibition in the United States by noting that in countries like Italy, which did not have temperance organizations or crusades, public drunkenness was nonexistent. In contrast in England and Ireland, where temperance groups abounded, public inebriation was a serious problem.[6]

Tensions Between Valentine and CK

CK's jocular prose in the *Bee* gave no indication of the anger and anxiety he felt during his entire trip. Even before he boarded the *Cedric* for the trip across the Atlantic, simmering tensions between him and Valentine erupted over control of the editorial policy at the *Bee*—and underlying that, the succession of the McClatchy children at the *Bee*.

The two brothers were very different men with very different work personalities. Phebe Briggs McClatchy, Carlos's wife, summarized the feelings of her socially prominent family, and perhaps the way many other Sacramentans may have felt, about the two brothers: "My mother and father were more fond of V.S. than they were of C. K. and his family—I don't know why—they were easier to deal with. V.S. was a very attractive man, and relaxed and easy to deal with. C. K. was rather stiff and not easy to talk to, somewhat forbidding."[7] As noted earlier, Valentine was always disdainful of his younger brother's lifestyle. He begrudged CK's longer vacations (some of them apparently for therapeutic reasons), which saddled Valentine with a raft of extra work. CK noted that Valentine also took his leisure but not as far away or as expensively because he had a larger family. Both men and their wives were highly protective of their families and eyed each other warily.

Valentine

After graduating from Santa Clara, Valentine landed a job as a clerk in the office of the secretary of state—probably through his father's connections. But life in Sacramento had no allure, and in 1879 he moved to Oakland where he worked as a clerk at the Oakland Savings Bank. Sometime in 1880 he began courting Adeline Hanifen, the oldest daughter of Jeremiah Hanifen. Hanifen, like James McClatchy, was an Irish immigrant—but from County Kerry in the south. Hanifen began his career as a real estate speculator and hotelier in New York. He took a quick trip to California in 1852, then returned to the Empire State, where "Addie" was born. In 1858 he moved his family to San Francisco and made a small fortune in real estate. Ten years later the prospering Hanifen retired and moved across the bay to Oakland, where he dabbled in real estate and the liquor and wine business. The devoutly Catholic Hanifens had seven children, one of whom became a Holy Family nun. Valentine married Addie on February 9, 1881, and after a "bridal tour" to Monterey, the couple returned to Oakland, where Valentine was hired as a receipt clerk at the U.S. subtreasury.[8] They had eight children, one of whom, Claire, was developmentally disabled and spent her life in a Stockton asylum.

Valentine was a businesslike but loving father. He sent his sons away to Santa Clara and carefully monitored their spending, writing many worried letters about their academic progress and deportment. He did the same with his daughters. Valentine had no known addictions or vices—he drank but little and was faithful to his wife and family. He loved outdoor recreation and was a champion rower. He joined the McNeill singing club when it began in 1887 and not only sang baritone but managed its business affairs. He and his family loved to vacation around the pristine areas near Lake Tahoe—boating, camping, and swimming.

Thomas Fox—Family Friend

On most matters of public policy, the brothers were united. They agreed on government ownership of transportation and utilities, improvements to urban infrastructure, the maintenance of high tariffs, women's suffrage, and the crusade for a clean Sacramento. The *Bee*'s crusade against urban corruption flayed city administrations and certain officials for allowing graft and corruption to flourish. Sacramento had its share of petty swindlers and local vice lords, including Frank Rhoades, William Gerber, Bartley Cavanaugh, and Frank Daroux, not to mention the activities of the political agents of the Southern Pacific Railway. In many cases CK's hyperbolic writing had ginned up the outrage beyond proportion. Sacramento's kings of vice were petty thieves compared with Abe Ruef or "Blind Boss" Christopher Kelly of San Francisco. Still, CK kept after these "scoundrels," even occasionally his old friend Thomas Fox.

Thomas Fox was the longtime head of the Democratic Party of Sacramento County. During two Democratic administrations, Grover Cleveland's and Woodrow Wilson's, he held the position of city postmaster, a lucrative patronage job. Fox had grown up with the McClatchys and been a classmate of CK's in grammar school. Although he was a well-known insurance agent, his political opponents and the *Bee* always suspected him of shady real estate deals and corruption. The *Bee* also insisted he was a railroad hireling—a quiet boss who controlled patronage and money and did the bidding of the railroad. In short, Fox was the perfect villain for one of CK's Dickensian templates.

However, Fox was also a personal friend of the C. K. McClatchy family, especially of Ella. At some point he had taken Ella's ne'er-do-well brother James under his wing. When James's chronic unemployment and alcoholism began to take their toll, Fox took the dying man to a sanitarium in Stockton and visited him faithfully. Eventually he brought James to the McClatchy home to die. Fox's solicitude for "poor Jim" won him a debt of gratitude from CK's mother-in-law, Mrs. Kelly, and Ella. After Jim's death Fox continually visited and offered help to Mrs. Kelly. When CK was struck with a life-threatening bout of pneumonia, Fox and his wife visited Ella daily, generously promising financial help should CK pass away. In addition Ella had many charities to support and often tapped some of Sacramento's less virtuous citizens for donations. Fox knew these people and opened doors for her.[9] He was so close to the McClatchy children that they called him Uncle Tom.

CK was not a fan of Fox's politics. CK wrote to Carlos in 1913: "No scheme of Tom Fox's has ever been presented to this city [that] I have not fought; every municipal candidate he has groomed I have tried to defeat." But unlike many other Sacramentans who felt the sting of CK's editorial pen, Fox never held grudges or snubbed CK but kept up a devoted and seemingly selfless friendship despite the treatment. Valentine, however, believed Fox deserved harsher editorial treatment. "You asked me as a personal favor," Valentine wrote to his brother in March 1911, that "while conceding the truth of the statements, to leave out any further reference to Fox. The reason frankly given me was that the relation between the two families were [*sic*] such that the criticism of Fox would make serious embarrassment for you."[10] As soon as CK was out of town Valentine sought to right this wrong—and here the fight began.

The Rupture

Valentine accompanied CK and his family to New York to bid them farewell on their lengthy trip. As CK left, the *Bee* was on another one of its crusades against gambling in the city. Its chief target was Chief of Police William Ahern, who claimed he lacked authority to shut down the many illegal games going on in the city. The *Bee* published the names of the owners of gambling establishments, including old bêtes noire like Ed Kripp and Chinese gamesters like Foon Tong, and excoriated the rival *Union* for seeming to side with the gamblers.[11]

But Valentine believed the root of the gambling problem lay in Thomas Fox's protection of these illegal games through his handpicked city officials. With CK gone, Valentine decided to act. The front page of the January 25, 1911, edition of the *Bee* ran the first of a series of unflattering political cartoons about Fox, Mayor Marshall Beard, and Police Chief Ahern that suggested they were all in on the swag (graft) from local gambling interests. A few days later Valentine editorialized that local authorities possessed sufficient authority to crack down on the gambling but were unwilling to do so because they did not want to cut off the flow of "illegal contributions and hurt Tom Fox's feelings." Carlos sent these papers to his parents, and Ella was horrified to see the family benefactor abused on the front pages of the paper. CK was even more furious at the breach of understanding with his brother and Valentine's deviousness in attacking Fox while CK was absent. CK took it as an effort by Valentine to challenge CK's de facto control of editorial policy. Some even suspected that it was a form of retaliation against Fox, who had blocked the Lawrence Stone Company, in which Valentine had a controlling interest, from obtaining a contract to build a new county jail. Before he sailed for Europe, CK bitterly protested the *Bee* editorial and cartoon. He registered his shock and dismay at the disloyalty of his brother and reminded Valentine of all the kindnesses Fox had done his family, noting that everyone in town knew about them. In running the cartoon Valentine had made CK seem like an ingrate, "I think you have done injustice to myself and to yourself—to yourself in that you have condemned [the] man and declared him guilty without proof; to myself in that I stand before the people of Sacramento as the editor of the *Bee,* as having been guilty of gross ingratitude." He defended Fox, noting that other prominent Sacramentans had more guilt: "There probably isn't anywhere near as much circumstantial evidence that Fox is back of gambling in Sacramento than there is that [George] Peltier, Fred Kiesel, [F. J.] Ruhstaller, [Arthur M.] Seymour et al are back of the dives in Sacramento. . . . And in comparison with the crime charged against Tom Fox their crime stinketh to high heaven." He concluded, "I am not pleading for mercy to Tom Fox. I am asking only for justice and for right—for justice to me if no one else."[12]

As the ocean liner steamed across the Atlantic and into the Mediterranean, and CK failed to receive even so much as an acknowledgment from his brother, CK seethed. When Valentine finally responded in mid-February, he tried to tamp down his brother's rage and assure him he was doing nothing underhanded but merely exercising his rights as coeditor. He acknowledged he could not prove his allegations against Fox in a court of law, but he would not back down from the attack on Fox's minion Marshall Beard. Valentine reminded his brother that they and everyone else in Sacramento knew that Fox controlled Beard and that members of the police force were beholden to him. "On the face of conceded facts," he lectured his brother, "I regard Tom Fox as the most dangerous menace to good government in Sacramento." Failure to condemn Fox when the trail of urban corruption leads to him, Valentine insisted, would mean "we are placing ourselves in the same position as the citizens of San Francisco whom we scathingly denounced for falling away from the graft prosecution when it touched the higher ups."[13]

Valentine swept away CK's invocation of Fox's kindnesses to his family and viciously suggested they were done to muzzle or silence criticism from Sacramento's foremost newspaper. Valentine lectured his brother: "You carry your loyalty to friends, I think too far, or are not willing to believe ill of them. . . . This same unwillingness to believe ill of one who professes himself your friend, has, I think, led you into error in connection with several individuals and their treatment in The *Bee*."[14]

Sitting a continent away from his brother and reading and rereading this long-delayed letter, perhaps under the influence of alcohol, CK seethed with anger and self-pity. The rest of the trip through Europe must have been an emotional nightmare for him. All he could do was stew and compose additional letters both in his head and on paper, replying to his brother's insults and misrepresentations. Val's action broke loose a reservoir of anger and resentment CK had stored over many years. This episode nearly destroyed their working relationship. For all the perfumed Victorian slush of mutual affection they professed in their letters to one another, it was now clear that these two men disliked and distrusted each other.

In his isolation and away from the action, CK became morose and gloomy. He was angry that Val had waited nearly six weeks before answering him and then seemed to dismiss his complaints. CK now became convinced Val was using his protracted absence to either drive him from the *Bee* or so rearrange working conditions as to make it impossible for him to return and continue to work there. His suspicions were further aroused when he learned that editorial positions were now being produced in conferences—a practice he was not likely to continue after he returned. He secretly wrote to the business manager, John Chambers, inquiring about the meetings and wondering fearfully "if the business department runs them." In a letter to Carlos CK declared, "If things continue as they are, there is absolutely nothing left in honor for me to do but leave The *Bee*."[15]

Carlos, who kept his father abreast of matters in Sacramento, also formed a distrust of Valentine that remained with him for the rest of his life. CK railed against his treatment by his older brother. "The complaint is this," he protested to Carlos, "That being Editor of The *Bee* I have been treated as though I had no right whatever to dictate its editorial policy or even to be considered therein—unless I am always there to watch and superintend. Val knew my relations with Tom Fox. It has been told to him half-a-dozen times . . . he knew it would cut me to the quick and put me in the light of an ingrate to have Fox assailed as bitterly as he was assailed."[16]

CK's exasperation spilled over into one of his letters to his mother, whom he usually shielded from business matters. When she wrote him in Rome reminding him that poor Val was "almost worked to death" by his absence, a vexed CK replied,

> My dear, dear Mama, I think it rather unfair to me that every time I go away for a needed vacation or a trip of any kind, I am invariably reminded that Val is 'almost worked to death.' It would seem that my absence must be looked upon as burdening his shoulders with a wonderfully extra amount of work. This my dear, dear Mama is unjust to me. There is no more reason under the heavens why Val should work himself almost to death when I am away than I should work myself almost to death when he is away—as he has been for at least three months out of every year for some years past.

He harrumphed, "I have now put in considerable more years on The *Bee* than Papa did. I have written for it for 36 years almost, during 26 years of which I have been its editor [--] for years its only editorial writer ever. I choose to spend money in traveling. Val prefers to put his in automobiles, pleasure boats, etc. . . . . As I grow older, I hope to travel more and more."[17]

On March 3, 1911, still angry that Valentine had not replied to the two letters he had written in February, CK delayed a trip from Rome to Florence to wait for a reply. While waiting, CK also penned a lengthy letter to his friend Father Robert Kenna of Santa Clara, laying out the case in great detail and telling him that he was through with the *Bee*. Although there is no record of a reply, Kenna probably urged him to calm down. CK wrote two more letters to his brother. One, a rambling twenty-seven pages, and a second of shorter length. Years of stored-up bitterness flowed out. At one point his frustration seemed to point to ending his relationship with the *Bee*: "But what's the use? I am worn-out, weary and heart-sick. There is absolutely nothing to be gained by any further discussion. It would be impossible for me to continue in The *Bee* after what has happened. Therefore, as soon as I return home I shall begin to plan to sell out with the least friction possible. It was in order to give you plenty of time for consideration that I cabled you yesterday." The second letter defended himself from Valentine's earlier charge that he shielded Fox.[18]

Finally a long-awaited letter from Valentine arrived. He apologized to his brother for not replying sooner, blaming his fragile health, and went on to explain that other issues were on his plate. He admitted, "Frankly, I put aside a full answer to your letter because it seemed to me of less immediate importance than these other matters." His reasons for going after Fox were, he said, "seemed to me justified and even demanded by the facts, and existing conditions." He loftily reminded his brother who was in charge: "In considering the matter, I shall expect you to assume that those who are here can better judge conditions than you who are in Europe." And in his usually steely way Valentine recapped the realities of *Bee* governance:

> You have doubtless explained to him [Fox] that, while you are nominally, respectively Editor and publisher, we are in fact joint editors and publishers! And that you have as little right to saddle the paper of which I am half-owner and co-manager with an editorial policy or financial obligation or business course opposed to agreed policy or my wishes as I would to do any of these things without your

approval; and that in the absence of one of us, the other is in sole charge, responsible only to the law, to his co-manager and to his own conscience.[19]

In a second letter of nineteen pages, Valentine sounded a conciliatory note, rejecting the idea of breaking up the partnership:

> A separation would be bad for the business, for ourselves, for our boys. While either of us can successfully continue The *Bee* on its upward course, the name and counsel of both, even if not very active in management, will be of value. A sale of the whole property, or of one-half to outsiders would have to be made at a price representing much less than the amount on which interest is now shown and only a fraction of that on which in a comparatively few years, and under present direction, returns could be produced. For these reasons, and even if you are certain that you wish to dissolve—I would not consider it until I have seen you personally and laid before you the probable results of various plans on which you might decide. I hope it is needless for me to say that I shall strenuously oppose separation as a matter of affection and sentiment as well as for weighty business reasons.[20]

Valentine took the occasion to air his irritation at the impression that CK was the sole editorial voice. Alluding to CK's protestation that James McClatchy had not shared editorial control of the *Bee* with anyone, including his partner, J. F. Sheehan, Val declared: "Our father controlled absolutely the editorial expression of the *Bee* in his late lifetime. But he did it first because he was sole owner, and afterwards because in admitting Sheehan to partnership he expressedly [*sic*] stipulated that Sheehan should have no voice in editorial expression. There is certainly no condition of this kind in our case. We bought the paper jointly, sharing equally. Any authority which anyone received to speak or act for us must come equally from both."[21]

Returning to the accusations against Fox, Valentine offered an olive branch: "It is possible that I may have gone too far. I concede this is a matter of judgment and that I am not infallible. But I believe that I am right." Nonetheless, he offered, "I shall . . . eliminate, until you return, suggestions that Fox is directly receiving blackmail or graft from the conditions for which he is responsible—a charge by the way The *Bee* has never yet made." Still, he insisted, "As to the main point in the present case—whether Fox's name should be used and his methods and responsibility for existing conditions criticized I submit that you cannot insist on silence in the matter without stultification and violation of one of The *Bee*'s cardinal principles." He insisted that if CK wanted to exercise his right to change principles, and even the *Bee*'s crusade to "criticize the causes of bad government when and where we can find them," he would have to do so by means of a cable, and Val would then refrain, "though I shall do so under protest."[22]

CK refuted several of his brother's assertions, correcting him on the ownership of the *Bee* by noting that "James McClatchy was never at any time nor under any circumstances 'sole owner' of The *Bee*. He never owned a majority thereof. He was an employee from 1857 to 1866. We refer to him as founder of the *Bee*—and he was, because he was undisputed editor thereof at all times and he laid the policy formation for all subsequent years." But, CK coldly observed: "Your letters to me, combined with your actions, prove that, no matter what your attitude outwardly, in your heart you are not and have not been satisfied with me or my editorial work. You have said it in so many words—you practically repeat it again."[23]

In the midst of their ongoing quarrel, Valentine. brought up the subject of Carlos and questioned his degree of readiness for the editorship, complaining that he, like his father, did not know numbers well or the practicalities of the newspaper business. CK rose to his son's defense:

> I am proud to say that no college professors have yet weakened him one iota in the great principles which James McClatchy instilled into me during nine years of drilling at The *Bee* desk, and which I implanted in Carlos. . . . I told [Carlos] bluntly that if he ever became weaned from the doctrine of the Man before the Dollar, or ever looked upon himself as aught else than a servant of public righteousness and the welfare of God's poorest creatures—he never with my consent would succeed me as Editor of the *Bee*; nor would I permit him during my life to hold a position of editorial trust and responsibility thereon. . . . I am proud . . . to say that Carlos is, if anything even more intensely democratic than I am.[24]

One result of the brothers' heated and defensive exchange was the recognition that the *Bee*'s management policies had to be clarified. When he returned home, CK put together a specific written agreement spelling out the respective responsibilities of each partner—essentially formalizing his understanding that he was, and eventually Carlos would be, the sole voice of the paper, with Valentine and his progeny charged with running the business side of things. Valentine balked at signing the document. He tenaciously refused to surrender his right to control editorial content if he so chose—according it to CK "by delegation" but not irrevocably. "I know . . . of no good reason why such a division should be made; or why either of us should resign the right which he has held to approve or disapprove of measures for which his name as half owner must stand responsible," Valentine reasoned.[25] This all became further complicated when factoring the now-maturing McClatchy offspring into the equation.

The following September, all three James McClatchy grandsons officially became part of the family business. CK had written to the business attorney Milton Green, "Would it be very difficult or take much 'red tape' to increase the number of directors of The *Bee* to seven from five? Jedd is on there now, Carlos is going, so I thought it no more than right and proper that Jim McClatchy should also be there. I suggested this to V.S. yesterday. . . . He said he had no objections and would like it very much, indeed, but did not want to suggest it himself."[26]

Eventually, after CK returned to Sacramento and to work, the whole business of editorial control ended with a whimper. Once CK again felt himself securely at the helm, he acknowledged the efforts of his brother to give him a wide berth and to be sensitive to his feelings about his role at the business. The undertone of the entire incident had been a subtle dispute about succession at the paper. Although the matter seemed to have been resolved, it only went underground, to surface again in 1923. However, the tensions and misunderstandings of 1911 would not be forgotten. For CK's children and likely for Ella they were a painful warning of how devious and underhanded Valentine could be. All the McClatchy children regarded Valentine with mistrust from that time on. Carlos in particular remained resolutely loyal to his father's insistence that attacks on Fox were not to be entertained.[27]

In mid-1911 CK turned his attention back to state politics while he traveled abroad. As noted earlier, he had missed one of the most productive legislative seasons in California history as a raft of Progressive bills were enacted, significantly transforming the Golden State into one of the "laboratories of Democracy." CK returned to the editor's chair and devoted himself to promoting Johnson's program and political career. He and Ella also supervised the building of their new home on Twenty-fourth and U streets and moved in 1912.[28]

Carlos McClatchy

Carlos Kelly McClatchy was supposed to be named after his father, but Ella did not want another Charlie in the house, so they settled on the Spanish version of the name. As per his father's insistence on democratic education (that is, going to school with children of all social classes), Carlos attended the Sacramento Grammar School, where he finished the eighth grade in 1904. He completed Sacramento High School in three years, and in 1907—probably at the urging of Father Kenna—he joined his cousins at "dear old Santa Clara." His grades were average, but he made his first efforts at public writing with two short stories, "What's in a Name" and "For the Children's Sake," published in the *Redwood,* Santa Clara's literary journal. He also contributed brief informational pieces describing the activities of the various classes.[29]

Perhaps like his father, he was unhappy with the discipline of the college, so he transferred to Columbia University in New York in 1908, where he studied history. At Columbia he joined his cousin Brown Maloney. Although his parents were in favor of the move, they worried about the influence of cousin Brown, who apparently was quite immature and did not share McClatchy family politics. Carlos, who had already demonstrated an extraordinary ability to size people up, allayed these fears. He wrote home in 1909: "Do not fear that Brown ever influenced me with any of his eccentric ideas. I have always considered Brown, though he is a nice fellow, as an amusing crank whom it was interesting to listen to as an example of how a man may pervert the gift of thinking." Carlos, who shared his father's hostility to concentrated wealth, added, "I could place no credence in the statements of a man who considers every robbing corporation infallible and impeccable." At one point Carlos planned a European bicycle trip with a graduate student named Martin, who had a law degree from the University of Texas. The two hoped to experience the life of ordinary people. "He practiced in his father's business in Uvalde, Texas. . . . I have learned quite a lot of law from him." The European trip did not materialize, but Carlos did tour the South and West with Martin—and may have confided his preference for law over journalism. The trip to the West included a long train ride to New Orleans, where he boarded a steamer back to New York. "The trip across was hot, dusty, disagreeable and dirty. . . . The people on board were uninteresting or unsociable save a few." He observed, "New Orleans is a quaint, old place, very interesting to visit but I should think it a poor place to live in. They seemed very much behind the times." By his own accounts he did well in college but had difficulties with physics and dropped

German.[30] We know little about his coursework and grades apart from a few preserved college papers. At Columbia he joined the Epsilon Alpha Eta fraternity and finished his coursework in 1911.

During his childhood Carlos seemed to be a normal boy in every way, but Ella fretted endlessly about him. For example in November 1899, when CK and Ella were in San Diego, Carlos contracted a cold, and his older sister Charlotte sent distress signals to her parents. Even though Uncle Valentine (who had his own brood of children) looked in on the children at their Tenth and O Street home, Ella became upset and insisted the family doctor, Dr. Sutliff, check on the boy regularly. Valentine wrote: "I saw Dr. Sutliff today. He says Carlos is entirely recovered and no more trouble. He was very kind going three times a day to the house for the two days not because he thought there was any danger, as he says, but out of personal regard for you and that he might promptly advise me if there should be any change that was not favorable. I am sorry to hear that Ella was disturbed by Charlotte's reports."[31]

CK protected Carlos from too much interference from Ella. In the summer of 1904, when Carlos went off to visit Ella's sister, Mary Frances White, and her family in Colfax, Washington, a horse threw him. When Mary Frances wrote to CK of his son's mishap, he took it in stride: "Such things are to be expected." But, he added, "I shall certainly not tell Mrs. McClatchy anything about it. She would only worry over the matter, it would do her no good and it might result in her calling Carlos home when I know that he needs plenty and plenty of out-door air and exercise."[32]

The Education of an Heir: Carlos

Carlos apparently was expected from birth to become a journalist—a career he may not have wanted. In a moment of bitterness later in life, Carlos recalled: "I did not select newspaper work nor go to work upon The *Bee* purely of my own choice. I would have preferred being a lawyer, but I became a newspaperman as the result of your wishes and my mother's counsel, running as far back as my memory can go. . . . When I thought of entering the law my mother pointed out to me how you planned all your life how I would succeed you and that if I did otherwise you would be broken-hearted."[33]

On November 12, 1908, CK wrote to Colvin Brown, a former reporter for the *Bee* then serving on the California Promotion Committee in New York City, telling him:

I have this day written to Carlos asking him to try his hand, now and then, at a New York letter, and also asking him to see if he can't occasionally furnish a signed article for the editorial page. I want to see what the boy is made of, and also I want to try to encourage him along. But I wish you would see the youngster and give him some points about what you think would be interesting to write about, etc., etc. and tell him some news that would be of interest to the people over here and help him along in various ways.[34]

Carlos did write for the *Bee*.[35] At one point he considered transferring to Harvard University and traveled up to Boston to check out the possibility.[36] At Columbia he was a man in a hurry. Even though he hit some difficulties with physics, he was able to secure the credits he needed to graduate ahead of schedule in 1911. The yearbook for 1911 carried a darkly handsome picture of the graduate and a delightful tribute:

He came because Columbia is in the East, and he wanted to see it; but that it was better? No. Let any man who has 'grown-up' west of the Rocky Mountains remain in the East for a thousand years and he will never admit that it is better than his Pacific-washed coasts. And a son of California? Not in a hundred thousand years. So because we know we cannot make an Easterner out of him we wish him all success in his work in the vocation of his father, and because of his efforts we wish new glory and honor to the Sacramento *Bee*.[37]

The original plan did not include bringing Carlos back to the *Bee* after graduation. CK thought a period of tutelage in the world of New York journalism would help better prepare his son. He twice approached his friend Robert H. Davis, editor of *Munsey's Magazine,* to see if Carlos could land a slot on the *New York Sun*. Before that might have been arranged, apparently CK decided to take Carlos right into the business. "I have changed all my ideas about Carlos," CK wrote to Davis. "I propose to keep him here on The *Bee* where I hope before many years he will take my place."[38]

But it was not clear that Carlos wanted to do this. Alva Johnston, a *New York Times* reporter, was the son of CK's close friend the state printer Al Johnston, and Alva also a friend of Carlos's. He urged the recent graduate to remain in New York to work. CK learned of Johnston's advice when he inadvertently opened and read one of Carlos's letters. Angrily he wrote to Alva:

I want to say to you, however . . . that I can scarcely credit your conduct in this matter. You knew I did not want Carlos to go to New York; you knew my ambition was to have him succeed me here as Editor of The *Bee*; and you should have at least credited me with judgment enough, sense enough and experience enough to know what is proper training for a young man of twenty-one to succeed his father as editor of the paper. Even if you did not know what my ideas were upon the subject, you should have at least been just enough and fair enough with me to advise me upon the subject and not constantly be egging Carlos on to go to New York and be your companion; advising him that there is a place where he can get a proper foundation for journalism. Some day or another, when you are ten or twenty years older, you will recognize the fact that there are other journals in the United State besides the *New York Times*. . . . Carlos will not get any finish in New York that will be any aid to him in his equipment when he takes charge of The *Bee*; in fact Carlos will never be permitted to take charge of The *Bee*, if he should come back from New York with such ideas as seem prevalent there. Carlos is learning more about real newspaper business in California today than he could learn under the methods prevailing in New York. . . . He is now going from town to town in the Northern part of this state, becoming acquainted with the people, being the guest of the correspondents and writing news and sketches. . . . I have written Carlos that he can go to New York if he wants to; but that if he does he will lose all the time on advancement on the *Bee* he is putting in to no purpose.[39]

It is unclear whether Carlos seriously considered Alva Johnston's invitation, because whatever he may have wished to do, he dutifully returned to Sacramento and began his formal apprenticeship with the *Bee*. To get a feel for local conditions, he traveled through the *Bee's* various circulation districts—including the small towns and communities of the northern part of the state (Superior California). Also in 1913, just as the Woodrow Wilson administration began, CK sent his son to Washington, D.C., where he understudied the *Bee* reporter Ernest G. Walker and, with the help of letters of introduction written by his father, learned to cultivate sources and access in the nation's capital. Carlos initially stayed with Marion and Minnie De Vries at the Woodward Apartments. CK put Carlos to work running errands for him in the capital. "I have not received any information of any character from you concerning that request I asked you to make of Representative [William] Kent," he scolded his son in one letter. Insisting that Carlos be organized, he urged, "You should keep a memo book in which you put these requests, either from myself, or from Mr. Chambers or from V.S., and scratch each memo out only when you have finished the detail." Even when CK traveled, he fretted about his son and urged Walker to discreetly keep an eye on Carlos.[40]

CK made sure Carlos's observations of Washington received top billing in the *Bee*. Writing to the assistant editor John Chambers from Milwaukee, CK complained,

> I notice in The *Bee* the other day . . . that a letter from Carlos was put on an interior page with a very poor head on it. I do not object to the interior page at all, but I think the article itself was of vast importance to the fruit growers and to the producers, generally, of California; in fact, although Carlos wrote it—I think it was one of the most interesting things that had appeared in The *Bee* for many a day. I do not believe in cutting down the heads on such an important matter. If Carlos has been correctly informed, the tips which he gave to the producers of California were of the utmost importance.[41]

Young Carlos eventually moved from the De Vries's apartment to stay with Congressman Kent, which was helpful and tested the young man's skills as a mediator. Carlos helped arrange a critical meeting between Kent and Hiram Johnson—who did not like or trust each other—that helped dispel some of the tensions between them.[42]

But Carlos had his missteps. With Senator Henry Cabot Lodge as his source, he reported prematurely that a touchy provision of a Japanese immigration bill had been resolved and cited the name of the Japanese ambassador in this context. The story, picked up by the Associated Press and angrily denied by Ambassador Sutemi Chinda, had to be retracted. Valentine reassuringly wrote to Carlos, "In the matter of the interview with Senator Lodge and your explanation thereof to the Associated Press, I am very glad to see that throughout this matter, and with one very slight and immaterial exception, you have been entirely right—the exception being the excusable use of Ambassador Chinda's name in connection with the first article. . . . San Francisco originally wired Washington that Chinda had approved the language in question on the strength of our statement, based on your original article."[43] Lodge later backed down from his suggestion that Japan had approved the controversial clause of the treaty—and Carlos learned an important lesson about checking sources.

Carlos returned to Sacramento in late August or early September 1913, having thoroughly enjoyed his time in the nation's capital. Writing to his co-worker Ernest G. Walker, Carlos said, "I have been reading with much interest the good stories you have been sending out about [Thomas] Fox. A number of people have commented upon them to me. I sometimes wish I were making the rounds of the Capitol again with you or riding around in that little devil bus wagon of yours."[44] He continued writing for the *Bee*, working all around the upper valley of Superior California and preparing for the next gubernatorial bout in 1914.

In 1914 CK arranged to have Carlos follow Hiram Johnson's reelection campaign. In the summer of 1914, when one of the *Bee* general managers took a vacation at the same time CK and Ella were away, CK appointed Carlos to oversee the editorial work. CK wrote proudly to James Barry, "I notice in the recent Star that you pay quite a compliment to my son. I believe the kid is getting along splendidly. For five weeks he fully [managed] one-half of the editorial work with myself, while Mr. Lawson was away on vacation. Everybody says he did remarkably well." At the end of the summer Carlos accompanied Hiram Johnson on the campaign trail as he was battling for a second term against Democrat John Fredericks. Carlos turned in a series of well-written reports and gained a host of contacts around the state.[45]

After Johnson's reelection Carlos returned to the Superior California beat, investigating conditions all around the valley and the delta and even trying his hand at writing lurid articles that attracted readership.[46] Carlos took on more and more assignments and was regularly featured on the front page as "C. K. McClatchy, Jr."[47] In 1916 he accompanied his father to the state political conventions, and both father and son sent back their impressions of the events.[48] Carlos continued to cover the campaign, which found the *Bee* supporting Woodrow Wilson but with misgivings about his lack of leadership in the international crisis that had become the First World War. After the election Carlos offered commentary on the long-held plan to consolidate all state offices in Sacramento through the construction of new buildings near the capitol.[49] With growing confidence and the support of his parents and the *Bee* staff, Carlos began to prepare himself for the next great chapter of his life.

Chapter Fourteen
World War I

◆

CK KNEW LITTLE about other countries, except as a tourist. Nonetheless, he often ventured into foreign affairs generally, consistently advancing anti-imperialist viewpoints. However, as time went on, his willed ignorance of complex international relations suggested he had no real understanding that the United States was now a force in global affairs. Thus the *Bee* became an example of the ostrich press he condemned in other papers.

World War I began in August 1914, and shortly afterward Pope Pius X died. CK, who had been impressed with the pontiff, expressed his condolences to a friendly American priest in Rome: "We are all horror stricken at the war in Europe. It is believed over here that grief over this monstrous international crime hastened the death of the good Pope." CK's first reaction to the war was revulsion. The war was the fruit of a rotten diplomatic tree bred by European power politics, arrogance, and mindless nationalism. Referring to the warring nations of Europe, he noted, "The foreign policy of these nations has plunged a very great proportion of the civilized world into the most infamous crime in history. That was simply and solely for territorial aggrandizement, world influence and the extension of trade." Even before guns began blazing in August, the Sacramento editor predicted, "If war materializes, a new history will be made. The map of Europe will be changed. Great nations may be weakened and smaller nations made great. . . . Women in Europe . . . . will have the death of a father, brother or husband to mourn. . . . Wives who lived in the honor of their husband's eyes may sell their virtue to feed little mouths. For every stirring victory there will be thousands of corpses and as many desolate homes."[1]

As "lights went out all over Europe," CK applauded President Wilson's declaration of U.S. neutrality. Ever alert to compromised patriotism, CK cast a wary eye on "hyphenated-Americans" (for example German-Americans, Irish-Americans), insisting they foreswear their ancestral loyalties. "Columbia is a jealous mother," he lectured. "She demands from her sons and daughters—adopted as well as native—undivided allegiance."[2]

However, neutrality was hard to maintain. Reports of German atrocities in Belgium and elsewhere, many of them planted by British propagandists, reawakened CK's scorn for Kaiser Wilhelm, whom he lambasted as "crazed with war fever, insane with insatiable ambition and drunk with egotism."[3] The sinking of the *Lusitania* in May 1915 elicited a swell of patriotic support for President Wilson's stern words to the German government demanding respect for freedom of the seas.

As the war unfolded, the British declared an illegal blockade to which the Germans responded with U-boat activity. Anti-German feeling notwithstanding, CK spent much time criticizing the British, whose motives and behavior he always suspected. "This country cannot with self-respect allow England to dictate what we shall and shall not ship. . . . The United States is not a subsidiary ammunition factory and commissary department for Great Britain." He fervently maintained that America's neutrality on the high seas had to be respected by Great Britain. In fact he was so often critical of the British that when Valentine complained about the dearth of editorial outrage at Germany's behavior. CK retorted defensively: "You are in error regarding silence concerning Germany's course. *Bee* editorials thereon have been as strong as the English language could make them—not only concerning butchery on the seas but as well murder from the air."[4]

Through 1914 and 1915 McClatchy held fast to his neutralist position. He lamented the resignation of his friend William Jennings Bryan, who left the State Department in protest of Wilson's aggressive stand in the *Lusitania* sinking.[5] Privately and publicly CK criticized the belligerent declarations of former president Theodore Roosevelt, who was Wilson's most trenchant critic. "I firmly believe," he wrote in 1915, "that were Theodore Roosevelt president of the United States, we would not only be in a war with Mexico today, but we would be a participant in the great international crime which is now slaughtering hundreds of thousands in Europe."[6]

By 1916, however, CK began to moderate his reflexive distrust of Great Britain and edge away from his strict neutralism. He traveled to Washington, D.C., in the spring and from there wrote a series of articles praising efforts to keep both Germany and England on a short tether.[7] When his old nemesis Peter Yorke came to Sacramento for a church dedication and urged the mostly Irish American listeners to pray to the Virgin Mary for "their kith and kin who are fighting their ancient enemy [Great Britain] for the honor of God and the glory of Ireland," CK bellowed his disapproval on the front page of the *Bee*, lashing Yorke for calling for a German triumph over France and Britain.[8]

The Presidential Campaign of 1916

As the carnage mounted in Europe, CK worried that the United States might be drawn into the conflict. Hiram Johnson had declared his candidacy for the U.S. Senate and of course CK strongly supported him. However, CK was ambiguous about whom he would support for the presidency in 1916. He had certainly lost his early enthusiasm for Wilson (as he did with every public official except Hiram) but cherished no warm feelings for the potential Republican nominees, Theodore Roosevelt and New York governor Charles Evans Hughes. As the primaries and nominating conventions drew near, CK directed his staff: "Kindly refrain from anything that would sound like a preference for Wilson as against Roosevelt, or for Roosevelt against Wilson unless I shall give orders to the contrary. . . . Very few Americans of a decidedly independent cast of mind have today made up their minds as to exactly what they intend to do. So I do not want The *Bee* put in any position from which there can be no very satisfactory retreat."[9]

Before he and Carlos departed for the political conventions of 1916, he also instructed his staff about neutrality:

> The editorials should keep strictly to the line of neutrality in the European contest, being careful to show no signs of partiality to either the cause of the Allies or to the cause of Germany. Of course this does not mean that The *Bee* should not most zealously and most vigorously rebuke anything on the part of Germany or England, or any other fighting nation that interferes with the rights of American citizens or American commerce or that violates the principles of humanity. But always it should be kept in mind that The *Bee* plays no favorite in this European fight. . . . Its only hope is that no matter who is victor the ultimate result within a comparatively short period of time will be the extermination of kings from the face of the earth.[10]

Eventually the Republicans came together around Charles Evans Hughes, who began a spirited campaign to take the White House. However, when the Republican nominee came to a California hotel where Hiram Johnson was staying but did not meet or appear with him, CK deemed Hughes unsuitable for the presidency. On the eve of the election, CK wrote to Franklin K. Lane, "I have come to the conclusion that Wilson will be re-elected. I could not have been for Wilson had Hughes come out like a man on certain propositions; for there are a great many things about the Wilson Administration in connection with national and particularly Mexican affairs that I don't like at all. But I think the result will be in my present disgust with Hughes, that on November 7th little Charlie will walk up to the polls and cast a vote for Woodrow Wilson."[11] Wilson won the election after a cliffhanger of a campaign—and with the electoral votes of California sealing his victory. Some unhappy Republicans blamed the loss on Johnson's failure to work for the Hughes campaign in the Golden State.

The War Cometh

The talk soon turned again to war. Germany's decision to resume unrestricted submarine warfare tipped the position of the *Bee*. After the revelations of the famous Zimmerman note—a missive from the German foreign ministry to its emissary in Mexico—which urged Mexico to make war on the United States in league with Germany (and in early reports implicated Japan in the plot) surfaced, CK insisted that whatever sympathy existed for Germany among Americans "should be wiped out by the exposure of Germany's treacherous enmity . . . against a peaceful country."[12]

After reporting the rupture of diplomatic relations with Germany and the ongoing harassment of American vessels by German U-boats, CK finally cheered Wilson's call for war before a joint session of Congress on April 2, 1917: "A righteous war has been invoked for the safety of our citizens, the integrity of our Nation and the principles of humanity. . . . Let it be a fight to the finish between humanity on one side and the Kaiser's hellishness on the other." In words he would later regret, he noted in the next day's editorial, "All our past prejudices and established principles concerning entangling alliances must for the moment disappear in the face of a common danger and in ridding the world of a common enemy."[13]

When the United States entered the war, CK gave instructions to his reporters: "During the continuance of this war I desire as little as possible [written] that would hurt the feelings of the Germans as a race of people. Smash as hard as you like at the Kaiser, at the Hohenzollerns, and at Kaiserism, but have a good word occasionally for the German people whose greatest enemy is not in the field of armed opposition to Wilhelm, but is in the personality of Wilhelm himself." When the word *Hun* was used in the *Bee* to refer to Germans, CK sent a stern memo: "The Prussian, or the German, or the Hohenzollern army is never under any circumstances to be called the Hun and that the Germans are not to be described as Huns. . . . Kindly cut it out." CK also avoided hyping the horror stories about German military tactics that British propagandists fed to American newspapers.[14]

CK would become caught up in wartime hysteria, but at the outset he was skeptical of those who profited from the war. In a slap at the Chamber of Commerce, whose members tagged laborers wanting better pay as disloyal, CK had no patience for "the very Pecksniffs bewailing loudly the 'disloyalty' of the working classes, [who] were themselves not so intensely 'patriotic' that they permitted their 'loyalty' to interfere with their thrift. These were the institutions and the men that . . . thought it a very opportune moment to take England by the throat and compel her to submit to a most outrageous multiplication of prices for coal, for shipping, and for other indispensable commodities and carriers."[15]

When he heard later that Liberty Bonds, many of which had been purchased by ordinary Americans, would be devalued, CK demanded answers from William Kent, who represented the Sacramento area in Congress. "The trouble with the financial policy of the government, however, is, my dear Kent, that it doesn't run its own finances but lets Wall Street and the bankers run such policy for it for the benefit of Wall Street and the bankers. The patriotism of Wall Street in general, and the bankers also, is largely bunk." At CK's urging, another member of Congress from California, Charles Curry, drafted remedial legislation. In his reply to Curry CK quoted Curry's words acknowledging the editor's role in shaping the legislation: "'My bill, a copy of which I enclose, which almost in its entirety was prepared by you or under your direction, would effectually prevent gambling in Liberty Loan or other war bonds.'" CK continued, "I would like in this matter, my dear Curry, if you don't object, to take a certain portion of the credit for that bill. . . . I don't care a cent about that for myself, but all those kinds of matters are good advertisements for The *Bee*. . . . I want to have The *Bee*, if possible, recognized all over as one of the great papers of the Pacific Coast; and every little thing of this character helps."[16]

CK, who also wanted to make sure the pain of fighting the war did not fall on enlistees alone, supported the draft. He telegraphed Johnson: "General sentiment here favors conscription. Mothers and Fathers do not want their sons volunteering while others remain at home since war opened, demand for conscription is becoming universal. The people generally here hope you will see your way clear to vote for conscription without any provision for volunteers for that will only make still another precedent to perpetuate [an] unfair and inefficient volunteer system." After Congress approved the draft in 1917 and draft boards were established, CK denounced any able-bodied Sacramento boy who tried to duck conscription. Whenever CK heard of an exemption of an able-bodied man (particularly from a wealthy family), he raised doubts about the person's patriotism and occasionally printed his name in the paper. Such was the case of Henry Heilbron Jr., the scion of a wealthy local German American family, who, CK noted in a letter to Bert Meek, "is to be exempted. . . . Now the Heilbrons are wealthy. . . . And incidentally, for your own information, it might be mentioned that any man in Sacramento who knows the Heilbrons will tell you that they have been all along intensely pro-German, if not anti-American."[17]

One casualty of the war was CK's appreciation of President Wilson. Everything, from preparedness to mobilization, became the subject of increasingly harsher criticism. Here he no doubt was also influenced by the almost pathological hatred Johnson held for the president. When Johnson all but accused Wilson of cowardice after the declaration of war—maintaining "Wilson does not intend really to get into war. His purpose is to fight with our dollars to the last Frenchman and Englishman"—CK readily agreed, even though soldiers and airmen were already being trained. Since neither of these armchair generals had ever been in combat and had no idea of the complexities of mobilization in the decentralized economy of the United States, they became impatient with the lack of action. Their complaints were petty and personal; CK even did an ideological back flip when Wilson turned down Theodore Roosevelt's grandstanding request to lead a regiment overseas. CK had spilled gallons of ink complaining about Roosevelt's narcissism and shoot-first-ask-questions-later approach to foreign relations. Now he criticized Wilson for "playing very poor, low-down, peanut politics."[18]

The Personal Toll of the War

The war took its toll on *Bee* staffers—including Carlos, who enlisted in the military, making the editor's job even more intense. In response to a June 1918 request from Johnson to come to Washington for a long stay, CK had to say no: "Everything has happened just wrong. Carlos is away; Lawson is sick half the time; we have a variegated collection of men on the staff of the garden variety—most of whom don't know Sacramento and some of whom don't seem to know anything of any character—and we are all shot to pieces." He also informed Hiram that Valentine "has been ordered away by his doctor for a couple of months—whether he will go or not is a question; all these damned fool McClatchys are stubborn—and you will see why I can't very well get over there." Val then extended his leave to six months and in November took a fateful trip to Asia that would solidify his already negative feelings about Japanese immigration.[19] CK and the managing editor, J. Earl Langdon, ran the day-to-day affairs of the paper.

Carlos Goes to War

The war's awful reality hit home as the McClatchy sons of both families enlisted in the armed forces—the first of the clan to see combat. In 1916 cousin J. V. McClatchy, a member of the National Guard, began serving on the Mexican border. At the beginning of July 1916, twenty-six-year-old Carlos reported for a month of training at the National Guard training camp in Monterey. "I go to the Monterey army camp tomorrow," he wrote Hiram Johnson on July 8, 1916. His temporary stint ended quickly, however, and in August he was back at the *Bee*. "The training camp at Monterey afforded very good training and gave me an insight of military matters I had not had before," he wrote to his uncle. He also observed, "I became very much interested during the slight glimpse of army life we had at Monterey—enough, however, to make me a firm believer as I have been before, in the justice and the necessity of universal military training."[20]

Carlos opened up a channel to William T. Haley, a quartermaster at Nogales, where a number of Northern California soldiers were deployed:

> I want to have all news of any interest concerning any of the Sacramento and Superior California companies, in the way of promotion, sickness, or any little camp gossip about their doings that will interest 'the home folks.' The *Bee* also wants stories on conditions in camp in the way of food, poor lodging, or bad treatment in any way, when actual facts justify such publication. The paper, however, does not want unfounded criticisms on trivial annoyances that cannot be helped where so many men have to be taken care of. But it does want to give a just account of any conditions that should be remedied.[21]

Later Carlos ran a straw poll on the subject of compulsory military service among the Californians at the Mexican border.[22] At his urging the paper began to talk up the cause of preparedness and better planning for an eventual increase in the number of men under arms.

Once America entered the war in 1917 Carlos reported to the Presidio in San Francisco, where he underwent basic training in the Reserve Officers' Training Corps. CK heard regularly from his son and began to pass on Carlos's complaints about camp conditions to government officials. One typical letter to Johnson raged about military procurement: "Down at the Presidio where Carlos is, things are in such a delightful state of 'preparedness' that the Commissary Department hasn't even any socks for the 2500 young men in the Reserve Officers Training Corps." Carlos survived the sockless summer and in August was assigned to Camp Lewis in Washington State, where he became part of the Ninety-first Division of the 362nd Infantry—known variously as the Wild West Division, the Powder River Division, and the Pine Tree Division. He wrote to his mother: "Everything is going finely. I am getting healthier every day and with a heavier tan. Half past five seems [a] fairly natural hour now [to rise], or [at] least I am reconciled to it as a necessary evil. Yesterday and today I was corporal in charge of my squad, a job that rotates. I had a lot of fun putting them through the manual of arms and marchings."[23] In August 1917 CK noted proudly to his friend Ulric Collins,

> Carlos has been awarded a First Lieutenancy after a drastic course of treatment by regular army officers at the Presidio. Mrs. McClatchy and I feel a bit elated over the matter, since we did not expect the boy to get anything but a Second Lieutenancy and would have been perfectly satisfied with that. In fact Carlos himself stated that even if he did not get a Second Lieutenancy, he was not going to shirk . . . but would go in the second camp and if he failed there he would enlist somehow even if he chanced to be a high private.[24]

The days at Camp Lewis were long, and the poor conditions spread influenza and other communicable diseases. When Johnson inquired about the camp during a Christmas visit to California in 1917, CK replied, "Primarily, the Government of the United States made an ass of itself in selecting that site—or rather in accepting it. . . . The place in winter is a bog. The parade ground is to a large extent a pond. It rains incessantly and minimizes very much the opportunities for drill and all kinds of practice. Besides, the atmosphere is depressing to a great many of the boys. But the sanitary conditions there are most admirable. The boys not in the hospital never looked so well in their lives."[25] Carlos remained at Camp Lewis for the remainder of 1917 until he shipped out to France on July 6, 1918. Life in the service seemed to agree with the personable young man. He was also ready to make another profound change in his life. While waiting to ship over to France, he decided to marry Phebe Briggs on January 19, 1918.

Phebe Briggs was born November 8, 1892, in Sacramento, the daughter of a local ophthalmologist, William Ellery Briggs, and Grace Rideout.[26] The Briggs family was quite active in local cultural and social affairs and financially well off, thanks to the wealthy Rideout connections. The family was prosperous enough to travel abroad and to send Phebe to a Miss Ransom's school in Piedmont, a finishing school for young women. Following in her mother's footsteps, she enrolled at Vassar College, graduating Phi Beta Kappa. Phebe was an energetic young woman, hailed as a genuine hero when she saved four of five Vassar classmates from drowning after their toboggan careened down the campus's Sunset Hill and smashed through the thin ice of an artificial lake on the Vassar campus (one of the young women became caught under the ice and perished). Phebe met Carlos during her senior year when she was working on a thesis about the Industrial Workers of the World in the Wheatland Riot of 1913. In order that she might learn more firsthand, her parents introduced her to Carlos, who had covered the IWW for the *Bee* and knew many of its leading members. The McClatchys and the Briggses knew each other socially. CK and William Briggs regarded each other warily. Briggs was a devout nondrinker and openly censorious about CK's periodic bouts of public intoxication, which Briggs noted regularly from his office window. Briggs was also quite progressive in his politics—even further to the left of the generally progressive CK.[27] Briggs was also an atheist, a matter that CK was content to leave in peace but that did not accord with his own spiritual path.

The issue of religion loomed large, especially for Ella, when the young couple fell in love and planned marriage. Even though Carlos, like his father, was a fallen-away Catholic, he had to contend with his mother's insistence that her children be married in the presence of a priest. The couple decided around New Year's 1917 to marry before Carlos went overseas. On January 15, 1918, Carlos sent a telegram to his mother from Camp Lewis: "Phebe and I are engaged. Plans to be married this Saturday. Though a hard trip I want you and the family to be here ever so much. If date impossible will change it. Just decided all this so couldn't let you know before. I know CK and you will like your new daughter."[28]

The telegram hit the McClatchy household with a thud. Not only were CK and Ella reluctant to endorse a wartime marriage, but Ella was doubly distressed that they did not plan to be married by a priest. That she refused to attend under those circumstances astounded Phebe, who remarked to her fiancé, "Well, that's too bad; you're her only son and you're going away to war. She ought to be at your wedding." Phebe ultimately mollified Ella and agreed to be married by a priest. Carlos found a priest from Seattle and rapidly completed church forms for a dispensation for "mixed religion" (granting a Catholic permission to wed a non-Catholic). The two were married in the Washington Hotel in Seattle—with the McClatchys, including Ella, in attendance. But the addition of a priest changed the plans of Phebe's grandmother Rideout, who disapproved of organized religion and for a time cut her granddaughter out of her will. She later relented and not only restored Phebe but would later contribute to the fund that saved the *Bee* for CK and Carlos. CK approved of the match. To Johnson he wrote: "Ella and I are both delighted. Phebe Briggs is a remarkably fine girl." He and Ella overcame their misgivings about a wartime marriage, telling Johnson: "If anything happened to Carlos over in France and he and Phebe would not wed, she would never forgive us for having pleaded that the marriage be put over until after the war."[29]

When Carlos's departure overseas was imminent, CK and Ella took Phebe into their household for a time. "Carlos' wife has been down here for a few days," he wrote to Senator Johnson in May 1918, "and he has telegraphed her. That is the only symptom—if it can be one—that I have seen anywhere that would tend to show a spirit of coming alacrity in the moving of the troops. For months and months the boys have been expecting to go next week; but they are still here."[30]

Over There

On July 6, 1918, the Ninety-first Division sailed from New York in fourteen camouflaged ships "packed with doughboys jammed down in the holds, in four and five tier bunks." Arriving in Liverpool, the troops were temporarily parked in a "rest camp" and then made their way to Southampton and from there to the port of Le Havre. Carlos's transfer to the front was nearly cut short when an engine going sixty miles an hour hit his train. A number of his comrades died even before reaching the front. Recovering from the disaster, the troops drilled and maneuvered for six weeks around Montigny-Le-Roi in Haute-Marne. The regiment was called up as a reserve for the St. Mihiel salient but never used. Finally, they were rolled into position to replace French troops at the Argonne—a stalemated battlefield "of trenches and defensive works that had resisted for four years all the efforts of the French." Carlos was in the Argonne from September 22 to October 12—twenty days of hell. Telling the story in a series of serialized articles that later appeared in the *Bee,* Carlos painstakingly reconstructed the details of the battle. He movingly described the mood before the attack began, the horrible pounding of the artillery, and winced at the ill-considered comments of a chaplain who warned the men about hell the night before they attacked. In dramatic terms Carlos recalled the moment of going over the top—at first meeting little or no resistance and then finally running into German machine guns and snipers. Worst of all was being caught in the fire of the American artillery: "The worst the most sickening part of the whole war which came nearer to ruining the morale more than anything else was when our artillery . . . began to fall short and came crashing among our own men."[31]

On September 26 the Ninety-first was ordered to attack the city of Gesnes, requiring American soldiers to break through some of the most formidable German defense works on the western front. Above Gesnes the Germans had placed deadly accurate artillery batteries that swept the open hills the Americans had to traverse. Off to the sides German snipers and riflemen were prepared to rake the American ranks. At 3:45 a.m. the command was given to attack. "Turning from the phone, the Colonel called the officers together. All of them knew as well as he what the order meant—the practical annihilation of the regiment. Few men could hope to survive that rain of fire alive and reach Gesnes," Carlos told the *Bee's* readers.[32] In a remarkable letter of October 24, 1918 to his in-laws, Carlos described his experience on September 26 only generically. The Gesnes assault required the regiment to advance across three open ridges, covered with heavy artillery and mines. He detailed for his in-laws a scene reminiscent of the Alamo:

> The Colonel, said he was going himself and wanted to know who was going with him, whereupon Carlos McClatchy, perhaps with a slight gulp for Phebe, said he was. So everybody lined up, whether it was their business or not, right down to regimental clerks and cooks. It was magnificent, glorious, that body of men marching bravely forward to take heavy artillery with rifles and bayonets across three

kms of shell swept area. . . . Men were dropping on every hand, but no one faltered. . . . To make a long story short, over half our regiment was left dead and dying on those ridges when the remnants reached and took the town, myself one of the remnants, by what fortunate chance I do not know.[33]

Here he revealed that he was an information officer shuttling information back and forth between the front and command—a prime target for snipers and susceptible to gas and artillery explosions. Carlos went back and forth many times during the bloody Argonne engagement. "The Colonel tells everybody I was under more shell-fire than anyone in the regiment, and I certainly know I had my share, for I went forward with each advance, and in addition was out on special missions that kept me exposed to shell-fire, machine gun barrages and snipers." He continued, "That night the Colonel sent me back to the General with a message for reinforcements. It was pitch dark, with the wounded on every hand. The glory of war there may be in the daytime, but at night it is obscured by the terrible sights and sounds of the battlefield."[34]

For his heroism Carlos received a battlefield promotion to the rank of captain. "I suppose by this time you have heard about Carlos's promotion to a Captaincy," CK crowed to Valentine, "for gallantry in battle. . . . We haven't heard any of the particulars yet, so know nothing more than what was in the telegram." But joy, accompanied by a champagne toast in the *Bee* office, turned to fear when no personal word arrived from Carlos. To allay Ella's fears, CK had the *Bee* correspondent in Washington contact Franklin Lane and Marion De Vries "to get some word over there to find out how Carlos is. . . . His mother thinks that he was wounded at that time and that is the reason she hasn't been able to hear from him." Finally, Carlos sent a message to his mother after the armistice was declared. A relieved CK wrote to William Kent, "Carlos states that he got out of the battle which assured his family that he was alive without a scratch, although he wonders now why he wasn't killed a dozen times."[35]

The 362nd—depleted in numbers, tired, hungry, and badly shaken—was given only a brief respite and on October 29 was ordered back into battle in Belgium, where the infantry was put under the command of the Belgian king and thrown into an attack on another open area—the Lys Scheldt offensive. They drove the Germans back and pursued them up to the very day of the armistice, November 11.[36] The division sustained 5,838 casualties, twenty-three were taken as prisoners of war.

Demobilization

Carlos returned to the United States in April 1919 and was welcomed home with relief and gladness. What had yet to be determined was the toll of the long months at the dank Camp Lewis and the period of waiting—November 1918 to April 1919—in cold and overcast Belgium after the war. Most important was the psychological impact of the horrors he had seen in the Argonne offensive and especially the annihilation of his regiment and friends at Gesnes. Gesnes had cost much American blood and valor—and in the end was evacuated. Even though the offensive itself helped end the war, this must have been disturbing. Robert Molander, who conducted research on Carlos in the 1980s, observed: "The war had been kind to him [Carlos] in that he was not wounded or killed, but he never forgot it. Like many who have been in the true thick of battle, he was not one to boast of his military service. But it remained in his thoughts and he was never able to erase it."[37] While it is impossible to be certain, the traumatic experiences of the war may have contributed to a propensity to alcoholism. His parents and others blamed the long wait in Belgium as the origin of his ultimately fatal addiction to drink. Even before he put on the uniform of the United States, Carlos was going on "Kellys"—as the family called his long periodic drinking sprees. No doubt he was, as many boys from upper middle-class families were, unprepared for the boredom and the peculiar dynamics of military life. The tensions of waiting and then the impending and real horrors of combat may have produced the kind of stress he could relieve only with alcohol—in much the same way as his father.

Carlos also grew up in an alcoholic household—with a father he saw inebriated and a mother who seemed to be in denial about many things in life. The expectations of the *Bee* and his family obligations were perhaps more than Carlos could bear. At any rate the war left an imprint on him, as it did on millions of veterans who endured the horrors of the front and survived. As Molander noted, Carlos rarely referred to his military experience—reluctant as many authentic combat veterans are to say much about what he had seen and experienced. But it is fair to surmise he was as much a casualty of war as those who lost life or limb. He wondered why he had been spared on those ridges at Gesnes—perhaps that question haunted him as he grew older and only the solace of drink allowed him to dim the memories.

Chapter Fifteen
Failed Dreams, Self-Imposed Exile

◆

THE PERIOD OF CK'S LIFE from the end of World War I until his death in 1936 consisted of a roller coaster of emotions and responsibilities. As the new decade dawned, CK fervently hoped he could hand over the day-to-day affairs of the newspaper to Carlos and spend months traveling abroad. But everything seemed to go wrong. The era of Progressive reform ended, and conservative governors and presidents kept him in a permanent state of apoplexy. Nowhere did the change hit him more than in the failure of his efforts to elect his friend Hiram Johnson president. In 1920 the nation elected the doltish Warren Harding, who was succeeded by the reactionary Calvin Coolidge. Although he left the country on several long trips abroad, CK's health was deteriorating badly. Each time he returned there was some crisis with the *Bee*. During this sad decade he broke relations with his brother and his brother's family. His dreams for a Progressive California and a peaceful transition of power to Carlos at the *Bee* also crashed and burned.

The Dying of the Light: Progressivism Wanes

CK never had any faith in Johnson's gubernatorial successor, William D. Stephens. A Progressive former member of Congress, Lieutenant Governor Stephens had been placed on the Republican-Progressive ticket in 1914 at the behest of Edward Dickson of the *Los Angeles Express*. Johnson disliked Stephens, and after Hiram was elected to the Senate, he deliberately strung out his transition of power until the last minute in order to embarrass the incoming governor. With his fingers crossed CK promised an open mind, telling Stephens he would "be judged fairly and squarely by your public acts." But CK had a higher loyalty to Johnson. The former governor was depressed and feeling rejected as he moved to Washington. CK consoled him: "You are entirely mistaken about the attitude of the people of California being: 'The king is dead. Long live the king.' I don't find any such feeling anywhere. I think you are a bigger man in this State right now than you ever were." But this heartfelt sentiment was not just about helping Johnson through one of his periodic slumps. CK believed that neither Stephens nor anyone else who sat in the governor's chair could ever replace Johnson in fortitude, grit, and true Progressive leadership. By late April 1917—hardly a month into the new governor's term—CK declared to Johnson that he had not met Stephens "and I have no desire to go out of my way to meet him." CK lamented: "I had hoped my impression of Stephens was erroneous—that he would prove to be better than he sounded at first. I think he will prove to be worse." CK dismissed those who thought "Stephens will make good," noting even his supporters admitted "he is lacking in punch; does not like to make enemies; has neither the force nor the inclination to push straight ahead through all barriers that you [Johnson] had."[1] CK sandbagged Stephens at every step, criticizing his decisions and holding him in contempt because he was not Hiram. Although Stephens would win election in his own right in 1918, CK opposed him and did whatever he could to undermine him, politically and otherwise. Stephens was a Progressive through and through but had one fatal flaw as far as CK was concerned: he wasn't Hiram Johnson. By undermining him CK brought about conservative rule, which he detested even more.

Johnson for President

While tending to Senate Affairs, Johnson, too, did his best to make Stephens's life miserable. Johnson, who also took a leading role in demolishing Woodrow Wilson's hopes for American participation in the League of Nations, entertained prospects of running for president in 1920. CK encouraged him, stating that Johnson had shown his abilities on the national stage when he was the Bull Moose Party's vice presidential candidate in 1912. Johnson's accession to the Senate in 1917 came just as the Progressive tide that had propelled him into office was cresting, and the national movement—including the Bull Moose Party—was fading away. "I motored down to Marion De Vries ranch Sunday," CK wrote to Johnson in June 1917, barely four months after he had entered the Senate. "He told me that it was his honest conviction that you would be the Republican nominee for president in 1920 and that you would be elected. And he told me that you had already obtained a wonderful hold over there with the Republicans who will have a great deal to say in the next National Convention."[2]

As usual, Johnson dithered about whether to run. But CK had no doubts and used his contacts with other journalists to drum up support for the senator. On April 17, 1919, CK published an often reproduced *Bee* editorial endorsing Hiram Johnson's candidacy. In "Issues in the Next Presidential Campaign and the Man for Standard Bearer," CK suggested that two issues would dominate the upcoming campaign: government ownership and "Americanism" (shorthand for the ongoing debate about the collective security aspects of the covenant of the League of Nations). CK sought to erase Johnson's sometimes abrasive and hypercritical image, and to focus attention on Johnson's dynamic and creative term as governor. CK also leaned heavily on Johnson's opposition to the league. Johnson was so successful, CK boasted, that even his former enemies now supported him.[3] Johnson managed to win a few primaries, stirring his hopes in the spring, but the mercurial solon never forged the campaign organization needed to propel him to the nomination. Many regular Republicans still blamed him for Hughes's loss of California to Wilson in 1916. CK ardently defended Johnson and used all his wiles but to no avail. The nomination went to Senator Warren G. Harding of Ohio.

Into Exile

By the time the historic 1920 election was held—the first in which all American women could participate—CK was already on a grand tour of Europe. CK and Ella took three major trips abroad in the 1920s: a sort of self-imposed exile, providing an escape from the Harding presidency and the advent of Prohibition. In 1920 CK was nearly sixty-one years old and had been writing and editing the *Bee* for almost thirty-seven years. Unlike his previous trip in 1911, on this trip CK did not have to worry what his devious brother might do to the *Bee* in his absence. Carlos was home and could look out for family affairs. The young man was eager to try his hand at administering the editorial department of the *Bee* and believed he had received enough tutelage to manage the business. CK was eager to "give the kid a try." Carlos was also ready to begin a family with Phebe.

Ella decided upon a lengthy European journey that would take the family (her, CK, and Eleanor and a companion) out of the country for nearly two years. The route first took them north to Washington State to visit their daughter Charlotte and her family, then through Canada to Quebec, where they boarded an ocean liner for London. From London, with the help of Cook's Tours, they planned an extensive itinerary "made in accord with seasonal and even more particularly political conditions." Before his departure CK wrote a sassy "Private Think," expressing his delight in escaping the "offensive and sometimes ridiculous Statutes [Prohibition], heavy with the oppressive atmosphere of slavery to Puritanism."[4] After a brief stay in England the route took them to the Continent, North Africa, Egypt, and the Holy Land.

CK was always a tourist, and most of the itinerary was typical of well-to-do Americans who flaunted their wealth in postwar Europe. However, in May 1921 the family traveled with reverence to the Meuse Argonne battlefront in France, where only three years before their son Carlos was in bloody battle. "Desolation met us on every side—village after village in ruins. The whole landscape, after we got into the battlefield region, was one seemingly unending mass of barbed wire and trenches, save where the work of rehabilitation had covered up Earth's sores, and where the nodding wheat was ripening in the kisses of the sun."[5] On May 9 they arrived at the Argonne Forest, also war-scarred: "Miles and miles of barbed-wire defenses are still to be seen; miles after miles of trenches; miles after miles of dugouts—while shell holes everywhere gave a pockmark effect to the face of Mother Earth." Pushing on through the battlefield forest, they finally came to Gesnes to look over the ground where the 362nd Infantry had charged. CK wrote a series of three poignant articles about his experience at the battlefields.[6] He described the devastation in ancient cities like Rheims as well as the villages, memorializing Gesnes and remarking on graffiti left by an anonymous doughboy—"To My Dear Mother." At the nearby cemetery they placed flowers on the graves of Captain Leon Martin and Edwin Elam, friends of Carlos's. In the final article from that site CK rehearsed the bitterness of Americans and Europeans who had fought to make the world safe for democracy and who ended up quarreling over the spoils of victory. Of course, he lost no opportunity to attack the League of Nations. From the battlefields the family went, no doubt at Ella's insistence, to the healing waters of Lourdes near the Pyrenees Mountains. CK did not take the baths but marveled at the faith of the people and the magnificent candlelight procession that took place with the thousands of pilgrims each night.[7]

After a trip to Constantinople, they returned to Vienna and had great difficulty finding a decent hotel, and at one point revolutionaries surrounded their lodging. In Vienna CK again repeated his belief, which he had first enunciated a year earlier, that economic relief should no longer be sent to Europe. Asked in early 1920 to contribute to the Near East Relief, CK wrote the petition-er: "With all due respect, I will have to say that I will not contribute anoth-er cent—for the present at least—to any cause of any character not confined to the United States. . . . We have been an easy mark too long . . . there is . . . plenty of poverty right here in the Immediate West. There are plenty and plenty of children in the City of Sacramento to be cared for, and they are very poorly cared for." In a diatribe for the *Bee* he wrote: "America is the largest in-ternational sucker that ever lived. We should quit playing Santa Claus and the Good Samaritan. This applies to Armenia and Austria. I found America feed-ing children that were rosy, healthy and athletic. Austrians are lazy and won't work, while America feeds Austrian children. Rich, profiteering Armenians in Constantinople don't contribute a cent to help their needy countrymen, but leave that to the United States."[8]

The second journey to Europe in 1926 combined sightseeing with periods of therapy at German baths and other therapeutic sites. CK wrote: "While the readers of The *Bee* are perusing these lines, the writer thereof will be on his way across the continent in sail from New York on the good ship *Homeric*. . . . His present intention is to be gone at least a year." This did not preclude regular communication with Johnson, "because I do not think it advisable for me to be in entire ignorance during all these weeks of those things I should know—some of which I might need as ammunition in the paper." After a brief stay in England, CK and Ella availed themselves of the waters at various baths and warm springs. In late September they went to Geneva, where he pretended to report objectively on the League of Nations. He and Ella took rooms at the Hotel Metropole, one block from the assembly hall of the league. Ella went first to the league gathering and pronounced it tedious. CK reported: "All I have seen and all I have studied and all I have read makes me more and more of the opinion that the United States would be all kinds of a jackass if she entered that body. She would not have the proverbial chance of a cat in hell without claws. The city is well packed with American shriekers for the League of Nations—particularly women . . . [who] flock to every meeting of the Assembly of the League of Nations, making themselves conspicuous by taking notes of all the proceedings and acting solemnly as if they were in some temple dedicated to the ever-living God."[9]

Without any acknowledgment of the role he played in defeating the league's effectiveness, CK accused it of hypocrisy for its inability to act decisively to "make the world safe for democracy." As evidence of its uselessness, CK pointed out the inaction of the body to protests filed by Abyssinia, Egypt, Syria, and the cause of the Arabs in the Holy Land. He continued to insist that the league was a creation of the British to keep their colonies.[10]

The high point of this trip was a dramatic meeting with the Italian dictator Benito Mussolini. CK and Ella both admired the Duce. "Personally, I do not care very much about [getting an interview]," he wrote somewhat disingenuously to Johnson, who helped arrange it, "but Mrs. McClatchy is a wild enthusiast over Mussolini and came to Italy practically to see him!" On October 16, 1926, CK and Ella were admitted to Mussolini's presence for a 6 p.m. meeting at Palazzo Chigi. They were escorted into a huge high-ceiling, frescoed room with scarcely any furniture, where they found Mussolini drinking coffee. As they entered Il Duce rose and gave the couple the stiff-armed Fascist salute. A bit perplexed, CK just nodded but realized that Mussolini had done this because Ella had given him the salute first. "As we walked around the room, he put down his cup and came to meet us. First he grasped the Madame's hands and kissed each twice, then shook hands vigorously with me."[11] CK was prepared, with favorable comments. He told the dictator they were from California, that his newspaper was friendly to "the sons of Italy," and that it had spoken out against the injustices of the Johnson immigration bill, which had restricted the number of Italians who could come to America.

CK told Mussolini that his "wife particularly was his enthusiastic admirer. At this he beamed all over Ella Kelly McClatchy and she was his. In fact, she had been his from the minute he kissed her hands, with all the grace of a knight of old." When CK told him that this was his third trip to Italy, Mussolini inquired, "And what difference do you find?" CK replied that "Italy was now orderly where before she was chaotic; that her people were now patriotic, where some years ago they seemed to have lost all loyalty; that the nation was progressing where before she was sliding to ruin; that Italy evidently was on the road to prosperity."[12] As they talked, CK again pressed for a message for the Italians of California, to which Mussolini consented. He then autographed three pictures of himself and presented them to the couple—again kissing Ella's hands and shaking CK's.

CK himself was swept away by the dictator's charm:

> We had not been in the room for more than a minute before I could tell that Mussolini, for some reason or another, had taken kindly to us. . . . Mussolini has the most piercing eyes imaginable; they reminded me of the midnight eyes of Edwin Booth. He seems to look

clear through into the soul of a man; and I believe it would be hard for anyone successfully to lie to Mussolini. . . . During the 'interview' he beamed and smiled all through and he has a wonderfully enchanting smile. . . . My honest opinion is that the good wife was the principal cause of the Premier's beaming manner. . . . Ah! Ella Kelly McClatchy certainly knows how to do some things.

As they turned to leave the room at the end of the appointment, Ella turned and offered another stiff-armed Fascist salute to Il Duce. He replied in kind.[13]

CK told Johnson, "It is wonderful the power and influence this man [Mussolini] has. His Fascisti is a splendid organization; it is not only composed of men, but even of children! Band after band of children were parading on the streets even last night. So Mussolini has built up a wonderful organization, not only for the present, but the future."[14] "When all is said," he wrote to Johnson in another letter, "Mussolini is undoubtedly the greatest man in Italy, if not the greatest man in the world today." CK was not alone in praising the Italian dictator. So too did William Randolph Hearst. However, CK was coldly realistic about the Italian's shortcomings and those of the Fascist Party. His admiration for the order it brought to Italy was diminished by his distaste for "fascism's methods, morality, and especially the eventual racial policies that arose in fascist Germany."[15] By the latter part of 1926 CK's infatuation with Mussolini had worn a bit thin—helped in part by Hiram Johnson's sobering reminders of the dictator's dismal record vis-à-vis individual liberties. "I note what you say about Mussolini," CK replied after one of these letters. "I am with you. I do not believe he can last. While he does last, however, he will do an immense amount of wonderful work in building up Italy."[16]

They arrived home on June 7, 1927, after having been away for more than a year. Before he left Europe CK had written to Johnson, "We have had a very pleasant time in Europe . . . but lately we have gotten a little bit homesick. Mrs. McClatchy says that when she gets home she will have enough sense to stay home." But, he added, "No telling what a couple of years may bring forth however."[17]

Chapter Sixteen
Reluctant Expansion and the Breakup

◆

ON MONDAY, APRIL 21, 1919, Sacramento's streets were lined with golden poppies and packed with lively crowds as the city prepared to welcome home the soldiers of the 362rd Infantry of the "Fighting Ninety-first" and the 847th Field Artillery. The schools had been closed in honor of the event, and 150 white-frocked young "Minute Girls" strewed handfuls of poppies along K Street in front of four trainloads of conquering heroes of the Argonne Forest. In his speech Governor Stephens promised, "All we have in California is yours, and we have strewn flowers in your pathway this morning to show you that we are going to strew jobs before you when you come back."[1] One of those missing from the parade that morning was Carlos Kelly McClatchy, who would not be mustered out until the latter part of the month in Wyoming. But he already had a job.

After Carlos returned, he joined the newly formed branch of the American Legion in Sacramento. These veterans likely would gather to reminisce and help plan a permanent memorial to the sacrifice of their fallen Sacramento brothers in a new memorial auditorium on J Street. But the memories of the war left their mark on Carlos. They are still hard to gauge because, like most authentic World War I (and II) combat veterans, he rarely spoke about it—except in the objective writing he did for the *Bee*. The blood, horror, confusion, and fear were nothing anyone—even real heroes—wanted to dwell on. One can only surmise that surviving the hell of the Meuse-Argonne offensive must have left deep wounds in his soul. Once back in Sacramento, he threw himself back into his work, aware that now he had a wife and home to care for and a newspaper editor's responsibilities to assume.

Carlos reentered the pace of work at the *Bee* with scarcely a break. In September 1919 CK wrote proudly to his friend Ulric Collins, "You will be glad to know that Carlos has been put in the way to take my place. He is practically in charge of the paper—of course, with limitation, which limitation will be taken off gradually. With exception of one editorial he has done all the leading editorial work for about ten days now and he will continue to do it." Two months later CK announced to the staff: "On January 1, next, C. K. McClatchy, Jr. will be placed in the published roll of *Bee* heads as assistant to the editor. He will assume practically my duties, as I intend to leave all details to him, and hereafter to confine myself—while I am in Sacramento—solely to special editorial work." CK noted his relief at handing the job over to Carlos in a letter to R. M. Richardson, president of Sacramento's Farmers and Merchant Bank. CK said he was "ridding . . . [myself] of looking into and bothering about details; of wandering around and finding out if other people on the paper are doing what they ought to do; of practically holding the reins of the Editorial and News Departments—that part of the job I have turned over to Carlos. . . . Carlos will have to be not only my lieutenant but my buffer."[2]

Valentine had also begun to groom his twin sons, James (JV, or Jim) and Harold (Jedd) for a future role on the *Bee* staff but with less success. As early as 1908 Jedd had his apprenticeship on the local desk of the *Bee*. Grateful for the opportunity, he wrote to his father: "You have mapped out a bunch of work, which I can readily realize will be of immense service to me in the future. As you know, I have a very good general knowledge of the office, matters which I have picked up from you in your handling of affairs and various conditions as they arise." Valentine had urged his son to accompany him on a trip to San Francisco and Oakland to look "through the newspapers in these cities and study . . . their methods. . . . A knowledge of how other men do the same thing as you do in a different way, but all striving for the same goal . . . should not help but educate a man if the foundation is there. . . . I guess you'll find me on deck this time next year fairly well qualified. I hope so at least." But Jedd was not a good money manager and was quite introverted. Valentine later sought to place Jedd at the *Chicago Tribune*. When Harrison Parker of the *Tribune* suggested instead a reporter's job at the *North American*'s new office, Valentine replied, "Jedd . . . has decided he is not fitted for the news end of the paper. He had a year or more's [*sic*] experience in our local room and what he apparently needs most, in his judgment and in mine, is some of the experience Jim has had, but more particularly learning the value of a dollar and has to overcome his diffidence in meeting people." Parker then landed Jedd a job in the *Tribune* composing room, for which Valentine thanked him, observing, "The outside work will tend to correct the defect in him . . . lack of confidence in meeting the public and lack of initiative."[3]

Jedd's twin, Jim, was a bit more successful but also had work ethic issues. Valentine found Jim a job in the classified department of the *Chicago Tribune*. Writing to Harrison Parker, Valentine praised Jim's new self-discipline and "how clearly he appreciates the benefit he is deriving from the work and experiences." He proudly noted that the young man had even refused subsidies from home, "saying that if the other fellows can get along on the salary he will do it."[4] Jim (JV) would take the lead in journalism. His brothers Ralph and Leo would also follow their father into the field—but none of them could surpass their cousin Carlos.

Establishing the *Fresno Bee*

Carlos was a born newsman—brimming with ideas and energy and raw talent. In 1922, while his father was in Europe, he helped inaugurate the *Bee's* first radio station, KVQ, which broadcast from Sacramento. Although the station did not last long, Carlos was soon in the forefront of other radio purchases. Eventually the *Bee* founded KFBK, a station the McClatchys owned until the 1970s.[5]

After he returned from the war, he began to discuss bold plans for the future of the *Bee*. According to the *Bee* historian Steve Wiegand, before CK left Sacramento for Europe in August 1920, Carlos managed to win his father's reluctant consent to add another newspaper operation to the company. CK and Valentine had considered adding other newspapers but had rejected the move up to this point. In the late 1890s they had nearly purchased the *Los Angeles Express*. Valentine even considered moving down to Los Angeles to assume full-time control of the paper. However, disputes about management, and general opposition from the Southern Pacific Railway, killed the deal. A few decades later the need for fresh venues to employ the next generation of McClatchy sons pushed forward plans for expansion.

Fresno was the unofficial capital of the San Joaquin Valley, a community of forty-five thousand in 1920, with a strong agricultural economy and good prospects for future growth and development. The possibilities—and the downward spiral of Fresno's two newspapers—intrigued Carlos. The *Fresno Republican*, long the perch of CK's irritant Chester Rowell, had been sold in

1920 to George and Chase Osborn, sons of a former Michigan governor and industrialist—neither of whom had any journalistic experience. The Osborns had also purchased Fresno's evening newspaper, the *Herald*. The McClatchys had tendered an offer to buy the *Herald* but were refused. So they decided to establish an entirely new newspaper and vie with the *Republican* and the *Herald* for circulation and advertising. On April 15, 1922, the very day CK cabled his friend Hiram Johnson with the news about the business, a front-page ad appeared in the *Sacramento Bee* announcing the founding of the *Fresno Bee* with Carlos as editor, J. V. "Jim" McClatchy as publisher, and Ralph McClatchy as circulation manager.[6] Veterans from the *Bee* office in Sacramento filled other jobs, while Fred Moore, a former city editor of the *Los Angeles Times,* was selected as city editor in Fresno.[7] Shortly after he returned from Europe, CK traveled to Fresno with Valentine, Carlos, and H. R. McLaughlin, an assistant city editor at the *Bee*, to inspect the new site of the newspaper plant.

In later retellings of the circumstances, Valentine insisted that control of the Fresno operation be shared in a similar manner to the *Bee* in Sacramento—with the oldest McClatchy sons assuming joint control of the editorial and business management staffs of the paper. Carlos gave his approval to the idea, assuming that it would work in Fresno as it had in Sacramento—and that he would have de facto control of the editorial end. His cousins would tend almost exclusively to the business side of the paper.

Shared responsibility, however, did not materialize. Carlos took a strong lead, investing maximum amounts of energy, enthusiasm, and oversight in the project. The project required erecting a new *Fresno Bee* building as well as putting together a team of editors, reporters, and managers. These endeavors were financially risky but would eventually catapult the *Bee* over its local rivals and ultimately to dominance in the southern part of the Central Valley. The amount of sweat equity Carlos invested in the *Bee's* second newspaper gave him a sense of entitlement. He also wanted control—independence from his extended family: Uncle Val, whom he had mistrusted since the blowup of 1911, and his cousins, who had nowhere near the expertise or enthusiasm that Carlos did for running a newspaper. He also wanted some distance from his parents. Carlos was determined, purposeful, and at times even devious—but always clear about his path: the McClatchy newspapers were to be his, and their future was in his hands. He had good business sense and was not as skittish as his father about taking risks that he believed would pay off.

CK no doubt supported the new paper but privately lamented to Johnson, "I expected practically to retire from work when I got back this time—although my wife has constantly said that I have not got the sense to retire—but now that Carlos has decided that he wants to build up a new paper, to be called the Fresno *Bee*, I feel that I must go back into the editorial arena."[8]

His willingness to "turn matters over" to his son notwithstanding, CK was determined to have some say in the management and direction of the new paper. From the start he nixed any compromise with those he considered his enemies, especially Chester Rowell. CK wrote to Carlos, who was moving with his young family to Fresno: "You say the announcement of the Fresno paper has received considerable enthusiasm in the San Joaquin Valley. I am glad to hear of it." However, to Carlos's suggestion that the paper include a column written by CK's irritant Chester Rowell, CK replied, "The more I look into the matter, the less I am impressed with the idea of featuring Chester Rowell in the Fresno *Bee*. I want to make the people of the San Joaquin Valley forget Rowell and accept the McClatchys. . . . Our policy should be to let him drop gradually out of sight."[9] Eventually, however, CK had to accept Rowell's columns even in the *Sacramento Bee*—nervously explaining to Hiram Johnson (who had broken with Rowell) why this was necessary for the paper's financial success. Accepting Rowell stretched the limits CK could go, even with his son.

But the new *Bee* posed more serious internal issues than featuring the irritating Rowell. Establishing and managing the *Fresno Bee* reopened the old family wounds of the brouhaha of 1911—especially the issue of editorial control. This time, however, the stakes were different. Although CK had seemed to accede to Valentine's insistence that he could alter the editorial policy of the *Bee* at will, by 1922 CK had become even more insistent that his son have absolute editorial sway. He was proud of Carlos, who had stepped out of an army uniform and right back into a demanding civilian job. CK also realized his own professional days were numbered, and he wanted to make sure Carlos had a free hand to run the paper. In addition the company had undertaken a tremendous risk in building a newspaper literally from the ground up. CK had for years resisted buying other newspapers—not only because of the stakes involved but because he did not want the *Bee* to become a huge impersonal chain like the Hearst papers. He no doubt worried (and drank) about the expense and the time it would take to make the Fresno operation financially independent. Nonetheless CK had gone along with the idea, not because he was convinced of its soundness but because he wanted it for his son, who was to have undisputed control of its content. Carlos himself was also a factor. He was no longer the young college kid who had watched his uncle Val tie his father into knots in 1911. He was literally battle hardened, tempered, and tested by his work with the *Bee* before World War I. He had ably managed affairs while his father was vacationing abroad and displayed something of his father's obstinate streak. He believed he had no obligation to compromise with his uncle or, cousins whom he considered less talented.

Tensions Build

In the summer of 1922 CK climbed back into the editorial saddle. While he spent much of his energy helping the ever-pessimistic Hiram Johnson win a second term as California's senator, CK also now had to do battle over the governance of the new paper. He was not amused when he learned Valentine had insisted that the *Fresno Bee* was to have a corporate board consisting of representatives from both families. This board, dominated by members of Valentine's large family, would control the business affairs of the newspaper. Valentine had also insisted the paper mirror the organizational arrangements of the *Sacramento Bee*: editorial and business power was to be split between CK's and Valentine's families. That meant both Carlos and J. V. McClatchy were listed as "editor" and "publisher," as were their fathers in the Sacramento organization. This was not a problem, but what became the sticking point was Valentine's insistence that the editorial policy was also to be hammered out by Carlos and JV, functioning as an "editorial board." This was unacceptable to Carlos and to CK—and reopened the editorial control issue of 1911.

CK and Valentine had made their agreement in 1911 work because although Val never renounced his rights to editorial oversight, he tried not to interfere with his brother's dominance in this area. Valentine had started holding editorial board meetings in CK's absence, but CK stopped them as soon as he returned home. In fact, as CK later recalled, Val appeared to have little interest in the editorial work of the *Bee*—with the exception of the Japanese "question" (Valentine was violently opposed to Japanese emigration to the United States) and water reclamation issues (he was president of the state reclamation board). CK gladly ceded these topics to his brother, while he ranged around politics, city life, trees, isolationism, public morality, the content of school textbooks, and his other editorial hobby horses. Valentine's insistence on making provisions for his less qualified sons irritated both Carlos and CK. Carlos complained bitterly about his cousins, who could not match him in energy or intelligence. He wanted to work with other, more qualified, newsmen and businessmen, and such men were available—ready, willing, and eager to work in harness with the dynamic and innovative Carlos McClatchy, who at thirty-two had plenty of energy.

During the summer of 1922 CK and Carlos challenged Valentine about the joint editorial control decision at the *Fresno Bee.* Carlos insisted he should not be subservient to his cousin JV, who had limited understanding of the demands of editing a major newspaper. Valentine contended that Carlos had to learn to work in tandem with his cousins. The disagreement raged throughout the late summer and fall of 1922, with CK voicing extreme unhappiness about the arrangement. If Carlos were forced to work with the less skilled JV in the detested regular editorial meetings, it would spell disaster for the new venture. CK maintained in two letters (July 31 and August 2, 1922) that he had not agreed to joint control of editorial and business affairs in Fresno. On August 8, 1922, Valentine penned a lengthy and methodical reply—laced with sarcasm—in which he rejected CK's "extraordinary statements and demands, which I cannot reconcile with facts." He explained some of the business arcana, which CK claimed not to comprehend. Valentine also laid out the legal issues related to the new corporate structure (making no mention that his side of the family would control the board of directors). But on the issue of joint control he was adamant. "I said from the start," Valentine lectured, "that unless the plan provided for this policy, I would not even consider it." Valentine contended CK had been consulted about joint control and insisted that Carlos, who had power of attorney for CK, had heard about the policy and approved of it, or at least never objected. As supporting evidence, Valentine used bits and pieces of correspondence with his brother in Europe. Quoting from a letter he had sent CK in Paris on March 16, 1921, Val noted that he had stipulated joint editorial and business governance, a "free hand" for the boys but with veto power by the two patriarchs. He also pointed out the "Provision in the Fresno organization for effective teamwork, partly through frequent regular conference of the heads of departments, and a weekly majority conference of Carlos and Jim, with their managing editor, circulation manager, advertising manager, etc. at which general information will be exchanged." CK had cabled "ALL RIGHT" to this missive, seeming to approve the arrangement. But to CK's concern that this would diminish the quality of the paper and thereby jeopardize his considerable investment, Valentine cavalierly urged him to sell out and leave it all to him. He added condescendingly: "I still will be glad to have Carlos act as editor . . . if he wishes, and you will consent and provided, of course, he will adapt himself to the joint control policy."[10] CK must have seethed as he read this communication, his mind filling with misgivings about the whole Fresno enterprise. Nonetheless the *Fresno Bee* set up shop in temporary quarters in September 1922, and the juggernaut moved forward.

With sufficient guarantees of advertising in hand, the *Fresno Bee* put out its first edition—sixty pages of news and advertising—on October 17, 1922. At its basement facilities at Van Ness Avenue and Calaveras Street, one of the first subscribers threw the ceremonial switch that drove the presses, and drivers rushed to get the new copies to trains and conveyances for delivery all over the San Joaquin Valley—from Stockton in the north to Bakersfield in the south. A new multistory *Bee* building eventually would arise on this site. In the inaugural editorial Carlos repeated his father's principles: the *Bee* belonged to no political party, nor was it under the sway of any religious group. Its "primary purpose" was "to tell the news, to tell it fairly, simply, and impartially." But he also recognized that he was in a well-plowed field and struck a pose of humility: "The *Bee* comes to Fresno as not mentor to enlighten a benighted community . . . this community and The San Joaquin have builded well in which labor it [the *Bee*] intends to join as a willing worker, content to leave to time what part it shall play."[11] The new paper would eventually dominate Fresno and its environs. The *Bee* now circulated through a great deal of the San Joaquin Valley and began to challenge both the *Republican* and the *Herald*.

As their mutual energies focused on getting the *Fresno Bee* up and running, CK and Val observed a brief truce in the building tension between them. However, on Christmas Day 1922 Valentine surprised everyone by agreeing to sell his half of the *Fresno Bee*—but with provisos that CK at first accepted but then withdrew on the advice of his lawyer, Judge C. E. McLaughlin. CK and Valentine met in Fresno without Carlos present in January 1923. At this time CK rejected Valentine's offer to sell, so Val then tried to persuade Carlos that CK and Carlos should sell, suggesting "that you and he stay together for two or three years, so the ship would weather the storm. . . . He wanted me to say whether you would consider such an offer. I told him I did not think so, but that he should make it to you." Val did so and Carlos made his opinion of the proposal clear: "It would be worse than foolish in my opinion. The salvation of these two papers require quickly that some unified control come into effect to end the chaotic condition of uncertainly and confused control. Further delay may become very dangerous. The money market may tighten." Although Valentine had offered "full and complete and unchecked editorial control to you and to me, with business control to himself [Valentine]," Carlos was not in the mood for compromise. He wanted Valentine's family out of the *Bee* organization. He pressed his father, "I suggest that insistence be had that when V.S. returns to Sacramento that he and you remain in the city until the matter is fully completed . . . let a week's time be set for the completion of preliminaries and that definite signatures to whatever is to be done in all details be secured. . . . Neither Sacramento nor Fresno will run successfully under present conditions."[12] That did not happen, and the wrangling resumed. What finally pushed CK over the edge was not only Valentine's encroachment on an editorial position of the *Bee* but his willingness to bargain with ideological opponents.

At issue was a decision to locate a new naval base on Mare Island—the *Bee* supported it, while the San Francisco Chamber of Commerce opposed it vehemently and wanted it located in Alameda. Someone on the executive committee of the San Francisco chamber requested a discussion of the *Bee's* position. Valentine approached his brother in the hope they both could meet with the chamber and defend the *Bee's* position. CK unenthusiastically assented and sent J. Earl Langdon, the managing editor, to the session. The meeting was a grueling experience. In a letter to Carlos, CK wrote: "I find out from Mr. Langdon—that the *Bee* and himself particularly, were practically put on trial before this Committee of the Chamber of Commerce and that V.S. checked him every time he started to say anything battling for The *Bee's* position, as Langdon thought it should be battled for under the circumstances." Valentine then wrote to Robert Newton Lynch, the manager of the San Francisco Chamber of Commerce, reaffirming the *Bee's* position but indicating that "If . . . it is shown that we are mistaken and that the recommendation against Mare Island is based on entirely different grounds and those grounds are good against the facts and expert advice, we will be called upon fairly to modify our views and act accordingly." CK was angered that Valentine had opened the paper's editorial position to debate and turned to Carlos for advice. CK pondered whether he should say anything at all or "keep it as one of the numerous incidents which prove that I will be a darned fool to stay in the paper with him." In a draft of his protest to Valentine, CK accepted his part in the confusion: "I did not object to you or Mr. Langdon meeting the executive committee of the San Francisco Chamber of Commerce." But, CK insisted, "It belittles The *Bee* or any other paper to have its managing editor or any other representative of the Editorial Department, go down to another city to be put on the defensive by a committee of the chamber of commerce that always has been opposed to The *Bee*'s position."[13] Carlos traveled to Sacramento to discuss the matter with his father and urged him not to send the memo. But Carlos did note that it was "a repetition of things that were going on all the time." To Carlos "there was simply one thing at issue and that was the dissolution" of the long-term partnership of the two brothers.[14] In March 1923 the squabbling temporarily abated as ground was broken on the four-story *Fresno Bee* building. Carlos oversaw not only all the elements of the new building but the assembling of a first-rate editorial staff, including 130 correspondents.

Dissolving the Partnership

After these festivities the wrangling resumed into the spring of 1923. At some point the brothers reached the momentous decision to separate as business partners with ownership of the newspapers to be determined through a bidding competition. The basic legal structure of the dissolution was finalized on July 1, 1923, creating two separate companies: the V. S. Company and the C. K. Company, both of which competed to become the parent company of the newspaper company.[15] Bidding was not set until the last day of August, but in the meantime negotiations continued in the hope of ending the impasse. The intensity of the negotiations was such that it was impossible for CK to attend a long-scheduled meeting with Hiram Johnson at the Sacramento depot on August 25: "Am afraid will not be able to go up the road to see you next Friday," CK's telegram read. "May not be able even to say how do you do at the depot. Final decisive meetings on matters in dispute being held that day and evening." As rumors of the contention picked up, friends tried to intervene to keep the brothers together. Charles Dillman, president of D. O. Mills Bank, wrote imploringly, "I know nothing regarding your differences, but in the name of your Dear Good Father, isn't it possible to hold up matters and see if by the assistance of friends the difference cannot be ironed out so that you can manage to stick together the few remaining years allotted you both on this earth? . . . I cannot help but think it will wreck the lives of both of you if consummated. Charles, you both are too old to do it, the world will never be the same to either you or Val."[16] CK thanked Dillman for his concern but noted there was no turning back.

The brothers went to court on August 31, 1923. The bidding took place downtown in the appellate courtroom. CK's old friend Judge E. C. "Lije" Hart served as referee. CK and his attorney, C. E. McLaughlin, carefully bid higher and higher in increments of $1,000. Carlos was nearby to assure his father of a flow of money should the price go quite high—representatives of Amadeo Giannini's Bank of Italy were on hand to extend a line of unsecured credit, and Phebe's grandmother, Phebe Mason Rideout, and her parents donated $100,000, as did others (including a manager of the San Francisco Seals base-ball team).[17] The bidding took two hours. A relieved CK wrote to his daughter Charlotte, "[Finally] V.S. and his people and his attorney Will H. Devlin, went out; when they returned, V.S. came up and offered his hand to me and shook hands and said, 'Well, Charlie, you have won.' And that was the end of it." Bidding for the *Bee* stopped at $316,000 for both papers—plus a percentage of the profits of the *Bee* for a period of time. "At one time Carlos and myself and Judge McLaughlin were very much afraid we were going to lose," CK confided to his friend Marion De Vries. When the sale was finalized, Carlos had contrib-uted $140,000 of the total—all of it from his generous in-laws.[18]

The momentous decision was announced quietly. CK in particular main-tained a discreet silence (no doubt out of family loyalty but also from sadness at the break with his brother). "This is a matter on which I have said noth-ing even to my dearest friends," he wrote Hiram Johnson. Once the sale was completed, he reassured old friends and advertisers that all was well with the newspaper company. CK explained the breakup to Hiram: "The thing was in-evitable, Hiram. It had to come. The published accounts you may have seen in some papers concerning the alleged reasons are absolutely crazy. . . . It was sim-ply that he [Val] demanded joint editorial and [business] authority not only for himself, but for his boys. One instance of that was the unswerving demand on his part that J. V. McClatchy, who had no training in the editorial depart-ment, be equal co-editor with Carlos in The Fresno *Bee*, and that no policy be started or principle sustained or attacked, or editorials written to which J. V. objected." CK was not about to surrender editorial control to "two young men who, no matter what their abilities in other lines, have certainly shown none in the editorial branch."[19]

A Regrettable Spiral of Mutual Disdain

The settlement was unsettling, upsetting, and even anticlimactic. On September 6, 1923, all of Valentine's sons—Ralph and JV, who worked in Fresno, as well as Jedd, who worked as business manager in Sacramento, and the *Bee* librarian, J. Everett Johnson, who was married to Valentine's daughter,

Edna—resigned effective November 1.[20] CK quickly accepted all the resignations with short replies, perfunctory thanks, and the stylistic professions of affection and support typical of his personal correspondence. Valentine's son Leo, the *Bee*'s Washington correspondent, also resigned, but CK and Carlos asked him to stay on—which he did for several months.[21] All these children would later claim they had been ousted—a charge that deeply hurt CK but that Carlos ignored.

By October the bitterness between the two brothers grew even more intense. At one point, Judge McLaughlin, who was worried about cash flow, proposed selling the *Fresno Bee* to Valentine "if he would take it." McLaughlin discussed it with Carlos, who ceded the decision to his father. CK replied, "I have no desire to allow The Fresno *Bee* to go into the hands of the V.S. McClatchys. After all the trouble we went to get it we want to hang on to it to the last ditch. . . . A sale to V.S. would be a confession of weakness and failure." CK tended carefully to the fragile finances of the new operation, looking for ways to raise capital or save money, and considered selling a lot next to the *Bee* building but did not want the *Bee* to look bad.[22]

Afterward Valentine deeply regretted he had not outbid his brother and kept the *Bee*. In his mind the success of the paper was largely the result of his having invested a lifetime of work in the business. One can only imagine him waking up on his first full day of freedom from the *Bee* and its concerns and reading the newspaper he had helped guide for nearly forty years—now as an outsider. Members of his family turned their scorn on CK and his wife, Ella, whom they believed drove them out of the newspaper business. Among the most indiscreet was Valentine's wife, Adeline ("Addie"), whose venomous comments were picked up by the small-town gossips of Sacramento and repeated to CK's family. The Valentine faction directed bitter barbs at Ella, who seemed to order the hapless CK about like a child. CK began to keep notes on what he heard. At one point Adeline spoke to Carlos's mother-in-law, Mrs. Briggs, confiding "that CK's acts had [*sic*] made his brother broken-hearted." Following that, on a train trip from San Francisco, Adeline again found Mrs. Briggs and began a tirade against Ella. "[Adeline] said that Mrs. CK for years and years had had an inveterate hatred of V.S. and had always intended to do all she could to hurt him in every way; and now she had succeeded. She said Mrs. CK is the wife of a very hen-pecked husband who is of a very weak and vacillating character. . . . Then she said it was a disgrace the way, egged on by Ella, CK had treated her boys and driven them out into the streets." Mrs. Briggs then pointed out to Adeline that Valentine had done very well financially.[23]

Adeline also vented to a Mrs. Martin Beasley, who then reported to Mrs. Briggs, again accusing Ella of being the evil genius behind the C. K. Company's purchase of the *Bee*. In reality Ella was quite distraught about it all—prompting CK to beg family friend Minnie De Vries not to make a big issue of the separation with Ella for fear of upsetting her further.[24]

Ella

Some did blame Ella Kelly McClatchy for the breakup. Her detractors— mostly her in-laws—accused her of dominating CK and ordering him around, especially when matters came to a head in 1923. Some in Valentine's family portrayed the decision to separate as the battle of the two wives, Adeline versus Ella. What was the truth about Ella? Did she play the pivotal role in the break- up of the brothers? No evidence exists that she directly meddled or helped bring matters to an impasse. But she certainly was not passive on the issue of the *Bee* or her family, especially regarding Carlos, who often is mentioned in oral histories as "the apple of her eye." She also had witnessed over time the condescending manner with which Valentine treated her husband and was not going to permit her hardworking, war hero son to be passed over or marginal- ized in any bureaucratic shuffle.

Ella was not shy. Recollections of her suggest that she could be rather prim and starchy—so much so that her grandson James confided he did not like visiting his Grandmother McClatchy because life at the McClatchy home seemed so overly formal and reserved. She certainly ruled the household. Her daughter-in-law recalled: "Grandmother McClatchy was a strong personali- ty. You were never in doubt about what she thought about anything and she didn't hesitate to express it. She was agreeable. She was nice looking, plump . . . dressed conservatively but elegant . . . a very respectable kind of wom- an." Indeed she could be forceful and decisive and even a bit intimidating. Although she does not appear to have meddled much in her husband's busi- ness, her politics matched his—and in 1920 she volunteered to be a delegate for Hiram Johnson at the Republican National Convention and in 1924 was a delegate to the Progressive Party conclave that nominated Robert La Follette for the presidency. She never appeared to take no for an answer and often ob- tained permissions and privileges to do and see things abroad that might not have been open to others. Of her ability to finagle a deal, her daughter Eleanor once asked in admiration, "Mama, what is your fatal charm?"[25]

Raising money for private charities was one of Ella's outlets. She had a particular interest in struggling youth. She continuously raised funds for Sacramento orphans, and holidays often found her distributing gifts at one or the other of Sacramento's orphanages. Both she and CK took into their home the five orphaned children of their next door neighbors, the William B. Russells, after both parents died.[26] CK was the executor of the estate while Ella became the children's guardian.[27]

Religion was a particularly sore spot between the couple. While Ella was willing to let CK go his way with respect to religion, she was hurt when her children strayed. She insisted all their weddings take place in the presence of a Catholic priest. In 1909, when daughter Charlotte eloped with James Maloney, CK sought to sooth Ella's deep disappointment by going directly to Bishop Thomas Grace of Sacramento for a dispensation for the "kids" to marry as Catholics. In a letter to Maloney's father CK confided: "When she [Ella] was in a grieved spirit . . . a woman in that condition magnifies everything. Every little thing that is not exactly to her own very sterling notions becomes an additional barb to prick and wound her."[28] As noted earlier, she insisted that Carlos be married in the presence of a priest and hosted a lavish backyard ceremony when Eleanor married an aviator. When Eleanor's marriage ended in divorce, Ella made sure the Catholic Church annulled it.

Time and again CK sought to shield Ella from life's unpleasantness and to defer to her wishes on certain matters pertaining to the household and any problems with the children. For example, when Eleanor developed a problem with her eyes while away at boarding school, CK wrote to an official of the school, Etta Bagley: "I wish you would send these letters concerning Eleanor's health to me," he asked. "Be sure to address them care of The *Bee*, and not to my home—then I can use my judgment as to whether I will submit them to my wife. . . . I believe there are occasions when no harm will be done if the mother does not know every little thing."[29] When a horse threw Carlos during a summer vacation, CK urged that the matter be kept from Ella, and had doctor bills sent to him at the *Bee* to avoid Ella's prying eyes.

But was CK henpecked? Setting aside the implicit sexism of such a charge, the simple answer is no. CK genuinely loved his wife—although probably in the rather reserved Victorian way of his time. He saved his sentimentality and affection for letters. He was never unfaithful to her, and she seemed to tolerate a good deal of his occasionally troubling behavior, from his formal rejection of Catholicism to his alcoholism. That she appeared to rule the household was largely by mutual consent. CK did not have a good grasp of, or deep interest in, the practicalities of daily life. Since he was often absorbed in his work, his books, and the theater, he tended to surrender vast areas of his personal life to her direction. Did she materially assist in the breakup of the brothers? Not directly. If CK needed a strong push to uncouple from his brother, it probably was administered by Carlos, not Ella—although she would have concurred. But CK himself had endured enough from Valentine and was not about to surrender his son's rights to a career for which he had prepared and for which he had superb qualifications. Neither he nor Carlos would tolerate a position that made him subservient to his less-skilled cousins.

Family Squabbles Continue

CK moved with care as the McClatchy children and in-laws submitted their resignations. He graciously accepted the resignation of J. Everett Johnson, the librarian of the *Bee* (and Valentine's son-in-law), assuring him of his "sincere regard and deep affection . . . if at any time you need a friend, you will come and see me." But CK moved swiftly to remove one of Valentine's pet projects, the Japanese Exclusion League, which he had formed in 1920. This lost its *Bee* support and ultimately was ejected from office space in the *Bee* building. The pettiness raged on. At one point CK worried about the loyalty of his business manager, W. H. James (on whose expertise he relied more than ever). James had worked closely with Valentine and no doubt felt some pangs of loyalty toward him. CK became suspicious of their ongoing relationship, and at the end of October 1923, he wrote to Carlos, "V.S. has been up here for some time and James has had dinner with him quite frequently, as I understand it, being with him and Jedd, or with V.S. alone, for several hours at a time. I know James is as loyal as can be, but V.S. would pump anybody in The *Bee* office in order to get anything he wants to know and he is not entitled to know anything at all about the business except what is given to him in the semi-annual reports." After urging Carlos to get to the bottom of it, CK noted, "I want one thing thoroughly understood and that is that nobody in The *Bee* office is to tell V.S., directly or indirectly, anything about the business."[30] James would remain at the *Bee* until his retirement in the 1930s. Despite his connections with Valentine, he remained steadfastly loyal to CK, whom he also admired greatly.

Problems emerged as well from Valentine's sons, who also probably regretted their resignations—and the haste with which they were accepted. In the fall of 1923, Ralph McClatchy returned a check that Carlos had paid him, feeling he was not entitled to it. But when Carlos insisted he take it, Ralph accepted it gratefully and seemed to be open to future visits with his cousin. JV, in contrast, left the family business by proclaiming flamboyantly in his official announcement that he had "supervised the construction of the handsome four-story reinforced concrete home for the new paper. . . . Under his direction the circulation of the paper was built to over 17,000 in less than a year and the paper acquired large advertising accounts, both national and domestic." When Carlos shared the clipping with his father, CK snorted, "The thing is done, but I do not think it was a good thing to make it so strong . . . for he can never live up to the reputation this gives him. Besides, I think a thing like that should have some semblance of truth."[31]

Leo McClatchy remained for a time as the Washington correspondent, a decision that earned him the opprobrium of his father and brothers. CK noted, "Leo would never be working for either *Bee* today had it not been for myself. His father didn't want to speak to him anymore; had ordered him not only away from The *Bee*, but also away from Sacramento. I was the party who fixed the thing up and Leo said he would never forget me and what I had done for him, etc., etc." However, Leo's loyalties to the family eventually trumped his uncle's kindnesses to him. He burned his bridges by making uncomplimentary references to Hiram Johnson that were not amusing to the thin-skinned senator —a serious violation of McClatchy editorial policy. In late November 1923 Leo abruptly sent "a seven day ultimatum" notice to his cousin and uncle, informing them that he was setting up his own independent bureau through which he would do business with the *Bee* if they chose to use his services. The suddenness of this move threatened to leave Carlos and CK without a bureau reporter in the nation's capital. Carlos was upset not only by the problem it posed for the *Bee* but also that Leo had apparently put his bureau together while working on *Bee* time. In retaliation Carlos and CK did what they could to dry up sources for the renegade cousin by urging congressmen Charles F. Curry and John Raker not to give him any interviews. Leo managed to hang on for a while with interviews from Senator Samuel Shortridge and was able to hawk his dispatches to a few *Bee* rivals in Northern California (including the *Fresno Republican* and the *Sacramento Union*).[32]

At the end of 1923 the rancor between the two brothers erupted again over the financial support of their sisters, Fanny and Emily. Neither of the women derived any direct benefit from the *Bee,* but the paper paid both an allowance—as it had Mother McClatchy—that allowed them to lead comfortable lives. The paper also picked up the fixed expenses related to their living spaces. Since both brothers no longer jointly operated the *Bee,* the question of support for their sisters was not resolved. Apparently the matter had been discussed early in the split, but, not surprisingly, resolution fell through the cracks until December 1923, when Valentine discovered that Emily and Fanny were encountering financial difficulties. The two women owed nearly $7,000 for taxes, improvements, and the like. Valentine sent his sisters a copy of a memo on the issue he had sent to CK; the implication was that CK was holding out on them. CK reacted with indignation, questioning the agreement and countering, "I have the plain statement of Jedd—made after the sale—that . . . it was the intention of the V.S. McClatchy family, if it succeeded in getting the two papers, to call such indebtedness at once to the attention of Fannie and Emily, with a suggestion that these sums could gradually be paid up out of their increased allowance." CK protested his love for his sisters but insisted that he was doing only what Jedd had told him was "the plan." "The burden is now on my shoulders," CK protested. "I do not know whether I have the moral right to throw away nearly $7,000 of the assets of the papers, when such large sums are due other people."[33] He suggested that the two brothers split their sisters' indebtedness and pay it off.

The controversy provoked intense bitterness from Valentine, who lashed out at his brother: "In your intense eagerness to oust me and my sons from a business which had been built up in large measure through my efforts, you blindly assumed burdens when you lacked the experience, the commercial standing and apparently the resources (though I assumed you had Mrs. Rideout's backing) necessary to carry them. And you would make the burden thus assumed an excuse for failing to do something which would have been done by others in your place."[34]

Valentine's criticisms of the whole transaction continued. He upbraided his brother for mortgaging the real estate and the printing plants, as well as for selling a piece of property reserved for a new building "and a lasting monument to our father." Nonetheless, since he felt that "my oversight in not making provision for the matter in the contract is responsible for the present situation, I will stand half the amount" to be paid to the sisters, but he determined to pay in installments rather than a lump sum. Valentine sent a copy of this to the sisters. CK reacted with equal vitriol right after Christmas, damning Valentine for the financially precarious position of the *Bee* and refuting Valentine's accusations that he (CK) was incompetent in business matters.[35]

In the meantime CK found himself confronting an income tax snafu of monumental proportions. CK, befuddled by the income tax, had made an incorrect payment in 1917. After the brothers' partnership was dissolved, an audit by the Internal Revenue Service in 1923 determined that the McClatchy Company owed $22,000 in back taxes. CK found the reasoning nonsensical. "The *Bee* owes this additional money because 'the stock of the corporation was owned by the partners of the James McClatchy Company and not by the partnership proper.'" Although the *Bee* had supported and endorsed the implementation of a federal income tax, CK now heartily concurred with Secretary of the Treasury Andrew Mellon's tax-cutting policies. "It is outrageous that so long after the war is over we have to pay such enormous taxes." CK complained. "It is scarcely profitable to run The Sacramento *Bee*, for instance, much as its natural profits are; and there is no reason why we should be billed so outrageously when multi-millionaires put their money in tax free securities."[36]

The Struggle About the History of the *Bee*

CK's reaction to the dissolution was at first sorrow and even embarrassment. He was so sheepish when asked about the split that he did not attend the formal dedication of the *Fresno Bee* building in October 1923, worrying that "there would be a few at least who would want to open up the inquiry as to the dissolution."[37] However, as time went on CK and his family grew angrier and angrier at Valentine. Two articles written by Valentine soon appeared in the trade journal *Editor and Publisher*. The first, "Newspaper Making a Merchandising Business," was published in the December 29, 1923, issue, followed by the second on January 5, 1924, "Newspaper Creation or Building? The First Year of the Fresno *Bee*." CK and Carlos found the tone and some of the assertions of the articles offensive. What ensued was a major dispute about the history of the *Bee*—CK's version clashed sharply with Valentine's. Since both men took their own particular historical narrative quite seriously, this further alienated the brothers from each other.

Valentine wrote the articles in his logical and thorough style. The first emphasized his business methods in helping to make the *Sacramento Bee* a circulation leader. Naturally he made his role appear central to the success of the paper. Valentine took a swipe at his brother's competence in business affairs by noting "that any competent businessman could come in now and run The *Bee* in all departments." Valentine had strongly implied that if his business methods were followed, the paper would be a success. But "if it fails, it will fail simply because it was not properly managed."[38] Naturally, given his low estimation of his brother's managerial skills, one might conclude the paper was on the slow road to doom.

CK was furious at Valentine's bragging and the narcissistic suggestion that he alone had been responsible for the success of the *Bee.* In a letter to Carlos on January 3, 1924, CK took aim at Valentine's assertion that "the newspaper was managed under a system of joint control" and retorted that it was "not true, as everybody in The *Bee* office knows. In fact, Mr. V.S. McClatchy is against government ownership [of certain public entities, such as utilities]—one of the strongest principles of The *Bee*'s editorial policy. He is against The *Bee*'s views on the subject of prostitution; he is against The *Bee*'s views on the subject of prohibition. In fact, in that paragraph he gives the reader to believe that he was as much the editor of The *Bee* as I ever was." He scored his brother for joining the Elks, thereby violating their mutual pledge not to join fraternal associations. CK also took after Val for seeking public office, revealing that "at one time he moved heaven and earth to be appointed postmaster of Sacramento, and he was for seven years Chairman of the Board of Reclamation. . . . Outside interests kept him away from The *Bee* office most of the time the last twelve years." Valentine had also galled CK by taking exclusive credit for the creation of the Superior California Department, a popular feature of the newspaper, "which was the idea of John S. Chambers, [who] first broached to me. In fact, years before Chambers suggested that, I tried to get something of that kind . . . but V.S. wouldn't have it saying, in the first place, it was not a good idea, and, in the second, it would cost too much money." CK harrumphed, "Now, he lets everybody believe he was the inspiration for the Superior California Department."[39]

CK wanted to stop the second *Editor and Publisher* article penned by his brother, but Carlos and G. C. Hamilton, the C. K. Company's business manager, advised against it. Carlos counseled. "V.S.'s article is gall unlimited, but

I cannot see anything practical that you can do, either to object to the first or forestall the second, that latter of which is already off the press." Carlos urged his father to move on, writing, "I can see nothing else to do than to forget it, remembering that V.S. only has the shell of these petty revenges while you have the whole nut." He admitted, "I have some curiosity to see what he will say about the *Fresno Bee*, but outside of that I wipe it out of my mind." The second Fresno article was comparatively pedantic, a simple restatement of the facts of place and foundation. But it hit a sore spot when Valentine asserted, "The enterprise was conceived, planned, and inaugurated by the home office under the direction of the publisher and his assistant W. H. James, in the early part of 1922 during the latter part of a two-year European trip of the editor."[40] This time CK not only informed the representative of *Editor and Publisher*, Harry Drummond, of his displeasure but directed his staff to reinforce the message by cutting off advertising in trade publications.

Drummond reported to his superiors, "The whole *Bee* outfit are sore at us." The *Editor and Publisher* flap continued, and at one point CK began to suspect his office staff of disloyalty. Once again CK singled out the business manager, W. H. James.[41] Carlos dismissed his father's fears about disloyalty in the shop and warned him about bothering James:

> I have the fullest trust and confidence in James and am absolutely certain he would not do anything to help V.S. to such a presumptuous appearance in print. Much of the success of the two papers depends upon the good relations between James and yourself and I regret exceedingly the slightest chance of impairment of such relations, especially in such a case as this. . . . We must remember also that nothing would please V.S. better than to drive a wedge between James and yourself, for that would be a serious disarrangement in the machinery of the paper's success. I personally, as I think you do, bank entirely on James' whole hearted support of your regime. Were anything to disturb the relations between you two, the effect would be decidedly bad.[42]

CK quickly put a damper on any follow-up in *Editor and Publisher*, assuring the editor, James W. Brown, that Drummond's gossipy report of conditions at the *Bee* was blown out of proportion. In bringing the *Editor and Publisher* controversy to a conclusion, CK wrote a bland note to his brother assuring him of his right to say whatever he wanted. To Carlos, CK confided, "I want to work this thing around without any friction anywhere in the office, but I want to have it so shaped that there will hereafter be no answers to Mr. V.S. McClatchy from anybody in the office on anything that is none of Mr. V.S. McClatchy's business."[43]

CK actively sought to isolate Valentine from his former associates. CK continued to make his displeasure known in enough journalism circles so Valentine would hear. To John Francis Neylan, now editor of the *San Francisco Examiner,* CK related the erratic nature of Valentine's editorial interventions, singling out his detestation of Japan and the Japanese: "For during all 40 years we were together V.S. became a 'specialist' only on reclamation work when he was chairman of the Reclamation Board, and on Japan after he had made his Oriental trip [1919]. Prior to that he was for the Japanese and I, as Editor of The *Bee,* lambasted them during the Russo-Japanese war and subsequently, against his decided opinions if not his protests." CK concluded: "I do not think the man to write the history of the Sacramento *Bee* should have been the one whose property it is." CK ratcheted up the antagonism by refusing to run articles Valentine had submitted about his pet project of Japanese exclusion and had provided no budget or office space for Valentine's anti-Japanese activities. In retaliation Valentine produced editorials on the subject and sent them to papers other than the *Bee.* CK insisted on having the first right of publication, and when Valentine refused, his articles did not appear in the *Bee.* Valentine observed snidely: "I may say casually, that the particular article which the *Bee* failed to publish because the *Union* used it first appeared in the *S. F. Examiner* of Sunday last four or five days after publication in the *Union.*"[44]

The Final Rupture

The aftermath of this dust-up produced the incident that permanently poisoned relations between the two men and their families. On February 3, 1924, the brothers accidentally ran into each other late on Sunday morning in San Francisco. As CK related in a memo circulated to family: "CK asked V.S. how he was getting along and put out his hand. V.S. never extended his one inch and said: 'I do not feel a bit that way.' To which CK responded: 'Well, by God, Val, you ought to feel that way.' With a sneer on his lips, V.S. turned away." CK seemed to take it in stride but later received a hateful note from his brother demanding to know why CK expected him (Valentine) to shake his hand after he had been treated so shamefully. CK circulated the note among close friends and family. Despite requests from his son and wife that he put Valentine out of his mind, CK never really recovered from the hostility and ill will. Ironically, one who seemed impervious to the insults and antagonism (and even threats of physical violence and legal action) from those he gored with his acerbic pen or who blamed him for exposing their public faults seemed to crumple emotionally under the blows of his angry and sarcastic brother, sister-in-law, and nephews. Nonetheless the *Bee* had been preserved for Carlos. CK moved forward to replace Valentine on the Associated Press board with the Oakland publisher William Knowland. Carlos tried to console his father, writing, "Perhaps it is just as well that V.S. shows his true colors and his real spitefulness. . . . For the last fifteen years at least he has had no brotherly affection, but has been so intent on his own aggrandizement that he sacrificed you and your interests. . . . Your record as a brother is clear . . . let him go his way." Later Carlos expressed his own bitterness toward Valentine: "V.S. deliberately in my opinion is doing everything he can to wound you. . . . No brother would have treated you as he did in 1911 and had love in his heart. . . . He neither has affection for you and deserves not the slightest bit from you. You are hated by V.S. and by nearly all his family, not for any wrong you ever did them, but because you resisted the wrongs he would have done you. . . .Why not let us write V.S. from memories just as he disappeared from the salary roll. You have a wife, two daughters and myself who ought to be able to supply you with the affection that V.S. never had for you."[45]

But the breakup with Val crushed and hurt CK, and he sometimes poured out his heart to his family—most likely his daughter Eleanor. Indeed twelve years later, in a bitter exchange with her uncle, Eleanor threw up his cruelty as "the epitome of all the hurts you thrust at my father—that unforgettable day in San Francisco when you harshly and ruthlessly refused my father's hand. That I shall never forget." However, CK may have reconciled with his brother. In 1936, when a *Bee* radio station planned to place portraits of both CK and Valentine in the lobby, Eleanor vetoed the idea. Valentine took offense at this and also for the paper's slighting of his role in building the *Bee*. In a letter to his niece, he noted: "It was CK's wish that past differences be buried. . . . Whatever fault rested with CK or myself in connection with our business separation was freely forgiven on both sides a few years ago." Val maintained that he had not insisted on having his picture next to his brother's but that the suggestion had come from the *Bee* business manager G. C. Hamilton, who had received such a request from CK himself. "The photograph was not sent to Mr. Hamilton until after C. K. in personal conversation had told me of those instructions."

Valentine took his brother's gesture "as a characteristically generous and frank one intended to convey from his sickbed a message to the public that all differences between himself and V.S. had been healed."[46] It is not clear that Eleanor believed this rendition of events, but she later fired Hamilton.

CK nonetheless continued to keep tabs on the rumors spread by Valentine's family, noting that Leo had told someone or other that the two papers were in financial straits and that his father would have to take over the papers again. Leo McClatchy remained in journalism, running a new agency out of Washington for many years and working at the *Stockton Record* for a time. He vented his anger at his uncle through occasional potshots at Hiram Johnson.[47] As Leo's criticisms continued, CK sadly noted to Hiram,

> I really begin to believe it would be useless for you to attempt to do anything on the Leo proposition—that is, at least until you come to California. Judge McLaughlin told me only the night before last, that two different Californians . . . who have returned from Washington, told him that Leo tells the nastiest tales of and concerning myself to all Californians who will listen. You can see from this that Leo will probably hit anybody I like. . . . I am afraid he intends to continue right along in the same line. I am sorry to say it because I heretofore have liked Leo very much. I never thought there was such a streak in him.[48]

Moving Forward

Even though the *Fresno Bee* still was not making money, Carlos spied an easy purchase of a long-standing Modesto paper to round out McClatchy press dominance from the Oregon border to Bakersfield. Negotiations had begun while CK was in Europe and culminated in early August 1924. The *Bee* purchased the *Modesto News-Herald* for $321,509 and updated it with additional news reporters, clearer type, and four pages of comics. The paper, headed by Fred Moore, would not change its name to the *Modesto Bee* until 1933. In Fresno Carlos bought out his two competitors, the *Fresno Herald* in 1923 and the *Fresno Republican* in 1926. In 1932 he merged the latter with the *Bee*.[49]

In 1928 CK received an interesting offer. CK described the terms in a letter to Johnson: "I have been offered ten times the net profits of the McClatchy Publications for ten years for the properties in Sacramento, Fresno and Modesto—the payments to be made at once and all in cash." The offer had come from the Copley Newspapers, which would buy a number of California dailies—including the *Sacramento Union*. The chain had purchased two or three in Southern California and a handful in the Midwest. "Copley is a multi-millionaire head . . . or something . . . of the electric trust so you can see what the gang is doing." The fear for CK, however, was that "if the public utilities under private ownership . . . [bought] the McClatchy publications there wouldn't be a voice that I can call to mind . . . that wouldn't be practically the mouthpiece of what Arthur McEwen [chief editorial writer of the *New York American*] used to call the plunderbund."[50]

Troubles with Carlos

As CK was battling his brother, he also had to think about reorganizing the papers in a way that would ensure he could pass them on intact to his son. At the end of 1923, hoping to give Carlos a raise, he consulted with his attorney, Judge McLaughlin. "I would like to have it so arranged that Carlos would get $15,000 a year to date from the time when we took over the papers on September first last. . . . Of course we couldn't pay the money now, under the agreement, and I do not think Carlos would take it under any evasive way until such time as we are situated better financially." On the subject of ownership CK declared,

> When that time comes, I want Carlos to be known as co-owner of the paper, or papers, as well as co-editor, with a salary equal to my own. . . . I have not changed my views about the will. . . . I think the property I have if my wife should die also, should be divided equally among the three children. I want it definitely fixed, however, that nobody shall interfere with Carlos in the management of the two papers; that he shall have supreme control and that he may pass that supreme control over to his son, if he may deem that advisable.[51]

But Carlos had never thought he would one day be anything other than the single head of the *Bee* enterprise. In a lengthy letter to his father, he explained that "it had been your life-time ambition to have me on The *Bee* as your successor; that you intended to make it up to the girls [Charlotte and Eleanor] otherwise. I cannot remember a time when this was not told me." He commented bitterly, "The first word I ever had contradicting what I can remember from childhood was your conversation the night before the bidding. It more than stunned me." He rejected vehemently the offer of one-third ownership: "I haven't the slightest interest in pledging my life work so that larger and larger sums could be made by The *Bee* so two thirds of its revenues would be spent in idle luxury. Life is too short, the work is too hard, the motive too futile." He noted that he could command a higher salary elsewhere and urged his father to divide the property any way he wished but that he, Carlos, was free to take his labor elsewhere—for his own well-being and that of his young son, James. CK replied to Carlos the same day: "I am sure you make a mistake in your idea that I ever said that you were to have the whole *Bee* property and I intended to making [*sic*] it up to the girls on the outside. I couldn't do that if I would; for I have nothing with which to do it." He pleaded with Carlos to reconsider his opposition, to consider the honor of running his own paper rather than being a vassal of someone else. CK pleaded with Carlos to consider the future of the company and agree to share with his sisters. Then in May CK wrote again: "Your mother, Judge McLaughlin and self had a lengthy séance today which wound up in nothing; your mother being very strongly opposed to the girls having no stock whatever—not a trace of connection with the paper. . . . And I don't believe your mother likes the annuity business, etc. for her. It seems absolutely impossible to agree on anything and Judge McLaughlin has given it up as a bad job. . . . I have not spoken to Eleanor upon the subject; but I understand she feels considerably as her mother does." Because McLaughlin had "given it up as a bad job," CK found another lawyer, who found the right language for the agreement. In the end Carlos would receive the papers and reserve for his mother a guaranteed annual income of $26,000, and his sisters $250,000 each in trust, payments derived from stock in the paper. Carlos appeared to be satisfied. His hard work and energy would count for something.[52] But his problems with his father would only get worse.

Carlos at the Helm: Micromanaged to Distraction

The separation of the McClatchy brothers had serious implications for CK. Gone now were his long-anticipated hopes of a placid retirement—dabbling in politics, plotting with Hiram and his California cronies against the forces of reaction, and reaping the rewards of his long years in the publishing and political worlds. CK had purchased forty acres in rural Carmichael in 1919 and created a gentleman's farm there called Casa Robles. There he planted trees and orchards and took refuge from the tedium and demands of daily city life. With the help of his friend Bert Meek of Oroville, CK produced an olive oil "from mission trees." Japanese caretakers tended the trees and vines. A rural cottage

(CK referred to it as a shack) was erected on the property, primarily for the use of CK—and it would be the place where he died. CK's hopes to use this rural Shangri-la as his retirement villa never materialized. The *Bees* all required tending—as did his brilliant but increasingly distracted son.

With the battle with Valentine behind them, Carlos expected his father to give him full control of the *Fresno Bee*, while CK managed the Sacramento enterprise. At first CK seemed to think this was the way to handle the two newspapers. When Carlos invited him in October 1923 to an open house celebrating the Fresno plant's first anniversary, CK begged off. "I think it a better policy for me to remain away. You already suggested you didn't think it would be good policy to play up an absentee owner—stating that Fresnans are rather sensitive about that matter. . . . I would rather the Fresno people got the idea that the paper is run entirely by your people down there, especially by you." When Hiram had asked something about Fresno, CK told him to direct his query to Carlos. "One," he pointed out, "you will save at least a day, if not two days thereby. Two, Carlos knows exactly what I want and how I want it done; and therefore, I leave everything in the Fresno section in his hands; and it puts a deeper feeling of pride into him if he feels that I can pass over anything and everything to him without first considering it myself."[53] But that was a short-lived promise. Despite protestations to the contrary, CK kept a close watch on Carlos and his *Bee* management. CK, in fact, was now the editor of both papers and expected Carlos to run the Fresno paper in strict conformity with his wishes. Moreover CK was worried that his son spent too much money and took too many risks.

A few days later he sent Hiram a note thanking him for "writing directly to Carlos. I think it is the better way concerning anything connected with that section of the country." But, CK added, "it might be just as well, however, when you do so to send me a carbon copy of your letter so I can keep in touch with whatever is going on down there." Of the constant requirements for consultation with the elder McClatchy, Phebe Briggs McClatchy recalled that her husband, Carlos, "went [that is, drove] back and forth often . . . so much [that] he wore himself out driving and we finally had to get a driver." She also remarked that "Carlos found that his father did not always agree with what he wanted to do at The *Bee*. . . . The things he wanted to start and promote. . . . I can just remember he would go up to Sacramento with a big idea and come back discouraged. And that went on a lot."[54]

Absent Valentine's reassuring hand, CK fretted constantly about company finances and occasionally second-guessed members of his staff. He was rightly concerned about the huge debt the *Bee* had taken on to purchase other papers. He grew even more anxious when, as I noted earlier, the *Bee* purchased its only remaining evening rival in Fresno, the *Herald*, in late 1923 (for a mere $33,604). Although this left the *Fresno Bee* in exclusive control of the afternoon market, CK was anxious about the finances. No amount of assurance that this was in the end an economical move could allay his worry. In fact he became so querulous on this subject and questioned the business manager William H. James to such a degree that the loyal James became offended. CK wrote to Carlos expressing misgivings about the purchase. The *Herald*, CK worried, was not being liquidated fast enough to help with the overall financial picture and the *Fresno Bee* was still losing $15,000 a month. CK worried about a circulation war with the still-strong *Fresno Republican* and snorted his unhappiness at James's defensiveness about the purchase— and CK's suggestion that James might be responsible for the potential failure of the *Fresno Bee*. CK harrumphed: "It is . . . unfortunate . . . that I cannot make pertinent inquiries into my own business without somebody being offended."[55] Despite his father's misgivings, Carlos continued to innovate in Fresno, introducing a Sunday edition in September 1924. But even this unsettled CK. Other difficulties developed between father and son, increasing Carlos's frustration.

Acquiring the *Star*

In 1925 the *Bee* announced yet another expansion of the newspaper's reach with its purchase of the *Sacramento Star*, a rival paper that for years had an evening circulation of about ten thousand. CK and Carlos paid $52,728 to the *Star*'s parent company, the Scripps Howard chain, for the acquisition. There were other changes as well. In June 1925 Carlos obtained a license to begin radio station KMJ in Fresno. That August, by using the license from an earlier attempt to open radio station KVQ, the *Bee* began operating radio station KFBK in Sacramento and beyond. CK regarded the radio with some suspicion. One year before his death he wrote: "The radio is a wonderful thing in many ways probably God-sent. But certainly in others it is the devil diverted. . . . The greater portion of its time is given over to emanations of spurious and deplorable wit and bastard humor."[56]

Eleanor McClatchy

Amid all the personal and professional bitterness resulting from the break-up, a shaft of light shone through in 1924—the marriage of Eleanor to Raymond Crozier. Crozier was a World War I aviator who had been stationed at Mather Field. Eleanor, who volunteered for Red Cross war work, met the dashing airman with other Sacramentans who had come to welcome the pilots to the state capital. Phebe McClatchy recalled him as "nice looking—he wasn't distinguished looking but he was nice looking . . . an agreeable non-descript man." Crozier, a college graduate, was from Madison, Indiana, and he dreamed of starting an aircraft manufacturing firm. "Eleanor never had many beaus," recalled Phebe McClatchy, who was with her sister-in-law when she met Crozier.[57] A courtship ensued, and in early May 1924, Eleanor and Raymond announced plans to be married. Bishop Patrick Keane of Sacramento presided at Eleanor's August 7, 1924, garden wedding, with Carlos as Crozier's best man, while her best friend, Eunice McLaughlin Dunn, served as matron of honor, and little James Briggs McClatchy was a ring bearer.

The couple moved to Pasadena, where Raymond tried (with the help of McClatchy money) to found an aircraft manufacturing firm. However, Crozier turned out to be an abusive alcoholic who made Eleanor miserable. Her sad letters home brought the intervention of Carlos, who packed her up and brought her back to Sacramento, while he sent Crozier on his way. To avoid publicity and because of its more liberal divorce laws, Eleanor terminated her marriage in 1928 in Fallon, Nevada (avoiding Reno, where the *Bee* circulated). Crozier made one last effort to hang on, writing in a letter from Phoenix dated August 5, 1928: "Though it breaks my heart to think of you doing it, I loved you enough to promise that when that time comes, I will do nothing to interfere. Most of all I do not wish to cause either you or your family any further trouble. . . . I have grown to hate liquor and the airplane business as they have broken up our home. . . . I have learned my lesson now when I am afraid it is too late tho [*sic*] I have hopes of someday being worthy of you. May I have one last chance?"[58] Eleanor refused to discuss reconciliation and finalized the divorce just before Christmas 1928. Nonetheless she kept the letter and the elaborate wedding albums until she died. The stock of Crozier's ill-fated aircraft company was sold, and he disappeared, never to be heard of again.

In early 1929 the newly single Eleanor joined the Briggs family on a tour of Africa, remaining with her brother's in-laws until a chance came to break off and tour with friends she had met aboard a cruise ship. Phebe recalled, "Eleanor just suddenly popped off and left them, to go with some people she had met on the trip to Yugoslavia, and they felt very much hurt the way she just abandoned them without apparently giving any thought to thanking them for giving her such a good trip or anything like that—she just saw a better opportunity and took it."[59]

Eleanor had had a challenging youth. Plagued by health problems, she was particularly close to her parents and more religiously observant than her siblings. When she was barely six years old in late 1901, she had a serious operation for an unspecified reason. Although she had access to the best medical care available in Sacramento and San Francisco, she had a recurring speech impediment. Phebe Briggs, Eleanor's childhood friend and later sister-in-law, recalled, "She stuttered dreadfully. . . . She could hardly talk and she was very friendly and very happy apparently and wanted to be with you but she was timid and a terrible stutterer which was enough to make anyone timid—that would blight her life very much."[60] Eleanor's embarrassing stutter sent the McClatchys on a nationwide search for a doctor who could cure her. CK himself tried, using the technique of the famed ancient Greek orator Demosthenes, as the editor explained to a friendly San Francisco physician:

> I have been having her read to me with a handful of marbles in her mouth for fifteen minutes every evening since she has been home. I find this thing to be true: That when she takes the paper and reads to me she stutters and hesitates and stammers and practically goes to pieces. When I read the paper to her, sentence by sentence, she will repeat it after me as clearly and distinctly as I enunciate it myself. She never stuttered once in all the time I have tried it that way, but just as soon as she takes up the paper herself and reads to me, the same old trouble goes all over again.[61]

At some point CK and Ella realized that the solution to Eleanor's problems might be a new environment where she could be on her own and take personal responsibility for her improvement. In 1913 CK and Ella decided to send her to a finishing school away from Sacramento. Ella worried that Eleanor might become too homesick and first tried schools in Washington, D.C., where the McClatchys had developed a network of friends and associates. However, the

Washington academy they inspected did not meet their expectations, and at the suggestion of friends the McClatchys decided upon the Bennett School in Millbrook, New York, a picturesque village on the Hudson. Bennett had been founded in 1890 by May F. Bennett, an educator in Irvington, New York, and was dedicated to "finishing" young women.

The school had grown gradually to a six-year institution—the first four roughly equivalent to a high school curriculum and the last two made up of "feminine studies"—music, art, literature, history, economics, ethics, domestic arts, and sciences. In 1907 Bennett moved the thriving academy to a failed summer resort hotel in Millbrook called Halcyon Hall. Set on a hill fifteen miles east of the Hudson River, the twenty-two-acre school had plenty of space for physical activity and a stable of forty horses. It attracted students from all over the United States who came for Bennett's healthy mix of academics and physical activities, which included running, calisthenics, and equestrian pursuits. Academics were stressed, but the primary emphasis was on personal development: "Its upper classes are designed to equip the student for her place in life without the long, arduous college course."[62] Eleanor enjoyed the beautiful rambling old resort building, which was school and dormitory, and the prospect of pursuing her equestrian interests. As time went on her confidence grew, and she apparently became an accomplished rider, participating in the various competitions and shows the school had. In 1916 she won a silver cup and blue ribbon for being the best rider in her class. The personal attention of the staff helped to some degree with her self-confidence and speech, but improving her speech proved to be a lifelong quest—one she never quite mastered. Once Eleanor came home for the summer in 1914, her stuttering returned.

The only fear CK had in sending his daughter to an elite girls' academy in the East was that she might forget her Sacramento roots. "We had seen so many returned California girls whose noses were turned heavenward, even if their minds were not, and who seemed to be bored with life in this 'neck of the woods' and we would rather have Eleanor not go to school at all than return with an air superior to her surrounding and distaste for her old friends." But his fears were not realized. Eleanor "is as democratic, if not more democratic, than ever. . . . She is the same to everybody with no airs, no overlooking old friends, no desires to forget any of the old scenes, and with as much love for Sacramento as she ever had," her father happily reported to May Bennett.[63]

Indeed Eleanor never forgot her western roots. In 1915 Bennett's literary publication, the *Hexagon,* featured an article by Eleanor, "Helpful Hints to

Young Farmers," in which she described an idyllic ranch "on thirty acres of riverland" that she and her Japanese servants (Togashura and Hecuba) turned into a profitable enterprise as Rancho del Pricio de Fancie (Fancy Price Ranch). With its evocations of flood lands and Japanese servants, she evoked a nostalgia for her home turf that could not have been lost on her Bennett School companions. She would return to California, never to leave.[64]

Chapter Seventeen
The Last Roar of the Aging Lion

◆

HERBERT HOOVER'S NOMINATION for president in 1928 elicited nothing but disdain from CK. Unwilling to stomach "Herbert Chrysanthemum," CK endorsed Democrat Alfred E. Smith, the New York Democrat he had admired for many years. Smith shared CK's belief in public ownership of utilities and the use of government for improving the commonweal. Hiram Johnson was practically blackmailed into endorsing Hoover—a quid pro quo in which Johnson received Hoover's support for reelection to the Senate. CK naturally forgave his old friend. "Personally, I do not know how you could have done otherwise," CK assured Johnson. "There was absolutely no other avenue to take. As the hero in Led Astray is made to say by the dramatist, 'if there is but one road, one must take it, lead through what ways it will.'"[1]

Hoover won in a landslide, and Hiram received another six-year term, making this his third consecutive Senate victory. CK blamed part of Hoover's triumph on women's suffrage, complaining to Johnson, "I do not believe it has purified politics in any manner, shape or form. I do not believe it has led us into better governmental ways—quite the contrary. . . . So far woman suffrage has been a great failure in this State of California when it is considered in connection with either sensible or reformatory legislation."[2]

But women were not the issue. Although he had never held elective office, Hoover was genuinely popular as an efficiency expert-in-chief. Moreover he was able to maneuver deftly around the anti-Catholic bias directed at Smith during the campaign. Hoover himself condemned religious intolerance but was able to take advantage of the edge it gave him in the election. Even the reach of the McClatchy news empire could not deliver California to Smith. Most disappointing was that Sacramento County went for Hoover by a solid

1,000 votes. CK lamented: "We did the best we could and we got licked. That is all there is to it. But I tell you Hiram, I feel a thousand times better right now defeated than I would feel if I had thrown aside my principles and come out for the winner."[3]

Shortly after the election yet another opportunity for European travel opened up. By the end of 1928 CK and Ella had followed their younger daughter, Eleanor, who had joined the W. E. Briggs family for another trip abroad. Carlos would be in charge of the three newspapers, but this time there was more apprehension than ever about leaving him alone with the business.

Concerns About Carlos

CK continued to worry about the financial condition of the newspapers. When CK returned home from his European vacation of 1926–27, he was not totally happy with his son's business performance. Carlos had added columnists who called into question *Bee* editorial policies. One took issue with several *Bee* positions and criticized CK's (and Ella's) infatuation with Mussolini. In response to Carlos's plans to travel abroad and write about international conditions, especially affairs in the Soviet Union, CK grumped to Johnson, "I was under the impression that Carlos wanted to get into Russia, but I think he is making a mistake in starting to make this trip one of hard work, reading, writing, interviewing, and everything else instead of making it one of pleasure. But Carlos has an obstinate mind of his own. I do not know where he could have got it." Carlos also promoted the reprint of a *Vallejo Chronicle* editorial dismissing the chances of Buron Fitts, a former lieutenant governor and now Los Angeles County district attorney, who was challenging Hiram Johnson for the Senate in 1928. CK dissented "with Carlos entirely on this subject." CK even nixed Carlos's efforts to bring operatic music to Fresno—something he had underwritten with *Bee* money. In 1929, when Carlos proposed bringing the Scottish-born soprano Mary Garden to perform, CK vetoed the idea because previous concerts had lost money. Besides, CK insisted, such high culture did not appeal to the "average working man and the average working woman" whose friendship was necessary for the success of the papers. Ordinary citizens likely did not care "very much whether Mary Garden comes to California or not."[4] This letter must have been deeply disappointing to Carlos.

Beneath the anxiety about finances and particular editorial decisions lay fears of Carlos's increasing dependence on alcohol and his sometimes erratic personal behavior. CK, too, had struggled with alcoholism, but the needs of his children and concern for his wife apparently had been enough to bring this vice under control. Even before their marriage, Phebe knew her husband had problems with alcohol. Phebe speculated her husband had started drinking as a teenager when he worked for a time with stevedores on the Sacramento docks. After the birth of their first son, James, in 1920, Carlos, she recalled, "went on the first of the devastating sprees that I had experienced." Phebe's brother had found Carlos and brought him home, where she "nursed him and comforted him and we both thought it would never happen again." But it was only the beginning. She later confided to her sons that when Carlos's drinking became bad, she would remove the children from his presence. At one point Carlos asked if she wanted him to stop drinking, and she instead left it up to him—something she later regretted. Carlos's addiction to drink grew stronger during his years in Fresno. Even during Prohibition days he managed to obtain fine liquor smuggled in from Canada. He allowed parties at the *Bee* offices in Fresno, where spirits were readily available. As with his father, people with whom he worked noticed his bouts with the bottle. His father and mother received reports of Carlos's public intoxication and odd behavior from staff. Many did not understand how Carlos, with a lovely wife and now three sons, could manage to be drunk for days on end. But who would have the temerity to confront the boss? Indeed alcohol had begun to take its toll on his judgment and work. One rumor, repeated by the *Bee* historian Steve Wiegand, was that Carlos had botched a promising Bakersfield acquisition because he had been drunk on the day of the closing.[5] Still, CK tried to balance his concerns with his belief in Carlos's abilities and his track record of solid judgment in many areas. But now CK relied increasingly on his staff, including J. Earl Langdon, Walter Jones, and their Fresno counterparts, to keep him informed about his son's behavior and to note deviations from CK's rules in the daily copies of the other *Bee*s in the valley.

CK by now was feeling the burden of his seventy years, and although both he and Ella were sick with bad colds, they steamed for Europe one final time in 1928. When they reached Naples, he was put to bed and was unable to get around for nearly two weeks. Carlos kept him abreast of state and national politics—and also took the momentous step of sending Walter Jones to Washington, D.C., as the *Bee*'s full-time correspondent there. Jones, who was destined to become CK's replacement as editor, had joined the *Bee* staff in

1925 when it merged with the *Star*. Bright, energetic, and wholly sympathetic to CK's vision, he soon became the most trusted of the McClatchy lieutenants. When Hiram Johnson informed CK that Jones was appearing regularly at his office, CK remarked, "This is the first I have known that Walter Jones has been sent over to Washington to represent the '*Bee*'; but I am glad that he is over there." Carlos later explained that sending Jones was yet another chapter in the ongoing saga of the Valentine-CK feud since the rival *Sacramento Union* had hired Leo McClatchy to do its congressional reporting in Washington. Carlos had dispatched the astute and hardworking Jones to counter Leo's efforts—especially as they related to Hiram Johnson. Johnson, like CK, came to admire and respect Jones's judgment and his forthright writing style.[6] Eleanor McClatchy would keep him as her right hand until his death in 1974.

Eleanor joined her parents in May and continued to travel with them throughout Western Europe. In the fall they met Judge Charles McLaughlin while traveling in England. Sadly, McLaughlin suffered a stroke, and CK and Ella arranged doctors and nurses for him until his daughter Eunice arrived from the States to take her father home. The trip was a nightmare for the McClatchys as CK was seriously ill much of the time and spent extended periods in European hospitals. The couple returned home in November 1929, with Ella still suffering from a lingering respiratory problem. When Johnson welcomed them back, CK's physical deterioration surprised him. Johnson confided to his son: "Mr. and Mrs. C. K. McClatchy came here. . . . The ravages of the years show very plainly now. He is seventy-one years old and he and Mrs. McClatchy have just returned from a year's absence abroad. I can't for the life of me see how they could very greatly enjoy themselves, and particularly so when I found that he was in the hospital in Paris for three weeks, and again in Munich for a considerable time. The old boy says that his wanderings are now over." Johnson tried to cheer him up by praising the way the *Bee* had been handled during his absence. At that the hopeful CK opined, "I consider Carlos a better general, all-round newspaper man than I ever was. The reason for that is this—in modern newspaperdom two qualities in a thorough newspaper man should be amalgamated—one the editorial and the other the business. . . . Carlos has both qualifications splendidly developed."[7] CK would take one last trip, to the Far East—but without Ella. Whatever hopes he had that Carlos was ready to run the entire McClatchy newspaper operation were soon dashed, and what followed were several years of personal agony.

Back to the Grind

CK and Ella had arrived home in 1929 about a month after the calamitous crash on Wall Street had plunged the nation into the Great Depression. Although the economic shock waves took time to reach the Pacific Coast, by early 1931 Sacramento and the rest of California were witnessing a steady decline in business life. Farmers and orchardists experienced a falloff in production (the result of a terrible cold snap) and also in demand. This of course affected the canneries, box companies, and railroad, which had to lay off workers. Carlos met with his father after he arrived in Sacramento and briefed him on various conditions at the newspapers. They also met with CK's friend Bert Meek to hear the status of affairs in Governor Clement Young's administration.

CK's support for Young had already begun to wane as the new governor came into office in 1927. Although Young had done some good things, the governor's reluctance to tie himself too closely to Johnson and his decision to support Hoover in 1928 were seen as acts of treason. Young had particularly irritated CK by refusing to keep all the state government offices in Sacramento and allowing annexes in Los Angeles and San Francisco. Even though Johnson himself had endorsed Hoover, CK and Johnson decided to keep Young at arm's length, believing his support for the Republican candidate had permanently alienated Progressives.

Carlos continued to be a source of concern. When he traveled to Washington, D.C., on behalf of the radio stations the *Bee* owned, he managed to spend time with Johnson but did not seek his help. CK had worked hard to cultivate the tempestuous Johnson. Carlos now apparently thought he could do business without the senator.

Johnson kept CK abreast of the legislative activity of the early Hoover administration. Their letters were filled with contempt and scorn for newspapermen who supported the new president. CK and Johnson referred to them as Knights of the Napkin, as they appeared to be easily flattered by invitations to White House luncheons and dinners and gave the White House favorable press coverage. In California CK continually scoured the horizon for signs of opposition to Senator Johnson, regularly sending him clippings from various California newspapers and serving as his surrogate in the senator's ongoing battles with the *Los Angeles Times,* which had opposed him throughout his career.

However, CK's energy faltered in early 1930. He recalled Walter Jones from the Washington, D.C., beat and turned over to him more and more of the precious political analysis CK so loved—taking Jones to meetings with friendly state politicians who were often pleading for an endorsement or a bit of publicity in the *Bee*. Jones eventually became CK's alter ego. But the unpleasant realities surrounding Carlos—his increasingly erratic, alcohol-induced behavior—created leadership and administrative difficulties at the Fresno papers and affected the general conduct of all the McClatchy enterprises. Things became so bad that at one point CK planned to remove him some time in 1930, but both Ella and Phebe tearfully begged him not to. The sentimental CK gave in. But worries about the management of the *Bee* and Carlos's condition weighed on his mind. CK's escape consisted of long rides in the country, often with a dragooned *Bee* staffer he took with him on chauffeured jaunts to Woodland or Folsom. Among those he corralled on these afternoon trips was Roy V. Bailey, a *Bee* employee since 1919 who occasionally outlined editorials for CK. Bailey later would help Eleanor compile a memorial book of his "Private Thinks."[8]

Problems continued into 1931 as Carlos again became vocal about who was to inherit the *Bee*. CK temporized and extended the trust that governed the management of the *Bee* for another five years. He had contracted Johnson's services to represent him in all matters pertaining to the *Bee,* and Johnson had asked his California law partner, Theodore Roche, to assist.[9] However, CK found problems were growing worse. "Things have not been going very well," he confided to Johnson. "In fact they are in a very bad condition so far as the principal point is concerned. You know what I mean. I have come to the conclusion that I must alter the trust deed very materially for the protection of all parties concerned. I do not favor making a will because its provisions would have to be made public, and I do not want that."[10] For both personal and professional reasons, Johnson would be kept apprised of developments during CK's final years.

The conflict with Carlos, which would become acute, then subside throughout 1931, added to CK's woes. To make matters worse, in late May CK fell through an uncovered manhole while waiting for Eleanor at the train station in Davis. The fall shattered his shoulder, leaving him without the use of his right arm and in nearly constant pain. The impact of the tumble on the seventy-two-year-old newsman was devastating. It required surgery and a painful convalescence and set in motion a long chain reaction of illnesses that kept him immobilized for nearly the rest of his life. For all intents and purposes, CK's effective career as editor of the *Bee* was finished on that May day—but he would not give up or step down before enduring even more severe emotional pain.

As Bert Meek would say at his funeral in 1936: "Our friend has been walking toward the sunset since the accident several years ago."[11]

CK convalesced all summer long at home and at his Citrus Heights ranch.[12] Later, with therapy, he was able to use his arm from the hand to the elbow— and handwrote his *Private Thinks,* which recommenced in 1932.

Tragedy Strikes

Things seemed to improve for Carlos in the fall of 1931.[13] By the late fall, with Carlos seemingly stable, CK decided, on his doctors' advice, to take another trip abroad, this time to the Far East. Ella chose not to accompany him, and he booked passage on the Canadian steamship *Empress of Canada* for Hong Kong and Japan. The disabled CK was wheeled aboard and began his journey, which would last several weeks. Johnson wrote to him (a letter he did not receive), saying, "I am praying for your good health and speedy recovery. I confess that your long trip rather frightened me, but I recognize that you and your doctors knew much more about what was good for you than I did." In early December CK wired his personal secretary, Gladys Cunningham, that "he was feeling better." But CK returned to Sacramento just before Christmas to find that Carlos had once again gone on one of his "wild sprees." CK wrote dejectedly to Johnson: "I am very sorry to say that the thing that has troubled the Madame and myself recently at present is worse than ever. I have suggested to the Madame that probably the only way to do under the circumstances, is to pension the party. If things go on as they are now, the papers probably will get into a great deal of trouble." He added, "Kindly tear up this letter."[14] This crisis passed, but no sooner were things back on track when influenza struck CK. Gladys Cunningham now also monitored his health and reported to Johnson.

Despite optimistic predictions that CK would be up in a matter of days, he was still bedridden at the end of February 1932. Further difficulties ensued as CK, whose illness may have dimmed his perceptions, contemplated running portions of a book entitled *The Rise of Herbert Hoover* by the crusading journalist Walter W. Liggett. Carlos and others tried hard to dissuade CK because the tone of the book and its sources did not seem sound. CK informed Johnson: "I wanted to rush to publication of these things, beginning tonight, but Carlos seems to be timid about the matter. He fears a libel suit."[15] A brief moment of sunshine appeared when the *Fresno Republican,* the last remaining competitor to the *Fresno Bee,* was finally shuttered (it had been purchased in 1926 but kept running for a time). CK exulted, "The purchase of the Fresno Republican is a great tribute to the talent and shrewdness of Carlos. . . . This purchase . . . settles the problem in Fresno. It saves the Fresno *Bee* $100,000 a year in one line alone, and undoubtedly Fresno hereafter will report a profit all along the line." The problems with Carlos abated for at time, and Johnson wrote to CK about meeting with another *Bee* attorney, Alex Ashen, regarding the radio business. After Johnson and Ashen talked, Johnson wrote CK: "I was immensely pleased with what he told me about Carlos, and I rejoice with you that Carlos is doing so well. I know what a load must have been lifted from you when he settled down. He is a marvelous man, and Ashen explained to me from the newspaper standpoint he probably had no equal on the coast. We can all rejoice that he is himself again."[16]

CK was still bedridden in May, and by mid-June Gladys Cunningham wrote anxiously to Senator Johnson, revealing that CK's problems were cardiac. "His heart is in bad shape," she reported, "and he cannot do anything to tire himself. . . . He seems to be worried about Carlos and told me he knew he was drinking again, although so far he has covered it up pretty well." Cunningham also worried that CK was not being well served by Johnson's partner, Theodore Roche, and mentioned her apprehension "that Carlos is grooming another man for his assistant—when he gains control of the papers—a man who has no connection with the papers, who knows nothing of C. K.'s policies, etc." But even more ominously she lamented, "I was told the other day that the doctors who took care of Carlos feel there is no hope for him; that he is a mental case now and that it is only a matter of time until he will be drinking hard again. . . . Carlos has told CK that if he gives away the stock to anybody but him, he will resign and have nothing more to do with the papers." Cunningham appended a note to another letter to Johnson two weeks later, "Things are not going along in good shape. We are very much worried and so are CK and Mrs. CK. Will be glad when you finally get to California."[17]

A few days later CK confirmed the renewed tension: "I am sorry to say," he wrote Johnson, "that things do not look at all well. The person in question [Carlos] is more obstreperous than ever, taking the attitude that he has been wronged and that he hasn't been treated right at all. I really do not know what in the name of heaven to do." Johnson wrote back sympathetically, "He [Carlos] is such a wonderful man, of really extraordinary ability, already at the top of his profession, that the thought of the ruin of it all by an utter lack of restraint, is simply terrible." He noted, "I fear little can be done. If the situation continues as you indicate in your note, you simply will have to rely on the splendid organization you have built up during the years and steel yourself to a break."[18] The remainder of 1932 was an ongoing nightmare for CK and Ella as Carlos became increasingly unmanageable.

CK tried to keep his mind on the impending presidential election of 1932 in which he strongly supported the candidacy of Franklin D. Roosevelt. When Roosevelt received the nomination, CK sent a congratulatory telegram to which FDR replied warmly with a handwritten note, "I look forward to seeing you a little later on." In fact CK actively collaborated with the Roosevelt campaign, dispatching the *Bee*'s political editor, Walter Jones, to follow the campaign train on a late September swing through the Golden State. Jones reported from Dunsmuir, in the northern Sacramento Valley, that "they asked me for suggestions on a speech in Sacramento." Jones advised them to praise hometown boy Hiram Johnson and to allude to a speech the senator had delivered on progressivism before the California Federation of Labor Convention in Modesto the day before. "Governor Roosevelt and his advisers willingly accepted my suggestion and prepared the speech he delivered in Sacramento and gave it out to the 25 correspondents on the train prior to its delivery here."[19]

Roosevelt's victory brought CK some rejoicing, as did the new administration's feeler to his friend Johnson to join the cabinet, but CK continued to decline. If he allowed himself any observation, it was a smattering of his life-long curmudgeonly misogyny, this time directed at the new first lady, Eleanor Roosevelt. In his opinion she was entirely too full of public comment: "I think it would be better for Mrs. Roosevelt, and all women like her, to shinny on their own side and let their husbands take care of the affairs of the nation." Johnson sent an end-of-year greeting to the decrepit CK with the sincere wish for "a surcease of the worries that have been yours, some real measure of improved health and that 1933 may be good to you in every aspect."[20]

The New Year, however, brought the tragic denouement of the problems with Carlos. According to the *Bee* historian Steve Wiegand, Carlos took off on another drinking binge on New Year's and had to be hospitalized once again.[21] On January 11, CK wrote to Johnson from Fresno: "I am down here because things have gone as far as they could go. The party has been put in the sanitarium with a little doctor who was attending him and after he gets thoroughly sobered up, he is to be told he will have a vacation from the McClatchy Newspapers for a year. During that time, he will have to take treatment and his future is with himself." CK finally poured out on paper all that had happened over the past fourteen months:

> I held out on this matter as long as possible, but now I think I should [have] done a year or two ago what I find now has to be done. I had that purpose in mind more than once, but, first my own wife and then Carlos' wife begged me not to do it, but to hold on as there probably would be a goodly prospect of reform. There hasn't been any. Things are in an awful condition. I have found it necessary to relieve him of everything in the offices and I have appointed G.C. Hamilton as General Business Director, and J.E. Langdon as General Editorial Director of all the newspapers, leaving everything else just as it is. I do not intend to take Carlos' name away from the top of the staff which we publish in The Sacramento *Bee* every Saturday and which I intend to publish in the other papers. His name will remain under mine as General Manager of the McClatchy Newspapers, followed by the name of Langdon and Hamilton. I thought it would be a very poor policy not only from a family stand point of the paper itself to haul down his name from the masthead.[22]

Carlos did not take the demotion quietly. CK was disconsolate, even as he found the energy to assume control.[23]

A week later Carlos was dead. Details of Carlos's death are sketchy. Official reports say he died at 10:30 a.m. on January 17, 1933, at the home of a friend in San Mateo as physicians worked to save him. Apparently he had caught a bad cold from a night out in the rain that developed into full-blown pneumonia. CK brought down a cadre of Sacramento physicians, including Dr. Philip Brown King, chief of the medical staff of the Southern Pacific Hospital.[24] All to no avail: Carlos died in the presence of his father, wife, and mother-in-law. Monsignor Thomas A. Horgan of Sacramento's Cathedral of the Blessed Sacrament conducted the funeral services at the McClatchy home.

A letter to Ella from a former priest of the cathedral indicated Carlos had received the last rites of the church before he died—at least this is what CK and Phebe told her. Carlos was the first of his family to be interred in a family plot in Sacramento's East Lawn Cemetery. Later Ella and Eleanor had windows designed, and dedicated in his honor, for the chapel of St. Patrick's Orphanage (today St. Rose Church) on Freeport Boulevard in South Sacramento. In his memory his sisters, Eleanor and Charlotte, commissioned the *Bee's* artist-in-residence, Dunbar Dyson Beck, to craft fourteen stations of the cross—memorials of the stages of Jesus's ascent to Calvary, his death, and burial—to be displayed in the church. The grateful pastor acknowledged the grief of the prominent, but nonchurch-going family, as "a lasting monument to their beloved brother, a monument that will serve to keep his memory green in his native Sacramento."[25] Later, windows memorializing other members of the family and an elegant reredos were installed in the church.

CK and Ella plunged into deep grief. However, CK's remarkable willpower made it possible for the couple to move on. He was even able to summon enough energy to console Johnson—whose own son Archibald committed suicide in August 1933. CK and Ella pondered what had happened to their only son. CK confided to Johnson: "The Madam always contended that Carlos' troubles sprang from the war. I didn't think so at the time, but as the days go on, I am more and more convinced she was right."[26]

As painful as Carlos's death was, it also ended CK's worries for his only son's safety and the handling of the businesses. Assuming control of the organization temporarily reinvigorated him, but he was careful to marshal his strength. Even before Carlos's death CK had wanted to make sure that his administrative team could deal with the issues at hand. Writing to H. R. McLaughlin, who was now running the Fresno paper, CK addressed his long-held fears that the paper was bleeding the company's revenue. Still, the Fresno paper would go on, and he insisted the Fresno staffers follow the chain of command through either Hamilton or Langdon—particularly Langdon for "questions approaching *Bee* policies," but, "I do not want to be troubled with anything more than is absolutely necessary."[27]

After Carlos's death CK and Ella drew up their wills. CK's will specified that half of everything would go to Ella, and he apportioned the other half to leave money to Eleanor, Charlotte, and a trust fund for Carlos's three sons. When Ella died, her estate would be parceled out in the same way.[28]

Final Years

To help recover from the shock of Carlos's death, CK, Ella, Eleanor, and a traveling nurse decamped from Sacramento in early March 1933 and took a circuitous route to the Mayo Clinic in Rochester, Minnesota. They first steamed through the Panama Canal and up to New York City, where they checked in at the Roosevelt Hotel.[29] Before going to Rochester, he made the trek down to Washington, D.C., where Johnson arranged a quick visit to the White House so CK could meet President Roosevelt. Roosevelt was in the second month of what would become the famous Hundred Days and suffering from a bad cold. Yet he welcomed the meeting with his California supporter on April 19.

Since CK was by this time too weak to climb stairs, arrangements were made for him to meet the president on the lower level of the White House. CK wrote glowingly to Cunningham: "He was graciousness itself. He is really a marvelous man, probably not one man in ten thousand could have done what he did with his indomitable will when all his lower limbs are paralyzed." Johnson praised CK to the new president. "In introducing me to the President, Senator Johnson said some very complimentary things concerning myself," CK told her. "And the President agreed with him and thanked me very heartily for what the papers had done for him in California. So I was considerably embarrassed at the bouquets."[30] The meeting was fairly substantive—CK related to Cunningham that the president talked quite a bit about his decision to stop the flow of gold to Europe. The veteran White House usher Ike Hoover gave CK a tour of the executive mansion, and CK marveled at the new buildings Coolidge had erected along Pennsylvania Avenue.

The support of CK and the *Bees* for FDR would remain fairly steady, although the aging editor continued to take a dim view of Eleanor Roosevelt's highly publicized activities and worried openly about the internationalist tendencies of the Democratic president. CK would not live to see the eventual slide into war that would occur in FDR's second term.

From Washington the McClatchys went by railroad to the Mayo Clinic, where the staff thoroughly examined the ailing editor. They definitely diagnosed CK's heart problems and told him he must drastically reduce his workload and seriously restrict his movements. He was relieved by the prognosis and told Hiram that "I have there [sic] declaration that I ought to live ten years or more longer provided I am not run over by an automobile or something of that kind."[31] By late May all three McClatchys were back home in Sacramento.

Nonetheless, despite the recurrent optimism about his health and longevity, CK from this point on was a virtual invalid. He was still able to wield a pen now and then, but he turned over effective administration of the *Bee* to his longtime associates Guy Hamilton and J. Earl "Lang" Langdon. However, in late 1934 "Lang" unexpectedly retired, and Walter Jones replaced him and became the primary conveyor of CK's ideas and ideology and the guardian of the McClatchy legacy. CK attempted to trudge on and did his best to spice up the paper with his waspish observations. He noted with joy the final repeal of Prohibition in June 1933: "Yours truly will arrogate to himself no peacock feathers. . . . He will not be Sir Chanticleer startling the air with crescendo crows. But he thinks he has earned the right to say 'I told you so.'"[32]

But CK had scant sympathy for the growing numbers of unemployed Sacramentans and endorsed the harsh measures taken by the city welfare officer, Mary Judge. He applauded especially her heavy hand with the poor, whom he lumped together as the "pest and plague of professionally unemployed blatherskites, wind bags, and 'sons of rest'—men [on] whose sensitive nerves a sawbuck has the same chilling effect as [a] snake has upon the average woman." Judge's harsh tactics, which included berating and physically ejecting the poor, finally ended when riots broke out in her offices, and homeless men and women refused to be intimidated by her authoritarian ways. Later, when Hoovervilles rose up in various sections of Sacramento, he endorsed Judge's questionable assertion: "Over 90 percent of able-bodied single men available to enroll in federal relief camps from what is [*sic*] known as Hoovervilles have refused to do so." He backed Judge's request that relief for all men younger than sixty—with exceptions—be discontinued." His disdain for the unemployed was tempered by his understanding that "the Depression has brought want and suffering to thousands of worthy aged people many of whom laid away a nest egg for their declining days, only to see it pilfered by those in whom they had put trust." But he had little faith in social welfare programs such as the Townsend Plan, which promised old age assistance, fearing "it would teach a wholesale lesson of idleness. It would relegate thrift into the background. It would create [a] vast army of loafers who would look upon work as degrading."[33]

The remainder of 1933 was trying for both family and associates as CK's health declined even more. He tried to return to some kind of normal work pattern but was unable. In September his worried secretary wrote Johnson that CK was sneaking whiskey into the car for his daily automobile rides. Even more, his heart was giving out; despite top-notch care, CK's heart problems defied easy prognosis. To avoid the problem of stairs and to provide a more serene environment, CK repaired to his ranch, where he remained for much of the fall of 1933. He put the final touches on the new arrangement at the *Bee,* with him as president and Hamilton and Langdon assuming key duties. He remained a loyal supporter of President Roosevelt's. The key issue of 1933 was funding the Central Valley Water Project. Many importuned CK to press Senator Johnson for the project. Feeling Johnson out on the implications of the bill, he trod gingerly, knowing the project would heavily favor the northern part of the state and might displease Johnson's Southern California constituents. "Whatever you do will be O.K. with me, of course," wrote CK. "The *Bee* is going to fight all it possibly can for the acceptance by the electorate of this plan; but it does not want you to do a single thing that would in any way mitigate against your re-election to the United States Senate."[34]

Despite his deteriorating health and mobility, CK observed approvingly as his reporters scrutinized the appointment of two judges in Nevada—William Woodburn, a Reno attorney, to the U.S. Circuit Court of Appeals, and Frank Herbert Norcross to the U.S. District Court. *Bee* reporters then unleashed a series of articles condemning the two men as minions of the local Nevada boss George Wingfield.[35] An editorial blast against their nominations followed and was widely reproduced and circulated by Senator William Gibbs McAdoo of California. These stories would eventually end the careers of both men and Wingfield and win the *Bee* its first Pulitzer Prize, in 1935. CK likely played only a marginal role in this signal honor to the paper.

In early January 1934 the still bedridden CK continued to feed information and documents to Johnson, attacking appointments, warning of their damage to Roosevelt, and cautioning him to be wary of Senator Patrick McCarran, the Nevada Democrat. CK also weighed in on the National Industrial Recovery Act and its codes of fair competition. He advised Johnson, who was up for re-election, to form a new political coalition called the Progressives that would link Democrats and progressive Republicans behind his candidacy. February 1934 brought a confession from CK to Hiram that his health had deteriorated further. Nonetheless he mustered the energy to send his first warning to the Roosevelt administration: "I am sorry to say that I fear The *Bee* and Mr. Roosevelt will part company before long, for I believe he will not stand by the propagandists of America against the European countries, but will yield to internationalists as represented by such men as Newton Baker and Chester Rowell. If so, 'I lifts up my hat, and I say goodbye.'"[36]

At his ranch CK began to feel a bit better and had time to engage in local California politics. As in times past, all state politics evolved around a single issue for CK: public ownership of utilities. He framed the issues the way he always did: through the dichotomies of darkness and light, evil and good. In 1934 a campaign for governor was underway. The incumbent, James Rolph, had badly managed the oncoming depression, and the poor were in desperate straits. Rolph died in office and former governor Clement Young sought endorsements for another run. Although Young had committed the unforgivable sin of supporting Hoover in 1928, he hoped to win Johnson's backing for the primary, but the senator begged off, insisting he didn't participate in primary politics. Young approached CK and swore solemn assurances he was a loyal supporter of Johnson's. McClatchy advised Young that he should run against the corporations, but with the full effects of the Depression now hard on California, Young instead held that he had to do something about the unemployment and serious economic distress besetting the Golden State. CK would have none of it. When Young declared his candidacy on the radio and promised relief, CK (still thinking it was 1920) wrote to Young, "If you will pardon me for saying so, I could not find . . . any definite program on which a real Progressive should fight. There wasn't a line in there of the domination of the people of California by the privately-owned public utilities." He concluded wryly, "I suppose however, that you are holding your powder upon this thing for a more auspicious occasion."[37] To Johnson CK wrote that the crisis of the Great Depression was "not the great question before the people of the State of California." Rather the issue was the power of the private utilities—"Pacific Gas & Electric Company, the Southern California Edison Company, and birds of that stripe."[38] His disdain for Young grew: "The more this man flits about and flirts about the more disgusted I am. . . . If he is a Progressive, why doesn't he say so?"[39]

CK then threw his support to the futile candidacy of John Quinn, who ran a weak campaign. This drew votes away from Young, who lost the nomination and left the field to two radicals: Senator Frank Merriam and the muckraking journalist Upton Sinclair. CK wrote Johnson that it "appears probable now, the nominees will be F.F. Merriam, the crook, and Upton Sinclair, the crazy sky-rocket." The editor seemed to regard the whole episode with amusement, promising to endorse the hopeless candidacy of Raymond Haight, "for I would rather lose all the papers than say a word for either Upton Sinclair or F.F. Merriam as a gubernatorial candidate."[40] The 1934 election campaign was a defeat for the McClatchy position, elevating the conservative Frank Merriam, a former state Assembly speaker who won a solid victory over Sinclair and Haight, who split the Progressive vote. CK took the defeat lightly; his only moment of drama came when yet another of his old Progressive friends defected from the "tents of Israel" and lined up with the detested Merriam.

In the fall Cunningham noted, "I was out at the ranch and worked with CK this morning. He doesn't sleep well and hasn't much strength. The nurse is hoping that as soon as the hot weather is gone he will begin to feel better again. The doctor here does not permit him to walk very much. It gives all of us old-timers on the *Bee* a heart ache when we think of CK as he is and CK as he was a few short years ago. He has a wonderful spirit though and complains but little."[41] The year 1935 was a difficult one for C. K.

McClatchy began to think seriously about succession at the *Bee*. Martin Maloney, his oldest grandson, had already gone to work in the business department of the Sacramento paper. In a letter to H. R. McLaughlin a year later, in November 1935, CK touched on the question of another grandson, Brown Maloney. "Brown wants to work on The Fresno *Bee*, or, rather, he wants to work for the McClatchy Newspapers. I chose Fresno for him because I do not want Martin and him to be on the same paper. He is crazy to be a newspaperman, and I think he has inclined to the business department. I would much rather he would go on with the news and editorial side as Martin is on the business side in Sacramento; and I honestly think Brown would be very much better out in the news room." CK put young Brown under McLaughlin's demanding eye and insisted he receive $25 per week, "but only $15 of that will be paid by The *Bee*. I will furnish the other $10 privately out of my own pocket because I do not want any of my relatives to be treated by The *Bee* with any more kindness or generosity than anybody else who applies for a position." Earlier in the year the family had a brief respite of joy as CK and Ella celebrated their fiftieth wedding anniversary with a honeymoon trip to Monterey. After the trip McClatchy confessed to Johnson he was feeling well but lazy. By late May CK was suffering new problems with his leg. He traveled to Stanford University Hospital for a lengthy hospitalization and felt weak until July. Back at home, fighting the oppressive heat of the state capital, he recalled to Johnson, "You know Hiram, when we were younger, we never cared about the summer climate in Sacramento, and it is only since my accident that the doctors have told me I must avoid my city in the blistering hot summer months."[42]

By early December 1935 CK was back in the Stanford hospital. He returned home to Sacramento in late December and described himself both candidly and optimistically to Hiram: "I have not been well enough lately even to dictate, but I am feeling very much improved and am going out riding every afternoon and now Miss Cunningham 'takes her pen in hand' to help me out." Despite his steady decline CK kept at it, taking aim at those he felt had departed from the true faith of progressivism. Concerning Roosevelt, he had written Johnson in early 1935: "I can confide to you . . . that I have lost a great deal of my admiration for one Franklin Delano Roosevelt and the lack of admiration I always have felt his wife has been added to."[43] Nonetheless he was alarmed at the actions of the Supreme Court, which had struck down certain New Deal laws. He noted to Johnson: "You will notice The *Bee* has taken the ground that the constitution should be amended so as to provide for the recall of decisions and to clip the talons of the Supreme Court—something that you and Theodore Roosevelt fought for some years ago." But even here his energies waned. When Johnson sent information about neutrality legislation, CK admitted: "I note what you say about the neutrality bills. I haven't had a chance to look into them very much for I am still weak and do very little reading and no writing. I dictate a lot of stuff by telephone but only the skeletons of things." Chester Rowell, however, could still get his juices flowing. When Johnson sent something Rowell had written, CK snapped: "Chester has become about as mean and untrustworthy as any of them."[44]

On February 22, 1936, CK had finally decided to make arrangements to transfer the *Bee* to his daughter Eleanor. "When I depart from The *Bee*," he wrote Eleanor, "I want you to take my place." With Carlos gone CK had hoped that young Martin Maloney might be able to step in with the aid of Jones and Hamilton. But, as CK explained in some frustration to his younger daughter, "I am sorry to say that Martin has shown himself to be utterly irresponsible. If I were doing my duty today he would not be on The *Bee*, but tears and appeals have knocked my judgment out of me and I am putting him in a new position on the same *Bee*. . . . I cannot rely on Martin to direct anything. I do not know that Brown would be capable of it. . . . I fear he is too timid." But knowing that this would disrupt Eleanor's dreams of being a playwright—dreams resumed after her divorce from Crozier—he begged her to return from Pasadena, where she was working, and come back to take over. Indeed his decision was ironic—given his misogyny—but Eleanor was the only option. "Everybody connected with us thinks you ought to come into The *Bee* and learn the various propositions—not to interfere, but to have a knowledge of everything that is going on when I pass away, so that in after years, when the time comes you may be thoroughly equipped to manage matters." CK expected that it would be "some years . . . before you can pass from an observer to a real director." But he urged her, "As the boys [Carlos's sons] grow up I want you and the other trustees to pick out the one most available and the best armed to direct the course of the paper." A chauvinist to his dying day, he concluded, "I think a man ought ultimately to be in charge."[45]

As CK and Eleanor worked to settle the matter of succession, Eleanor wrote to her father on February 24, calling him "Dearest Chickie." "I want to explain to you that my own ambition in life now, as always, is play writing. Due to many unfortunate circumstances from the time I was divorced and left [for] Pasadena—I was really getting a good start in it—till these last two years I have had no opportunity to go into it as I wanted." Sacramento was full of distractions, and she needed to be away from it all. "Play writing is my main interest and I do not feel it would be fair to have me put off again the thing I have been wanting to do and have been diverted from by necessity each time I seem to be reaching a goal." Nonetheless she agreed to come north and talk more about her potential role at the newspaper but only on the proviso "that my own life and personal ambitions and freedom are not entirely taken up."[46]

Ultimately Eleanor caved in and agreed to begin her tutelage at the *Bee* under Hamilton and Jones. This was a rare moment for the shy, sickly, stuttering girl on whom her parents had showered so much concern and anxiety. This likely made "Chickie" very happy. Eleanor could "hold the fort" until Carlos's sons were old enough to take over. At least that was the plan.

Throughout April CK was virtually bedridden. Aware that his end was coming, he may have reconciled with his brother before death took him on April 27, 1936, at his Citrus Heights ranch. Monsignor Thomas Horgan from the Catholic Cathedral was called and administered the last rites of the Catholic Church. "It made me happy to hear that he died in the Faith I always felt he would," wrote the Reverend Thomas Hayes, a former pastor at the cathedral, to Ella. Tributes flowed into the McClatchy household, one of which appeared in the *Oregon Spectator* and was preserved by Franklin Hichborn and sent to the *Bee* in 1952. It summarized what many thought of the tenacious publisher. Bearing the headline "Fighter for Truth," it read, "Characterized by fearless expression, indifferent to criticism, indomitable in his courses, inflexible in his beliefs, unhesitant in his searing denunciation, he was at the same time a drama critic, a philosopher, an essayist, and, above all, as he said himself a 'mere plain, ordinary man, and therefore only human.'"[47] Bert Meek, his old fellow

Progressive and rancher, offered the eulogy. Laid to rest in East Lawn Cemetery next to his beloved son, this complex yet purposeful man had changed and been changed by Sacramento and California. Quietly some of his aging companions may have whispered in private eulogy what CK often said to encourage fellow newsmen and those whose values he shared: "More power to your elbow, CK."

Epilogue

CK WAS ALWAYS Sacramento's son. Sacramento was where his life began, his family was born, where he would find his best friends and his worst enemies. There they laid him to rest. Even though he had his doubts, he controlled a powerful newspaper organization that became the voice of the Central Valley. Always uncomfortable with the expansionist plans of his brother and his son, he would have been content to be the hometown editor of his beloved Sacramento—the one place on the planet he truly loved. He never ceased to "boom" Sacramento, promoting its economic advance, supporting its beautification, and knitting its citizenry together by his sharing of the highs and lows of city life. Fiercely regional, he promoted the great valley as Superior California.

Although a proud Californian, CK grew up in an era of intense nationalistic fervor—attachment to the cause of the Union and its martyred icon, Abraham Lincoln; resistant to imperialism as a violation of the national creed of self-determination; militant in defending American liberties and freedoms; and the bane of any he suspected of being less than faithful to America. Until his death CK handed out an amalgam of news and moral exhortation that reflected the journalistic values of his younger years. His numerous columns and articles repeated endlessly his deepest feelings and prejudices: away with culture-mongering missionaries and American expansionists; to hell with radicals and anarchists who would destroy social order; a pox on the house of any who subverted representative government to their own greedy or illegal ends. He kept his philanthropy private but did allow his personal generosity to go public when he erected flagpoles to fly Old Glory. These he placed on the cathedral grounds and the campus of Grant Union High School. His wife, Ella, would erect another in his memory at Sacramento's second high school. His estate was valued at $1.5 million, and his heirs reaped the fruit of his labors and built on the foundations he and his brother had constructed. The *Bees* survived and thrived.

In October 1936 Sacramentans approved a bond issue to erect a new high school. In February 1937 J. E. Lynn of the Sacramento Board of Education proposed naming the new high school in honor of CK: "C. K. McClatchy was an outstanding citizen of Sacramento and he did everything he could to keep Sacramento in the forefront. He fought to make our city beautiful, to preserve our splendid shade trees." Another board member, Mrs. P. D. Bevil, seconded the motion: "C. K. McClatchy was not only an outstanding Sacramento figure, he was a national figure." Another board member lauded CK for his "opposition to anything that would lead to the introduction of religion into the schools of Sacramento. . . . In doing him an honor we do ourselves an honor."[1]

The new $800,000 building, designed by Starks and Flander, was paid for with the proceeds of a bond issue and a grant from the Public Works Administration in Washington, D.C. On May 20, 1937, with eleven hundred junior high students in attendance, the city's Masonic Lodge members laid the cornerstone. Inserted in it was a biography of CK, copies of the *Sacramento Bee* and the rival *Sacramento Union* of the day "and other documents." Ella and her family had a Catholic aversion to Masons and did not attend. But on Sunday, September 19, 1937, a thousand people gathered in the capacious auditorium of Sacramento's newest school. The Native Sons of the Golden West hosted the solemn ceremony, which included a band and a procession led by the local fire chief. The American flag was raised on CK's memorial flagpole, and a commemorative plaque was dedicated. Ella was present with her daughters, Eleanor and Charlotte, and Charlotte's family. One wonders what CK would have thought of the assembled orators. Judge Peter Shields (who would remain on the bench past his hundredth birthday), whom CK had derided over the years, spoke eloquently: "He believed in education as an agency for freedom and for justice and for the attainment of those ideals which America has set herself to attain. He was the champion of unpopular causes. He was the friend of the friendless multitudes. He was the leader of people who needed leadership to attain their objectives." Sam Pepper, the school's principal, quoted CK's tribute to teachers: "This nation owes more to her schools than it does to her soldiers. Arms and the man never have conferred the hundredth part as much benefit on this country as books and teachers." This beautiful new building was not the only tribute to CK. In March 1944 Eleanor traveled to the port of Wilmington, California, to break a ceremonial bottle of champagne over the bow of the USS *C. K. McClatchy*, a 10,500-ton Liberty ship built for the U.S. Maritime Commission.[2]

One by one the members of CK's family passed to eternity. Valentine died at the age of eighty in May 1938, and a few months later his wife, Addie, followed. Ella died in September 1939 and was memorialized in a Requiem Mass at the Cathedral of the Blessed Sacrament.[3] Hiram Johnson lived until August 1945, dying the same day the atomic bomb was dropped on Hiroshima.

It was left to the reluctant Eleanor, the aspiring playwright and theater critic, to carry on for her father. At first unsure, she relied heavily on the cadre of close associates CK had gathered around him, especially Walter Jones, who best articulated the editorial philosophy of CK. However, Eleanor was fiercely protective of her father—of his principles but also his passions. With the help of a *Bee* staffer, Roy V. Bailey, she produced a volume of her father's favorite themes.[4] Not given to the same dramatic or colorful invective as her father, she nonetheless could be tough when it came to certain issues in the company. She once again tangled with her uncle Valentine, who protested when she vetoed placing his own portrait next to CK's in a *Bee* radio station. She ruled gently but could be quite forceful when necessary. She dismissed CK's trusted business manager, G. C. Hamilton, during a dispute in the early 1940s.[5] Others who challenged her authority were banished. Unlike her father, she often mingled with workers in the *Bee* plant; they were often pleased to have "Miss McClatchy" sit down with them in the *Bee* cafeteria. Thanks to her brother Carlos and the excellent staffs in Sacramento, Fresno, and Modesto, the *Bee*s had good leadership and continued to dominate readership in the Central Valley. The flagship paper itself grew larger and more readable, and in 1952 Eleanor built a new, modern plant at Twenty-first and Q. Another building was erected at the same time in Modesto.

The editorials were not quite as colorful, but Walter Jones made every effort to remain faithful to CK's traditions. Eleanor was fortunate to preside over the McClatchy Company's growth years of the postwar era. California became a favorite place to live, and those who relocated to Sacramento had a choice of newspapers, but most preferred the *Bee*.

Like her father, Eleanor seemed to cherish the things of the spirit. Her love for Sacramento grew as she moved home for good in 1936. As her companion, she took in the artist Dunbar Beck, who lived with her and performed various decorating and artistic functions for the *Bee*. Beck oversaw the interior design of the new *Bee* building and produced the religious art that memorialized Carlos at a local Catholic church. Beck and Eleanor were not involved romantically, but he was a reliable public partner who would escort her to events and speak to her of art and culture. She continued her father's passion for urban beautification and local theater—a patron of the arts, promoting and supporting local theater and homegrown talent (so much so that honored young Sacramento artists receive an Elly Award for excellence in several categories). Her face is on a plaque in the courtyard of the California Musical Theater, home of the Music Circus, a theater in the round that still provides summer entertainment for Sacramentans today. When freeway construction threatened to wipe out the oldest part of the city in the early 1960s, she helped mobilize local support to preserve part of the old town, noting the connection of the old families of the city—like her own—to the beginnings and ongoing development of the city.

The paper now is a huge corporation, and family members are still involved. It must gratify them that many of CK's hopes for a more equitable and socially conscious California and America came to be. Others of his ideas (such as those about homosexuality or civil liberties) would be socially repugnant today. C. K. McClatchy's life offers a retrospective on an era of journalism that will never return. Even with his contradictions, biases, and sometimes erratic behavior, CK believed he was grasping for truth. That so many agreed and allowed themselves to be led and educated by this sensitive, yet at times belligerent, man validates to some degree what he hoped to do with his life—and his understanding that an editor had a social and moral responsibility to educate, challenge, and even inspire those who read his words.

Notes

———————◆———————

Introduction

1. "The Jellyfish Tells What An Editor Should Not Do," in Eleanor McClatchy and Roy V. Bailey, eds., *Private Thinks by C. K.* (New York: Scribners, 1936), 9.

2. "New School Named for C. K. McClatchy," *Sacramento Bee,* February 16, 1937, 1 and 4.

3. C. K. McClatchy to Carlos McClatchy, January 8, 1924, box 1, folder 052, Charles Duncan Files, McClatchy Papers, Center for Sacramento History. Unless otherwise noted, all citations to McClatchy Papers refer to the vast collection at the CSH.

4. C. K. McClatchy, "The Ideals of Journalism," undated clipping of an excerpt from his toast at the 1901 "Santa Clara Golden Jubilee," copy in box 12, folder 14, McClatchy Papers.

5. C. K. McClatchy to Valentine McClatchy, March 3, 1911, box 56.1, folder 8, McClatchy Papers.

6. C. K. McClatchy to Franklin Hichborn, April 9, 1916, Editorial, 11/02/1915–12/26/1916, p. 347, McClatchy Papers. See also C. K. McClatchy to Josephus Daniels, April 24, 1918, Editorial, 12/20/1916–07/27/1918, p. 825, McClatchy Papers.

7. "Parasites and McClatchyism," November 5, 1927, box 19, folder 9, McClatchy Papers. This was a letter directed to no one in particular.

8. C. K. McClatchy to Carlos McClatchy, January 8, 1924, box 1, folder 052, Duncan Files, McClatchy Papers.

Chapter One Sacramento's Son

1. *Sacramento Age*, November 4, 1856; "Married," *Sacramento Daily Union,* November 5, 1856, 2.

2. Charlotte McClatchy to Mrs. Irving, March 2, 1858, box 009-41-3, folder 044-3-13, McClatchy Papers; "Emily McClatchy Dies in Bay City," *Sacramento Bee*, August 26, 1946, 4.

3. Avella, *Sacramento: Indomitable City.*

4. C. K. McClatchy to William Moreland, November 16, 1898, General Correspondence, 10/14/1898–01/04/1899, p. 310, McClatchy Papers; "A City of Homes," *Daily Bee*, May 10, 1887, 2; "Sacramento Must Rid Herself of Provincialism," *Saturday Bee*, February 14, 1903, 9.

5. "Sacramento Slurred," *Daily Bee*, March 3, 1894, 4; "Notes," *Daily Bee*, July 27, 1887, 2; "Stand by Your Town!" *Daily Bee*, September 13, 1892, 4.

6. C. K. McClatchy to James D. Phelan, November 16, 1915, Editorial, 11/02/1915–12/26/1915, p. 23, McClatchy Papers.

7. C. K. McClatchy to Dr. W. A. Briggs, March 3, 1916, Editorial, 11/02/1915–12/26/1916, p. 238, McClatchy Papers; "Tom Fox Warrior? Sure, But He Didn't Tote Gun in Strife," *Sacramento Bee*, September 15, 1915, 4.

8. "City Intelligence: Dedication of the Franklin School House," *Daily Union*, March 19, 1858, 3.

9. C. K. McClatchy to Phebe McClatchy, September 12, 1935, box 009, folder 056, McClatchy Papers.

10. C. K. McClatchy to Robert H. Davis *(Munsey Magazine),* January 14, 1913 (Milwaukee), and "Scatteration vs. Segregation," 009, 01/03/1913–03/20/1916, p. 30, both in McClatchy Papers.

11. C. K. McClatchy to Franklin Hichborn, March 17, 1916, "Scatteration vs. Segregation," 01/03/1913–02/05/1920, p. 165, McClatchy Papers. See also Hichborn, "Social Evil Under Hot Fire," *Sacramento Bee*, January 30, 1913, 1 and 4.

12. C. K. McClatchy to Mrs. A. C. Hart, January 8, 1917, Editorial 12/20/1916–07/27/1918, p. 22, McClatchy Papers.

13. For the history of Santa Clara, see McKevitt, *University of Santa Clara.*

14. McKevitt and Giacomini, *Serving the Intellect, Touching the Heart,* 45–46, 67.

15. Philhistorian Debating Society, Archives of the University of Santa Clara (hereafter AUSC).

16. James Campbell, letter to the editor, *Redwood* (student publication), June 1907, 407, AUSC;; McKevitt, *University of Santa Clara,* 102.

17. See McKevitt, *University of Santa Clara*, 130–35, 148.

18. C. K. McClatchy to Rev. William Borland, S. J., August 4, 1915, C. K. McClatchy Personal Correspondence, 08/14/1914–08/14/1915, p. 421, McClatchy Papers.

19. C. K. McClatchy to V. S. McClatchy, n.d. [1911], box 56-1, folder 9, McClatchy Papers; Gerald McKevitt to author, July 10, 1997; C. K. McClatchy to James Barry, May 15, 1896, General Correspondence, 03/06/1896–07/30/1896, p. 440, McClatchy Papers.

20. Cesar Aguayo Garcia, "Jesuit Higher Education in the Mid-Nineteenth Century: A View Through Two Student Diaries," paper delivered at Duquesne University History Forum, October 20, 1978, copy in AUSC; McClatchy Travel Diary, 1926, p. 42, McClatchy Papers.

21. "The Bible," *Daily Bee*, December 9, 1886, 2; "Notes," *Daily Bee*, December 13, 1893, 4. CK often invoked Ingersoll. A sample of this is "A Lay Sermon," *Daily Bee*, December 11, 1886, 6.

22. "CHARLES K. McCLATCHY has this day been admitted to the firm of James McClatchy and Co., proprietors and publishers of the Daily and Weekly *Bee*," notice in *Daily Bee,* November 3, 1879, 2.

23. Valentine McClatchy, "The Crusades," *Owl,* November 1872, 95–97; "Ships and Ship-Building," *Owl,* January 1873, 161–69; "Alchemy and Alchemists," *Owl* February 1873, 221–23; "Sunrise," *Owl,* March 1873, 263; "The Knights of St. John," *Owl,* May 1873, 320–25.

24. "McClatchy Properties," document in McClatchy Papers. This compendium of James's financial dealings provides salient details of the predeath transactions, the will, and the eventual takeover of the *Bee* by the two brothers. See Valentine McClatchy Personal Correspondence, 09/18/1905–11/28/1906, pp. 167–72, McClatchy Papers.

25. Ella was the youngest of seven children. Her siblings were Mary Frances (1840–1911), Kate (1843–1870), John Austin (1846–1895), Sophia (1848–1927), Frank Patrick (1853–1917), and James Carolan (1855–1896). I am grateful to Jill White for this genealogical information.

26. The history of the Sisters of Mercy is contained in M. Evangelist Morgan, *My Song Is of Mercy* (San Francisco: Fearon Press, 1957).

27. Phebe Briggs McClatchy (widow of Carlos McClatchy), interview by Adair McClatchy and C. K. McClatchy, September 1984, Fresno, California, box 3, in folder labeled "Rideout/Phebe Conley Recollections," James and Susan McClatchy Collection, McClatchy Papers.

28. The McClatchys valued their privacy, so accounts of Ella's religious faith and CK's lack of religious observance are anecdotal. The source of whatever we know is the recollections of Phebe McClatchy. The baptismal registers of St. Rose Catholic Church in Sacramento carry the records of the baptisms and the marriages of most McClatchys.

29. "Married," *Daily Bee*, February 12, 1885, 3; C. K. McClatchy to J. M. Maloney, October 2, 1909, box 56-1, folder 3, McClatchy Papers.

30. Jedd McClatchy to Valentine McClatchy (at Hotel Breslin in New York), April 17, 1908, Valentine McClatchy Personal Correspondence, 01/22/1908–12/09/1908, p. 238, McClatchy Papers.

31. In the city of Sacramento alone, Valentine's holdings consisted of entire blocks between Thirtieth and Thirty-first, and between Q and R, S and T, T and U, and U and V. He also owned property in Orangevale, as well as in Los Angeles, Lassen, and Butte counties. See "Memorandum as to Condition of Property," February 5, 1906, Valentine McClatchy Personal Correspondence, 09/18/1905–11/28/1906, p. 169, McClatchy Papers.

32. "Memorandum of Real Estate Owned by V. S. McClatchy," January 1, 1906, p. 167, and "Memorandum as to Personal Property," n.d., p. 172, both in Valentine McClatchy Personal Correspondence, 09/18/1905–11/28/1906, McClatchy Papers.

33. Sandul and Swim, *Orangevale,* 7–10. See also Sandul, *California Dreaming.*

34. Valentine McClatchy to J. W. Brittain, January 8, 1896, Valentine McClatchy Personal Correspondence, 09/23/1895–07/20/1896, p. 155; "Memorandum for V. S.'s

Personal Book as to lease of the Japanese of Sutter County Land," p. 34, both in McClatchy Papers.

35. Valentine McClatchy to L. B. Schei, Sacramento Suburban Fruit Lands Co., September 3, 1912, Editorial, 10/01/1911–10/02/1912, p. 894, McClatchy Papers.

36. *Daily Bee,* March 15, 1893, p. 4.

37. This anecdote was pushed into circulation by Frank Snook, a local driver for CK who insisted that this Curry-McClatchy clash was true. See Frank G. Snook recollections, n.d., in a folder of oral histories titled "C. K. McClatchy Recollections," box 01, folder 03, 17–47, McClatchy Papers.

38. Phebe Briggs McClatchy interview.

39. Valentine McClatchy to "My dear Jennie" (Leila J. Lindley), n.d. [ca. 1889]; Valentine McClatchy to C. K. McClatchy, August 28 and August 24, 1889, all in box 15, folder 15, McClatchy Papers.

40. Valentine McClatchy to H. D. Gamble, February 20, 1890, box 15, folder 15, McClatchy Papers.

Chapter Two An Editor's Vision

1. Early samples of his "Notes" column include *Daily Bee,* March 6, 1877, 3; *Daily Bee,* March 8, 1877, 2; *Daily Bee,* November 27, 1877, 2; and *Daily Bee,* January 30, 1879, 2. The first use of the phrase "Merely a Private Think" may have appeared in the *Daily Bee,* August 7, 1894, 3.

2. Hugh Mohan, "Representative Men," 1880, C. K. McClatchy Biographical File, California State Library, Sacramento.

3. C. K. McClatchy to Hiram Johnson, August 1, 1918, Editorial, 07/29/1918–06/07/1919, p. 8, McClatchy Papers, CSH; "Merely Some Private Thinks," *Sacramento Bee,* August 8, 1922, 2.

4. C. K. McClatchy to Professor Walter Williams, October 16, 1917, Editorial, 12/20/1916–07/27/1918, p. 483, McClatchy Papers.

5. Ibid.

6. In 1917 he sent a note of regret to a Shakespeare scholar on the faculty of the University of Nebraska who had addressed city high school students on the Bard of Avon. "Had I been here, it would not only have delighted me to listen to your remarks about which I have heard so much, but also have had a member of the staff there to have written out for the paper at least a column of your very interesting statements." C. K. McClatchy to Charles W. Wallace, February 19, 1917, Editorial, 12/20/1916–07/27/1918, p. 114, McClatchy Papers.

7. C. K. McClatchy to E. J. Devlin, December 27, 1919, C. K. McClatchy Personal Correspondence, 06/18/1916–02/05/1920, p. 602, McClatchy Papers; "Literary Sacrilege," *Daily Bee,* September 27, 1894, 3.

8. "One Hundredth Anniversary of Charles Dickens' Birth," *Sacramento Bee,* February 7, 1912, 4.

9. CK's preference for the King James Version of the Bible was solely because of its English, not the accuracy of its translation. He often quoted the literary critic James

Anthony Froude, who declared that the King James Version "was as remarkable for the inaccuracy of its translation as the majesty of its English." C. K. McClatchy to John S. Chambers, July 29, 1911, Editorial, 12/24/1910–10/07/1911, p. 830, McClatchy Papers.

10. A good overview of the history of Sacramento's nineteenth-century theaters and the thespians who frequented their stages is Charles Vernard Hume, "The Sacramento Theater" (unpublished Ph.D. diss., Stanford University, 1955).

11. C. K. McClatchy to "Dear Mama," June 2, 1870, box 002-03, folder 19, McClatchy Papers.

12. C. K. McClatchy to Peter Wilson, Clunie Theater, July 4, 1913, Editorial, 10/01/1912–09/10/1913, p. 851, McClatchy Papers; C. K. McClatchy, "The Past Comes Back in Recollections of the Drama of Days Gone By," *Sacramento Bee*, September 27, 1924, reprinted as pamphlet, "Personal Recollections of Great Artists Who Have Appeared on the Sacramento Stage," by the *Sacramento Bee*, McClatchy Papers, CSH. Warde appeared often in Sacramento. See "A Treat to Come," *Daily Bee*, February 26, 1890, 3, in which CK suggests that Warde would be the successor to Edwin Booth, and "Stars of the Stage," *Saturday Bee*, April 21, 1894, 1. In addition to his performances in *Henry IV, Henry VIII, Julius Caesar, Richard III* and *Richelieu*, Warde occasionally gave public lectures on Shakespeare. See "Amusements," *Evening Bee*, March 28, 1895, 1; "Talk on Shakespeare," *Daily Bee*, March 30, 1895, 4; "Mr. Warde as King Lear," *Evening Bee*, March 21, 1896, 12; "The Study of Shakespeare," *Evening Bee*, March 21, 1896, 4.

13. *Daily Bee,* June 7, 1893, 3; "Some Private Thinks," *Evening Bee*, February 6, 1904, 11. See also "Booth in 'Hamlet,'" *Daily Bee*, April 9, 1887, 1.

14. "Each Municipality Should Have Its Own Theater," *Daily Bee*, September 20, 1887, 2.

15. This quote is taken from the "James McClatchy" edition of the *Bee,* which the brothers published to mark the twentieth anniversary of their father's death. "And the Sons Built a House to Their Father," *Annual of the Evening Bee—1903, James McClatchy Edition,* February 23, 1903, 17 and 32.

16. Ibid.

17. James McClatchy to Charles McClatchy, June 28, 1865; James McClatchy to Master C. K. McClatchy, August 13,1865; C. K. McClatchy to "Dear Mama," May 31, 1870, all in box 002-03, folder 19; and C. K. McClatchy to "Dear Mama," June 10, 1870, box 15, folder 15, all in McClatchy Papers.

18. He repeats this anecdote in his Travel Diary, 1926, p. 41, McClatchy Papers. He told a slightly different version of it earlier, in "Merely a Private Think," *Sacramento Bee*, August 14, 1914, 30. Judge N. Greene Curtis also paid tribute to the late editor's kindness to an African American at a Fourth of July celebration in 1885, relating "an affecting story of an aging darkey whom he had met on Decoration Day dragging himself out to the cemetery to place a few flowers on the grave of James McClatchy 'de bes' fren' dis darkey ever had.'" See "Feast of Reason—Flow of Soul," *Daily Bee*, July 6, 1885, 1.

19. C. K. McClatchy to "Dear Mama," August 26, 1871, box 002-03, folder 19, McClatchy Papers.

20. Occasionally the *Sacramento Record-Union* would quote James McClatchy to his son. An example of this involved support for higher levees in Sacramento, which James wanted but CK opposed. When the *Record-Union* did quote James to refute his son, CK always replied and attempted to reframe his opponents' arguments. For example, "Our esteemed contemporary has much to say this morning about what the late James McClatchy said about levees in 1881." See "The Levee Question Again," *Daily Bee,* February 19, 1884, 2.

21. McClatchy mythmaking also occurred in the 1903 "James McClatchy" edition of the paper and again in 1957 when the newspaper celebrated its centenary with a special centennial edition. "Centennial Issue of the *Bee,*" *Sacramento Bee,* February 4, 1957, n.p.

22. C. K. McClatchy to Edmund S. Kinyoun, February 16, 1916, Editorial, 11/02/1915–12/26/1916, p. 185, McClatchy Papers.

23. "Prominent Men of the Day," *San Francisco Call,* December 25, 1890, 11; "A Protest," *Evening Bee,* December 29, 1890, 1. CK compared Sheehan's relationship to James McClatchy to that of a box office agent to the great Edwin Booth.

24. Wiegand, *Papers of Permanence,* 34.

25. Wiegand offers interesting details on the supposed plot and James McClatchy's evolving role. Wiegand, *Papers of Permanence,* 46–47.

26. "How California Stands," *San Francisco Bulletin,* September 16, 1880, 2; "Unwritten History—Why General Sumner Came Secretly to San Francisco and How California Was Saved from the Horrors of the Civil War," *Evening Bee,* September 21, 1880, 2; "The *Bee* Through 100 Years: The *Bee's* Centennial Album, Part the Eighth, James McClatchy," *Sacramento Bee,* February 3, 1958, CC-12–CC-13.

27. "Unwritten History"; Jas. McClatchy Co. to Gen. W. T. Sherman, November 22, 1884, General Correspondence, 01/06/1884–08/22/1890, p. 334, McClatchy Papers; *Oakland Times,* May 24, 1894, 4. In "Saved to the Union," *Daily Bee,* June 2, 1894, 3, CK refutes this assertion by reiterating what James said in his 1880 article, "Unwritten History."

28. "California and the Union," *Evening Bee,* July 1, 1898, 4; C. K. McClatchy to Marion De Vries, August 3, 1898, General Correspondence, 06/23/1898–10/14/1898, p. 381, McClatchy Papers.

29. C. K. McClatchy to Judge C. C. Goodwin, August 31, 1903, General Correspondence, 07/29/1903–10/15/1903, p. 405, McClatchy Papers. The first account of this story in the *Bee* came in 1880. See "Unwritten History"; "The *Bee* During the Great Civil War," *Annual of the Evening Bee—1903, James McClatchy Edition,* February 23, 1903, 2–3; "Story Told by James McClatchy by Sick Man Saves State of California to Union," *Sacramento Bee* (Days of '49 Edition), May 23, 1922, 24. In "Credit Should be Given Where Credit Is Due," *Sacramento Bee,* March 18, 1931, 1, CK took umbrage at the honor bestowed on Thomas Starr King, whose likeness had been chosen to represent California in Statuary Hall. King was a San Francisco

minister whose oratory had been credited with saving California for the Union, but CK insisted that King had never spoken for the Union unless he was paid. The story was also recounted in the *Argonaut*, a San Francisco magazine, by an anonymous author writing as "Franciscoer." CK, who probably wrote the article himself, touted it in "McClatchy's Work to Foil War Plot," *Sacramento Bee*, February 15, 1935, 4; "The *Bee* Through 100 Years: The *Bee's* Centennial Album, Part the Eighth, James McClatchy," *Sacramento Bee*, February 3, 1958, CC-12–CC-13.

30. Benjamin F. Gilbert, "The Mythical Johnston Conspiracy," *California Historical Society Quarterly* 28, no. 2 (June 1949): 165–73.

31. Barker, *Henry George*, 76.

32. C. K. McClatchy to Henry George Jr., April 8, 1899, General Correspondence, 04/01/1899–08/11/1899, p. 74, McClatchy Papers. McClatchy ran a substantial article by George in 1876. See "The Press," Daily *Bee*, February 17, 1876, 1, and February 18, 1876, 1.

33. "The Rise of Henry George," *Daily Bee*, September 25, 1886, 4.

34. George, *Life of Henry George*, 173.

35. C. K. McClatchy, letter to editor, *Century Magazine*, March 18, 1899, General Correspondence, 01/05/1899–04/01/1899, p. 830; C. K. McClatchy to Henry George Jr., April 25, 1899, General Correspondence, 04/01/1899–08/11/1899, p. 175, both in McClatchy Papers. CK later retracted his correction to the Brooks article in *Century Magazine* with a letter to the editor, *Century Magazine*, May 9, 1899, General Correspondence, 04/01/1899–08/11/1899, McClatchy Papers.

36. Barker alludes to the dispute between CK and Noah Brooks. See Barker, *Henry George*, 75–76.

37. "Little Harry George," *Daily Bee*, September 1, 1886, 2. A strong defense of George's ideas about land, and a comparison of them with similar ideas of James McClatchy's, is in "Henry George's Candidacy," *Daily Bee*, September 11,1886, 2. A rationale reinforcing George's argument that the city should own its transportation system is found in "Unnecessary Agitation," *Daily Bee*, October 14, 1886, 2.

38. C. K. McClatchy to Albert M. Johnson, February 8, 1897, General Correspondence, 12/09/1896–04/06/1897, p. 583, McClatchy Papers. CK did differ with George on the question of the tariff, rejecting George's free-trade ideas and advocating high tariffs to protect America from an inundation of cheap goods made from "pauper labor" in England. See *Daily Bee*, November 2, 1888, 4.

39. "A Noble Tongue Silenced," *Daily Bee*, January 8, 1887, 4; "The Church After George," *Daily Bee*, January 11, 1887, 2; "George's Answer," *Daily Bee*, January 15, 1887, 6; "Pope and Priest," *Daily Bee*, January 20, 1887, 2; " A Great and Grand Man," *Daily Bee*, May 28, 1887, 2; "Brave Father McGlynn," *Daily Bee*, June 24, 1887, 2; "The Pope and M'Glynn," *Daily Bee*, June 25, 1887, 4. Reverend McGlynn visited Sacramento in 1890, and the *Bee* conducted an extensive and sympathetic interview, "Edward M'Glynn," *Daily Bee*, May 25, 1890, 8.

40. "Notes," *Daily Bee*, December 3, 1887, 4.

41. "Third Annual Banquet," *Evening Bee*, March 26, 1894, 1.

42. "The Duty of a Newspaper," *Daily Bee*, January 14, 1886, 2.

43. "The Blanket Sheets Must Go," *Daily Bee*, August 15, 1887, 2.

44. "Memo to Chambers, Stanford, Norman, Magill, Lawson, Eichler, Carroll, Anderson, Langdon, McLaughlin, Jones, Anderson, Davis, Standwick, Johnston," August 16, 1910, C. K. McClatchy Personal Correspondence, 04/28/1910–12/02/1912, p. 386, McClatchy Papers.

45. "Sneers at Any Race Not Tolerated in This Paper," *Evening Bee*, February 5, 1908, 4.

46. For example, see "Los Angeles Crowd Tries to Lynch Negro Who Assaulted Girl," *Sacramento Bee*, October 5, 1908, 1 and 8; "Two Negroes and Young Negress Are Burned by a Mob," *Sacramento Bee*, December 6, 1911, 1.

47. "The Negro's Right to Fair Play and a Square Deal," *Sacramento Bee*, August 18, 1908, 4.

48. "The '*Bee*' to Its Readers," *Daily Bee*, January 22, 1884, 2.

49. They often repeated the story of their purchase of the *Bee* with its debt and challenges. See "The '*Bee*'s' New Volume," *Daily Bee*, July 1, 1885, 1.

50. Valentine McClatchy to H. J. F. Berkeley, June 6, 1906, Valentine McClatchy Personal Correspondence, 09/18/1905–11/28/1906, p. 275, McClatchy Papers; "The Conduct of the '*Bee*,'" *Daily Bee*, August 11, 1887, 2.

51. "V. S. McClatchy Passes Away in Bay Home," *Sacramento Bee*, May 16, 1938, 1.

52. C. K. McClatchy to W. E. Gerber, February 9, 1912, Editorial, 10/01/1911–10/02/1912, p. 537, McClatchy Papers.

53. "Do Your Duty Col. Forbes and Do It Like a Soldier!" *Sacramento Bee*, March 14, 1908, 3; "A Dismal Failure," *Marysville Appeal,* March 13, 1908, 4.

Chapter Three Defenders of the Valley:
The Struggle with Hydraulic Mining

1. Still the best source for this controversy is *Gold vs. Grain*. See also Greenland, *Hydraulic Mining in California*.

2. "George Ohleyer Dead," *Evening Bee*, August 17, 1896, 1. Ohleyer eventually was elected to the California State Assembly and worked hard to advance Sacramento Valley claims in the legislature. See also "Mr. Cadwalader's Death," *Daily Bee*, April 29, 1884, 2.

3. "Who Will Move in the Matter?" *Daily Bee*, May 24, 1875, 2; "Needed Legislation," *Daily Bee*, February 2, 1878, 2; "The Mining Sediment," *Daily Bee*, February 6, 1878, 2; "Let Us Examine the Case!" *Daily Bee*, February 6, 1878, 2.

4. "Mining Tailings," *Daily Bee*, December 23, 1875, 2; "The Important Case—Miners vs. Farmers," *Daily Bee*, January 26, 1877, 2. See also "Miners vs. Farmers," *Daily Bee*, July 18, 1877, 2.

5. "Something That Must Be Considered," *Daily Bee*, February 9, 1878, 2. James makes the same argument in "Damage by Flood," *Daily Bee*, February 11, 1878, 2, and again in "Sunshine After the Storm," *Daily Bee*, February 21, 1878, 2. See also "California Bays," *Daily Bee,* May 18, 1878, 2.

6. "What Hydraulic Mining Has Forced Us to Do," *Daily Bee*, July 15, 1881, 3; Kelley, *Gold vs. Grain,* p 212–13.

7. "Judge Sawyer's Decision" and "The Farmers Win," *Daily Bee*, January 7, 1884, 2 and 3; "One Who Would Have Rejoiced," *Daily Bee*, January 8, 1884, 2; "The '*Bee's*' New Volume," *Daily Bee,* January 2, 1884, 2.

8. "Where There [*sic*] Interest Lies," *Daily Bee*, April 30, 1885, 2; "Some Light on Riparian Rights," *Daily Bee*, June 23, 1886, 2; "A Review of the Water Question," *Daily Bee*, June 26, 1886, 2.

9. "Mob Law in Northern California," *Daily Bee*, July 13, 1887, 2.

10. "More Talk of Dams," *Daily Bee*, May 11, 1885, 2; "Mr. Budd and Dams," *Daily Bee*, January 23, 1884, 2. See also "No Dams While Hydraulic Mining Is Still Possible," *Daily Bee*, January 29, 1884, 2; "Standing in Their Own Light," *Daily Bee*, February 4, 1884, 2.

11. "One Law for All," *Daily Bee*, April 10, 1884, 2; "The Policy of Silence," *Daily Bee*, April 11, 1884, 2; "Hydraulic Mining in Amador," *Daily Bee*, April 14, 1884, 2. The *Bee* urged all county boards of supervisors to sue any mining company that flouted the *Woodruff* decision. See "One Suit for All," *Daily Bee*, May 2, 1844, 2. CK believed the mere threat of a suit would bring an injunction that would effectively end all the hydraulic mining affecting the watershed of the Sacramento Valley. See "The Big Suit," *Daily Bee*, May 16, 1884, 2; "The Omnibus Suit Indorsed [*sic*]," *Daily Bee*, May 26, 1884, 2; "Nearing the End," *Daily Bee,* June 7, 1884, 2.

12. "A Falsehood Indorsed [*sic*]," *Daily Bee,* May 3, 1884, 2. CK reported on the impact of these "legal" mines on the watershed, computing at different times how many carloads of slickens they dumped into the rivers. Typical was "A Vast Aggregate," *Daily Bee*, May 28, 1884, 2.

13. "Give Them No Quarter," *Daily Bee*, March 26, 1884, 2. See also "Smite Them, Hip and Thigh," and "Rebelling Miners," *Daily Bee*, March 28, 1884, 2; "To This Complexion It Has Come at Last," *Daily Bee*, February 3, 1885, 2.

14. "Shall the Rivers and Bay Be Redeemed?" *Daily Bee*, March 1, 1884, 2; "River Improvement," *Daily Bee*, April 19, 1884, 2; "A Disgrace to the State," *Daily Bee,* July 15, 1886, 2. Hearst, who had made his fortune in both copper and silver ore mining, was sympathetic to the gold miners. CK attempted to have Hearst denied reelection to the Senate. See "Down with Hearst!" *Daily Bee*, November 6, 1886, 4.

15. "Inviting Punishment," *Daily Bee*, February 15, 1884, 2.

16. Valentine McClatchy to Hon. Joseph McKenna," July 16, 1884, General Correspondence, 007, 06/21/1884–02/23/1885, 77, McClatchy Papers. An editorial before this letter warmly commended McKenna's candidacy but lamented the weakness of the platform statement on hydraulic mining. See "Joseph McKenna," *Daily Bee*, July 15, 1884, 2.

17. "Apathy and Neglect," *Daily Bee,* July 17, 1884, 2; "A Great Opportunity," *Daily Bee*, July 19, 1884, 2. See also "The Flow of Debris," *Daily Bee,* July 22, 1884, 2; "Colonel Mendell's Report," *Daily Bee*, August 1, 1884, 2.

18. "California's Curse," *Daily Bee*, December 24, 1884, 2–5.

19. "An Infamous Bill," *Daily Bee*, February 7, 1885, 2. The *Bee* railed against this bill, which never made it out of the state senate. See "Laus Deo!" *Daily Bee*, March 5, 1885, 2.

20. "On with the Suits," *Daily Bee*, May 15, 1885, 2; "Hydraulic Mining Must Go!" *Daily Bee*, July 3 1885, 2; "An Eleventh Hour Appeal," *Daily Bee*, May 14, 1885, 2.

21. "Slickens Fat," *Record-Union*, August 19, 1885, 2. See also "Record-Union Melange," *Record-Union*, August 15, 1885, 4; "The '*Bee*' and Its Record," *Daily Bee*, August 19, 1885, 2.

22. Valentine McClatchy to Zach Montgomery, August 28, 1885, General Correspondence, 02/23/1885–10/19/1885, p 420–25, McClatchy Papers; "The Anti-Debris Litigation," *Daily Bee*, April 25, 1885, 2. See also "A Scandalous Document," *Daily Bee*, January 7, 1886, 2; "Some Questions for the People of the Mountains," *Record-Union*, January 9, 1886, 4; "Crawling in the Dust," *Daily Bee*, January 9, 1886, 2. Typical of the monitoring was close scrutiny of legislation the miners initiated. See "A Shameful Measure," *Daily Bee*, January 26, 1887, 2; "Kill This Bill" and "In the Path of an Avalanche," *Daily Bee*, February 8, 1887, 1. Likewise, the paper sympathetically covered the efforts of Assemblyman George Ohleyer, a stalwart in the antihydraulic fight, who introduced a bill in 1887 to further curtail the dumping of debris in the rivers. See "A Valiant Effort," *Daily Bee*, February 4, 1887, 2; "An Unmitigated Evil," *Daily Bee*, February 5, 1887, 2; "A Danger to the State," *Daily Bee*, February 7, 1887, 2; "Follow Up the Victory," *Daily Bee*, March 5, 1887, 2.

23. Editorial, *Daily Bee*, February 12, 1887, 2.

24. "An Editor on Trial," *Daily Bee*, January 31, 1887, 3; "The M'Whorter Trial," *Daily Bee*, February 1, 2, and 3, 1887, 3; "Sensational Testimony," *Daily Bee*, February 4, 1887, p 1 and 3; "Placid McWhorter," *Daily Bee*, February 8, 1882, 3.; "For the Defense," *Daily Bee*, February 9, 1887, 1; "For the Prosecution," *Daily Bee*, February 9, 1887, 3; "M'Whorter Acquitted," *Daily Bee*, February 10, 1887, 3.

25. "The McWhorter Trial," *Daily Bee*, January 28, 1887, 3; "The M'Whorter Trial," *Daily Bee*, January 29, 1887, 3.

26. "A Few Words for the Dead," *Daily Bee*, February 10, 1887, 1.

27. "Hobson's Homestead," "Today's Proceedings," *Daily Bee*, November 2, 1887, 3; "A Question of Technicalities," *Daily Bee*, November 3, 1887, 2; "The Prosecution Rests," *Daily Bee*, November 3, 1887, 3; "The Fifth Day," *Daily Bee*, November 4, 1887, 3; "Will Run into Next Week," *Daily Bee*, November 5, 1887, 8; "The Bee's Libel Suit," *Daily Bee*, November 7, 1887, 2; "Robinson on the Rack," *Daily Bee*, November 8, 1887, 3; "Eighth Day at Auburn," *Daily Bee*, November 9, 1887, 3; "Stories of Bribery," *Daily Bee*, November 10, 1887, 2; "The Evidence All In," *Daily Bee*, November 11, 1887, 2; "The Eleventh Day," *Daily Bee*, November 12, 1887, 8; "Judge Fulweier Talks," *Daily Bee*, November 14, 1887, 1; "A Great Speech," *Daily Bee*, November 4, 1887, 1–3; "The Thirteenth Day," *Daily Bee*, November 15, 1887, 3; "Hard Hits by Hart," *Daily Bee*, November 16, 1887, 3; "General Jo Hamilton," November 17, 1887, 3; "A Great Speech," *Daily Bee*, November 18, 1887, p 1–3;

"A Matter of Satisfaction," November 19, 1887, 2; "The '*Bee*'s' Victory," *Daily Bee*, November 21, 1887, p 1 and 3.

28. "'*Bee*'s' Victory"; "Receiving Congratulations," *Daily Bee,* November 21, 1887, 3; "Growling at the '*Bee*,'" *Daily Bee*, December 7, 1887, 1. See also "Another Libel Suit," *Daily Bee*, February 16, 1887, 3; "The '*Bee*'s' Libel Suit," *Daily Bee*, February 17, 1887, 2; "Is It a Concerted Movement," *Daily Bee*, February 19, 1887, 2; "Hobson of San Francisco," *Daily Bee*, February 22, 1887, 3.

29. On the Caminetti Act, see Kelley *Gold vs. Grain*, 271–300.

30. Smith, *Mining in Yuba County*, 83.

31. "Can This Be True?" *Daily Bee*, April 23, 1885, 2; "A Mischievous Error," *Daily Bee*, April 24, 1885, 2; "Impolitic Valley Zeal," *Evening Bee*, June 13, 1892, 3; Valentine McClatchy to W. C. Ralston, June 13, 1892, General Correspondence, 04/28/1892–09/06/1892, 168, McClatchy Papers.

32. "Great Hydraulic Mining Issue," *Evening Bee*, July 26, 1899, 2; "Criticism of Anti-Debris Association" and "Eager at All Times to Refer to the Courts," *Evening Bee*, November 20, 1900, 5 and 8; "Caminetti Act and the Valleys," *Evening Bee*, November 21, 1900, 1 and 5; "The Old Rebel Cry—All We Want Is to Be Let Alone," *Evening Bee*, November 21, 1900, 4.

Chapter Four A World of Trouble: Boycotts and Libel Suits

1. "Calico Is Timid," *Daily Bee*, March 13, 1886, 2.

2. Valentine McClatchy to F. K. Misch, January 31, 1890, General Correspondence, 02/06/1884–08/22/1890, p. 378, McClatchy Papers. The *Bee*'s wages for its compositors had come under attack as early as 1885 when members of the Knights of Labor accused the *Bee* of running a rat paper that did not pay fair wages to its compositors. CK and Valentine responded huffily that they did. See *Daily Bee*, editorial, December 12, 1885, 4.

3. V. McClatchy to F. K. Misch.

4. Philip Freshwater, "History of the *Bee*," unpublished ms., chap. 14, n.p., CD0002:010, McClatchy Papers; Valentine McClatchy to William McKenna, October 10, 1890, p. 136; Valentine McClatchy to Business Manager, *Marysville Appeal,* October 6, 1890, p. 122; and Valentine McClatchy to H. Z. Osborne, October 14, 1890, p. 165, all in General Correspondence, 8/22/1890–01/14/1891, McClatchy Papers.

5. Valentine McClatchy to William McKenna, October 10, 1890, General Correspondence, 8/22/1890–01/14/1891, p. 136, McClatchy Papers.

6. Valentine McClatchy to Getchel, October 7, 1890, p. 127; Valentine McClatchy to W. O. Cuthbert, January 7, 1891, p. 465, both in General Correspondence, 8/22/1890–01/14/1891, McClatchy Papers.

7. Valentine McClatchy to W. R. Hearst, October 16, 1890, p. 178; Valentine McClatchy to G. M. Brennan, October 14, 1890, p. 220, both in General Correspondence, 8/22/1890–01/14/1891, McClatchy Papers.

8. A copy of this flyer was inserted in V. S. McClatchy, "Private Personal Stunts," 09/1890–03/25/1898, McClatchy Papers.

9. Valentine McClatchy to G. M. Brennan, October 25, 1890, General Correspondence, 8/22/1890–01/14/1891, 220, McClatchy Papers.

10. Valentine McClatchy to Harris Weinstock, October 24, 1890, General Correspondence, 8/22/1890–01/14/1891, 215, McClatchy Papers.

11. "The Law and the Boycotters," *Evening Bee*, November 10, 1890, 2; Valentine McClatchy to Col. Harrison Gray Otis, November 14, 1890, General Correspondence, 8/22/1890–01/14/1891, p. 283, McClatchy Papers.

12. James McClatchy Co. to Chas. T. Kelly, December 18, 1890, p. 389; Valentine McClatchy to Victor F. Lawson, November 25, 1890, p. 315, both in General Correspondence, 8/22/1890–01/14/1891, McClatchy Papers.

13. "Why Not Print All of It," *Daily Bee,* February 11, 1891, 3. The original was "Two Ways of Looking at It," *Daily Bee*, March 13, 1886, 4. CK protested that portions of his supposedly hypocritical editorial were not included in the reprint.

14. Valentine McClatchy to C. H. Jones, November 26, 1890, General Correspondence, 8/22/1890–01/14/1891, p. 323, McClatchy Papers.

15. "Appreciation," *Daily Evening News,* December 27, 1890, 2; "There Is Room," *Daily Evening News,* December 29, 1890, 2.

16. Pioneer, letter to editor, *Daily Evening News,* January 5, 1891, 3.

17. Valentine McClatchy to Henry T. Scott, December 26, 1890, General Correspondence, 8/22/1890–01/14/1891, p. 409, McClatchy Papers.

18. "An Enemy of Labor," *Daily Bee,* January 21, 1891, 2. Typical of the dramatic way CK portrayed the boycott were his comparisons of it to the guillotine of the French Revolution and of the strike leaders to the leaders of the Reign of Terror. See "The Modern Guillotine," *Daily Bee,* February 3, 1891, 3; "The Boycott Must Go," *Daily Bee,* February 7, 1891, 2.

19. "Does It Boycott," *Daily Bee,* February 2, 1891, 2; "Public Pulse," *Daily Bee,* February 4, 1891, 1; "The Boycott Bill," *Daily Bee,* February 10, 1891, 3. The California State Senate heatedly debated the bill in February, and during the discussion it was asserted the bill had been introduced at the behest of the *Bee,* because it was feared that Judge Armstrong's injunction would not survive an appeal to the California Supreme Court. See also "Boycott Bill," *Evening Bee,* February 20, 1891, 1; "A Fair Bill," *Daily Bee,* April 9, 1891, 4.

20. Valentine McClatchy to Jud C. Brusie, February 23, 1891, General Correspondence, 01/15/1891–05/31/1891, p. 152, McClatchy Papers.

21. "Connect Your Dates," *Daily Bee,* February 9, 1891, 3; "Warde's Wolsey," *Daily Bee,* February 20, 1891, 3.

22. Valentine McClatchy to J. T. Garrison, Carpenters Union, February 24, 1891, p. 156; Valentine McClatchy to Executive Committee, Sacramento Typographical Union, April 4, 1891, p. 331, both in General Correspondence, 01/15/1891–05/31/1891, McClatchy Papers; "An End of Strife," *Daily Bee,* February 28, 1891,

2; C. K. McClatchy to Secretary of the Typographical Union, No. 46, May 2, 1893, General Correspondence, 04/03/1893–06/30/1893, p. 297, McClatchy Papers.

23. "The Printers Win," *Daily Evening News*, February 28, 1891, 3; "The Right Wins," *Daily Evening News*, March 2, 1891, 2.

24. "Barry and the *Bee*," *Daily Evening News*, January 31, 1891, 2; "Bold Buzzer," *Daily Evening News,* March 3, 1891, 2; "Just a Little Bug," *Daily Evening News*, April 6, 1891, 2. "The '*Bee*' Bill," *Daily Evening News*, April 13, 1891, 2, questioned the $1,537 contract the sheriff gave the *Bee* for printing.

25. Junius Brutus Harris had actually worked for the *Bee* at one time as a compositor and was unexpectedly given a reporter's beat. His writing talents served him well, and he worked for the *Bee* for nearly twenty years before joining the *Daily Evening News* and later the *Sunday News*. Harris had earlier worked in Truckee, where he was secretary of the Anti-Chinese League. See his obituary, "June Harris Dead," *Evening Bee,* June 19, 1897, 1.

26. "About the Boycott," *Evening Bee*, March 6, 1891, 3.

27. "Scattering Private Thinks," *Evening Bee*, May 25, 1907, 3; Landino, "Sacramento *Bee*'s Editorial Policies"; James H. Barry to C. K. McClatchy, October 9, 1917, James H. Barry Papers, BANC MSS 98/186 c, The Bancroft Library, University of California, Berkeley.

28. C. K. McClatchy to James H. Barry, November 7, 1912, James H. Barry Papers, BANC MSS 98/186 c, The Bancroft Library, University of California, Berkeley. A copy of the night letter to Gompers and Morrison, dated November 9, 1912, is in this file as well.

29. "A Government by Labor Unions," *Evening Bee*, May 14, 1903, 4.

30. "The '*Bee*' Denounced," *Record-Union*, March 13, 1893, 3; "A Great Outcry" and "Meeting of Citizens," *Evening Bee*, March 13, 1893, 1.

31. This quasi-apology appeared first in an editorial, "State Capital Removal," *Evening Bee,* March 13, 1893, 4.

32. James McClatchy Co. to A. M. Johnston, Secretary Board of Trade, March 30, 1893, General Correspondence, 12/21/1892–04/03/1893, 470, McClatchy Papers.

33. "A Board of Trade Boycott," *Evening Bee*, March 20, 1893, 1; "Legitimate Result of Sensational Journalism," *Record-Union*, March 14, 1893, 2.

34. "It Told but the Truth," *Evening Bee*, March 15, 1893, 4.

35. From the start the *Bee* had dismissed the prospect of moving the capital. Likewise, the paper noted the horrendous costs of transferring the state capital offices and the potential fate of the capitol building, which would become a huge white elephant in the center of Sacramento. See "How It Was Done" and "What the Papers Say," *Evening Bee*, March 14, 1893, 1.

36. A copy of this statement is found in a two-column block on the front page of the *Evening Bee* on March 15, 1893; see also "The *Bee*'s Turn" in the same edition.

37. Valentine McClatchy to O. M. Ramsey, April 7, 1893, General Correspondence, 04/03/1893–06/30/1893, 36, McClatchy Papers. The McClatchys never forgave Grove

Johnson. See C. K. McClatchy to Grove Johnson, November 16, 1914, Editorial, 007, 09/16/1914–11/02/1915, p. 286, McClatchy Papers.

38. "Where Do They Stand?" *Evening Bee*, March 21, 1893, 4.

39. For the history of the American Protective Association, see Kinzer, *An Episode in Anti Catholicism.*

40. One of these cartoons appeared on the front page of the November 1, 1895, edition of the *Evening Bee.*

41. "Reynold's Deposition," *Evening Bee*, October 24, 1893, 1; "Royster's Libel Suit," *Evening Bee*, October 27, 1893, 1; "Wanted $20,000," *Saturday Bee,* October 28, 1893, 1. An earlier case involved a local glove maker, Emma Dodge, who was represented by Grove Johnson; she accused the McClatchys of libeling her. In fact the paper had printed misinformation about her derived for an unsubstantiated source. "The Libel Suit," *Daily Bee*, March 21, 1893, 8; "'The *Bee's*' Libel Suit," *Evening Bee*, March 23, 1893, 1. Dodge's case ended in a hung jury, unable to prove the *Bee* guilty of malice in inaccurately reporting on her divorce. See "Failed to Agree," *Evening Bee*, March 24, 1893, 1.

42. A copy of this anonymous letter, signed by "Sacramento Mechanics" and dated April 4, 1892, is in General Correspondence, 01/04/1892–04/27/1892, p. 429, McClatchy Papers.

43. "Insult to Labor," *Evening Bee*, April 16, 1892, 1; "Mr. Gilman's Disclaimer," *Daily Evening News*, April 16, 1892, 1.

44. "A Widow's Story," *Evening Bee*, August 20, 1892, 8; "The Gilman Case," *Evening Bee*, 23 August 1892, 2; "Gilman Is Held," 24 August 1892, *Evening Bee,* 2; "Gilman Discharged," *Evening Bee*, September 24, 1892, 2; "Now It Is Gilman," October 11, 1892, 1. A front-page story announced the suit and included a two-panel cartoon entitled "Gilman Goes A-Fishing—Where Will He Most Likely Land?" It depicted Gilman as an angler hoping to snag a fish with $50,000 and landing in a bowl of soup in the second panel.

45. "An Alleged Libel," *Evening Bee*, January 23, 1894, 1; "The Gilman Case," *Evening Bee*, January 24, 1894, 2; "Barry as a Witness," *Evening Bee,* January 26, 1894, 1 and 2; "Gilman Libel Case," *Evening Bee,* January 27, 1894, 8; "Gilman on the Stand," *Evening Bee,* January 30, 1894, p 1 and 2; "The Law of Libel," *Evening Bee,* January 31, 1894, 2; "That Alleged Libel," *Evening Bee,* February 1, 1894, 2; "A Masterly Argument," *Evening Bee,* February 2, 1894, 1; "Bristling with Points," *Evening Bee,* February 5, 1894, 5; "The Libel Case," *Evening Bee,* February 6, 1894, 1 and 2; "The Libel Case," *Evening Bee,* February 7, 1894, 4; "The Search for Stella Truitt," *Record-Union*, January 25, 1894, 4.

46. "Concerning the Law of Libel," *Record-Union,* February 1, 1894, 4; "A Day of Long Waits," *Record-Union,* February 2, 1894, 4; "The Gilman-'*Bee*' Case," *Record-Union*, February 5, 1894, 5; "One More Argument to Come," *Record-Union*, February 6, 1894, 6; "Libelous Articles Denounced," *Record-Union*, February 7, 1894, 4.

47. "Five Hundred Dollars," *Evening Bee*, March 27, 1894, 1; "Is This the Law?" *Evening Bee*, March 28, 1894, 3; "An Unvarnished Recital," *Evening Bee*, March 31, 1894, 4; "Gilman Goes Under," *Evening Bee*, April 19, 1894, 2.

48. "Field for Parasites" originally appeared in the *San Francisco Post* and ran in the *Evening Bee* on March 29, 1894, 1. The *Saturday Bee* of March 31, 1894, quoted "If This Be the Law" from the front page of that day's *Fresno Expositor*. See also "The Catlin Decision," *Oroville Mercury Register,* April 7, 1894, 7; "Will Be Backed by the Press," *Oakland Tribune,* April 9, 1894, 3; "An Absurd Doctrine," *El Dorado Republican,* April 12, 1894, 4; "The Gilman Decision," *Chico Chronicle-Record,* April 14, 1894, 1. for CK's reaction to the reporting of the *Record-Union* on this decision see "Don't Cloud the Issue," in the *Evening Bee*, March 30, 1894, 3.

49. "Wail of Solomon Solon," *Evening Bee*, April 2, 1894, 3; "Libel—Some Misconceptions," *Record-Union*, March 30, 1894, 2; *Record-Union*, editorial, March 31 1894, 2. The paper followed up on the editorial by reprinting a lengthy letter to the editor from Gilman's attorney, Solomon Solon Holl; see *Record-Union*, April 2, 1894, 3. CK responded angrily in a back-page editorial, "The Ignorant Editors," *Evening Bee*, April 14, 1894, 8. For the *Bee's* response, see "Ye Brethren of the Press" and "A Widow's Story," *Saturday Bee*, April 14, 1894, 1; "A Judas in the Ranks," *Evening Bee,* April 14, 1894, 4; "The *Bee*-Gilman Case," *Evening Bee*, April 18, 1894, 1.

50. "The Law of Libel," *Evening Bee*, November 19, 1895, 1; "Case of C. H. Gilman Versus the *Bee*, on Appeal," *Evening Bee*, March 21, 1896, 1; "The Gilman Decision," *Evening Bee*, April 22, 1896, 1; Valentine McClatchy to A. J. Bruner, April 22, 1896, General Correspondence, 03/06/1896–07/30/1896, p. 260, McClatchy Papers. See also CK's editorial, "Gilman Decision."

51. "Come Out from Behind Your Ambush," *Evening Bee*, May 11, 1896, 1. The McClatchys also lashed out at the *Record-Union*, accusing it of cowardice in reporting sexual crimes. See "The Gilman Case Again," *Evening Bee*, May 18, 1896, 1.

52. "Gilman Case Decided," *Evening Bee*, 11 March 1897, 1; C. K. McClatchy to Reddy, March 13, 1897, General Correspondence, 12/09/1896–04/06/1897, p. 773, McClatchy Papers.

53. The first report of the Talmadge marriage was "C. V. Talmadge's Bride," *Evening Bee*, October 30, 1895, 6. The reporter hints at Marta's unsavory background, describing her circle of friends as "gentlemen of a sportive disposition."

54. "Court and Editor," *Evening Bee*, May 30, 1896, 9; "A Czar in the Courts" and "Hail A. P. Catlin, Czar!" *Evening Bee*, May 29, 1896, 5.

55. "A Direct Question," *Evening Bee*, June 1, 1896, 8; "Court and Editor"; "Cited for Contempt," *Evening Bee*, June 2, 1896, 1; "Contempt Case Is On," June, 4, 1896, 1; "Hail A. P. Catlin, Czar," *Evening Bee,* June 5, 1896, 1; "The Czar Hath Spoken," *Saturday Bee*, June 6, 1896, 1; C. K. McClatchy to Gil R. Osmun, July 7, 1896, 03/06/1896–07/30/1896, p. 826, McClatchy Papers; Oscar Lewis, "The Sacramento *Bee*, 1857–1957," 113, unpublished ms., box 6, folder 2, McClatchy Papers. Osmun was editor of the journal *Chicago.*

56. For examples of his editorials see "The Rights of Man," *Evening Bee,* June 20, 1896, 1, which discusses the arguments offered in the state Supreme Court case; "The Court and the Editor," *Evening Bee,* June 29, 1896, 4; "Massachusetts Press on the Catlin Decision," *Evening Bee,* June 30, 1896, 4; "The Unvarnished Truth About a

Recent Contempt Case," *Evening Bee,* October 22, 1896, 8; "It Is Now in Order for Judge A. P. Catlin to Fine Himself," *Evening Bee,* October 28, 1896, 1; "The Defeat of Catlin," *Evening Bee,* November 4, 1896, 4.

Chapter Five Creating a Press Monopoly

1. *Daily Evening News,* editorial, July 6, 1891, 2; "Unhappy 'Bee' Editors," *Daily Evening News,* February 16, 1892, 2.

2. "The Iowa Hill Matter," *Daily Evening News,* November 5, 1891, 2. See CK's response in "The Enemy in Camp," *Evening Bee,* January 6, 1892, 3.

3. "The Mysterious Organ Grinder's New Tune," *Evening Bee,* February 23, 1892, 1.

4. These reports relating information from the mysterious "Rob" are to be found in V. S. McClatchy, in The *Bee* Sacramento, 12/26/1896–unknown ending date, McClatchy Papers.

5. "Behind the Fence," *Daily Evening News,* February 24, 1892, 2. For the McWhorter-Robinson allegations see "What Was It All For," *Daily Bee,* October 15, 1886, 2. CK denied the accusation, pointing out that the *Bee* was already steadfastly against hydraulic mining by 1880. See *Daily Bee,* October 16, 1886, 2.

6. *Daily Evening News,* editorial, February 26, 1892, 2; "Living on Blood Money," *Daily Evening News,* March 3, 1892, 2.

7. "City Water Supply," *Evening Bee,* March 16, 1893, 4; "It Gave Up the Ghost," *Evening Bee,* September 12, 1893, 2. See also "It Had a Fair Test," *Daily Bee,* September 13, 1893, 3. It is hard to document the so-called agreement on the use of the printing machinery. One can only surmise that this was part of the agreement to shutter the News because CK was so angry that this machinery had been used to produce the Sunday News, which was edited by Sheehan.

8. "And Thereby Hangs a Tale," *Galt Weekly Gazette,* September 16, 1893, 2; "A 'Mortal Cinch,'" *Galt Weekly Gazette,* September 23, 1893, 2.

9. C. K. McClatchy to N. Kirtley, September 22, 1893, General Correspondence, 06/30/1893–11/02/1893, p. 329, McClatchy Papers; "The Elusive Rumor" and "Steinman and 'the *Bee*,'" *Saturday Bee,* November 4, 1893, 1.

10. V. S. McClatchy, "Report on Sunday January 17, 1897," pp. 185–85, in The *Bee* Sacramento, 12/26/1896–unknown ending date, McClatchy Papers.

11. *Sunday News,* editorial, January 17, 1897, 2, copy in Center for Sacramento History, hereafter CSH.

12. "Ghouls of the Press," *Sunday News,* March 7, 1897, 1, copy in CSH.

13. "A Leper of Journalism," *Evening Bee,* March 6, 1897, 4.

14. Ibid.

15. This information appears in the written reports of "Rob" in V. S. McClatchy, Personal Correspondence, 12/26,1896–no terminal date given, McClatchy Papers.

16. The entire sequence of the von Arnold sting is related in "A Detective Story," *Saturday Bee,* March 13, 1897, 1. This was written before the McClatchys knew that

von Arnold was a fraud. See also "Von Arnold Affair," box 009, folder 61.2 (actually three folders) in the McClatchy Papers.

17. V. S. McClatchy to C. J. Stilwell, December 30, 1896, and V. S. McClatchy to C. J. Stilwell, January 6, 1897, Valentine McClatchy Personal Correspondence, 7/22/1896–09/07/1898, pp. 139–40, McClatchy Papers. Valentine was quite concerned about keeping his association with the sting quiet and keeping only a few people in the know. Instead of having a secretary type the letters, he carefully handwrote most of his correspondence with Stilwell.

18. John Weil was a minor player in this drama but had run afoul of the McClatchys and had ample reason to want to strike back at them. A successful crockery businessman he had run for mayor in 1893 against the McClatchy favorite, Benjamin Steinman.

19. "A Detective Story," *Saturday Bee*, March 13, 1897, 1.

20. Valentine McClatchy to C. J. Stilwell, February 2, 1897, Valentine McClatchy Personal Correspondence, 7/22/1896–09/07/1898, pp. 176-78, McClatchy Papers. Valentine monitored these letters, offering edits where necessary.

21. See the letter to John Weil published on the front page of the *Evening Bee*, March 11, 1897; the letter to Wachhorst, written in German, appeared in the *Evening Bee*, March 16, 1897, p. 1.

22. Weinstock was interviewed by *Bee* reporter Colvin R. Brown on February 26, 1897, and in this interview asserted his disinterest in any of the schemes presented by von Arnold. See affidavit of Colvin B. Brown, von Arnold Files, box 009, folder 61.2, McClatchy Papers.

23. "Gigantic Combine!" *Evening Bee*, March 3, 1897, 1. See also "More of the Combine," *Evening Bee*, March 4, 1897, 1 and 2; "Rounding Them Up," *Evening Bee*, March 5, 1897, 1 and 2; "The Combine's Daily," *Evening Bee*, March 8, 1897, 1 and 2. This story was so big it pushed the inauguration of President William McKinley to page four of the newspaper. "Our New President," *Evening Bee*, March 4, 1897, 4.

24. "Grove L. Was in It," *Evening Bee*, March 12, 1897, 1.

25. "Ghouls of the Press," *Sunday News*, March 7, 1897, 1; "Von Arnold Is Amused," *Evening Bee*, March 15, 1897, 1.

26. "Herr Carl Von Arnold," *Evening Bee*, March 13, 1897, 4.

27. "Thief, Liar and Fraud," *Sunday News*, March 14, 1897, 1.

28. "The Scoundrels on the Run," *Sunday News*, March 14, 1897, 2; See also "Herr Carl Von Arnold," *Evening Bee*, March 15, 1897, 1.

29. "A Baron's Tough Career," *Sunday News*, March 21, 1897, 1; "Read This, C. E. Leonard!" *Evening Bee*, March 15, 1897, 1; and "Letter to Wachhorst," March 16, 1897, 1; "Hubbard on the Rack," March 17, 1897, 1 and 2; "Accumulating Corroboration," March 18, 1897, 1; "Corroborating Von Arnold," March 19, 1897, 1; "The Combine's Conspiracy," March 20, 1897, 1; "Leonard and the Fire Alarm," March 22, 1897, 1; "Stilwell Will Stand No Nonsense," March 23, 1897, 1; "Will Weinstock Pull Chestnuts Out of the Fire," March 24, 1897, 1; "Men and Women Blackmailed by Sheehan," March 26, 1897, 1; "Case of the Combine," March 27,

1897, 1; "Proof of Guilt," March 30, 1897, 1; "He Played Private Secretary," March 31, 1897, 1; "A Bit of Retrospection," April 1, 1897, 1, all in the *Evening Bee.*

30. "Let Us Be Honest," *Evening Bee*, March 18, 1897, 4.

31. Weinstock defended himself vigorously against any and all accusations that he had colluded with von Arnold. A good summary is "Weinstock on the Stand," *Sacramento Daily Record-Union*, February 11, 1898, 3.

32. "Rounding Them Up," *Evening Bee,* March 5, 1897, 1.

33. "Memorandum of conversation had this Monday, March 8th [1897] at 9 A.M. in private office of V.S. McClatchy between himself and Dr. Chas. Van Norden of Auburn," Valentine McClatchy Personal Correspondence, 07/22/1896–09/07/1898, p. 185, McClatchy Papers.

34. "H. Weinstock Sues the *Bee*," *Record-Union*, March 21, 1897, 3; "He Asks for $50,000," *Evening Bee*, March 22, 1897, 4. George W. McMillin—whom the McClatchys accused of being the go-to man for Sheehan's various shakedowns in articles that ran in the *Bee* on March 6 and 26, 1897—filed his own libel suit against the McClatchys in May. "And Now McMillin," *Evening Bee*, May 10, 1897, 5. McClatchy taunted Charles Leonard and Sheehan to join McMillin in suing the *Bee*. See *Evening Bee*, editorial, May 11, 1897, 4.

35. "Mr. Weinstock's Statement," *Record-Union,* March 21, 1897, 3; "Reply to H. Weinstock," *Record-Union,* March 22, 1897, 5; "And This Is Honorable Journalism," *Evening Bee*, March 22, 1897, 5; "Why Weinstock's Connection Is Concealed," *Evening Bee*, March 25, 1897, 1.

36. "Submitted to the People," *Evening Bee,* April 2, 1897, 4.

37. C. K. McClatchy to editor, *News Modesto,* April 3, 1897, General Correspondence, 12/09/1896–04/06/1897, p. 992, McClatchy Papers.

38. "Johnson Is Again Fishing," *Evening Bee*, April 13, 1897, 4.

39. Weinstock is mentioned in "Von Arnold Is a Bigamist," *San Francisco Examiner*, April 14, 1897, 1–2. See also "Is It Von Arnold," *Evening Bee*, April 12, 1897, 1; "Carl Von Arnold," *Evening Bee*, April 13, 1897, 1; "The False Baron and the Lady," *San Francisco Examiner*, April 13, 1897, 1–2.

40. "Don't Worry About Us," *Evening Bee*, April 18, 1897, 4.

41. Deposition of I. W. Lees and Edward F. Moran, May 22, 1897, von Arnold Files, box 009, folder 61.2, McClatchy Papers; "Was Lees Outwitted?" *Evening Bee*, May 10, 1897, p. 6.

42. "Weinstock-McClatchy Case," *Evening Bee*, February 1, 1898, 2; "Argued over the Admission of Evidence," *Evening Bee,* February 9, 1898, 1 and 8; "Have a Right to Make Its Case," *Evening Bee,* February 10, 1898, 1 and 5; "Contradictory Mr. Weinstock," *Evening Bee*, February 11, 1898, 1 and 5; "Explanatory Mr. Weinstock," *Evening Bee,* February 12, 1898, 1; "Weinstock Versus Weinstock," *Evening Bee*, February 16, 1898, 1 and 5; "Boodling and Blackmailing," *Evening Bee,* February 18, 1898, 1 and 5; "A Plain Tale Unvarnished," *Saturday Bee,* February 19, 1898, 1 and 11.

43. "He Got Four Hundred," *Evening Bee*, February 28, 1898, 1; "He Wishes He Hadn't," *Evening Bee*, February 28, 1898, 4.

44. "Harris Weinstock Arrested for Violating the U.S. Postal Laws," *Evening Bee*, November 28, 1899, 5; "Prosecution Said to Be Spite Work," *Evening Bee*, November 29, 1899, 5; "El Dorado Officials at Outs over the Weinstock Case," *Evening Bee*, December 9, 1899, 8.

45. "The Weinstock Mail Case," *Evening Bee*, December 4, 1899, 4. A copy of the *Sunday News* carrying the original story has not survived.

46. V. S. McClatchy to David Lubin, July 16, 1906, Valentine McClatchy Personal Correspondence, 09/18/1905–11/28/1906, p. 311, McClatchy Papers.

47. Harris Weinstock to David Lubin (copy), July 17, 1906, p. 317; Harris Weinstock to David Lubin, July 30, 1906, p. 365; C. K. McClatchy to V. S. McClatchy, August 9, 1906, p. 364, all in Valentine McClatchy Personal Correspondence, 09/18/1905–11/28/1906, McClatchy Papers.

48. C. K. McClatchy to David Lubin, n.d., Valentine McClatchy Personal Correspondence, 09/18/1905–11/28/1906, p. 375, McClatchy Papers.

49. Peter Shields to Harris Weinstock, July 21, 1908, box 56-1, folder 5, McClatchy Papers. Shields's injection of himself into this painful personal matter also earned him some scorn from the McClatchys. C. K. McClatchy to Ernest G. Walker, February 19, 1917, Editorial, 12/20/1916–07/27/1918, p. 112, McClatchy Papers. See also Peter Shields to C. K. McClatchy, February 7, 1933, box 19, folder 11, McClatchy Papers.

50. "A Popular Idea," *Daily Bee*, September 28, 1887, 2.

51. Valentine McClatchy to William H. Mills, May 3, 1901, General Correspondence, 01/29/1901–07/16/1901, p. 75, McClatchy Papers.

52. Valentine McClatchy to William H. Mills, June 1, 1901, General Correspondence, 01/29/1901–07/16/1901, 426, McClatchy Papers.

53. Valentine McClatchy (from New York City) to H. J. F. Berkeley, February 20, 1906, Valentine McClatchy Personal Correspondence, 09/18/1905–11/28/1906, p. 184, McClatchy Papers.

54. "Memo for Mr. Robbins and Mr. Burroughs," January 15, 1907, p. 649; Valentine McClatchy to L. E. Bontz, January 15, 1907, p. 651, both in General Correspondence, 10/08/1906–02/18/1907, McClatchy Papers.

55. "Thomas D. Calkins," in *History of Merced County, California* (Los Angeles: Historic Record Co., 1925), 569–70.

56. CK noted the work of the Calkinses already in 1893. See *Evening Bee*, editorial, March 23, 1893, 4.

57. Dinkelspiel, *Towers of Gold*, 275–76.

58. For information on Leonard Calkins, see "Leonard Sayler Calkins," in *Memorial and Biographical History of Northern California*, 302; "L. S. Calkins Dies at Lincoln," *Sacramento Bee*, July 23, 1931, 5. The announcement of the takeover, "Willard Calkins and Staff in Sacramento," appeared on the front page of the February 23, 1908, edition of the *Union*.

59. "Col Edwin Emerson Resigns," *Fresno Morning Republican*, March 14, 1908, 1, an editorial by Chester Rowell that CK reprinted in the *Bee*. See also "Calkins Syndicate and Problem in Induction," *Sacramento Bee*, March 18, 1908, 4.

60. Here Is One Good Reason Why Corruption Flourishes," *Saturday Bee*, February 1, 1908, 11.

61. "The Calkins Answer to the Accusation of Being a Railroad Tool," *Evening Bee*, February 12, 1908, 4.

62. "Declaration of Intentions," *Sacramento Union*, February 23, 1908, 4.

63. "The Deadly Blight upon the Syndicated Union," *Sacramento Bee*, June 18, 1908, 4; "The Morning Herrin Really Becomes Quite Wearisome," *Sacramento Bee*, October 6, 1908, 4.

64. "A Belated Denial from the Syndicated Calkins' Union," *Evening Bee*, February 25, 1908, 4; "Assembly Man Root, Under Oath, Declared Calkins Sent Removal Letter," *Sacramento Bee*, October 6, 1908, 1.

65. "Mayor White Should Redeem His Pledges to Sacramento," *Sacramento Union*, June 25, 1908, 6; "Plain Word to Mayor White about Sacramento Deadfalls," *Sacramento Union*, June 26, 1908, 6.

66. "Boycott Used as a Threat to Muzzle Union," *Sacramento Union*, June 27, 1908, 1; "'It Is Not Policy to Attack the Dives" and "You Must Either Stop This or Lose Advertising," *Sacramento Union*, June 27, 1908, 1 and 6.

67. "A Vicious Slander Against the City," *Sacramento Bee*, June 26, 1908, 1; "Indignant Citizens Meet to Denounce Sacramento Union" and "Chief Sullivan Makes Answer to the Union," *Sacramento Bee*, June 27, 1908, 1; "Committee Says Calkins Promised to Make Amends," *Sacramento Bee*, June 29, 1908, 1.

68. "The Calkins Stinger—Why Used and How Extracted," *Sacramento Bee*, June 29, 1908, 4; "Where the Union Stands," *Sacramento Union*, June 30, 1908, 1.

69. "The Psalmist David Evidently Visioned the Calkins Syndicate," *Sacramento Bee*, October 8, 1908, 4; "Edward Insley Was 'Beastly Drunk,'" *Sacramento Bee*, December 14, 1908, 1 and 8; "Enough Said About Edward Insley," *Sacramento Bee*, December 15, 1908, 1.

70. "Calkins Syndicate Papers Are Railroad and Graft Journals," *Sacramento Bee*, March 14, 1908, 1; "Merry War of the Editor vs. Syndicate," *Sacramento Bee*, March 16, 1908, 5.

71. "A Rascally Pack Yelping at Chester Rowell's Heels," *Sacramento Bee*, April 15, 1908, 12.

72. "Discharged Editor of Fresno Herald Makes False Explanation of Cause," *Sacramento Union*, March 15, 1908, 1; "The Bouncing of Colonel Edwin Emerson," *Sacramento Union*, March 16, 1908, 6.

73. "Memo for C. K.," July 8, 1908, Valentine McClatchy Personal Correspondence, 01/22/1908–12/09/1908, p. 285, McClatchy Papers.

74. "Calkins Syndicate in More Trouble," *San Francisco Call*, December 6, 1908, 41.

75. "Memorandum of Statement Issued by Calkins Syndicate for Dunn and Bradstreet," April 1, 1908, Valentine McClatchy Personal Correspondence, 01/22/1908–12/09/1908, p. 291; Valentine McClatchy to C. K. McClatchy, March 27, 1909, Valentine McClatchy Personal Correspondence, 12/07/1908–09/29/1909,

p. 217, both in McClatchy Papers. See also "Utter Failure of Calkins Syndicate," *Sacramento Bee*, March 27, 1909, 1.

76. "Calkins Reaped a Harvest in Yuba," *Sacramento Bee*, March 30, 1909, 1 and 12; "Willard P. Calkins Sued for Divorce," *Sacramento Bee*, May 8, 1909, 1. CK revealed the grisly details of Calkins's physical brutality to his wife and floated a rumor that his dalliance with a switchboard operator from his office, known as "Baby Doll," had precipitated his divorce. See "'Baby Doll' May Be with Calkins," *Sacramento Bee*, January 22, 1910, 9. An equally fulsome account is "Divorce Asked for Brutality of Publisher," *San Francisco Call*, May 9, 1909, 45.

77. "The Union Purchased by L. E. Bontz," *Sacramento Union*, November 6, 1910, 1; "Union in New Hands," "Salutatory," and "The Retiring Editors," *Sacramento Union*, August 14, 1918, 4; "Sacramento Union Sold to Wooster," *Editor and Publisher*, August 24, 1918, 20; C. K. McClatchy to Valentine McClatchy, August 19, 1918, Editorial 07/29/1918–06/07/1919, p. 39, McClatchy Papers.

78. C. K. McClatchy to John Francis Neylan, February 20, 1924, and John Francis Neylan to C. K. McClatchy, February 23, 1924, McClatchy Papers; John Francis Neylan to C. K. McClatchy, March 6, 1928, "*Bee* History, Union Sacramento *Bee* Criticism," folder 19.09, McClatchy Papers.

79. "Memo to Miss McClatchy," April 30, 1943, Sacramento Union Loan—1929, box 56, folder 8, McClatchy Papers, Center for Sacramento History (CSH).

80. Wiegand, *Papers of Permanence*, 154.

81. C. K. McClatchy to Hiram Johnson, September 30, 1931, box 33a, folder 1148, McClatchy Newspapers and Broadcasting Collection, McClatchy Papers, CSH.

82. Valentine McClatchy to Mitchell Nathan, December 14, 1904, General Correspondence, 12/14/1904–04/17/1905, p. 1, McClatchy Papers.

83. V. S. McClatchy to W. H. Porterfield, January 12, 1906, General Correspondence, 01/09/1906–04/05/1906, p. 11, McClatchy Papers.

84. "To the Membership of the McNeill Club," n.d., Valentine McClatchy Personal Correspondence, 009, 09/18/1905–11/28/1906, p. 425, McClatchy Papers; "Music," *Sacramento Star*, September 26, 1906, 2; Valentine McClatchy to Peter Wilson, September 27, 1906, p. 430, and "To the Editor, the Star," September 27, 1906, p. 431, both in Valentine McClatchy Personal Correspondence, 09/18/1905–11/28/1906, McClatchy Papers.

85. Carlos McClatchy to Roy W. Howard, October 11, 1923, box 2, folder 052, Charles Duncan Files, McClatchy Papers; "The *Bee* Merges the Star with Itself and Plans Striking Improvements," *Sacramento Bee*, February 7, 1925, 1.

Chapter Six A Tribune of Reform

1. Valentine McClatchy to L. B. Schei, Mgr. Sacramento Suburban Fruit Lands Co., September 3, 1912, Editorial, 10/01/1911–10/02/1912, 894, McClatchy Papers.

2. For example, in September 1887 Valentine appeared before the Sacramento Board of Trustees as a representative for property owners on K and O streets and contested a transportation franchise awarded to R. S. Carey. Valentine insisted that

amendments to the deal be added to ensure the work would be completed and that the lines would be sufficient in number. His efforts here failed, in part thwarted by the opposition of Grove Johnson, who defended Carey's interests. "Our Autocratic Trustees," *Daily Bee*, September 12, 1887, 5.

3. "Sample Silurians," *Daily Bee*, September 6, 1887, 1

4. Valentine McClatchy to William Mills, November 24, 1885, General Correspondence, 10/19/1885–03/27/1886, p. 81, McClatchy Papers. He also put in a similar request with the California Immigration Association. See Valentine McClatchy to C. H. Street, November 24, 1885, p. 83, in the same letter book.

5. Valentine McClatchy to E. G. Walker, January 18, 1911, Editorial, 12/24/1910–10/07/1911, p. 65, McClatchy Papers.

6. "A Case Decided," *Daily Bee*, May 1, 1886, 2.

7. Valentine McClatchy to W. A. Webster, August 17, 1908, Editorial, 06/08/1908–05/25/1909, p. 188, McClatchy Papers.

8. "Sacramento of the Future," *Evening Bee*, March 21, 1893, 4; "Sleepless Vigilance Necessary," *Evening Bee*, March 24, 1893, 4; "A Glance Backward," *Evening Bee*, September 10, 1895, 4.

9. *Where the California Fruits Grow, Resources of Sacramento County: A Souvenir of the Bee* (Sacramento: H. S. Crocker, 1894), 80. See also "The *Bee*'s Souvenir," *Saturday Bee*, March 10, 1894, 4.

10. An example of this press taunting of Hubbard is "This Is Refreshing Gall," *Evening Bee*, February 9, 1897, 4.

11. This was a long-standing position of the McClatchys'. See "A Live Question," *Daily Bee*, February 13, 1884, 2; "Quod Erat Demonstrandum," *Daily Bee*, December 14, 1888, 2. "License Gambling," *Daily Bee*, December 15, 1888, 4, alludes to an article that appeared "several years ago," wherein Sacramentans were asked if gambling should be legalized and all but five said it should. See also "The Gambling Question," *Daily Bee*, December 20, 1888, 1.

12. "Licensing Gambling," *Daily Bee*, April 14, 1880, 2; "A Ministerial Slander," *Daily Bee*, February 23, 1885, 2.

13. "Assemblyman Jones in Wrong Path," *Daily Bee*, January 24, 1885, 4; "Assemblyman Jones' Gambling Bill," *Daily Bee*, February 6, 1885, 2; "Gambling in Sacramento," *Daily Bee*, February 9, 1885, 1. See also "The Question of Licensing Gambling," *Daily Bee*, February 20, 1885, 2; "They All Favor It," *Daily Bee*, February 21, 1883, 5; "They All Talk the Same Way," *Daily Bee*, February 23, 1885, 3; "A Last Word upon the Subject," *Daily Bee*, March 13, 1885, 2.

14. "They Do Not Know It," *Record-Union*, July 16, 1885, 2; "Is Gambling Conquered," *Daily Bee*, July 16, 1885, 2; "License Gambling," *Evening Bee*, January 16, 1891, 3. See also "It Must Be Licensed," *Evening Bee*, April 13, 1893, 8.

15. C. K. McClatchy and Valentine McClatchy to H. H. Markham, March 20, 1891, General Correspondence, 01/15/1891–05/31/1891, p. 253, McClatchy Papers; "License Gambling," *Daily Bee*, January 4, 1894, 3. This article discusses the existence

of gambling in the town of Oroville, but it accurately depicts CK's attitude toward similar circumstances in Sacramento.

16. "Passing of Prominent Figure in the Political Life of the Capital City," *Evening Bee*, December 6, 1905, 4; "Flowers Were Banked over 'Bart' Cavanaugh's Grave," *Evening Bee,* December 8, 1901, 1.

17. C. K. McClatchy to Mrs. A. C. Hart, January 25, 1912, Editorial, 10/01/1911– 10/02/1912, p. 466, McClatchy Papers; "Judge Hart Rules Against Pool Selling Ordinance," *Evening Bee*, December 11, 1899, 8. See also "To Stop Pool-Selling in Sacramento," *Evening Bee*, December 14, 1899, 4; "Pool Sellers Said to Use Money to Corrupt Officials," *Evening Bee*, December 19, 1899, 5. The term *pool selling* referred to bookmaking.

18. "The Pool Rooms Must Go," *Evening Bee*, December 20, 1899, 4; "Sensational Accusations Against Mayor-Elect," *Evening Bee*, December 22 ,1899, 5.

19. "Wipe This Giant Evil from Among Us," *Evening Bee*, January 20, 1900, 4; "Pool Room Fight Now Fairly On," *Evening Bee*, January 23, 1900, 2; "Stamp Out These Vicious Pool Rooms," *Evening Bee*, January 24, 1900, 5; "Pool Rooms a Blight on the Community," *Evening Bee*, January 25, 1900, 5; "Citizens Determined to Rid the City of a Curse," *Evening Bee*, January 26, 1900, 4; "Either the People or the Poolrooms," *Evening Bee*, January 27, 1900, 4; "The Battle of the People Against the Poolrooms," *Evening Bee*, January 27, 1900, 5; "The Clergy Will Battle Against the Vicious Poolrooms," *Evening Bee*, January 27, 1900, 8; "Churches Resound with Denunciations of Pool Rooms," *Evening Bee*, January 29, 1900, 4; "Break Down those Kripp Doors Chief!" *Evening Bee*, January 29, 1900, 4; "Kripp and Egan Promise to Close," *Evening Bee*, January 29, 1900, 5; "Right Will Triumph; Battle Will Be Won," *Evening Bee*, February 5, 1900, 2.

20. "The Clergy Will Battle Against the Vicious Poolrooms," *Evening Bee*, January 27, 1900, 3; "Father Quinn Gives His Views," *Evening Bee*, January 29, 1900, 6. At the same time the *Bee* began to sound out the city trustees for their votes and found only one who would vote against it, one who refused to say how he would vote, and a third who was ill and would not be able to vote. "The Battle of the People Against the Poolrooms," *Evening Bee*, January 27, 1900, 4; "Youth Corrupted; Manhood Wrecked," *Evening Bee*, January 30, 1900, 2.

21. "Mayor Clark Orders Closing of All Gambling Houses," *Evening Bee*, January 27, 1900, 5. "Assembled Citizens Demand Close of Poolrooms," *Evening Bee*, February 10, 1900, 1; "Closing Rallies Against the Poolroom Curse," *Evening Bee*, February 12, 1900, 2; "Trustees Pass Poolroom Ordinance" and "They Will Be Hoisted by Their Own Petards," *Evening Bee*, February 13, 1900, 2 and 4; "To the Good People of Washington Across the River," *Evening Bee*, March 1, 1900, 4.

22. "A Minister Deals Hard Blows Against the Pool Room Evil," *Evening Bee,* July 16, 1900, 2; "Mayor Clark and the Poolrooms," *Evening Bee*, July 30, 1900, 8; "The Mayor and His Mind," *Evening Bee*, July 31, 1900, 4.

23. "Mayor Clark Says No," *Evening Bee,* November 12, 1900, 8; "A Few Questions About the Poolrooms in Sacramento," *Evening Bee,* November 13, 1900, 4; "Mayor

Clark and the Chief Know Nothing About Poolrooms," *Evening Bee*, November 14, 1900, 4; "The Poolroom Industry in City of Sacramento," *Evening Bee*, November 15, 1900, 4; "This Is Respectfully Dedicated to Mayor George H. Clark," *Evening Bee*, November 19, 1900, 1.

24. "Not Even a Faded Flower from Mayor G. H. Clark," *Evening Bee*, January 19, 1901, 3; "Our Marvelous Mayor and His Patent Hot-Air and Faith Hypnotic Treatment," *Evening Bee*, July 14, 1901, 4. The information about the mortgage loan appears in a letter, C. K. McClatchy to Valentine McClatchy, March 3, 1911, box 56-1, folder 8, McClatchy Papers.

25. *Daily Bee*, editorial, December 30, 1893, 4.

26. C. K. McClatchy to Robert H. Davis [Milwaukee], January 14, 1913, "Scatteration vs. Segregation," 01/03/1913–02/05/1920, p. 30, McClatchy Papers. See also C. K. McClatchy to W. A. Lawson in Milwaukee, January 13, 1913, "Scatteration vs. Segregation," 01/03/1913–02/05/1920, p. 34, McClatchy Papers.

27. C. K. McClatchy to Eugene I. Fisher, March 4, 1913, "Scatteration vs. Segregation," 01/03/1913–02/05/1920, p. 94, McClatchy Papers. See also "Merely Some Private Thinks," *Sacramento Bee*, July 30, 1932, S-6.

28. C. K. McClatchy to Franklin Hichborn, December 5, 1912, "Scatteration vs. Segregation," 01/03/1913–02/05/1920, p. 27, McClatchy Papers. (This letter was misfiled but can be found in the file given.)

29. C. K. McClatchy to Bob Davis, January 3, 1913, Editorial, 10/01/1912–06/26/1913, p. 241, McClatchy Papers; C. K. McClatchy in Milwaukee to John S. Chambers, January 3, 1913, "Scatteration vs. Segregation," 01/03/1913–02/05/1920, p. 24, McClatchy Papers.

30. Valentine McClatchy to Mrs. Mary F. Hawley, January 10, 1913, Editorial, 10/01/1912–06/26/1913, p. 251, McClatchy Papers; L. T. Hatfield, "Remedies Suggested for the Social Evil," *Sacramento Bee*, January 8, 1913, 2. For Valentine's refutation see V. S. McClatchy, "The Social Evil and Society," *Sacramento Bee*, January 11, 1913, 30; "The Venereal Plagues—A Menace to the Human Race," *Sacramento Bee*, January 18, 1913, 28. See also C. K. McClatchy to Valentine McClatchy in Milwaukee, January 14, 1913, "Scatteration vs. Segregation," 01/03/1913–02/05/1920, p. 34, McClatchy Papers.

31. C. K. McClatchy to Mayor, Cheyenne, Wyo., January 21, 1913, p. 39; C. K. McClatchy to Mayor, New Orleans, January 21, 1913, p. 40; C. K. McClatchy to Victor Rosewater, editor, *Bee*, Omaha, February 17, 1913, p. 44; C. K. McClatchy to Brand Whitlock, March 1, 1913, p. 86; and C. K. McClatchy to Newton D. Baker, March 1, 1913, p. 87, all in "Scatteration vs. Segregation," 01/03/1913–02/05/1920, McClatchy Papers.

32. The array of proposed legislation is laid out in Franklin Hichborn, "Measures Before the 1913 California Legislature," *Sacramento Bee*, February 12, 1913, 2.

33. "How Should the Legislature Deal with the Social Evil?" *Sacramento Bee*, February 3, 1913, 6; "Shall It Be Segregation or Shall It Be Scatteration?" *Sacramento*

Bee, February 7, 1913, 2; "Again: Beware of Scatteration," *Sacramento Bee*, February 15, 1913, 30; "Strong Testimony for Segregation Policy," *Sacramento Bee*, February 21, 1913, 5; Dr. S. Goldman, "Segregation Is the Best Way of Dealing with the 'Social Evil,'" *Sacramento Bee*, February 25, 1913, 11; "Beware of the Scatteration of the Social Evil," *Sacramento Bee*, February 8, 1913, 30. See also "Milwaukee Has Effectively Suppressed the Social Evil," *Sacramento Bee*, February 12, 1913, 7.

34. C. K. McClatchy to Frank Havenner, February 15, 1913, "Scatteration vs. Segregation," 01/03/1913–02/05/1920, p. 20, McClatchy Papers. Havenner, a member of the San Francisco Board of Supervisors and a McClatchy friend, produced an article advancing the cause of segregation in San Francisco, "Proper Segregation Minimizing Evils Object Aimed at by Municipal Clinic," *Sacramento Bee*, March 4, 1913, 18.

35. C. K. McClatchy to E. S. Birdsall, February 15, 1913, "Scatteration vs. Segregation," 01/03/1913–02/05/1920, p. 7, McClatchy Papers. See also C. K. McClatchy Jr., "The Social Evil Cannot Be Done Away with by the Passage of Laws," *Sacramento Bee*, March 6, 1913, 10; C. K. McClatchy, "Merchant Admits Girls' Low Wages Cause Immorality," March 8, 1913, 1 and 5.

36. C. K. McClatchy to A. E. Boynton, February 15, 1913, "Scatteration vs. Segregation," 01/03/1913–02/05/1920, p. 14, McClatchy Papers; "Social Evil Bill Goes Forward," *Sacramento Bee*, March 14, 1913, 1 and 18; "Abatement Bill Has Clear Road to Statute Books," *Sacramento Bee*, March 20, 1913, 1 and 5; Franklin Hichborn, "Women Force Passage of Bill," March 21, 1913, 1 and 18; "Redlight Abatement Will Become the Law," *Sacramento Bee*, March 21, 1913, 6.

37. V. S. McClatchy, "The Social Evil—Shall We Try Suppression or Regulation," *Sacramento Bee*, March 22, 1913, 32; C. K. McClatchy Jr., "It Is Absolutely Impossible to Suppress Prostitution," *Sacramento Bee*, March 25, 1913, 4 and 15; "Red Light Is Debated in Senate," *Sacramento Bee*, March 28, 1913, 1 and 4; "Abatement Bill Passes Senate," *Sacramento Bee*, March 29, 1913, 1 and 7; "Red Light Bill Is Signed," *Sacramento Bee*, April 7, 1913, 1. When a referendum to repeal the bill was proposed, CK argued against it, insisting, "The law should be given a full, fair, and thorough trial." See "Let the Abatement Law Have a Fair Trial," *Sacramento Bee*, April 18, 1913, 6.

38. "Memo from C. K. McClatchy for Messrs. Langdon, Carlos McClatchy, McLaughlin, Davis, Kenneth Campbell, Clayton Campbell, Jones, Gimball, Christian, Turner and Putnam, Goodwin, Davis, McGougan," December 19, 1914, Editorial, 09/16/1914– 11/02/1915, p. 361, McClatchy Papers.

39. C. K. McClatchy to Franklin Hichborn, April 9, 1916, Editorial, 11/02/1915–12/26/1916, p. 347, McClatchy Papers. See also C. K. McClatchy to Josephus Daniels, April 24, 1918, Editorial, 12/20/1916–07/27/1918, p. 825, McClatchy Papers.

40. C. K. McClatchy to Valentine McClatchy, July 22, 1913, "Scatteration and Segregation," 01/03/1913–03/20/1916, p. 124, McClatchy Papers.

41. "Flying School Site Approved," *Sacramento Bee*, February 20, 1918, 1.

42. C. K. McClatchy to Ernest G. Walker, April 8, 1918, Editorial, 12/20/1916–07/27/1918, p. 797, McClatchy Papers; "Sacramento Must Proceed to Clean Up," *Sacramento Bee*, April 10, 1918, 1 and 3; C. K. McClatchy to Major Bascom Johnson, April 13, 1918, Editorial, 12/20/1916–07/27/1918, p. 807, McClatchy Papers.

43. C. K. McClatchy to Newton D. Baker, June 19, 1918, Editorial, 12/20/1916–07/27/1918, p. 929, McClatchy Papers.

44. C. K. McClatchy to Charles F. Curry, June 2, 1918, Editorial, 12/20/1916–07/27/1918, p. 896, McClatchy Papers.

45. "The Vital Question Now Before Sacramento," *Sacramento Bee*, May 18, 1909, 4; C. K. McClatchy to W. E. Gerber, February 9, 1912, Editorial, 10/01/1911–10/02/1912, p. 537, McClatchy Papers.

46. The best overview of the full scope of Prohibition in California is found in Ostrander, *Prohibition Movement in California, 1848–1933*.

47. C. K. McClatchy to Carl Von Wiegand, February 21, 1914, p. 463; C. K. McClatchy to H. F. Stoll, secretary, California Grape Protective Assn., February 21, 1914, p. 466; C. K. McClatchy to David Lubin, February 26, 1914, p. 474, all in Editorial, 09/12/1913–09/16/1914, McClatchy Papers.

48. C. K. McClatchy to G. E. Cecato, September 13, 1916, p. 629, and C. K. McClatchy to H. F. Stoll (California Grape Protective Association), April 1, 1916, p. 307, both in Editorial, 11/02/1915–12/26/1916, McClatchy Papers.

49. C. K. McClatchy to Edgar M. Sheehan, September 13, 1916, Editorial, 11/02/1915–12/26/1916, p. 627, McClatchy Papers.

50. C. K. McClatchy to S. Heinrich, July 25, 1916, Editorial, 11/02/1915–12/26/1916, p. 524, McClatchy Papers.

51. C. K. McClatchy to Edgar M. Sheehan, October 2, 1916, Editorial, 11/02/1915–12/26/1916, p. 728, McClatchy Papers.

52. C. K. McClatchy to Ernest G. Walker, October 5, 1916, p. 750; C. K. McClatchy to Marion De Vries, October 6, 1916, p. 751; and C. K. McClatchy to Alison Ware, November 11, 1916, p. 894, all in Editorial, 11/02/1915–12/26/1916, McClatchy Papers.

53. C. K. McClatchy to Franklin Hichborn, April 6, 1916, Editorial, 11/02/1915–12/26/1916, p. 315, McClatchy Papers. See also C. K. McClatchy to Franklin Hichborn, October 23, 1916, Editorial, 11/02/1915–12/26/1916, p. 826, McClatchy Papers.

54. C. K. McClatchy to W. B. Hooker in Winburne, PA, May 12, 1917, p. 248, and C. K. McClatchy to Dr. Edward Huntington Williams, June 23, 1917, p. 309, both in Editorial, 12/20/1916–07/27/1918, McClatchy Papers.

55. Ullman, *Sex Seen*, 61–63.

56. Eugene Fisher to C. K. McClatchy, "Homosexual Issue," November 30, 1914, CD001:002:060, Duncan Files, and C. K. McClatchy to Eugene Fisher, November 30, 1914, Editorial, 09/16/1914–11/02/1915, p. 321, both in McClatchy Papers. See "Alleged Social Vagrancy Cases Up in long Beach," *Sacramento Bee*, December 7, 1914, 4.

57. Eugene Fisher to C. K. McClatchy, November 20, 1914, "Homosexual Issue, 1910–1915," CD1 002 060, and C. K. McClatchy to Eugene I. Fisher, December 26, 1914, Editorial, 09/16/1914–11/02/1915, p. 385, both in McClatchy Papers; Clayton Campbell, "Legislature Should Enact Some Law to Punish This Most Debasing Practice," *Sacramento Bee,* December 21, 1914, 1 and 10; "Wide Spread of Debasing Practices Make Punitive Legislation a Necessity," *Sacramento Bee,* December 22, 1914, 1 and 10; "Herbert N. Lowe Case Calls Attention to Crying Need of Action by Legislature," *Sacramento Bee,* December 23, 1914, p 1 and 12; "*Bee*'s Publicity Light on Great Vice of Day Shows Need of Punitive Measures," *Sacramento Bee,* December 24, 1914, 1 and 10; "California Codes Should Penalize This Infamy," *Sacramento Bee,* December 26, 1912, 28.

58. C. K. McClatchy to Newton D. Baker, December 26, 1914, Editorial, 09/16/1914–11/02/1915, p. 384, McClatchy Papers.

59. Newton D. Baker to Chas. K. McClatchy, December 31, 1914, "McClatchy, C. K.: Homosexual Issue, 1900–1915," box 002, folder 060, Duncan Files.

Chapter Seven Railroad Politics and Populist Upheaval

1. White, *Railroaded*; Orsi, *Sunset Limited.*

2. Valentine McClatchy to William H. Mills, November 9, 1900, General Correspondence, 04/27/1900–02/11/1903, p. 115, McClatchy Papers.

3. "Mills for Senator," *Evening Bee,* June 27, 1893, 3. See also *Evening Bee,* editorial, October 24 1894, 3. Mills had made the passes available to members of the McClatchy family and various employees of the *Bee.* See Valentine McClatchy to William H. Mills, February 3, 1897, General Correspondence, 12/09/1896–04/06/1897, p. 546; Valentine McClatchy to William H. Mills, July 13, 1898, General Correspondence, 06/23/1898–10/14/1898, p. 192; C. K. to William H. Mills, December 21, 1899, General Correspondence, 12/19/1899–04/27/1900, p. 32, all in McClatchy Papers.

4. "Stanford Steps Down," *San Francisco Examiner,* April 10, 1890, 3; "A Blow to the People," *Evening Bee,* April 10, 1890, 2.

5. "The Hand of Huntington," *Evening Bee,* October 18, 1890, 4.

6. During the period of railroad control of the *Record-Union,* the *Bee* occasionally threw bouquets at its morning contemporary. See "To Our Neighbor," *Evening Bee,* February 25, 1893, 4.

7. William D. Mills to Collis P. Huntington, February 4, 1893, series I, reel 52, Huntington Papers. Mills did not have direct control of the editorial policy of the *Record-Union,* and several editors did mix it up with the McClatchys over the years until the railroad finally sold the paper. For example, the *Record-Union* excoriated the *Bee* during the "Thank God" episode of 1893 in "The Action of the Legislature Saturday Night," *Record-Union,* March 13, 1893, 2; "Legitimate Result of Sensational Journalism," *Record-Union,* March 14, 1893, 2. In response CK wrote "That Funny Old Lady," *Evening Bee,* March 16, 1893, 4.

8. William D. Mills to Collis P. Huntington, January 11, 1896, series I, reel 53, Huntington Papers.,

9. "A Glorious Banner," *Evening Bee*, April 19, 1894, 1; "Will Not Disband," *Evening Bee*, April 20, 1894, 1. See also "Has Gone Far Enough," *Evening Bee*, April 20, 1894, 3.

10. "The Pauper Welcome," *Daily Bee*, May 3, 1894, 3; "Trouble in the Air," *Daily Bee*, May 16, 1894, 3.

11. "The Strike in California," *Evening Bee*, June 29, 1894, 1.

12. "Cool Judgment Needed," *Evening Bee*, June 29, 1894, 4; See also "Trade Is a Victim," *Evening Bee*, July 2, 1894, 1.

13. "Merchants Meet," *Evening Bee*, July 3, 1894, 1; "Will Be Suicidal," *Evening Bee*, July 10, 1894, 4; "The Laws Must Be Obeyed," *Evening Bee*, July 10, 1894, 4; "Troops in Town," *Evening Bee*, July 4, 1894, 1; "The Troops Come" and "Without a Shot," *Evening Bee,* July 11, 1894, 1; William H. Mills to Collis P. Huntington, August 15, 1894, series I, reel 53, Huntington Papers.

14. "Foully Murdered," *Evening Bee*, July 11, 1894, 1; "In Death's Shadow," *Evening Bee,* July 12, 1894, 1; "Harry Knox Arrested," *Evening Bee,* July 14, 1894, 1; "Thoughts upon the Strike," *Evening Bee,* July 12, 1894, 3; "A Prolonged Think," *Evening Bee*, September 22, 1894, 4.

15. William D. Mills to Collis P. Huntington, July 27, 1894, series I, reel 53, Huntington Papers.

16. William D. Mills to Collis P. Huntington, February 9, 1893, series I, reel 52, Huntington Papers. CK saw the merit on both sides of the funding controversy—both the creditors and the debtors. He believed that the only lasting solution would be the nationalization of the Pacific rail lines. See "Not Refunding, But What?" *Evening Bee*, January 4, 1897, 4. The McClatchys supported the funding bill, which wrote down the massive interest owed by the railroads—a great financial boon to them. But the McClatchys also floated the idea that the rail lines should be nationalized.

17. A sample of *Bee* invective against Grove Johnson is found in the wake of his efforts to organize a boycott against the *Bee* after the "Thank God" flap. See "Run to Earth, Grove L. Johnson Pilloried by The *Bee*," *Evening Bee,* March 27, 1893, 1; "Unearthed at Last," *Evening Bee*, March 27, 1893, 4; "A Local Skunk," *Evening Bee*, March 30, 1893, 4.

18. "In a Common Cause," *Evening Bee*, September 29, 1892, 4.

19. "The Libel Case," *Evening Bee*, February 6, 1894, 1.

20. Grove Johnson's political positions (e.g., women's suffrage) often aligned with the McClatchys'. He even denounced the Reilly Bill in Congress. In this he and the *Bee* agreed. See "Reilly Bill Defeated," *Daily Bee*, February 4, 1893, 3.

21. Valentine McClatchy to Collis Huntington, January 7, 1897, p. 280, and Collis P. Huntington to Valentine McClatchy (copy), p. 547, January 23, 1897, both in General Correspondence, 12/09/1896–04/06/1897, McClatchy Papers.

22. Wm. Mills to Valentine McClatchy, October 24, 1898, p. 862, and Valentine McClatchy to William H. Mills, October 25, 1898, p. 863, both in General Correspondence, 10/14/1898–01/04/1899, McClatchy Papers.

23. Valentine McClatchy to William Mills, November 9, 1900, General Correspondence, 10/30/1900–01/29/1901, p. 115, McClatchy Papers.

24. "To the Western Pacific Railway Co.," December 5, 1907, Valentine McClatchy Personal Correspondence, 11/30/1906–02/02/1908, p. 441, McClatchy Papers.

25. Valentine McClatchy to M. E. Hornlein, February 4, 1908, Valentine McClatchy Personal Correspondence, 1/22/1908–12/09/1908, p. 54, McClatchy Papers.

26. Walters, "Populism in California, 1889–1900."

27. Ibid., 155–56.

28. "Free Trade!" *Daily Bee*, December 6, 1887, 1. In the editorial in that issue, CK accurately predicted Grover Cleveland's loss in the 1888 election, erring only in his guess that James Blaine would be the next president. See "Good News For Republicans," 2.

29. "What It Means," *Evening Bee*, August 11, 1892, 3; C. K. McClatchy to Edward Eldridge, December 9, 1892, General Correspondence, 09/04/1892–12/20/1892, p. 455, McClatchy Papers.

30. "Let Us Have the Truth," *Evening Bee*, April 10, 1899, 4.

31. "Some Private Thinks," *Evening Bee*, May 25 1895, 8.

32. "Listen Silver Men!" *Evening Bee*, March 7, 1896, 4; C. K. McClatchy to "Dear Sir," March 13, 1896, General Correspondence, 007, 03/06/1896–07/30/1896, p. 46, McClatchy Papers; "The *Bee*'s Nonsense," *Evening Bee,* March 21, 1896, 4; "Let McKinley Come to Silver," *Evening Bee,* March 30, 1896, 4. CK also solicited endorsements of free silver from a variety of correspondents. See Henry V. Morehouse, "Straight Talk from the Shoulder," *Evening Bee,* March 31, 1896, 4; "'Frank Rhoades' on Silver Question," *Evening Bee*, April 1, 1896, 4; "Protection and Free Silver the Cry," *Evening Bee*, April 6, 1896, 4; "Ex-Gov. Markham on Silver," *Evening Bee*, April 22, 1896. 4. See also "The *Bee*'s Silver Supplement," *Evening Bee,* April 24, 1896, p1–4.

33. C. K. McClatchy to E. L. Colnon, May 23, 1896, General Correspondence, 03/06/1896–07/30/1896, p. 514, McClatchy Papers. However, in CK's solicitation of leading opinion makers in the state, he did open up the columns of the *Bee* to those who favored retention of the gold standard. Of the *Woodland Democrat*'s E. E. Leake, whose columns CK disagreed with but admired, he noted, "Leake particularly is using the column of this paper extensively to batter down the walls of the silver cause." C. K. McClatchy to Raleigh Barcar, May 23, 1896, General Correspondence, 007, 03/06/1896–07/30/1896, p. 511, McClatchy Papers.

34. "They Want Him Anyhow," *Evening Bee*, March 12, 1896, 5; "The West Sat Upon; Pacific Coast States Bull Dozed by Gold Bugs," *Evening Bee,* June 17, 1896, 1; "For Free Silver," *Evening Bee,* June 18, 1896, 5.

35. Valentine McClatchy to Daniel Meyer, June 11, 1896, General Correspondence, 03/06/1896–07/30/1896, p. 657, McClatchy Papers.

36. "The Parting of the Ways," *Evening Bee,* June 27, 1896, 4; Oscar Lewis describes CK's transition to populism in "The Sacramento *Bee*: 1857–1957," p150–51, unpublished manuscript, box 6, folder 2, Eleanor McClatchy Collection, Center for Sacramento History.

37. "For Bryan and the Right," *Evening Bee*, July 27, 1896, 4.

38. C. K. McClatchy to Editor, *Atlanta Constitution*, July 13, 1896, General Correspondence, 007, 03/06/1896–07/30/1896, p. 872, McClatchy Papers.

39. Valentine McClatchy to C. K. McClatchy, July 15, 1896, General Correspondence, 03/06/1896–07/30/1896, p. 866, McClatchy Papers; "Listen To-Night to a Great American" and "William J. Bryan, Sacramento's Guest," *Evening Bee*, March 26, 1900, 4, 8; "The *Bee* Will Again Champion Bryan," *Evening Bee*, July 7, 1900, 10.

40. "Marion De Vries, Former Judge Is Taken by Death," *Sacramento Bee,* September 12, 1939, 12; Federal Judicial Center, "Marion De Vries," Biographical Directory of Federal Judges, http://www.fjc.gov/servlet/nGetInfo.

Chapter Eight California Lion

1. See Maguire, *Ireland and the Pope*. Barry was a supporter of Maguire's and became a close friend of CK's.

2. Staniford, "Governor in the Middle," 26.

3. C. K. McClatchy to Valentine McClatchy, August 28, 1898, General Correspondence, 06/23/1898–10/14/1898, p. 531, McClatchy Papers .

4. "Religion in Politics," *Daily Bee*, August 22, 1892, 4.

5. Brusher, "Father Yorke Versus the A.P.A.," parts 1 and 2.

6. "The Foundations of Government," *San Francisco Monitor,* June 1, 1895, 5.

7. *Evening Bee,* editorial, December 5, 1895, 4. See also "Yorke Selects Foote," *Evening Bee*, December 9, 1895, 2; "An Alien American," *Evening Bee*, December 17, 1895, 4.

8. Valentine McClatchy to Peter C. Yorke, June 12, 1896, General Correspondence, 03/06/1896–07/30/1896, p. 674, McClatchy Papers .

9. "Editorial Notes," *Monitor*, March 21, 1896, 4.

10. CK reprinted this telegram exchange on the front page of the *Bee*. "Father Yorke's Personal Fight," *Evening Bee*, November 2, 1898, 1.

11. "What a Fall There Was My Country Men," *Evening Bee,* November 2, 1898, 4.

12. Melendy and Gilbert, "Henry T. Gage," 259–71, in *Governors of California*. See also "Gage's Great County Majority," *Evening Bee*, November 9, 1898, 8.

13. "The Defeat of Maguire," *Evening Bee*, November 9, 1898, 3.

14. Valentine McClatchy to H. T. Gage, January 16, 1899, p. 179; Valentine McClatchy to H. T. Gage, January 19, 1899, p. 225, both in General Correspondence, 01/05/1899–04/01/1899, McClatchy Papers.

15. "Legislature Names Bard for Senator," *Evening Bee*, February 6, 1900, 1.

16. "Signature Bill Signed by Gage," *Evening Bee*, March 21, 1899, 1.

17. C. K. McClatchy to R. A. Carothers, April 7, 1899, General Correspondence, 04/01/1899–08/11/1899, p. 57, McClatchy Papers.

18. CK ran an entire issue titled "Silly Season for Signatures Is Now Open" that included signed articles from a number of papers, most of them quite absurd. CK's remarks appear in that same issue, *Evening Bee*, April 19, 1899, 4.

19. "Business Almost at a Standstill," *Evening Bee*, July 22 1901, 1; "Strikers Clubbed by the Policemen," *Evening Bee*, July 25, 1901, 1 and 8; "Injunction Against Picket Men," *Evening Bee*, July 26, 1901, 8; "Non-Union Teams in Evidence," *Evening Bee*, July 29, 1901, 1 and 5; "Strikers Sent to the Hospital," *Evening Bee*, July 30, 1901, 1; "Many Non-Union Men Are at Work," *Evening Bee*, July 31, 1901, 1 and 8; "Can Factory Strike May Close Canneries," *Evening Bee*, July 31, 1901, 8; "Mayor Phelan Calls a Meeting," *Evening Bee*, August 1, 1901, 1 and 8; "Mayor's Efforts Not Successful," *Evening Bee*, August 3, 1901, 1 and 5; "A General Strike to Be Called Monday Next," *Evening Bee*, August 3, 1901, 8; "No More Men Have Been Called Out," *Evening Bee*, August 5, 1901, 1; "Strike of the Hoisting Men," *Evening Bee*, August 6, 1901, 1 and 8; "Employers Reply to Mayor Phelan," August 6, 1901, 6; "Situation in San Francisco," *Evening Bee*, August 8, 1901, 1; "Condition in San Francisco," *Evening Bee*, August 9, 1901, 1 and 8; "Thousands Will Walk Out This Afternoon" and "No Change in Teamster's Strike," *Evening Bee*, August 10, 1901, 1 and 8; "A General Strike in San Francisco May Be Called Within the Next Few Days," *Evening Bee*, August 12, 1901, 1; "Serious Situation in San Francisco," *Evening Bee*, August 13, 1901, 1 and 8; "Teamster's Strike in San Francisco," *Evening Bee*, August 14, 1901, 1; "All Is Quiet in San Francisco," *Evening Bee*, August 19, 1901, 1 and 8; "Battling with Renewed Energy," *Evening Bee*, August 22 1901, pp. 1 and 8.

20. "Father Yorke on Union Rights," *San Francisco Examiner*, August 8, 1901, 1. A sketch of the meeting, showing Yorke addressing the audience, was on the second page. See "Father Yorke's Notable Address," *San Francisco Examiner*, August 8, 1901, 2 and 6. See also Gribble, "Peter Yorke and the 1901 Teamsters and Waterfront Strike," 141–58; Sarbaugh, "Father Yorke and the San Francisco Waterfront."

21. "Peter C. Yorke Fishing for Converts with a Red Piece of Flannel," *Evening Bee*, August 10, 1901, 3; "Various Matters of Local Labor Interest," and "The Sympathetic Strike—The Weapon of Anarchists," *Evening Bee*, August 5, 1901, 4 and 5. CK had reporters interview "labor leaders" in Sacramento. Those who supported the strike were deemed heated or intemperate. See "Labor Leaders on 'Sympathetic Strikes,'" *Evening Bee*, August 6, 1901, 2. CK did permit the strikers to have a say in a solicited editorial by Walter MacArthur of the *Seacoast Journal*, "The Great Strike in San Francisco Viewed from a Labor Union Standpoint," *Evening Bee*, August 19, 1901, 4. A rebuttal came from an editorial of the *San Francisco Call* headed by McClatchy foe John D. Spreckels, whose steamship lines in San Francisco were adversely affected by the strike. See "The Labor Strike and the Press," *Evening Bee*, August 22, 1901, 4. CK tried to position himself as a moderate in this, but in fact he was deadly opposed to the strike in every way. He made this point again after the *Record-Union* criticized him for running the MacArthur piece. See "A Few Words to an Anonymous Critic," *Evening Bee*, August 23 1901, 4. See also "A Labor Leader on the Great Strike," *Evening Bee*, August 24 1901, 8.

22. "Henry T. as a Mediator," *Evening Bee*, August 14, 1901, 8; "The San Francisco Strike Seems to Be as Far as from a Settlement as Ever," *Evening Bee*, August 15, 1901, 1; "The Employers Association Will Not Meet the Strikers Half-Way," *Evening Bee*, August 16, 1901, 1; "Labor Controversy in San Francisco," *Evening Bee*, August 16,

1901, 1 and 5; "Attitude of Both Sides of Controversy," August 16, 1901, *Evening Bee,* 4; "Organized Attempt to Break the Strike," *Evening Bee,* August 16, 1901, 8; "Strike Situation Is Unchanged," *Evening Bee,* August 17, 1901, 1.

23. "Men Who Said 'Go Out' Now Say 'Come Back' The Teamsters Preserve Their Union Right to Organize Labor Is Fully Recognized [*sic*]," *San Francisco Examiner,* October 3, 1901, 1.

24. "The Rev. Father Yorke Points with Emphasis to the Misrepresentations of the 'Chronicle' and 'Call,'" *San Francisco Examiner,* September 30, 1901, 3; "Father Yorke Arraigns the City's Police Chief," *San Francisco Examiner,* October 1, 1901, 3.

25. "The 'Soggarth Aroon' of Virginia City, and the 'Soggarth' Without the 'Aroon' of San Francisco," *Saturday Bee,* September 28, 1901, 4; "Father Yorke Appears as Orator," *Evening Bee,* January 29, 1902, 1.

26. "Working Laborers and the Church for Henry T. Gage," *Evening Bee,* January 29, 1902, 4; "The Genesis of Reverend Peter C. Yorke—Likewise Some of His Revelations," *Evening Bee,* March 12, 1902, 4.

27. "Father Yorke on Editor McClatchy," clipping from the speech quoted in the *San Francisco Star,* March 1, 1902, Yorke Papers, Archives of University of San Francisco.

28. "A Few Boquets [*sic*] from Rev. Peter C. Yorke in His Usual Friendly Style," *Evening Bee,* February 18, 1902, 4; "The Political Priest and His Present Crusade," *Evening Bee,* February 19, 1902, 4.

29. "Reverend Peter C. Yorke Presents a Second Batch of Arguments," *Evening Bee,* March 11, 1902, 4.

Chapter Nine Public Health and Urban Corruption in San Francisco

1. Many of the details here are in Marilyn Chase's journalistic account, *Barbary Plague.* A more race-centered narrative is Shah, *Contagious Divides.* See also Kalisch, "Black Death in Chinatown." A good survey of contemporary literature on the plague is in Barde, "Plague in San Francisco." See also Barde, "Prelude to the Plague."

2. *Daily Bee,* February 13, 1884, 2; "A Great Chance for the Clergy," *Daily Bee,* February 23, 1886, 2. An example of the *Bee's* stance against Chinese immigration is "Stop Employing the Chinese," *Daily Bee,* December 11, 1885, 2.

3. "May Be Bubonic Plague" and "Four New Cases of Plague Reported," *San Francisco Call,* February 16, 1900, 11; "Startling Disclosures of Condition of Chinatown," *San Francisco Call,* February 17, 1900, 2; "Plague Again at Honolulu," *San Francisco Call,* February 27, 1900, 12; "The Plague in Hawaii," *San Francisco Call,* March 6, 1900, 11; "Dr. Brown on the Plague," *San Francisco Call,* March 23, 1900, 2; "Hilo Reports No New Cases of Plague," *San Francisco Call,* March 8, 1900, 2. The *San Francisco Call* reported that the Hawaiian plague stories were false in "Bubonic Plague Never Existed in the Islands," *San Francisco Call,* March 30, 1900, 12.

4. "Health Board Quarantines Chinatown," *San Francisco Bulletin,* March 7, 1900, 1; "Police Block All Entrances to Chinatown," *San Francisco Examiner,* March 7, 1900, 4; "Quarantine of Chinatown Is Completed," *San Francisco Examiner,* March 8, 1900, 2; "Police Keeping Quarantine Guard over Chinatown," *San Francisco Call,*

March 7, 1900, 12; "Waiting on the Menagerie Experiments," *San Francisco Bulletin*, March 8, 1900, 1.

5. "Plague Fake Part of Ploy to Plunder," *San Francisco Call*, March 8, 1900, 3. See also "Consul Utters Veiled Threat" in the same edition. Articles in the *Call* tended to link the plague episodes with poor administration by Mayor Phelan, who had helped rewrite the city charter to create a more powerful mayoralty. See "Darkness, Plague and Bankruptcy," *San Francisco Call*, March 10, 1900, 6.

6. "Is This a Plot to Destroy the City for Money," *San Francisco Bulletin*, March 8, 1900, 6; "The Bubonic Board," *San Francisco Call*, March 12, 1900, 18; "Chinatown Quarantine Is Removed," *San Francisco Bulletin*, March 9, 1900, 1; "Plague Force Is Over and Health Board Quits the Stage," *San Francisco Call*, March 10, 1900, 12; "Health Board Is Forced to Abandon Its Bubonic Bluff," *San Francisco Chronicle*, March 10, 1900, 7; "Quarantine of Chinatown Raised, All Fears Proving Groundless," *San Francisco Examiner*, March 10, 1900, 14.

7. "Health Board Inspecting Chinatown," *San Francisco Examiner*, March 11, 1900, 34; "Bubonic Scare Is Revived" and "Another Meeting of Health Board," *San Francisco Bulletin*, March 12, 1900, 2; "Death of Pig Rouses Health Board to Action," *San Francisco Call*, March 12, 1900, 10; "Chinese Scatter to Avoid a Threatened Quarantine," *San Francisco Call*, March 13, 1900, 4. "Dr. Kinyoun Says Plague Caused Death," *San Francisco Examiner*, March 12, 1900, 2; "Health Board Guarding the City Against the Plague," *San Francisco Examiner*, March 13, 1900, 7.

8. "No Need for a Scare" and "Health Board Watching for Sick Chinese," *San Francisco Examiner*, March 14, 1900, 6 and 8; "Ask for More Men for Work in Chinatown," *San Francisco Examiner*, March 15, 1900, 12; "In and Out of Kinyoun's Quarantine," *San Francisco Examiner*, March 16, 1900, 12; "Chinese Must Obey Health Regulations," *San Francisco Examiner*, March 17, 1900, 2.

9. The front-page denunciation appeared in "Our City Is Blacklisted All over America as a Plague Ridden Spot," *San Francisco Bulletin*, March 26, 1900, 1. Other articles denouncing Hearst can be found in the following: "Leading Citizens Declare Hearst Has Outraged City" and "Hearst's Life Work Is to Tear Down," *San Francisco Bulletin*, March 27, 1900, 1; "Phelan Denies the Story of a Plague" and "Health Board Is in Despair," *San Francisco Bulletin*, March 27, 1900, 5; "Horrors of the Hearst Plague," *San Francisco Bulletin*, March 27, 1900, 6; "Cost of Hearst's Bubonic Fake," *San Francisco Bulletin*, March 28, 1900, 6; "Examiner's Plague Lie Kills Trade," *San Francisco Bulletin*, March 29, 1900, 12; "Businessmen Fear Loss of Arctic Trade," *San Francisco Bulletin*, March 30, 1900, 1; "Merchants Confer on Plague Fake," *San Francisco Bulletin*, March 31, 1900, 3; "Some Bubonic Effects," *San Francisco Call*, March 23, 1900, 6; "The Yellow Plague," *San Francisco Call*, March 25, 1900, 18; "City Plague Scare a Confessed Sham," *San Francisco Call*, March 27, 1900, 1; "Examiner-Journal Plague Condemned by Press," *San Francisco Call*, March 31, 1900, 6.

10. "The Yellow Plague," *San Francisco Morning Call*, March 25, 1900, 18.

11. "Chinese Quarter Receiving a Most Thorough Cleansing," *San Francisco Examiner*, March 22, 1900, 3. Hearst also issued a strong defense of the board of

health in "Enemies to the City," *San Francisco Examiner*, March 23, 1900, 10; "Health Authorities Increase the Vigor of Their Conflict with Chinatown Germs," *San Francisco Examiner*, March 23, 1900, 12; "The Mayor Inspects the Work of Inspectors," *San Francisco Examiner*, March 25, 1900, 18.

12. "Would Counteract Report of Plague" and "Health Men Still at Work in Chinatown," *San Francisco Bulletin*, March 24, 1900, 8.

13. "Strict Quarantine Chinatown District," *San Francisco Examiner*, May 31, 1900, 3; "Board of Health Called upon to Provide for Quarantined Inhabitants of Chinatown," *San Francisco Examiner*, June 1, 1900, 3; "No Need to Be Alarmed," *San Francisco Examiner*, June 1, 1900, 6; "Strict Quarantine to Bar Street Cars from Chinatown; Board of Health Rebukes All Interfering," *San Francisco Examiner*, June 4, 1900, 3; "Leading Merchants of This City Advise That Attacks on the Board of Health Should Cease at Once," *San Francisco Examiner*, June 5, 1900, 3; "Preparing the Detention Station," *San Francisco Examiner*, June 6, 1900, 2; "Board of Health Awaits Decision of Court," *San Francisco Examiner*, June 7, 1900, 3; "Court Decrees the Raising of the Quarantine," *San Francisco Examiner*, June 16, 1900, 5.

14. "Chinese Sue for Right to Keep Going," *San Francisco Examiner*, May 26, 1900, 2. One of the attorneys for the Chinese was James Maguire.

15. "Local Health Authority Being Set Aside, Federal Quarantine Is Enforced Against San Francisco," *San Francisco Examiner*, June 17, 1900, 3; "Surgeon General Ordered the Federal Quarantine," *San Francisco Examiner*, June 18, 1900, 5; "All Quarantine Orders Have Been Suspended," *San Francisco Examiner*, June 19, 1900, 8.

16. "Bubonic Scare in San Francisco," *Evening Bee*, March 8, 1900, 1; "Stamping Out Bubonic Plague," *Evening Bee*, May 22, 1900, 1; "The Question of the Bubonic Plague," *Evening Bee*, May 24, 1900, 8.

17. C. K. McClatchy to John P. Cosgrave, May 21, 1900, General Correspondence, 04/27/1900–07/19/1900, p. 284, McClatchy Papers.

18. C. K. McClatchy to J. W. Williamson, May 24, 1900, General Correspondence, 04/27/1900–07/19/1900, p. 332, McClatchy Papers.

19. "The Plain Truth About the Bubonic Plague," *Saturday Bee*, May 26, 1900, 1 and 5; "The Bubonic Plague and Its History," *Saturday Bee*, May 26, 1900, 10; "Health Officials Say There Are Too Few Deaths," *Evening Bee*, May 28, 1900, 2; "San Francisco Merchants Change Their Attitude," *Evening Bee*, May 29, 1900, 1–3; "May Be Another Case of the Plague," *Evening Bee*, May 30, 1900, p 1 and 2; "Little Doubt Caused Latest Death," *Evening Bee*, May 31, 1900, 1; "General Belief in Necessity of Care," *Evening Bee*, June 1, 1900, 1; "Merchants to Clean Up Others' Yards," *Evening Bee*, June 2, 1900, 1; "Health Board Claims Another Plague Case," *Evening Bee*, June 4, 1900, 1 and 5; "The Plague Situation Still at a Critical Stage," *Evening Bee*, June 9, 1900, 3 and 4; "Bribe Charges in Connection with Plague," *Evening Bee*, June 9, 1900, 5; "Governor Henry T. Gage and the Plague," *Evening Bee*, June 14, 1900, 4; "Quarantine at the State Line," *Evening Bee*, June 16, 1900, 1 and 8; "Kinyoun Gets Word from Washington," *Evening Bee*, June 18, 1900, 1; "Shameful Attack upon Dr. Kinyoun," *Evening Bee*, June 18, 1900, 4.

20. "The Ostrich Press of the Metropolis," *Evening Bee,* May 30, 1900, 4. See also "The Plain Truth About the Bubonic Plague," *Evening Bee*, May 25, 1900, 1 and 5; "The Bubonic Plague and the Press," *Evening Bee,* May 25, 1900, 4.

21. James McClatchy Co. to Secretary, State Board of Health, Denver, Co., August 8, 1900, General Correspondence 07/19/1900–10/30/1900, p. 205, McClatchy Papers; "Plague Reports from Washington," *Evening Bee*, July 30, 1901, 5, and editorial comment on page 4.

22. "Public Records Denied the Public," *Evening Bee*, August 3, 1900, 1; "Denied Access to Public Documents," *Evening Bee*, August 3, 1900, 8; "Public Documents Belong to Public All the Time," *Evening Bee,* August 8 1900, 2 and 3; "The Law Is Above the Governor," *Evening Bee*, August 8, 1900, 4; "State Board of Health Appeals from 'The *Bee's*' Victory, *Evening Bee*, August 10, 1900, 5.

23. "The *Bee's* Position on Bubonic Plague Publicity," *Evening Bee*, August 10, 1900, 7; "Plague Again in San Francisco," *Evening Bee*, August 13, 1900, 1; "Truth About the Bubonic Plague in the City of San Francisco," *Evening Bee*, August 15, 1900, 1 and 9; "The Ostrich System in Public Matters," *Evening Bee,* August 15, 1900, 4; "Colorado upon the Plague Suppression," *Evening Bee,* August 16, 1900, 1; "Manifesto Checked by Latest Plague Case," *Evening Bee,* August 16, 1900, 8; "Let the People Have the Plain Facts," *Evening Bee,* August 17, 1900, 4.

24. James McClatchy Co. to J. J. Kinyoun, M.D., October 15, 1900, General Correspondence 07/19/1900–10/30/1900, p. 823, McClatchy Papers.

25. C. K. McClatchy to Paul Cowles, October 19, 1900, General Correspondence, 07/19/1900–10/30/1900, p. 868, McClatchy Papers.

26. C. K. McClatchy to Paul Cowles, October 23, 1900, General Correspondence, 07/19/1900–10/30/1900, p. 896, McClatchy Papers; "History of the Last Three Plague Cases," *Evening Bee*, November 10, 1900, 1; "The Medical Society of Northern California Unanimously Declares That the Bubonic Plague Exists in San Francisco, and Demands That Steps Be Taken for Protection," *Evening Bee,* November 14, 1900, 1. See also "The Bubonic Plague at San Francisco," *Evening Bee,* November 14, 1900, 8; "State Board on Record Confirming Plague Cases," *Evening Bee,* November 15, 1900, 2; "Medical Times on the Existence of the Plague," *Evening Bee,* November 15, 1900, 7.

27. C. K. McClatchy to Marion De Vries, December 4, 1900, p. 360, and C. K. McClatchy to Colvin Brown, December 21, 1900, p. 639, both in General Correspondence, 10/30/1900–01/29/1901, McClatchy Papers; Kalisch, "Black Death in Chinatown," 127.

28. "Truth Is Mightier Even Than California's Executive," *Evening Bee,* January 10, 1901, 2 and 7. CK subjected Gage's message to withering scorn and ridicule in "The Plague Message as Boiled Down," *Evening Bee,* January 10, 1901, 4.

29. "Another Case of Plague Found in San Francisco," *Saturday Bee*, January 12, 1901, 1. See also "And the Bubonic Plague Still Pursues the Governor," *Evening Bee*, January 17, 1901, 1; "'Plague Take the Thing!' Says Governor Gage," *Saturday Bee,* January 19, 1901, 1.

30. C. K. McClatchy to Alfred Harrell, January 19, 1901, General Correspondence, 10/30/1900–01/29/1901, p. 900, McClatchy Papers, and James McClatchy Co. to Henry Hildreth, M.D., Delano, March 15, 1901, p. 524; Dr. Cross, Visalia, March 15, 1901, p. 525; Dr. Carson, Bakersfield, March 15, 1901, p. 526; Dr. Hare, Fresno, March 15, 1901, p. 527, all in General Correspondence, 01/28/1901–04/26/1901, McClatchy Papers.

31. "Three More Cases of Plague Discovered in San Francisco," *Evening Bee*, February 14, 1901, 1; "Where Bubonic Plague Cases Were Discovered," *Evening Bee,* February 15, 1901, 1; [Indecipherable] to Charles A. Briggs, *News*, Tacoma, Washington, March 15, 1901, General Correspondence, 01/28/1901–04/26/1901, p. 518, McClatchy Papers.

32. "Federal Plague Commission Has Practically Finished," *Evening Bee,* February 18, 1901, 1.

33. "Bubonic Plague Exists," *Evening Bee,* March 6, 1901, 1.

34. "Infamous Compact Signed by Wyman," *Evening Bee,* March 6, 1901, 1. CK declared that the plague was more widespread than ever.

35. "Plague Report at Last Sees the Light of Day," *Evening Bee*, April 15, 1901, 1.

36. Chase, *Barbary Plague*, 86.

37. "Latest Plague Case Came from Sacramento," *Evening Bee*, March 1, 1901, 1.

38. H. A. French to Chester A. Lord, managing editor, *Sun,* New York, March 19, 1901, General Correspondence, 01/28/1901–04/26/1901, p. 582, McClatchy Papers.

39. James McClatchy Co. (*Bee* reporter H. A. French) to G. E. Tyler, secretary, state board of health, Denver, March 19, 1901, General Correspondence, 01/28/1901–04/26/1901, p. 585, McClatchy Papers.

40. James McClatchy Co. (*Bee* reporter H. A. French) to managing editor of Washington, D.C., *Star,* March 19, 1901, p. 615, and James McClatchy Co. to Hon. W. F. Blund, March 19, 1901, p. 589, both in General Correspondence, 01/28/1901–04/26/1901, McClatchy Papers.

41. C. K. McClatchy to James Barry, April 3, 1901, General Correspondence, 01/28/1901–04/26/1901, p. 747, McClatchy Papers; "Plague Report at Last Sees the Light of Day," *Evening Bee*, April 15, 1901, 1 and 2; "State Medical Society Says There Is Plague," *Evening Bee,* April 18, 1901, 2.

42. "Bubonic Plague Breaks Out in San Francisco, *Evening Bee,* July 9, 1901, 1; "The Stricken Jap Is Still Alive," *Evening Bee,* July 10, 1901, 2; "Japanese Women Dead of Plague," *Evening Bee,* July 11, 1901, 1; "Another Plague Case Among the Japanese," *Evening Bee,* July 12, 1901, 1; "Another Jap Dead of Bubonic Plague," *Evening Bee,* July 17, 1901, 4.

43. "Here Is the Bubonic Plague Report of Dr. H.F.A. Ryfkogel, a Public Document Illegally Kept from the Public by the State Board of Health," *Evening Bee*, September 7, 1901, 1 and 3;. "More Plague Cases in San Francisco," *Evening Bee,* September 30, 1901, 1. See also "Details of Latest Cases of Plague," *Evening Bee,* October 1, 1910, 1; "Dr. Wyman and the Louisiana Quarantine," *Evening Bee,* October 8, 1901, 2; "More Plague Found in San Francisco," *Evening Bee,* October 21, 1901, 1; "Another Plague Case in San Francisco," *Evening Bee,* November 4, 1901, 1.

44. "State Board of Health Force to Go on the Record," *Evening Bee*, October 17, 1901, 1; "Dan Kevane's Bills and Those He Audits," *Evening Bee*, August 7, 1901, 2.

45. C. K. McClatchy to E. W. Hale, November 22, 1902, p. 83, and C. K. McClatchy to Louis A. Kengla, December 4, 1902, p. 185, both in General Correspondence, 11/17/1902–02/11/1903, McClatchy Papers. See also C. K. McClatchy to Louis A. Kengla, December 4, 1902 (different letter), General Correspondence, 11/17/1902–02/11/1903, p. 189, McClatchy Papers.

46. C. K. McClatchy to Hon. George C. Pardee, December 6, 1902, General Correspondence, 11/17/1902–02/11/1903, p. 219, McClatchy Papers. See also C. K. McClatchy to James H. Barry, December 8, 1902, General Correspondence, 11/17/1902–02/11/1903, p. 216, McClatchy Papers.

47. C. K. McClatchy to Patrick Scanlan, January 27, 1903, General Correspondence, 11/17/1902–02/11/1903, p. 766, McClatchy Papers.

48. Kalisch, "Black Death in Chinatown," 133–34.

49. Franklin Hichborn apparently began drafting chapters for a memoir. One of these chapters dealt with his investigation of the plague in San Francisco at the behest of CK. A copy of this chapter is to be found in the papers of CK's daughter Eleanor. Quotes are from copy titled "The Bubonic Plague," chap. 38 (hereafter referenced as Hichborn, "Bubonic"), box 09:45, folder 06-022, "Hichborn Franklin Recollections of C. K. McClatchy," McClatchy Papers.

50. Hichborn, "Bubonic"; "Fighting the Plague in San Francisco," *Evening Bee*, September 4, 1907, 13; "Telling the Truth About the Plague in San Francisco," *Evening Bee*, September 6, 1907, 4; "Making War on Rats and Fleas in San Francisco," *Evening Bee*, September 20, 1907, 9.

51. "Governor Gillett to Investigate Plague," *Evening Bee*, September 20, 1907, 1; "State Appropriates $1,500 to Fight Bubonic Plague," *Evening Bee*, September 24, 1907, 1.

52. Franklin Hichborn, "Plague Situation at the Bay Is Unchanged," *Evening Bee*, October 7, 1907, 5; Hichborn, "San Francisco Still Laboring to Crush Out Bubonic Plague," *Evening Bee*, October 21, 1907, 11; Hichborn, "Bubonic," 12.

53. "The Plague Situation—the Need of Publicity," *Saturday Bee*, February 8, 1908, 11.

Chapter Ten The Graft Trials and the Cause of Righteousness

1. One of the earliest blasts against corruption in San Francisco politics came in June 1884 when CK urged the introduction and passage of the Cities Civil Service Act by the California State Legislature. See "How San Francisco Can Be Saved," *Daily Bee*, June 3, 1884, 2

2. For additional background on the graft prosecutions, see Bean, *Boss Ruef's San Francisco* and Thomas's *A Debonair Scoundrel*. A concise overview of this episode is provided by Issel and Cherny, *San Francisco, 1865–1932*, 156–57.

3. For more on Older, see his autobiography, *My Own* Story, and Wells, *Fremont Older*.

4. Chester Rowell, "The Spreckels Family and the Graft Prosecution," *Fresno Republican*, reprinted in *Sacramento Bee*, March 19, 1908, 4.

5. "The Disgrace of Republicanism Is the Opportunity of Democracy," *Saturday Bee*, September 8, 1906, 12.

6. CK ran this picture on the front page on October 13, 1906, with a bold headline, "No Editorial Is Necessary Here." The *Bee* ran the photo again on October 27, 1906, and on November 3, 1906.

7. "Exactly the Right Thing at Precisely the Right Time," *Evening Bee*, September 13, 1906, 4.

8. "If Ruef Spells Rottenness It Also Spells Gillett," *Saturday Bee*, October 27, 1906, 3. See also "Gillett Stands To-Day as the Handiwork of Abraham Ruef," *Evening Bee*, October 29, 1906, 4; "Gillett as Ruef's Man," *Evening Bee*, October 31, 1906, 1.

9. "Schmitz and Ruef Indicted," *Evening Bee*, November 15, 1906, 1; "The Indictment of Schmitz and Ruef," *Evening Bee*, November 16, 1906, 4; "Father Yorke Welcomes Schmitz Back to California Metropolis," *Evening Bee*, November 29, 1906, 10.

10. An account of first contacts between CK and Hichborn appears in Franklin Hichborn to Eleanor McClatchy, April 24, 1953, box 13, folder 3, McClatchy Papers.

11. The first of these reports is Franklin Hichborn, "Heney May Drag Herrin into the Net," *Evening Bee*, March 26, 1907, 1 and 12.

12. "Abe Ruef Is Forced to Confess His Guilt," *Evening Bee*, May 16, 1907, 14; "Overdoing the Lachrymose in the Case of Ruef," *Evening Bee*, May 18, 1907, 13.

13. "Influences at Work to Save Bribers," *Evening Bee*, May 31, 1907, 4.

14. "Shameful Spectacle in San Francisco," *Evening Bee*, June 6, 1907, 4. For an even lengthier denunciation of the various social classes and civic leaders who were now opponents of the prosecution, see "Most Discouraging Signs in San Francisco," *Evening Bee*, June 12, 1907, 4; Franklin Hichborn, "Fight Against Langdon Is Key to Political Situation at San Francisco," *Evening Bee*, October 5, 1907, 11; Franklin Hichborn, "The Defeat of Langdon Would Be a Greater Blow for San Francisco Than the Defeat of Mayor Taylor," *Evening Bee*, October 19, 1907, 10; Franklin Hichborn, "Confusion of Political Situation at the Bay Is to the Advantage of the Bribers," *Evening Bee*, October 26, 1907, 3.

15. *Evening Bee*, editorial, July 18, 1907, 4. See also Franklin Hichborn, "Mayor Taylor's Job More Difficult Than Fabled Labors of Hercules," *Saturday Bee*, July 20, 1907, 20.

16. The third trial's jury acquitted Ford after only two minutes of deliberation. See "Ford Acquitted at Third Trial," *Sacramento Bee*, May 2, 1908, 1.

17. "Ford's Little Joker," *Daily Bee*, February 2, 1895, 4. See also C. K. McClatchy to Franklin Hichborn, July 21, 1911, C. K. McClatchy Personal Correspondence, 04/28/1910–12/02/1912, p. 728, McClatchy Papers.

18. "Do 'the Best People' Desire to See Punished Only the Smaller Offenders?" *Saturday Bee*, December 21, 1907, 13.

19. "Appellate Court Releases Schmitz and Abe Ruef," *Evening Bee*, January 9, 1908, 1 and 5; "The Attack upon the Appellate Court Decision," *Evening Bee*, January 14, 1908, 4. See also "Appellate Court Releases Schmitz and Abe Ruef," *Evening Bee*, January 9, 1908, 1 and 5.

20. "A Deplorable Decision in the Schmitz Extortion Case," *Evening Bee*, March 11, 1908, 4; "The Schmitz Decision: What It Is and Exactly Why It Had to Be," *Sacramento Bee*, April 29, 1908, 1 and 9; "Heney Strikes Back Hard at Those Who Assail Him," *Sacramento Bee*, March 16, 1908, 4; C. K. McClatchy to Francis J. Heney, July 29, 1908, Editorial, 06/08/1908–05/25/1909, p. 165, McClatchy Papers.

21. "Maurice Haas [*sic*] Pulled the Trigger—Who Inspired the Deed?" *Sacramento Bee*, November 14, 1908, 12.

22. Hiram Johnson to C. K. McClatchy, December 1, 1908, box 34, folder 01, McClatchy Newspapers and Broadcasting Collection, McClatchy Papers, Center for Sacramento History. See also C. K. McClatchy to Hiram Johnson in the same collection.

23. "Ruef Is Guilty," *Sacramento Bee*, December 10, 1908, 1 and 5; "Justice Has Been Vindicated in the Case of Abraham Ruef," *Sacramento Bee*, December 11, 1908, 4.

24. "The Shameless Business Sentiment of San Francisco," *Sacramento Bee*, March 2, 1909, 4; "Society's Attitude Is a Shame to the State," *Sacramento Bee*, March 3, 1909, 4; "Coffey in San Quentin—Calhoun in Society's Bosom," *Sacramento Bee*, June 21 1909, 4.

25. *Sacramento Bee*, editorial, November 3, 1909, 4.

26. See Brusher, *Consecrated Thunderbolt*.

27. "A Rabbi Endeavors to Cloud the Issue," *Evening Bee*, November 22, 1906, 4.

28. "Most Discouraging Signs in San Francisco," *Evening Bee*, June 12, 1907, 4. See also "Grafting Pew Holders in the Various Churches," *Evening Bee*, November 15, 1907, 2.

29. "The Never-Failing Champion of the Public Thief," *Saturday Bee*, April 6, 1907, 11; "Father Peter C. Yorke Still Champions Eugene Schmitz," *Saturday Bee*, July 13, 1907, 12; "The Work of Two Years," *San Francisco Leader*, August 8, 1908. For a brief background on Yorke's role in the graft trials, see Gribble, "Peter Yorke and Corruption in San Francisco."

30. "Fiat Justitia," *Monitor*, November 26, 1908, 4; "One Catholic Voice Shameless— the Other Non-Committal," *Sacramento Bee*, November 26, 1908, 4.

31. "The Ravings of Civet McClatchy," *San Francisco Leader*, December 5, 1908, 4.

32. "The Plain Truth About Peter C. Yorke," pamphlet, copy in box 56-1, folder 10, McClatchy Papers.

33. "What His Townsmen Think of Him," *San Francisco Leader*, December 26, 1908, 1. Yorke reprinted portions of Insley's earlier article, Edward Insley, "McClatchy Point of View and One That Is Different," *Sacramento Union*, December 16, 1908, 4.

34. C. K. McClatchy to James H. Barry, December 15, 1908, Editorial, 06/08/1908– 05/25/1909, p. 573, McClatchy Papers.

35. James H. Barry to C. K. McClatchy, December 21, 1908, and C. K. McClatchy to James H. Barry, February 15, 1909, James H. Barry Papers, BANC MSS 98/186 c, The Bancroft Library, University of California, Berkeley.

36. "McClatchy Denounced by Knights of Columbus," *San Francisco Leader*, January 16, 1909, 1; "State Offices, A.O.H. [Ancient Order of Hibernians] Condemn C. K. McClatchy," *San Francisco Leader*, February 13, 1909, 8; "A.O.H. County Board Scores Civet McClatchy," *San Francisco Leader*, February 27, 1909, 8.

37. Untitled pamphlet, San Francisco, July 8, 1911, box 56-1, folder 10, and C. K. McClatchy to James Barry, December 5, 1911, C. K. McClatchy Personal Correspondence, 11/01/1911–12/02/1912, p. 20, both in McClatchy Papers. He also sent a copy of Lake's report to Yorke to Mrs. William Gormley, a niece of Sacramento's first bishop and the spouse of a prominent Catholic layman, William Gormley. See C. K. McClatchy to Mrs. Wm. F. Gormley, December 2, 1911, C. K. McClatchy Personal Correspondence, 11/01/1911–12/02/1912, p. 18, McClatchy Papers.

38. C. K. McClatchy to Patrick Riordan, December 8, 1911, C. K. McClatchy Personal Correspondence, 11/01/1911–12/02/1912, p. 27, and "Yorke Pamphlet and Tales Told by His Hired Detective, R. S. Lake," compiled by Warren and Norman E. Doan, 1911, box 56-1, folder 10, both in McClatchy Papers; "Father Yorke Dies at Home in San Francisco," *Sacramento Bee*, April 6, 1925, 11.

39. Michael Otis to C. K. McClatchy, December 18, 1908, box 163, Franklin Hichborn Papers (Collection 1242), Department of Special Collections, Charles E. Young Research Library, University of California, Los Angeles; Franklin Hichborn to Walter Jones, January 20, 1951, box 56.1, folder 5, McClatchy Papers.

40. The telegram sent by state senator Edward Wolfe to Wyman of January 4, 1909, reads, "The Republican Caucus has elected you Senate Chaplain. Please come." Wyman File, Paulist Fathers Archives, Paulist Administrative Center, Washington, D.C. (hereafter PFA).

41. "Frank J. Murphy Is Found Not Guilty," *Sacramento Union*, December 13, 1908, 1.

42. "Do Away Altogether with Legislative Chaplains," *Saturday Bee*, January 19, 1907, 11. See also "Blasphemy of Religion in the State Legislature," *Evening Bee*, January 22, 1907, 4; "The Jews in the Senate and the Prayers Therein," *Evening Bee*, January 23, 1907, 4.

43. Henry Wyman to Charles K. McClatchy, July 19, 1909, copy in box 163, Hichborn Papers.

44. Franklin Hichborn to C. K. McClatchy, n.d. (1909), and C. K. McClatchy to Franklin Hichborn, July 19, 1909, both in box 163, Hichborn Papers. See also C. K. McClatchy to Henry Wyman, July 20, 1909, copy in box 163.

45. "Some Paulist Fathers and the Cause of Public Honor in San Francisco," *Sacramento Bee*, July 20, 1909, 1; "The Various Churches and the Cause of Public Honor," *Sacramento Bee*, July 20, 1909, 4; Henry Wyman to C. K. McClatchy, July 21, 1909, and C. K. McClatchy to Henry Wyman, July 22, 1909, copies of both in box 163, Hichborn Papers.

46. Franklin Hichborn to C. K. McClatchy, July 30, 1909, box 163, Hichborn Papers; Henry Wyman to Henry Ignatius Stark, September 7, 1909, Stark File, PFA.

47. Biography of Henry Ignatius Stark, Stark File; Michael Otis to McClatchy, n.d., Otis File, PFA.

48. C. K. McClatchy to E. J. Devlin (Santa Cruz), October 7, 1911, p. 7, and C. K. McClatchy to James H. Barry, January 22, 1912, Editorial, p. 432, both in Editorial, 10/01/1911–10/02/1912, McClatchy Papers; "Fremont Older Still Working to Free Ruef," *Sacramento Bee*, March 19, 1913, 6. See also C. K. McClatchy to Franklin Hichborn, October 20, 1911, Editorial, 10/01/1911–10/02/1912, p. 52, McClatchy Papers.

49. "Ruef's Parole Is in No Way Irregular," *Sacramento Bee*, August 23, 1915, 6.

Chapter Eleven The Progressive McClatchy

1. The literature on progressivism is voluminous. Some of the classic works on California include Mowry, *California Progressives*, and Olin, *California's Prodigal Sons*. Deverell and Sitton, *California Progressivism Revisited*, a book of essays, surveys work in the field.

2. "Each Municipality Should Have Its Theater," *Daily Bee*, September 20, 1887, 2; "Wisconsin Will Continue Her Splendid Progressive Work," *Sacramento Bee*, January 4, 1913, 28; "The People Are Being Taught What the Government Can Do," *Sacramento Bee*, March 9, 1918, 32; "No Loss to Humanity in This Man's Death," *Sacramento Bee*, April 1, 1913, 6.

3. "Journalism's 'Weary Willie' Chides in the Argonaut," *Saturday Bee*, March 2, 1907, 13.

4. "Removal Is Beaten by Two to One," *Sacramento Bee*, November 5, 1908, 1; "Capital Removal a Dead Issue for All Time," *Sacramento Bee*, November 5, 1908, 4; "Let Us Be Honest with Ourselves," *Saturday Bee*, March 9, 1907, 11; "Now Will You Be Good?" *Evening Bee*, March 7, 1907, 1.

5. "Let the District Attorney Proceed with His Duty," *Evening Bee*, March 30, 1907, 12; "It's Straight Up to You District Attorney Wachhorst," *Evening Bee*, April 1, 1907, 4; "Wachhorst Will Not File Complaint Against Hatton," *Evening Bee*, April 4, 1907, 2; "There Was No Excuse for Not Indicting Hatton," *Evening Bee*, April 12, 1907, 4; "The Capital Removal Fight Will Be Made on Principle," *Evening Bee*, March 29, 1907, 4.

6. "Gambling Dens Operating Brazenly and Are Not Molested," *Evening Bee*, June 20, 1907, 1 and 12; "Policemen Levy Tribute on Fallen Women," *Evening Bee*, June 26, 1907, 1; "Love Letters of a Policeman," *Evening Bee*, June 27, 1907, 1 and 3; "Love Letters of a Policeman," June 28, 1907, 1 and 12; "How Radonich Got the Job," June 29, 1907, 3; "Two Disreputable Wretches Licensed to Run Saloon," *Evening Bee*, July 3, 1907, 4.

7. For CK's efforts to tar Beard, see "Southern Pacific Makes Fight for Beard," *Evening Bee*, November 7, 1907, 1 and 5. CK tied the Southern Pacific to gamblers and saloon keepers in a corrupt coalition formed to assure Beard's reelection in 1907.

8. Mahan, "Political Response to Urban Growth"; "Call upon Voters to Rid the City of Rule of Bosses," *Saturday Bee*, September 21, 1907, 1; "A Tower of Strength in Clinton L. White, and Not a Political Weakness," *Evening Bee*, October 4, 1907, 4.

9. "Clinton L. White Is Choice of Republicans," *Evening Bee,* October 4, 1907, 1; "Clinton L. White as Mayor Will Wear No Man's Collar," *Evening Bee,* October 11, 1907, 4; "Clinton L. White and the Saloon Element," *Evening Bee*, October 16, 1907, 4; "Clinton L. White," *Evening Bee*, October 23, 1909, 2; "Clinton L. White Stands for Independence and Progress," *Evening Bee*, October 24, 1907, 4.

10. "Give Us the Open Town for Competing Railroads," *Evening Bee,* October 7, 1907, 4; "Yesterday's Triumph Was but the Opening Victory," *Evening Bee*, October 28, 1907, 4; "Big Enthusiasm for White," *Evening Bee*, October 24, 1907, 3; "Vote for White for Mayor and for Unbossed Trustees," *Evening Bee,* November 4, 1907, 4.

11. "Sure, the *Bee* Loses!" *Evening Bee*, January 17, 1908, 9. See C. K. McClatchy to Clinton White, November 24, 1908, Editorial, 11 06/08/1908–05/25/1909, 503, McClatchy Papers.

12. "Sacramento's Proposed New Commission Charter," October 15, 1911, 32; "Crying Need of a Change in the Office of Mayor," *Sacramento Bee*, October 16, 1911, 4; "Sacramento Needs and Must Have the New Charter," November 4, 1911, 4.

13. "Franklin K. Lane Is Nominated for Governor," *Evening Bee*, September 3, 1902, 3; "The Tried and True Friend of 'the Common People,' for Governor of the State of California," *Evening Bee,* September 11, 1902, 1; "Franklin K. Lane Is the Toiler's Friend, but No Jack Cade or Demagogue," *Evening Bee,* September 13, 1902, 9; "A Speech Which Shows Forth the Conscience of the Speaker," *Evening Bee,* September 15, 1902, 4; "Franklin K. Lane's High Claims to the Confidence of the People," *Evening Bee,* September 16, 1902, 4; "Lane Talks to the Voters Through the *Bee*'s Columns," *Evening Bee,* September 16, 1902, 1; "The Voice of Union Labor Speaks Through the *Bee* for Franklin K. Lane," *Evening Bee,* September 19, 1902; 4.

14. "The People Have Spoken and George C. Pardee Is Elected," *Evening Bee*, November 6, 1902, 5. For Pardee's governorship, see Staniford, "Governor in the Middle."

15. "Theodore Bell Will Work Hard for His District If Elected," *Evening Bee,* September 18, 1902, 2; "Bell of Napa Who Is Running for Congress," *Evening Bee,* September 20, 1902, 16; "Enthusiastic Rally of Local Democracy," *Evening Bee,* October 17, 1902, 2.

16. "The Defeat of Theodore Bell," *Evening Bee*, November 9, 1904, 4.

17. "Adjourned—Thank God," *Fresno Republican,* March 13, 1907, 4.

18. "Lincoln-Roosevelt League Organized," *Evening Bee*, August 2, 1907, 9. Among the speakers at the event was Francis Heney, the lead prosecutor for the San Francisco graft scandals.

19. "Chester Rowell Flays Organization Bosses," *Sacramento Bee*, April 17, 1908, 2.

20. "William R. Hearst as a Patriot and a Moral Reformer," *Sacramento Bee*, April 11, 1908, 13.

21. Everett, "Chester Harvey Rowell."

22. "Every Honest Journal Should Put Principle Above Party," *Evening Bee*, March 14, 1907, 4; the reprint of the *Republican* article, "California Will Stand It No Longer," appears on the same page.

23. "Every Honest Journal."

24. "Vice President Roosevelt Has Lapsed into Obscurity," *Evening Bee*, May 6, 1901, 7.

25. "The New President of the United States," *Saturday Bee*, September 14, 1901, 10.

26. C. K. McClatchy to Hiram Johnson, January 26, 1916, Hiram Johnson Papers, BANC MSS C-B 581, The Bancroft Library, University of California, Berkeley.

27. "Keep Roosevelt in the White House," *Saturday Bee*, February 15, 1908, 1.

28. "Plain Reason Why the *Bee* Thinks as It Thinks," *Sacramento Bee*, May 4, 1912, 28; "Roosevelt and Clark Sweep the State," *Sacramento Bee,* May 15, 1912, 1 and 8; "It Was Great and Glorious—Governor Talks of Victory," *Sacramento Bee*, May 17, 1912, 1.

29. Californians to Lead Fight—Convention Battle Certain," *Sacramento Bee,* June 15, 1912, 1; "Issues Between Two Candidates Clean Cut," *Sacramento Bee,* June 18, 1912, 1 and 14; "Bolt by Roosevelt at Last Minute Now Seems Inevitable," *Sacramento Bee,* June 19, 1912, 1 and 10; "Cold Feet Among Delegates Threaten Roosevelt's Bolt," *Sacramento Bee,* June 20, 1912, 1 and 10; "Fighting Hard to Save Party," *Sacramento Bee,* June 20, 1912, 1; "Cold Feet Wave Spreading with California Firm," *Sacramento Bee,* June 21, 1912, 1 and 10; "Roosevelt Men Force Nomination of President Taft," *Sacramento Bee,* June 22, 1912, 1.

30. "An Outrage on the People of the State of California," *Sacramento Bee*, June 13, 1912, 4; "A Review of the Convention That Nominated Taft," *Sacramento Bee,* July 1, 1912, 10; "The Birth of a New National Progressive Party at Chicago," *Sacramento Bee,* June 24, 1912, 4.

31. "Democracy's Nominee Big Uncertainty," *Sacramento Bee,* June 24, 1912, 1 and 5; "Business Fights Bryan," *Sacramento Bee,* June 25, 1912, 1 and 3; "Bryan Still King-Pin of Convention with a Strong Following," *Sacramento Bee,* June 26, 1912, 1; "Bryan's Power Grows," *Sacramento Bee,* June 27, 1912, 1 and 18.

32. "Bryan's Masterly Stroke Forces Reactionaries to Swallow Bitter Pill," *Sacramento Bee,* June 28, 1912, 1 and 11; "Bryan Sits Unmoved, Ignoring Attack by New York Man," *Sacramento Bee,* July 1, 1912, 11; "Victory for W. J. Bryan," *Sacramento Bee,* July 2, 1912, 1 and 5; "The Man from Nebraska at the Baltimore Convention," *Sacramento Bee,* July 8, 1912, 1 and 2; "The Democratic Platform and Presidential Ticket," *Sacramento Bee,* July 3, 1912, 4.

33. "An Interview That Was Not an Interview," *Sacramento Bee*, July 9, 1912, 1 and 15.

34. C. K. McClatchy to editor, *Progressive News,* August 21, 1912, Editorial, 10/01/1911–10/02/1912, p. 878, McClatchy Papers.

35. "Roosevelt and His Platform—He Stands for the People," *Sacramento Bee,* August 23, 1912, 4. See also "Roosevelt to Be Here Tomorrow But 10 Minutes,"

Sacramento Bee, September 13, 1912, 1; "The People's Interests Surely Lie with Roosevelt," *Sacramento Bee*, October 12, 1912, 30; "The Power of the Trusts Is Thrown Against Roosevelt," October 21, 1912, 6; "Sacramento's Duty Alike to Herself and to Hiram W. Johnson," *Sacramento Bee*, October 28, 1912, 6.

36. "Hiram Johnson's Great Crusade Not Waged in Vain," *Sacramento Bee*, November 27, 1912, 6.

37. C. K. McClatchy to Hiram W. Johnson, November 28, 1912, Editorial, 10/01/1912–07/10/1913, p. 183, McClatchy Papers.

38. McClatchy to Johnson, January 2, 1913, Editorial, 10/01/1912–07/10/1913, p. 238, McClatchy Papers.

39. C. K. McClatchy to Valentine McClatchy, January 2, 1913, Editorial, 10/01/1912–07/10/1913, p. 235, McClatchy Papers.

40. *Daily Bee*, editorial, August 26, 1886, 2.

41. See Shapiro, "McNamara Case."

42. "And Abraham Lincoln Walks with God," *Sacramento Bee*, February 11, 1933, 5.

43. "Such Disloyalty Should Not Be Permitted in Our Public Schools," *Sacramento Bee*, December 2, 1911, 32. Varying reactions of the teachers were noted in "Pedagogues Divided on Attacks on History," *Sacramento Bee*, December 2, 1911, 5.

44. CK tied the issue to a debate about free textbooks for public school pupils in "Caminetti Denounces Textbook Plan That Promotes Adrianism," *Sacramento Bee*, December 6, 1911, 1 and 5. See also "Veterans Censure Adrian," *Sacramento Bee*, December 8, 1911, 1 and 16; "Inculcation of Patriotism Is the Very First Duty of a Public School Instructor," *Sacramento Bee*, December 9, 1911, 32; "Teachers Corroborate *Bee*'s Report of Adrian's Unpatriotic Address," *Sacramento Bee*, December 11, 1911, 1; "Teaching Disloyalty in Sacramento Public Schools," *Sacramento Bee*, December 11, 1911, 4; "Shall Sacramento Parents Submit to Such Things?" *Sacramento Bee*, December 12, 1911, 4; "High School Students Led Astray by False Teaching," *Sacramento Bee*, December 13, 1911, 4; C. K. McClatchy to Anna C. Weeks, December 13, 1911, Editorial, 10/01/1911–10/02/1912, p. 260, McClatchy Papers.

45. "Principal Williams of High School Objects to *Bee* Editorials," *Sacramento Bee*, December 9, 1911, 12.

46. CK printed a copy of the Declaration in the Christmas Eve edition of the *Bee*. See "Read to Children the Sacred Charter of Our Liberties," *Sacramento Bee*, December 24, 1911, 32.

47. "Adrianism Rebuked in Legislature," *Sacramento Bee*, December 14, 1911, 1. This article carries a copy of the concurrent resolution of the legislature introduced by McClatchy's friend state senator A. E. Boynton of Butte. See also "Resolution Condemning Adrianism Is Reported Favorably in the Senate," *Sacramento Bee*, December 15, 1911, 1. See also "California Senate Scores Adrianism," *Sacramento Bee*, December 18, 1911, 1.

48. Senate Concurrent Resolution No. 3 Relative to the Teaching of Patriotism in the Public Schools of California, *The Statutes of California and Amendments to the*

Constitution Passed at Extra Session of the Thirty-ninth Legislature, November 27, 1911–December 24, 1911, (Sacramento, 1912), 419–20.

49. C. K. McClatchy to Ernest G. Walker [night letter], December 15, 1911, Editorial, 10/01/1911–10/02/1912, p. 266, McClatchy Papers.

50. Stephens Is Scored for Attacks," *Sacramento Bee,* December 16, 1911, 4; "Cut Off Disloyal Teaching at Its Fountain-head," *Sacramento Bee,* December 18, 1911, 4; "Fountain Head of Disloyal Teachings Is U.C. Professor," *Sacramento Bee,* December 20, 1911, 1; C. K. McClatchy to A. L. Henry, December 18, 1911, Editorial, 10/01/1911–10/02/1912, p. 274, McClatchy Papers.

51. "Hysterical History," *Fresno Morning Republican,* December 14, 1911, 4. This was also reprinted in the *Union,* "*Bee's* Spasm over Adrian's Speech Ridiculed by Chester H. Rowell," *Sacramento Union,* December 15, 1911, 3. The *Union* also reprinted the defense of Adrian by the *Santa Barbara Independent,* "History and Good English," *Sacramento Union,* December 20, 1911, 4.

52. "Regent Rowell's Illogical Defense of Tory Teaching," *Sacramento Bee,* December 25, 1911, 4; C. K. McClatchy to Irving Martin, December 18, 1911, p. 278, and C. K. McClatchy to Mr. A. L. Banks, December 25, 1911, p. 294, both in Editorial, 10/01/1911–10/02/1912, McClatchy Papers. See "Lawmakers Say Disloyalty Must Not Be Taught," *Sacramento Bee,* December 23, 1911, 1. CK also reprinted the text of the Declaration of Independence under the headline "Is This All a Series of Lies?" *Sacramento Bee,* December 23, 1911, 3.

53. "Resolution by Boynton Sets the 'U' Men Agog," *San Francisco Call,* January 21, 1912, 1 and 42. See also "Is the State University Above Law and Regulation?" *Sacramento Bee,* January 25, 1912, 4.

Chapter Twelve Hiram

1. Hiram Johnson to C. K. McClatchy, March 18, 1918, and December 22, 1915, both in Hiram Johnson Papers, BANC MSS C-B 581, The Bancroft Library, University of California, Berkeley.

2. Lower, *A Bloc of One,* 1–45, provides a good overview of Johnson's early years through his gubernatorial term. Older accounts include Olin, *California's Prodigal Sons;* Mowry, *California Progressives;* Melendy and Gilbert, *Governors of California.* John Fitzpatrick III has written an interesting psychohistory of Johnson, "Senator Hiram W. Johnson." Fitzpatrick provides some important background material on Johnson's personal life and notes as well his reliance on CK for advice and friendship.

3. Fitzpatrick, "Senator Hiram W. Johnson," 26–30; "The Clark Aggregation in the Big Tent," *Evening Bee,* October 11, 1901, 4.

4. "E. J. Devlin Writes of Clark and Johnson Administration," *Sacramento Bee,* July 9, 1910, 2. Devlin, the *Bee's* city editor, reframed the history of the paper's relationship with Clark, making it more lighthearted and easy-going than it actually was.

5. "The Clark Forces Launch Campaign," *Evening Bee,* October 11, 1901, 2; "Clark Revival Service Draws Great Crowd," *Saturday Bee,* October 12, 1901, 2.

6. "Hiram Johnson Will Not Run," *Sacramento Bee,* February 8, 1910, 11.

7. "Johnson to Run for Governor," *Sacramento Bee*, February 19, 1910, 1; Hiram Johnson to C. K. McClatchy, February 20, 1910, box 32, folder 1130, McClatchy Newspapers and Broadcasting Collection, Center for Sacramento History.

8. C. K. McClatchy to Hiram Johnson, February 21, 1910, Johnson Papers, BANC MSS C-B 581, The Bancroft Library, University of California, Berkeley; "Hiram Johnson's Battle Is in the Public Interest," *Sacramento Bee*, February 21, 1910, 4; "Johnson Is Worrying Push," *Sacramento Bee*, February 21, 1910, 1; "Herrin Machine Divided Forces Find Itself Confronted with a Real Fight with Reformers," *Sacramento Bee*, February 25, 1910, 1 and 14; "No Safety in Numbers for the Regulars," *Sacramento Bee*, February 26, 1910, 1 and 25; "United Anti-Machine Republicans Face a Harassed 'Organization' Hopelessly Divided Against Itself," *Sacramento Bee*, March 5 1910, 1 and 11; "A Splendid Opportunity for California's Emancipation," *Sacramento Bee*, March 3, 1910, 1.

9. C. K. McClatchy to Theodore A. Bell, May 6, 1910, C. K. McClatchy Personal Correspondence, 04/28/1910–12/02/1912, p. 52, McClatchy Papers.

10. C. K. McClatchy to Hiram Johnson, June 10, 1910, C. K. McClatchy Personal Correspondence, 4/28/1910–12/02/1912, p. 94, McClatchy Papers.

11. For an example see C. K. McClatchy to Hiram Johnson, June 17, 1910, C. K. McClatchy Personal Correspondence, 4/28/1910–12/02/1912, p. 117, McClatchy Papers.

12. C. K. McClatchy to Theodore A. Bell, May 6, 1910, C. K. McClatchy Personal Correspondence, 4/28/1910–12/02/1912, p. 52, McClatchy Papers.

13. See Hiram Johnson to C. K. McClatchy, April 19, 1910; Hiram Johnson to C. K. McClatchy, May 2, 1910; Hiram Johnson to C. K. McClatchy, May 16, 1910, all in box 34, folder 001, McClatchy Newspapers and Broadcasting Collection.

14. C. K. McClatchy to Theodore Bell, September 1, 1910, and August 23, 1919, pp. 322 and 375, and C. K. McClatchy to Hensley S. Davis, September 1, 1910, p. 372, all in C. K. McClatchy Personal Correspondence, 4/28/1910–12/02/1912, McClatchy Papers.

15. C. K. McClatchy to Hiram Johnson, July 23, 1910, C. K. McClatchy Personal Correspondence, 4/28/1910–12/02/1912, p. 276, McClatchy Papers.

16. C. K. McClatchy to Theodore Bell, October 12, 1910, C. K. McClatchy Personal Correspondence, 4/28/1910–12/02/1912, p. 544, McClatchy Papers.

17. C. K. McClatchy to Franklin Hichborn, November 10, 1910, C. K. McClatchy Personal Correspondence, 04/28/1910–12/02/1912, p. 570, McClatchy Papers; Franklin Hichborn to C. K. McClatchy, November 12, 1910, box 163, Hichborn Papers, Department of Special Collections, Charles E. Young Research Library, University of California, Los Angeles; C. K. McClatchy to Franklin Hichborn, November 16, 1910, C. K. McClatchy Personal Correspondence, 04/28/1910–12/02/1912, p. 587, McClatchy Papers.

18. C. K. McClatchy to Francis J. Heney, December 26, 1910, C. K. McClatchy Personal Correspondence, 04/28/1910–12/02/1912, p. 592, McClatchy Papers.

19. C. K. McClatchy to Hiram Johnson, January 13, 1912, Editorial, 10/01/1911–10/02/1912, p. 391, McClatchy Papers.

20. Memo for C. K. McClatchy from "D" (perhaps Edward Devlin), October 24, 1911, p. 939, and C. K. McClatchy to Hiram Johnson, October 24, 1911, p. 955, both in C. K. McClatchy Personal Correspondence, 04/28/1910–12/02/1912, McClatchy Papers.

21. C. K. McClatchy to Theodore A. Bell, July 11, 1911, C. K. McClatchy Personal Correspondence, 04/28/1910–12/02/1912, p. 691, McClatchy Papers .

22. "Bryan Still King-Pin of Convention with a Strong Following," *Sacramento Bee*, June 23, 1912, 1.

23. C. K. McClatchy to Hiram Johnson, September 25, 1918, Editorial, 07/29/1918–06/07/1919, p. 99, McClatchy Papers; "Theodore A. Bell Dies Under Auto Near San Rafael," *Sacramento Bee*, September 5, 1922, 1 and 14.

24. C. K. McClatchy to V. L. Ricketts (*Goldfield News*), November 25, 1912, Editorial, 10/01/1912–07/10/1913, p. 174, McClatchy Papers.

25. C. K. McClatchy to H. J. McCurry, January 9, 1915, Editorial, 09/16/1914–11/02/1915, p. 410, McClatchy Papers .

26. Hichborn, *Story of the Session of the California Legislature of 1911*.

27. Valentine McClatchy to C. K. McClatchy, March 31, 1911, p, 416; C. K. McClatchy to Valentine McClatchy, August 1, 1911, p. 839; and C. K. McClatchy to Franklin Hichborn, August 4, 1911, p. 860, all in Editorial, 12/24/1910–10/07/1911, McClatchy Papers.

28. C. K. McClatchy to Valentine McClatchy, August 29, 1913, Editorial, 10/01/1912–09/10/1913, p. 959, McClatchy Papers.

29. A sampling of Carlos's articles includes "Fresno Republicans Help Clear the Campaign Issue," *Sacramento Bee*, September 24, 1914, 1 and 4; "Hiram Johnson Scores Hypocrisy of Fredericks," *Sacramento Bee*, October 1, 1914, 1 and 11; "Hiram Johnson Beards Spreckels in His Den," *Sacramento Bee*, October 2, 1914, 1; "The Splendid Workmen's Compensation Law," *Sacramento Bee*, October 20, 1914, 1 and 2; "Woman Suffrage Was a Johnson Achievement," *Sacramento Bee*, October 26, 1914, 1 and 15; "Johnson Leader in Anti-Alien Land Legislation," *Sacramento Bee*, October 27, 1914, 10; "Johnson Administration Greatly Helped Farmers," *Sacramento Bee*, October 28, 1914, 10; "Governor Johnson Combines Simplicity and Bigness," *Sacramento Bee*, October 31, 1914, 1 and 14.

30. C. K. McClatchy to Colvin B. Brown, September 26, 1914, p. 66, and C. K. McClatchy to Robert H. Davis, September 26, 1914, p. 65, both in Editorial, 09/16/1914–11/02/1915, McClatchy Papers. See also C. K. McClatchy to Robert H. Davis, October 20, 1914, p. 224 in the same letter book.

31. "Maximum of Good—Minimum Evil," *Sacramento Bee*, April 5, 1913, 32.

32. C. K. McClatchy to Harold J. Howland, February 28, 1914, Editorial, 09/12/1913–09/16/1914, p. 481, McClatchy Papers. See also Hansen, "Depoliticizing the California State Library."

33. C. K. McClatchy to Hiram Johnson, May 22, 1916, Johnson Papers, BANC MSS C-B 581, The Bancroft Library, University of California, Berkeley.

34. C. K. McClatchy to Hiram Johnson, September 6, 1916, box 33, folder 1133, McClatchy Newspapers and Broadcasting Collection, McClatchy Papers.

35. See Olin, "Hiram Johnson, the California Progressives and the Hughes Campaign."

36. Hiram Johnson to C. K. McClatchy, November 16, 1916, Johnson Papers BANC MSS C-B 581, The Bancroft Library, University of California, Berkeley.

Chapter Thirteen A New Era: Preparing the Heir

1. "McClatchy Home Was Set at $8,000," *Sacramento Union*, November 3, 1909, 1 and 8.

2. "Detention Home Still Unpurchased," *Sacramento Union*, December 7, 1909, 4; "Detention Matter up for Argument," *Sacramento Union*, February 8, 1910, 7; "Detention Matter Under Advisement," *Sacramento Union,* February 9, 1910, 3.

3. C. K. McClatchy to John S. Chambers, July 15, 1910, C. K. McClatchy Personal Correspondence, 04/28/1910–11/18/1911, p. 228, McClatchy Papers; "McClatchy Rent Claim Held Up," *Sacramento Union*, April 7, 1910, 4; "McClatchy Name Comes Up Again," *Sacramento Union,* July 8, 1910, 3; "Restrain Purchase of Detention Home," *Sacramento Union,* July 26, 1910, 2; "Detention Home Still in Court," *Sacramento Union,* August 6, 1910, 39; Detention Homes Bobs Up Again," *Sacramento Union,* August 7, 1910, 20; "Detention Home Claim Withdrawn," *Sacramento Union,* August 19, 1910, 7.

4. "Mrs. Ella K. M'Clatchy Dies in Home Here," *Sacramento Bee*, September 23, 1939, 1 and 3.

5. "Random Remarks About Sunny Italy," *Sacramento Bee*, March 30, 1911, 20; "Exceedingly Beautiful Is the City of Algiers," *Sacramento Bee*, March 15, 1911, 12.

6. "Beautiful Shade Trees on Paris Business Streets," *Sacramento Bee*, April 12, 1911, 1; "London Weather 'Beastly' but London Marvelous," *Sacramento Bee*, May 1, 1911, 8; "Dublin Is Dirty, but Has Pleasing Suburbs," *Sacramento Bee*, May 19, 1911, 2.

7. Phebe Briggs McClatchy, interview by Adair and C. K. McClatchy, September 1984, Fresno, California, box 3, in folder labeled "Rideout/Phebe Conley Recollections," James and Susan McClatchy Collection, McClatchy Papers.

8. Guinn, *History of the State of California*, 612–13. "Personal Notes" carries a brief account of the nuptials of Valentine and Adeline in the *Daily Bee*, February 9, 1881, 3.

9. C. K. McClatchy to Thomas Fox, February 7, 1919, C. K. McClatchy Personal Correspondence, 06/28/1916–08/24/1920, p. 415, McClatchy Papers.

10. C. K. McClatchy, telegram to Carlos McClatchy, June 12, 1913, box 33b, folder 1174, McClatchy Newspapers and Broadcasting Collection; Valentine McClatchy to C. K. McClatchy, March 26, 1911, box 108.2, folder 12, McClatchy Papers.

11. "Owners of Property Used for Gambling Purposes Guilty with Gamesters," *Sacramento Bee*, January 4, 1911, 1 and 3; "The Gambler's Apologist and Sacramento

Women," *Sacramento Bee*, January 7, 1911, 26; "Poolroom and Chinese Games Are Things Under Protection," *Sacramento Bee*, January 12, 1911, 2.

12. *Sacramento Bee*, editorial, January 31, 1911, 4; C. K. McClatchy to Valentine McClatchy, January 1911; box 12, folder 15, C. K. Family Letters, McClatchy Papers.

13. Valentine McClatchy to C. K. McClatchy, February 15, 1911, box 56, folder 8, Register Books, McClatchy Papers.

14. Ibid.

15. C. K. McClatchy to John S. Chambers, February 26, 1911, and C. K. McClatchy to Carlos McClatchy, n.d., both in box 56, folder 8, Register Books, McClatchy Papers.

16. C. K. McClatchy to Carlos McClatchy, February 28, 1911, box 56, folder 8, Register Books, McClatchy Papers.

17. C. K. McClatchy to "Dear Mama," February 28, 1911, box 56, folder 8, Register Books, McClatchy Papers.

18. C. K. McClatchy to Robert Kenna, S.J., n.d. (ca. March 1911), and C. K. McClatchy to Valentine McClatchy, March 2 and 8, 1911, all in box 56, folder 8, Register Books, McClatchy Papers.

19. Valentine McClatchy to C. K. McClatchy, March 2, 1911, box 108.2, folder 12, McClatchy Papers.

20. Ibid., March 26, 1911.

21. Ibid.

22. Ibid.

23. C. K. McClatchy to Valentine McClatchy, n.d. (probably sometime in early April 1911), box 108.2, folder 12, McClatchy Papers.

24. C. K. McClatchy to Valentine. McClatchy, n.d. (probably summer 1911), box 56.1, folder 9, McClatchy Papers.

25. Valentine McClatchy to C. K. McClatchy, May 29, 1911, box 108.2, folder 12, McClatchy Papers.

26. C. K. McClatchy to Milton J. Green, September 25, 1911, Editorial, 10/01/1911–10/02/1912, p. 954, McClatchy Papers.

27. C. K. McClatchy, telegram to Carlos McClatchy, June 12, 1913, box 33b, folder 1174, McClatchy Newspapers and Broadcasting Collection.

28. C. K. McClatchy to Valentine McClatchy, August 16, 1911, C. K. McClatchy Personal Correspondence, 04/28/1910–12/02/1912, p. 815, McClatchy Papers.

29. Articles by Carlos McClatchy in the Santa Clara student literary magazine, the *Redwood,* include "College Notes," 1907, 89–96; "Athletics," June 1907, 443–44; "The First Division Reading and Billiard Rooms," December 1907, 142–43; "For the Children's Sake," January 1908, 166–68; "What's in a Name," February 1908, 220–24, Archives of the University of Santa Clara.

30. Carlos to "Dear Papa," March 3, 1909, and Carlos McClatchy to "Dear Mama," September 7, 1909, and March 5, 1911, all in box 26.1, folder 7, McClatchy Papers.

31. Valentine McClatchy to C. K. McClatchy, November 25, 1899, Valentine McClatchy Personal Correspondence, p. 365, McClatchy Papers.

32. C. K. McClatchy to Mary F. White, July 29, 1904, General Correspondence, 01/01/1903–12/14/1904, p. 79, McClatchy Papers.

33. Carlos McClatchy to C. K. McClatchy, January 7, 1924, box 1, folder 052, Charles Duncan Files, McClatchy Papers.

34. C. K. McClatchy to Colvin Brown, November 12, 1908, Editorial, 06/08/1908–05/25/1909, p. 451, McClatchy Papers.

35. Carlos used the byline C. K. McClatchy, Jr. His articles include "Eastern and Western Spirit," *Sacramento Bee*, August 7, 1909, 13; "Store Workers Docked for Christmas Day," *Sacramento Bee*, January 3, 1910, 3.

36. Carlos McClatchy to "Dear Mama," March 25, 1910, box 26.1, folder 7, McClatchy Papers.

37. "A History of the Columbia College Class of Nineteen Hundred and Eleven," *Senior Year Book*, vol. 1, Columbia University Archives, New York.

38. C. K. McClatchy to Robert H. Davis, October 5, 1911, C. K. McClatchy Personal Correspondence, 04/28/1910–12/02/1912, p. 902, McClatchy Papers.

39. C. K. McClatchy to Alva Johnston, January 25, 1912, C. K. McClatchy Personal Correspondence, 04/28/1910–12/02/1912, p. 94, McClatchy Papers. Johnston won a Pulitzer Prize in 1923 for his *New York Times* articles on the convention of the American Association for the Advancement of Science. "Alva Johnston Wins Pulitzer Prize of $1,000," *Sacramento Bee*, May 14, 1923, 1 and 17.

40. C. K. McClatchy to Henry George Jr., January 2, 1913, p. 229; C. K. McClatchy to Carlos McClatchy, January 2, 1913, p. 230; and C. K. McClatchy to Ernest G. Walker, January 3, 1913, p. 246, all in Editorial, 10/01/1912–07/10/1913, McClatchy Papers.

41. C. K. McClatchy to John S. Chambers (from Milwaukee), January 10, 1913, Editorial, 10/01/1912–07/10/1913, p. 261, McClatchy Papers.

42. C. K. McClatchy to Franklin Hichborn, November 24, 1913, C. K. McClatchy Personal Correspondence, 08/30/1913–08/14/1916, p. 131, McClatchy Papers.

43. Valentine McClatchy to Carlos McClatchy, May 30, 1913, Editorial, 10/01/1912–07/10/1913, p. 719, McClatchy Papers.

44. Carlos McClatchy to Ernest G. Walker, September 6, 1913, Editorial, 10/01/1912–09/10/1913, p. 984, McClatchy Papers. Fox had been proposed for a local postmastership and was strongly opposed by local Republicans.

45. C. K. McClatchy to Hiram Johnson, August 26, 1914, p. 937, and C. K. McClatchy to James Barry, September 29, 1914, p. 88, both in Editorial, 09/16/1914–11/02/1915, McClatchy Papers. On behalf of Johnson's second term Carlos wrote: "Wipe Out Party Lines in State Politics," *Sacramento Bee*, August 8, 1914, 28; "Fresno Republicans Help Clear the Campaign Issue," *Sacramento Bee*, September 24, 1914, 1 and 4; "Hiram Johnson Scores Hypocrisy of Fredericks," *Sacramento Bee*, October 1, 1914, 1 and 11; "Hiram Johnson Beards Spreckels in His Den," *Sacramento Bee*, October 2, 1914, 1; "The Splendid Workmen's Compensation Law," *Sacramento Bee*, October 20, 1914, 1 and 2; "Woman Suffrage Was a Johnson Achievement," *Sacramento Bee*, October 26, 1914, 1 and 2; "Johnson Leader in Anti-Alien Land

Legislation," *Sacramento Bee,* October 27, 1914, 10; "Johnson Administration Greatly Helped Farmers," *Sacramento Bee,* October 28, 1914, 10; "Governor Johnson Combines Simplicity and Bigness," *Sacramento Bee,* October 31, 1914, 1 and 14; "Simplification of the State Government," *Sacramento Bee,* November 26, 1914, 1 and 2.

46. "Certainty of Murder at Orphanage Grows as Further Light Is Shed," *Sacramento Bee,* December 3, 1914, 1 and 2; "Cries of Boy Murdered Heard," *Sacramento Bee,* December 11, 1914, 1 and 2.

47. "Shall Hanging Be Nullified in California?" *Sacramento Bee,* September 14, 1915, 1 and 4; "Louis Bundy Was Most Brutal of All Murderers," *Sacramento Bee,* September 16, 1915, 1 and 9; "Sentimentalists Are Not Clamoring to Save Negro from Gallows," *Sacramento Bee,* September 18, 1915, 1 and 12; "Pleas for Murderers Really Are Efforts to Secure Their Freedom," *Sacramento Bee,* September 20, 1915, 1 and 9; "*Bee* Articles on Hanging Assailed as 'Unchristian,'" *Sacramento Bee,* September 22, 1915, 1 and 4; "Earl Loomis Is Again Painted as Unfortunate," *Sacramento Bee,* September 23, 1915, 1 and 12.

48. Carlos wrote "Hughes Statement Weak, Is but a Colorless Generality" and "Old Line Republicans Downcast, Stunned by Progressive Program," *Sacramento Bee,* June 6, 1916, 1; "Republican Situation Grows More Complex; Doubt Reigns," *Sacramento Bee,* June 6, 1916, 16; "Moosers Burn Bridges," *Sacramento Bee,* June 7, 1916, 1 and 2; "Pall of Indifference and Gloom Hangs over Republican Convention," *Sacramento Bee,* June 9, 1916, 1 and 5; "Horizon of Bourbons Convention Is Clear; Not a Fight in Sight" and "Bryan Probably Will Be Given Opportunity to Talk at St. Louis," *Sacramento Bee,* June 12, 1916, 1 and 5; "California Bourbons Minus Two Features—Wine and Tom Fox," *Sacramento Bee,* June 13, 1916, 1 and 2; "How to Keep Bull Moose Away from G.O.P. Ranks Is Democratic Problem," *Sacramento Bee,* June 13, 1916, 1 and 18; "Woman's Party Will Try to Wrest Ballot from Party in Power," *Sacramento Bee,* June 14, 1916, 3.

49. "Dividing the State Capitol," *Sacramento Bee,* December 9, 1916, 36.

Chapter Fourteen World War I

1. C. K. McClatchy to S. P. Conry (Rome), August 29, 1914, Editorial, 09/12/1913–09/16/1914, p. 950, McClatchy Papers; C. K. McClatchy to Hiram Johnson, April 5, 1915, Hiram Johnson Papers, The Bancroft Library, BANC MSS C-B 581, University of California, Berkeley; "War Is Almost Always an International Crime," *Sacramento Bee,* July 29, 1914, 6.

2. "Hyphenated Americans Are Not Wanted Here," *Sacramento Bee,* May 17, 1915, 6.

3. "A Crazy Man Plunges All Europe into War," *Sacramento Bee,* August 6, 1914, 6.

4. "America Should Treat England and Germany Alike," *Sacramento Bee,* June 26, 1915, 7; "England Also Must Be Made [to] Respect Our Rights," *Sacramento Bee,* July 13, 1915, 6; "America's Rights Must Be Respected on the Seas," *Sacramento*

Bee, November 8, 1915, 6; "The Un-American Assault Continued Will Re-Elect Woodrow Wilson," *Sacramento Bee*, December 3, 1915, 6; C. K. McClatchy, telegram to Valentine McClatchy, April 17, 1916, Editorial, 11/02/1915–12/26/1916, p. 371, McClatchy Papers.

5. "There Is but One Course to Follow No Matter Where It Leads," *Sacramento Bee*, May 31, 1915, 6; "Power to Punish Without Drawing the Sword," *Sacramento Bee*, June 2, 1915, 6; "Our President: May He Always Be Right. But Our President, Right or Wrong," *Sacramento Bee*, June 9, 1915, 6; "Was This Great Man Swayed by Heart More Than Head," *Sacramento Bee*, June 10, 1915, 6; "Neither the American People Nor Jesus of Nazareth Is with Bryan Today," *Sacramento Bee*, June 11, 1915, 6; "Every Stalwart American Stands Back of the President in Salute to the Flag," *Sacramento Bee*, June 12, 1915, 4.

6. C. K. McClatchy to Hiram Johnson, April 5, 1915, Hiram Johnson Papers, BANC MSS C-B 581, The Bancroft Library, University of California, Berkeley.

7. C. K. McClatchy, "Whether to Be Amused or Angered by the Note—That Is the Question," *Sacramento Bee*, May 8, 1916, 1 and 16; "'Caesar's Wife Should Be Above Suspicion' Wilson Should Now Rap Britain," *Sacramento Bee*, May 9, 1916, 1 and 18; "Bryan's Peace Treaty with Britain Not Bar to 'Freedom of Seas,'" *Sacramento Bee*, May 10, 1916, 1; "German Vote Not for Wilson or Roosevelt; Hoch der Kaiser and Herr Justice Hughes," *Sacramento Bee*, May 23, 1916, 1 and 15; "Mail Seizure Protest Is Very Fine and Very Strong; Now for Action to End Acts of Piracy," *Sacramento Bee*, May 27, 1916, 1 and 4; "Air of God Save the King Is as Close as America Will Get; No Alliance with Britain," *Sacramento Bee*, May 29, 1916, 1 and 14.

8. "Irish American Wind Bags Prove If St. Patrick Drove Snakes out of Ireland He sent Some to These Shores," *Sacramento Bee*, May 19, 1916, 1 and 10.

9. C. K. McClatchy to Ernest G. Walker, January 25, 1916, p. 146, and C. K. McClatchy Memo to Mr. Lawson, Carlos, and Langdon, January 27, 1916, p. 150, both in Editorial 11, 11/02/1915–12/26/1916, McClatchy Papers.

10. "Suggestions," n.d. [1916], Editorial, 11/02/1915–12/26/1916, p. 353, McClatchy Papers.

11. C. K. McClatchy to Franklin K. Lane, October 27, 1915, Editorial, 09/16/1914–11/02/1915, p. 850, McClatchy Papers.

12. "The Latest German Note Adds Insult to Injury," *Sacramento Bee*, August 25, 1916, 6; "Startling Exposure of Germany's Hostile Scheming," *Sacramento Bee*, March 1, 1917, 6.

13. "A Long-Suffering Nation Begins a Righteous War," *Sacramento Bee*, April 3, 1917, 6; "We Are at War. How Shall We Wage It?" *Sacramento Bee*, April 4, 1917, 6.

14. Memo for Langdon, Lawson and Carlos, April 6, 1917, p. 198; memo to Messrs. Lawson and Carroll, May 18, 1918, p. 862; C. K. McClatchy to Colvin J. Brown, October 24, 1917, p. 476,; CK to Ernest G. Walker, October 22, 1917, p. 478, all in Editorial, 12/20/1916–07/27/1918, McClatchy Papers.

15. C. K. McClatchy to Elliot Goodwin, March 27, 1917, Editorial, 12/20/1916–07/27/1918, p. 202, McClatchy Papers.

16. C. K. McClatchy to William Kent, December 3, 1917, p. 556, and C. K. McClatchy to Charles F. Curry, May 27, 1918, p. 875, both in Editorial, 12/20/1916–07/27/1918, McClatchy Papers.

17. "Men Released by Exemption Board," *Sacramento Bee,* September 4, 1917, 1; C. K. McClatchy, telegram to Hiram Johnson, April 24, 1917, Hiram Johnson Papers, BANC MSS C-B 581, The Bancroft Library, University of California, Berkeley; C. K. McClatchy to B. B. Meek, September 25, 1917, Editorial, 12/20/1916–07/27/1918, p. 427, McClatchy Papers.

18. Hiram Johnson to C. K. McClatchy, May 1, 1917, and C. K. McClatchy to Hiram Johnson, May 22, 1917, both in Hiram Johnson Papers, BANC MSS C-B 581, The Bancroft Library, University of California, Berkeley.

19. C. K. McClatchy to Hiram Johnson, June 24, 1918, p. 941, and C. K. McClatchy to Ralph Merritt, November 6, 1918, p. 187, both in Editorial, 07/29/1918–06/07/1919, McClatchy Papers.

20. Carlos McClatchy to Hiram Johnson, July 8, 1916, Hiram Johnson Papers, BANC MSS C-B 581, The Bancroft Library, University of California, Berkeley; Carlos McClatchy to Valentine McClatchy, August 8, 1916, p. 551, and Carlos McClatchy to Lt. H. R. Gimbal, August 31, 1916, p. 605, both in Editorial, 11/02/1915–12/26/1916, McClatchy Papers.

21. Carlos McClatchy to William T. Haley, August 15, 1916, Editorial, 11/02/1915–12/26/1916, p. 564, McClatchy Papers.

22. Carlos McClatchy to William T. Haley, September 16, 1916, Editorial, 11/02/1915–12/26/1916, p. 642, McClatchy Papers.

23. C. K. McClatchy to Hiram Johnson, May 22, 1917, Hiram Johnson Papers, BANC MSS C-B 581, The Bancroft Library, University of California, Berkeley; Carlos McClatchy to "Dear Mama," n.d., CD 001:002:52, Charles Duncan Files, McClatchy Papers.

24. C. K. McClatchy to Ulric Collins, August 13, 1917, C. K. McClatchy Personal Correspondence, 6/18/1916–02/05/1920, p. 197, McClatchy Papers.

25. C. K. McClatchy to Hiram Johnson, January 5, 1918, Editorial, 12/20/1916–07/27/1918, p. 624, McClatchy Papers.

26. The Briggs-Rideout union was featured on the front page of the *Bee.* See "Briggs-Rideout," January 2, 1892, 1. It included a lithograph of young Dr. Briggs.

27. "Local Girl Saves Four from Drowning in Vassar Lake," *Sacramento Bee,* February 6, 1913, 4; C. K. McClatchy to W. E. Briggs, March 17, 1904, General Correspondence, 01/01/1903–12/14/1904, p. 213, McClatchy Papers.

28. Carlos McClatchy, telegram to Mrs. C. K. McClatchy, January 15, 1918, Carlos McClatchy Papers.

29. Phebe McClatchy, interview by Adair and C. K. McClatchy, March 6, 1984, in personal files of the author, courtesy James B. McClatchy; C. K. McClatchy to Hiram Johnson, January 23, 1918, Hiram Johnson Papers, BANC MSS C-B 581, The Bancroft Library, University of California, Berkeley.

30. C. K. McClatchy to Hiram Johnson, May 28, 1918, Editorial, 12/20/1916–07/27/1918, p. 880, McClatchy Papers.

31. C. K. McClatchy Jr. [Carlos McClatchy], "American Doughboy a Devil-May-Care Happy Fighter," *Sacramento Bee*, May 20, 1919, 1 and 2; C. K. McClatchy Jr., "Chance of Battle Welcomed by Men of Ninety-first," *Sacramento Bee*, May 22, 1919, 1 and 10; C. K. McClatchy Jr., "Ninety-first Went into Action Lacking Proper Equipment," *Sacramento Bee*, May 24, 1919, 1 and 4; C. K. McClatchy Jr., "Ninety-first Goes into Greatest with Fight Smiles and Jokes," *Sacramento Bee*, May 27, 1919, 1 and 13; C. K. McClatchy Jr., "Ninety-first Division Found Decided Lack of Airplane Support," *Sacramento Bee*, May 29, 1919, 1 and 2.

32. C. K. McClatchy Jr., "Fateful Order Sent 362nd Regimen [*sic*] to a Fearful Slaughter, *Sacramento Bee*, May 31, 1919, 1 and 10.

33. Carlos McClatchy to "Mother Briggs," October 24, 1918, CD 001:002:52, Charles Duncan Files, McClatchy Papers.

34. Ibid. This account did not reach home until after the armistice. Another account taken from a letter to Ella McClatchy was published in the *Bee,* "Mails Bring Word of Trial of the 91st," *Sacramento Bee*, November 28, 1918, 1.

35. C. K. McClatchy to Valentine McClatchy, October 24, 1918, p. 349, and C. K. McClatchy to Ernest Walker, November 16, 1918, p. 357; C. K. McClatchy to William Kent, November 27, 1918, p. 360, all in C. K. McClatchy Personal Correspondence, 6/18/1916–02/05/1920, McClatchy Papers.

36. C. K. McClatchy Jr., "Attack in Belgium Soon Developed into a Spirited Marathon," *Sacramento Bee*, June 7, 1919, 1 and 2.

37. Bob Molander, "Carlos Kelly McClatchy," 1984, typescript, in the author's files.

Chapter Fifteen Failed Dreams, Self-Imposed Exile

1. C. K. McClatchy to William D. Stephens, April 7, 1917, Editorial, 12/20/1916–07/27/1918, p. 200, McClatchy Papers; C. K. McClatchy to Hiram Johnson, March 17, 1917, and April 21, 1917, both in Hiram Johnson Papers, BANC MSS C-B 581, The Bancroft Library, University of California, Berkeley; C. K. McClatchy to Hiram Johnson, April 29, 1917, Editorial, 12/20/1916–07/27/1918, p. 231, McClatchy Papers.

2. C. K. McClatchy to Hiram Johnson, June 12, 1917, Hiram Johnson Papers, BANC MSS C-B 581, The Bancroft Library, University of California, Berkeley. See also "Senator Hiram W. Johnson and The Presidency," *Sacramento Bee*, June 13, 1917, 6.

3. "Issues in the Next Presidential Campaign and the Man for Standard Bearer," *Sacramento Bee*, April 17, 1919, 20.

4. "*Bee* Editor Leaving on Trip to Europe," *Sacramento Bee,* August 21, 1920, 1; "A Parting Private Think," *Sacramento Bee*, August 21, 1920, 28.

5. C. K. McClatchy Travel Diary, May 8, 1921, n.p., McClatchy Papers.

6. All three of these articles have the same title, "Touring the Battlefields of Desolated France," *Sacramento Bee*, June 10, 1921, 1 and 12; June 11, 1921, 1 and 11; June 16, 1921, 1 and 11.

7. "Touring the Battlefields," June 11; C. K. McClatchy Travel Diary, May 9, 1921; "Touring the Battlefields," June 16; "Lourdes Is Certainly an Earthly Paradise," *Sacramento Bee*, June 21, 1921, 1 and 2.

8. "The Return to Vienna From Constantinople," *Sacramento Bee*, December 1, 1921, 1 and 11; "Austrian Visions Glare of Riotous Revolution," *Sacramento Bee*, December 3, 1921, 1 and 23; "Ship Your Charity Back to America!" *Sacramento Bee*, November 1, 1921, 1 and 10; C. K. McClatchy to J. Fontaine Johnson, February 23, 1920, C. K. McClatchy Personal Correspondence, 06/28/1916–08/24/1920, p. 676, McClatchy Papers; "America Feeding Lazy in Europe, Says McClatchy," *Sacramento Bee*, May 16, 1922, 2.

9. "Merely Some Private Thinks," *Sacramento Bee*, April 24, 1926, S6; C. K. McClatchy to Hiram Johnson, September 12, 1925, Hiram Johnson Papers, BANC MSS C-B 581, The Bancroft Library, University of California, Berkeley; C. K. McClatchy to Hiram Johnson, September 15, 1926, box 33a, folder 1143, McClatchy Newspapers and Broadcasting Collection, McClatchy Papers.

10. "League Convicted out of Its Own Mouth," *Sacramento Bee*, October 9, 1926, 1 and 9; "The League of Nations Is a Most Hypocritical Body," *Sacramento Bee*, October 11, 1926, 1 and 4; "What About These Protests Which the League Ignored?" *Sacramento Bee*, October 12, 1926, 1 and 19; "How the League of Nations Has Treated Poor Syria," *Sacramento Bee*, October 13, 1926, 1 and 12; "Treatment of the Arabs in the Holy Land," *Sacramento Bee*, October 14, 1926, 1 and 12; "The Oppressed Have No Chance Before the League of Nations," *Sacramento Bee*, October 16, 1926, 1 and 2.

11. C. K. McClatchy to Hiram Johnson, October 8, 1926, Hiram Johnson Papers, BANC MSS C-B 581, The Bancroft Library, University of California, Berkeley; C. K. McClatchy Travel Diary, n.d. (1926), p. 165.

12. C. K. McClatchy Travel Diary, n.d. (1926), 166.

13. Ibid., 165–69.

14. C. K. McClatchy to Hiram Johnson, October 29, 1926, Hiram Johnson Papers, BANC MSS C-B 581, The Bancroft Library, University of California, Berkeley. See also "Mussolini Is Italy; Italy Is Mussolini," *Sacramento Bee,* November 11, 1926, 1 and 15; "Something More About Benito Mussolini," *Sacramento Bee*, November 12, 1926; "Mussolini Holds Italy in the Hollow of His Hand," *Sacramento Bee*, November 23, 1926, 1 and 15.

15. C. K. McClatchy to Hiram Johnson, December 9, 1926, Hiram Johnson Papers, BANC MSS C-B 581, The Bancroft Library, University of California, Berkeley; Jane Elizabeth Barbier, "C. K. McClatchy's Private Thinks on Benito Mussolini," research paper, California State University, Sacramento, May 2000. McClatchy's affirmation of Mussolini was not unique. The historian John P. Diggins notes that the Italian dictator was eager to cultivate a good image in the international press. See Diggins, "Mussolini and America."

16. McClatchy to Johnson, December 9, 1926, Hiram Johnson Papers, BANC MSS C-B 581, The Bancroft Library, University of California, Berkeley.

17. C. K. McClatchy to Hiram Johnson, April 27, 1927, Hiram Johnson Papers, BANC MSS C-B 581, The Bancroft Library, University of California, Berkeley.

Chapter Sixteen Reluctant Expansion and the Breakup

1. "Homage Paid to Boys of the Fighting 91st," *Sacramento Bee*, April 21, 1919, 1 and 6.

2. C. K. McClatchy to Ulric Collins, September 8, 1919, p. 519; To *Bee* Heads and Employees—Greeting, November 29, 1919, p. 554; and C. K. McClatchy to R. M. Richardson, December 12, 1919, p. 586, all in Personal Correspondence, 06/18/1916–02/05/1920, McClatchy Papers.

3. Jedd McClatchy to Valentine McClatchy (at Hotel Breslin in New York), April 22, 1908, Valentine McClatchy Personal Correspondence, 01/22/08–12/09/1908, p. 241, McClatchy Papers; and Valentine McClatchy to Harrison Parker, January 4, 1909, p. 45; Valentine McClatchy to Harrison Parker, January 13, 1909, p. 60; Valentine McClatchy to Harrison Parker, January 27, 1909, p. 92, all in Valentine McClatchy Personal Correspondence, 12/07/1908–09/29/1909, McClatchy Papers.

4. Valentine McClatchy to Harrison Parker, January 4, 1909, V. S. McClatchy Personal Papers, 12/07/1908–09/29/1909, p. 45, McClatchy Papers.

5. For the development of the radio by the *Bee*, see Kassis, "A Buzz in the Ether."

6. CK was still in Europe when he cabled Johnson: "I presume you have heard that Val and I are going to start a paper in Fresno and that we will send Carlos down there to edit it and Jim to be the publisher. V.S. [Valentine], James [JV] myself and others will go down occasionally to counsel with the boys, but we expect to give them a rather free hand. We think the field is very excellent down there and we have thorough faith in our kids. They are considerably older now than we were when our father died and we had to take the Sacramento *Bee*, and each of them has the guts—you can't scare either one of them." C. K. McClatchy to Hiram Johnson, April 15, 1922, Hiram Johnson Papers, BANC MSS C-B 581, The Bancroft Library, University of California Berkeley.

7. "James M'Clatchy Co, to Establish Paper at Fresno," *Sacramento Bee*, April 15, 1922, 1.

8. McClatchy to Johnson, April 15, 1922, Hiram Johnson Papers, BANC MSS C-B 581, The Bancroft Library, University of California, Berkeley. CK and Ella wended their way slowly back to California, visiting with Hiram Johnson in Washington and then stopping in Washington State to spend time with his daughter and grandchildren. They finally arrived home to meet their new grandson, James Briggs McClatchy, who had been born to Carlos and Phebe in December 1920 and was already walking and talking.

9. C. K. McClatchy to Carlos McClatchy, April 27, 1922, copy in Hiram Johnson Papers, BANC MSS C-B 581, The Bancroft Library, University of California, Berkeley.

10. Valentine McClatchy to C. K. McClatchy, August 8, 1922, written at La Jolla, California, and typed at San Francisco, copy in box 2, folder 066, Charles Duncan Files, McClatchy Papers.

11. "The Fresno *Bee* Publishes First Number Today," *Sacramento Bee*, October 17, 1922, 1; "First Subscriber to the *Bee* Starts Press," *Fresno Bee*, October 17, 1922, 1; "The Fresno *Bee*," *Fresno Bee*, October 18, 1923, 6; "The Why and Wherefore of the Fresno *Bee*," *Fresno Bee*, October 17, 1922, 16.

12. V. S. McClatchy to William H. Devlin, January 7, 1923, copy in box 108.2, folder 3, and Carlos McClatchy to C. K. McClatchy, January 12, 1923, copy in box 12, folder 12, both in McClatchy Papers.

13. C. K. McClatchy to Carlos McClatchy, February 2, 1923; V. S. McClatchy to Robert Newton Lynch, February 1, 1923; and C. K. McClatchy to Valentine McClatchy, draft never sent but dated March 9, 1923, all in box 1, folder 052, Duncan Files.

14. See "Aide Memoire," February 3, 1923, box 1, folder 052, Duncan Files.

15. A copy of the final settlement can be found in box 12, folder 12, McClatchy Papers.

16. C. K. McClatchy, telegram to Hiram Johnson, August 25, 1923, box 108.2, folder 3, and Charles F. Dillman to C. K. McClatchy, August 26, 1923, copy in box 2, folder 066, Duncan Files.

17. James Briggs McClatchy, "Talk at Monterey Seminar of Board of Directors, McClatchy Newspapers, September 14, 1980," box 3, folder J, "McC Speeches," James and Susan McClatchy Collection, McClatchy Papers.

18. C. K. McClatchy to Charlotte Maloney, September 1, 1923, and C. K. McClatchy to Marion De Vries, September 2, 1923, both in box 2, folder 066, Duncan Files. CK did not seem to know just how much the Rideouts lent him to keep the *Bee*. In a letter about the payout schedule to Carlos dated November 21, 1923, CK alludes to the Rideout loan but seems to know nothing of its payback provisions, "What agreement was made with the Rideouts?" he asked. The letter is in box 1, folder 03, McClatchy Papers.

19. C. K. McClatchy to Hiram Johnson, September 2, 1923, copy in box 2, folder 066, Duncan Files.

20. Jedd McClatchy became a real estate agent and remained with the McClatchy Realty Company until his death in 1963. See "H. J. McClatchy Realty Man, Dies," *Sacramento Bee*, June 20, 1963, 1. Ralph McClatchy also joined the realty firm and worked there until his death in 1947. See "Ralph McClatchy Local Realtor, Dies," *Sacramento Bee*, November 25, 1947, 4; JV McClatchy continued in newspaper work after leaving the *Bee,* becoming general manager of the *Santa Barbara Press-News*. He later returned to Sacramento, where he too became involved in real estate. See "J. V. McClatchy, Realty Company Official Dies," *Sacramento Bee*, October 9, 1953, 1 and 8.

21. Leo McClatchy left the *Bee* in 1923 and opened his own independent news agency in Washington, D.C., that provided news to California and Hawaiian newspapers. In 1932 he became associated with the National Park Service and was stationed in Santa Fe, New Mexico. In 1943 he joined the staff of the *San Francisco Call-Bulletin* and died unexpectedly of a heart attack while working on an editorial for the paper.

"Leo A. McClatchy Dies Suddenly in San Francisco," *Sacramento Bee*, October 2, 1945, 4.

22. C. K. McClatchy to Carlos McClatchy, October 5, 1923, and C. K. McClatchy to Carlos McClatchy, October 1, 1923, copies of both in box 2, folder 066, Duncan Files.

23. Memo, October 15, 1923, copy in box 2, folder 066, Duncan Files.

24. Memo, Synopsis of Statement from Mrs. Martin Beasley to Mrs. W. E. Briggs, October 2, 1923, and C. K. McClatchy to Mrs. Marion De Vries, September 2, 1923, copies of both in box 2, folder 066, Duncan Files.

25. Phebe McClatchy, interview by Adair and C. K. McClatchy, March 1984, in the author's files. See also Phebe Briggs McClatchy, interview by Adair and C. K. McClatchy, September 1984, Fresno, California, box 3, in folder labeled "Rideout/ Phebe Conley Recollections," James and Susan McClatchy Collection, McClatchy Papers; C. K. McClatchy Travel Diary, 1926, p. 169, McClatchy Papers.

26. "Guardian Named for Russell Children," "Funeral of the Late Wm. B. Russell," *Evening Bee*, February 19, 1902, 4; "Estate of Late Wm. Bell Russell," *Evening Bee*, December 2, 1904, 12. CK resigned as trustee of the estate in 1904, and the task then went to Rev. John F. Quinn. CK grew annoyed with the free-spending ways of the Russell children, who never paid back debts owed to him but threw elaborate theater parties.

27. C. K. McClatchy to Edgar Williams, November 8, 1918, Editorial 11, 07/29/1918–06/07/1919, p. 196, McClatchy Papers; "Clifford Russell Is Killed in Yolo Auto Crash; W. I. Elliott Is Hurt" and "Russell, Born in City Was Leading Member of Bar," *Sacramento Bee,* October 23, 1937, 1 and 12.

28. C. K. McClatchy to J. M. Maloney, October 2, 1909, box 56.1, folder 3, McClatchy Papers.

29. C. K. McClatchy to Etta M. Bagley, December 2, 1913, C. K. McClatchy Personal Correspondence, 08/30/1913–08/14/1914, p. 140, McClatchy Papers.

30. C. K. McClatchy to J. Everett Johnson, September 6, 1923, and C. K. McClatchy to Valentine McClatchy, September 2, 1923, both in box 56.1, folder 4, McClatchy Papers; C. K. McClatchy to Carlos McClatchy, October 30, 1923, box 1, folder 03, McClatchy Papers.

31. Ralph McClatchy to Carlos McClatchy, n.d., box 56.1, folder 4; undated clipping, ca. October 1923; and C. K. McClatchy to Carlos McClatchy, October 3, 1923, box 108, folder 2.08, all in McClatchy Papers.

32. C. K. McClatchy to Carlos McClatchy, November 24, 1923, box 1, folder 03, and Carlos McClatchy to C. K. McClatchy, "Sunday" (not dated but ca. November 25, 1923), box 56.1, folder 4, both in McClatchy Papers.

33. Valentine McClatchy, memo to C. K. McClatchy, December 10, 1923, and C. K. McClatchy to Valentine McClatchy, December 18, 1923, both in box 108.2, folder 8, McClatchy Papers.

34. Valentine McClatchy, memo to C. K. McClatchy, December 10, 1923, and Valentine McClatchy, memo to C. K. McClatchy concerning his letter 12/18/23—and

the wiping out of book indebtedness of sisters, December 21, 1923, both in box 108.2, folder 8, McClatchy Papers.

35. Valentine McClatchy to C. K. McClatchy, memo of December 21, 1923; C. K. McClatchy to Valentine McClatchy, December 29, 1923, box 108.2, folder 8, McClatchy Papers.

36. C. K. McClatchy to Hiram Johnson, January 19, 1924, Hiram Johnson Papers, BANC MSS C-B 581, The Bancroft Library, University of California Berkeley.

37. C. K. McClatchy to Carlos McClatchy, October 13, 1923, box 1, folder 03, McClatchy Papers.

38. C. K. McClatchy to Carlos McClatchy, January 3, 1924, box 108.2, folder 08, McClatchy Papers.

39. C. K. McClatchy to Carlos McClatchy, another letter dated January 3, 1924, box 108.2, folder 08, McClatchy Papers.

40. Carlos McClatchy to C. K. McClatchy "Thursday" (not dated but probably January 4–5, 1924), box 1, folder 052, Duncan Files; V. S. McClatchy, "Newspaper Creation or Building? The First Year of the Fresno *Bee*," *Editor and Publisher,* January 5, 1924, copy in box 1, folder 03, McClatchy Papers.

41. Harry Drummond to "J.B.K.," January 24, 1924, and C. K. McClatchy to Carlos McClatchy, February 20, 1924, both in box 1, folder 03, McClatchy Papers.

42. Carlos McClatchy to C. K. McClatchy, n.d., McClatchy Papers.

43. C. K. McClatchy to James W. Brown, February 21, 1924, box 3, folder 3, and C. K. McClatchy to Carlos McClatchy, February 22, 1924, box 1, folder 03, both in McClatchy Papers.

44. C. K. McClatchy to John Francis Neylan, January 29, 1924, box 56.1, folder 20; Valentine McClatchy to J. E. Langdon, January 15, 1924, box 44.1, folder 47a, both in McClatchy Papers.

45. C. K. McClatchy, memorandum, February 6, 1924, repeated in C. K. McClatchy to Carlos McClatchy, February 6, 1924, and Carlos McClatchy to CK, n.d., "Thursday" (February 1924), both in box 46.1, folder 27a; Carlos McClatchy to CK, "Thursday" (ca. February 1924), box 1, folder 052, Duncan Files, all in McClatchy Papers.

46. Eleanor McClatchy to Valentine McClatchy, June 3, 1936, box 12, folder 12; Valentine McClatchy to Eleanor McClatchy, June 13, 1936, box 2.2, folder 15, both in McClatchy Papers.

47. Hiram Johnson to C. K. McClatchy, February 21 and February 23, 1925, and C. K. McClatchy to Hiram Johnson, March 2, 1925, Hiram Johnson Papers, BANC MSS C-B 581, The Bancroft Library, University of California Berkeley.

48. C. K. McClatchy to Hiram Johnson, March 12, 1925, Hiram Johnson Papers, BANC MSS C-B 581, The Bancroft Library, University of California Berkeley.

49. "The Modesto *Bee* and News-Herald Become This Paper's Name," *Modesto Bee*, July 26, 1933, 1; Wiegand, *Papers of Permanence*, 134.

50. C. K. McClatchy to Hiram Johnson, July 10, 1928, Hiram Johnson Papers, BANC MSS C-B 581, The Bancroft Library, University of California Berkeley.

51. C. K. McClatchy to Honorable C. E. McLaughlin, December 31, 1923, CD:001:002:52, box 1, Duncan Files.

52. Carlos McClatchy to C. K. McClatchy, January 7, 1924; C. K. McClatchy to Carlos McClatchy, January 7, 1924; and C. K. McClatchy to Carlos McClatchy, May 11, 1924, all in box 1, folder 052, Duncan Files; Wiegand, *Papers of Permanence*, 144.

53. C. K. McClatchy to Carlos McClatchy, October 13, 1923, box 108.2, folder 8, McClatchy Papers; "The *Bee* to Hold an Open House on Anniversary," *Fresno Bee*, October 15, 1923, 1; "The *Bee* Greets Throng at Anniversary, 'Open House,'" *Fresno Bee*, October 18, 1923, 1; C. K. McClatchy to Hiram Johnson, August 15, 1924, box 108.2, folder 1, McClatchy Papers.

54. C. K. McClatchy to Hiram Johnson, August 18, 1924, box 108.2, folder 01, McClatchy Papers; Phebe Briggs McClatchy interview, March 1984.

55. Wiegand, *Papers of Permanence,* 144; C. K. McClatchy to Carlos McClatchy, January 28, 1924, box 108.2, folder 09, McClatchy Papers.

56. "Merely Some Private Thinks," *Sacramento Bee*, February 26, 1935, 20.

57. Phebe Briggs McClatchy, interview by C. K. McClatchy, April 21, 1984, box 3, in folder labeled "Rideout/Phebe Conley Recollections."

58. Raymond Crozier to Eleanor McClatchy, August 5, 1928, box 41.3, folder 33, McClatchy Papers.

59. Phebe Briggs McClatchy interview, March 1984.

60. Ibid.

61. C. K. McClatchy to Dr. Charles Clinton, May 4, 1910, C. K. McClatchy Personal Correspondence, 4/28/1910–12/02/1912, p. 36, McClatchy Papers.

62. "The Part Country Life Plays in a Great School for Girls," ad reproduced in "Millbrook—Hudson Valley Ruins: The Bennett School for Girls (Halcyon Hall)" by Rob Yasinac, http://www.hudsonvalleyruins.org. See also Frank Hasbrouk, ed., *The History of Dutchess County, New York* (Poughkeepsie, NY: S. A. Mathieu, 1909), 485.

63. C. K. McClatchy to May F. Bennett, January 6, 1916, C. K. McClatchy Personal Correspondence, 08/14/1914–09/21/1916, p. 587, McClatchy Papers.

64. "Helpful Hints to Young Farmers," *Hexagon*, box 009:41.3, folder 091.3.29, Bennett School, McClatchy Papers. Enclosed in this folder is a program of Eleanor's participation in a horse show.

Chapter Seventeen The Last Roar of the Aging Lion

1. C. K. McClatchy to Hiram Johnson, October 12, 1928, Hiram Johnson Papers, BANC MSS C-B 581, The Bancroft Library, University of California, Berkeley.

2. Ibid., November 12, 1928, Hiram Johnson Papers, BANC MSS C-B 581, The Bancroft Library, University of California, Berkeley.

3. Ibid., November 22, 1928, Hiram Johnson Papers, BANC MSS C-B 581, The Bancroft Library, University of California, Berkeley.

4. C. K. McClatchy to Carlos McClatchy, November 2, 1927, box 56.1, folder 14, McClatchy Papers; C. K. McClatchy to Hiram Johnson, March 7 and 13, 1928, both in Hiram Johnson Papers, BANC MSS C-B 581, The Bancroft Library, University of California, Berkeley; C. K. McClatchy to Carlos McClatchy, May 5, 1929, box

4, folder "Charles K. McClatchy Diary," James and Susan McClatchy Collection, McClatchy Papers.

5. Wiegand, *Papers of Permanence*, 157.

6. C. K. McClatchy to Hiram Johnson, April 30, 1929, in Vienna; Hiram Johnson to C. K. McClatchy, April 16, 1929, both in Hiram Johnson Papers, BANC MSS C-B 581, The Bancroft Library, University of California, Berkeley.

7. Hiram Johnson to Hiram W. Johnson Jr., November 30, 1929, *Diary Letters of Hiram Johnson,* vol. 5, 1929–33, n.p.—arranged by date (New York: Garland, 1983); C. K. McClatchy to Hiram Johnson, November 16, 1929, Hiram Johnson Papers, BANC MSS C-B 581, The Bancroft Library, University of California, Berkeley.

8. C. K. McClatchy, memo to Hiram Johnson, January 27, 1930, and C. K. McClatchy to Hiram Johnson, September 26, 1930, both in Hiram Johnson Papers, BANC MSS C-B 581, The Bancroft Library, University of California, Berkeley; recollections of Roy V. Bailey, box 19, folder 19:03, Misc. Collection and Business Files, McClatchy Papers.

9. C. K. McClatchy to Hiram Johnson, March 11, 1931, box 33a, folder 1148, McClatchy Newspaper and Broadcasting Collection, CSH. CK signed the renewed trust papers on March 18, 1931. See C. K. McClatchy to Hiram Johnson, March 18, 1931, Hiram Johnson Papers, BANC MSS C-B 581, The Bancroft Library, University of California, Berkeley.

10. C. K. McClatchy to Hiram Johnson, March 28, 1931, box 33a, folder 1148, McClatchy Newspaper and Broadcasting Collection.

11. C. K. McClatchy obituary, *Sacramento Bee*, April 30, 1936.

12. C. K. McClatchy to Hiram Johnson, August 5, 1931, box 33a, folder 1148, McClatchy Newspaper and Broadcasting Collection.

13. C. K. McClatchy to Hiram Johnson, September 30, 1931, box 33b, folder 1148, McClatchy Newspaper and Broadcasting Collection.

14. Hiram Johnson to C. K. McClatchy, December 1, 1931; Gladys Cunningham to Hiram Johnson, December 5, 1931; and C. K. McClatchy to Hiram Johnson, December 24, 1931, all in Hiram Johnson Papers, BANC MSS C-B 581, The Bancroft Library, University of California, Berkeley.

15. C. K. McClatchy to Hiram Johnson, March 5, 1932, Hiram Johnson Papers, BANC MSS C-B 581, The Bancroft Library, University of California, Berkeley. Johnson later confirmed that portions of the book would be libelous, and CK withdrew his insistence it be published. The editorial team also urged CK to ease up on Hoover, who was already in deep political trouble, for fear of creating a sympathetic vote for him. Hiram Johnson to C. K. McClatchy, March 8, 1932; C. K. McClatchy to Hiram Johnson, April 5, 1932; C. K. McClatchy to Hiram Johnson, April 7, 1932, all in Hiram Johnson Papers, BANC MSS C-B 581, The Bancroft Library, University of California, Berkeley.

16. C. K. McClatchy to Hiram Johnson, March 23, 1932, box 33b, folder 1149, McClatchy Newspaper and Broadcasting Collection; Hiram Johnson to C. K.

McClatchy, April 24, 1932, copy in Hiram Johnson Papers, BANC MSS C-B 581, The Bancroft Library, University of California, Berkeley.

17. Gladys Cunningham to Hiram Johnson, June 2, 1932; note appended to a letter from C. K. McClatchy to Hiram Johnson, June 17, 1932, both in Hiram Johnson Papers, BANC MSS C-B 581, The Bancroft Library, University of California, Berkeley.

18. C. K. McClatchy to Hiram Johnson, June 23, 1932, box 33b, folder 1149, McClatchy Newspaper and Broadcasting Collection; Hiram Johnson to C. K. McClatchy, June 26, 1932, Hiram Johnson Papers, BANC MSS C-B 581, The Bancroft Library, University of California, Berkeley.

19. Franklin D. Roosevelt to C. K. McClatchy, July 21, 1932, box 009, folder 061:01/07 ; Walter Jones to C. K. McClatchy, September 26, 1932, box 56.1, folder 9, both in McClatchy Papers.

20. C. K. McClatchy to Hiram Johnson, December 14 and 16, 1932, box 33b, folder 1149, McClatchy Newspaper and Broadcasting Collection; Hiram Johnson to C. K. McClatchy, December 29, 1932, Hiram Johnson Papers, BANC MSS C-B 581, The Bancroft Library, University of California, Berkeley.

21. C. K. McClatchy to Hiram Johnson, January 3, 1933, box 33b, folder 1150, McClatchy Newspaper and Broadcasting Collection; Hiram Johnson to C. K. McClatchy, January 8, 1933, copy in Hiram Johnson Papers, BANC MSS C-B 581, The Bancroft Library, University of California, Berkeley.

22. C. K. McClatchy to Hiram Johnson, January 11, 1933, box 33b, folder 1150, McClatchy Newspaper and Broadcasting Collection.

23. Ibid.

24. "Carlos K. McClatchy Dies of Pneumonia in San Mateo," *Sacramento Bee*, January 17, 1933, 1.

25. P. F. Bennett, "Beautiful New Stations Give to St. Patrick's Home," *(Sacramento Catholic) Register*, October 29, 1933, 3, Superior California ed.

26. "Archibald M. Johnson Is Suicide at Bay Home," *Sacramento Bee*, August 1, 1933, 1 and 5; C. K. McClatchy to Hiram Johnson, August 15, 1933, box 33b, folder 1150, McClatchy Newspaper and Broadcasting Collection.

27. C. K. McClatchy to H. R. McLaughlin, January 11, 1933, box 56.1, folder 9, McClatchy Papers.

28. CK's will is in CD 001:002:065, Charles Duncan Files, McClatchy Papers. Ella's will is located in box 009, folder 041:3.1, McClatchy Papers.

29. C. K. McClatchy to Charles Mayo, April 13, 1933, box 56.1, folder 3, McClatchy Papers.

30. C. K. McClatchy to Gladys Cunningham, April 21, 1933, box 13, folder 1, McClatchy Papers.

31. C. K. McClatchy to Hiram Johnson, May 29, 1933, Hiram Johnson Papers, BANC MSS C-B 581, The Bancroft Library, University of California, Berkeley.

32. "Private Thinks," *Sacramento Bee*, June 22, 1933, 22. See also "Repeal, Racing Bill Passed by Landslide Votes," "Sacramento Goes Wet 10 to 1 with Heavy Balloting,"

Sacramento Bee, June 28, 1933, 1. The local vote on repeal of Prohibition was 14,222 in favor, 1,798 against.

33. "Private Thinks," *Sacramento Bee*, June 6, 1932, 6; "Mob of 100 Men Cause Near Riot at Court House," *Sacramento Bee*, January 17, 1933, 1; "Merely Some Private Thinks," *Sacramento Bee*, May 3 and January 5, 1935, S-4.

34. Gladys Cunningham to Hiram Johnson, September 11 and 26, 1933; C. K. McClatchy to Hiram Johnson, November 13, 1933, all in Hiram Johnson Papers, BANC MSS C-B 581, The Bancroft Library, University of California, Berkeley.

35. C. K. McClatchy to Hiram Johnson, January 2, 1934, Hiram Johnson Papers, BANC MSS C-B 581, The Bancroft Library, University of California, Berkeley.

36. C. K. McClatchy to Hiram Johnson, February 26 and March 17, 1934, Hiram Johnson Papers, BANC MSS C-B 581, The Bancroft Library, University of California, Berkeley.

37. Clement C. Young to C. K. McClatchy, April 3, 1934, and C. K. McClatchy to Clement C. Young, April 6, 1934, both in box 56.1, folder 9, McClatchy Papers. See also C. K. McClatchy to Hiram Johnson, April 4, 1934, Hiram Johnson Papers, BANC MSS C-B 581, The Bancroft Library, University of California, Berkeley.

38. C. K. McClatchy to Hiram Johnson, April 6, 1934, Hiram Johnson Papers, BANC MSS C-B 581, The Bancroft Library, University of California, Berkeley. See also C. K. McClatchy to Clement C. Young, April 9, 1934, McClatchy Papers.

39. C. K. McClatchy to Hiram Johnson, May 5, 1934, Hiram Johnson Papers, BANC MSS C-B 581, The Bancroft Library, University of California, Berkeley.

40. C. K. McClatchy to Hiram Johnson, July 15, 1934, box 33b, folder 1151, McClatchy Newspaper and Broadcasting Collection.

41. Message appended to a letter from CK to Hiram Johnson, October 7, 1935, Hiram Johnson Papers, BANC MSS C-B 581, The Bancroft Library, University of California, Berkeley.

42. C. K. McClatchy to H. R. McLaughlin, November 19, 1935, box 56.1, folder 9, McClatchy Papers; C. K. McClatchy to Hiram Johnson, February 23 and July 8, 1935, box 33b, folder 1152, McClatchy Newspaper and Broadcasting Collection.

43. C. K. McClatchy to Hiram Johnson, January 7, 1936, box 33b, folder 1153; C. K. McClatchy to Hiram Johnson, February 4, 1935, box 33b, folder 1152, both in McClatchy Newspaper and Broadcasting Collection.

44. C. K. McClatchy to Hiram Johnson, January 20, February 1, and February 10, 1936, box 33b, folder 1153, McClatchy Newspaper and Broadcasting Collection.

45. C. K. McClatchy to Eleanor McClatchy, February 22, 1936, box 3.1, folder 4, McClatchy Papers.

46. Eleanor McClatchy to "Dearest Chickie," February 24, 1936, box 41.3, file 44, McClatchy Papers.

47. Valentine McClatchy to Eleanor McClatchy, June 13, 1936, box 2.2, folder 17; Thomas J. Hayes to Ella McClatchy, April 27, 1936, box 56.1, folder 13; Franklin Hichborn to Walter Jones, October 29, 1952, box 56, folder 5, all in McClatchy Papers.

Epilogue

1. "New School Named for C. K. McClatchy," *Sacramento Bee,* February 16, 1937, 1 and 4.

2. "Ceremony of Laying C. K. McClatchy High School Cornerstone Is Conducted by Masonic Officers," *Sacramento Bee,* May 21, 1937, 4; "C. K. McClatchy School Is Dedicated to Truth, Liberty," *Sacramento Bee,* September 20, 1937, 4; "Liberty Ship Will Be Named for Late C. K. McClatchy," *Sacramento Bee,* March 15, 1944, 4.

3. "V. S. McClatchy Is Dead at 80," *Sacramento Union,* May 16, 1938, 1 and 3; "V. S. McClatchy's Widow Died in San Francisco," *Sacramento Bee,* November 10, 1938, 1; "Mrs. Ella K. McClatchy Dies in Home Here," *Sacramento Bee,* September 23, 1939, 1 and 3.

4. Roy V. Bailey and Eleanor McClatchy, comps., *Private Thinks by C. K. and Other Writings of Charles K. McClatchy* (New York: Scribners Press, 1936).

5. Eleanor McClatchy to G. C. Hamilton, n.d. (ca. May 23, 1942), box 61.2, folder labeled "McClatchy E., Hamilton, G.C.," McClatchy Papers.

Bibliography

———————————◆———————————

Collections Consulted

Archives of Santa Clara University, Santa Clara, CA
Archives of the Archdiocese of San Francisco, Menlo Park, CA
James Barry Papers, The Bancroft Library, University of California, Berkeley
Franklin Hichborn Papers, Special Collections, University of California, Los Angeles
Collis P. Huntington Papers, microfilm, California State Library, Sacramento
Hiram Johnson Papers, The Bancroft Library, University of California, Berkeley
McClatchy Papers, Center for Sacramento History, Sacramento
Paulist Fathers Archives, Washington, DC
Chester Rowell Papers, The Bancroft Library, University of California, Berkeley
Karl H. Von Weigand Papers, Hoover Institution Archives, Stanford, CA

Books, Journal Articles, Theses

Abbott, Carl. *How Cities Won the West*. Albuquerque: University of New Mexico Press, 2008.

Agresti, Olivia Rossetti. *David Lubin: A Study in Practical Realism*. Berkeley: University of California Press, 1941.

Avella, Steven M. *Sacramento: Indomitable City*. Charleston, SC: Arcadia, 2003.

Barde, Robert. "Plague in San Francisco: An Essay Review." *Journal of the History of Medicine and Allied Sciences* 59 (July 2004): 463-70.

———. "Prelude to the Plague: Public Health and Politics at America's Pacific Gateway, 1899." *Journal of the History of Medicine* 58 (2003): 153-86.

Barker, Charles Albro. *Henry George*. New York: Oxford University Press, 1955.

Bean, Walton. *Boss Ruef's San Francisco*. Berkeley: University of California Press, 1952.

———. "Ideas of Reform in California." *California Historical Quarterly* 51, no. 3 (fall 1972): 213–26.

Blessing, Patrick Joseph. "West Among Strangers: Irish Migration to California, 1850 to 1880." Ph.D. diss., University of California, Los Angeles, 1977.

Bogart, Victor. "Chester H. Rowell and the Lincoln-Roosevelt League, 1907–1910." Master's thesis, University of California, Berkeley, 1962.

Bonnet, Theodore. *The Regenerators: A Study of the Graft Prosecution of San Francisco.* San Francisco, Pacific Printing, 1911.

Brusher, Joseph. *Consecrated Thunderbolt: A Life of Peter C. Yorke of San Francisco.* Joseph F. Wagner, 1973.

————. "Father Yorke Versus the A.P.A." *Academy Scrapbook,* 2, no. 4 Academy of California Church History, Fresno (October 1951): 129–60.

————. "Father Yorke Versus the A.P.A." *Academy Scrapbook* 2, no. 5 Academy of California Church History, Fresno (November 1951): 175–92.

Bullough, William A. *The Blind Boss and His City: Christopher Augustine Buckley and Nineteenth-Century San Francisco.* Berkeley: University of California Press, 1979.

Burns, John F., ed. *Sacramento: Gold Rush Legacy, Metropolitan Destiny.* Carlsbad, CA: Heritage Media, 1999.

California Blue Book, 1850–2000. Sacramento: Office of the Secretary of State, 2000.

Chase, Marilyn. *The Barbary Plague: The Black Death in Victorian San Francisco.* New York: Random House, 2004.

Cherny, Robert W. et al., eds. *California Women and Politics: From the Gold Rush to the Great Depression.* Lincoln: University of Nebraska Press, 2011.

Clark, Thomas R. "Labor and Progressivism South of the Slot: The Voting Behavior of the San Francisco Working Class, 1912–1916." *California History* 66, no. 3 (September 1987): 196–207.

Cronin, Bernard Cornelius. "Father Yorke and the Labor Movement in San Francisco, 1900–1910." Ph.D. diss., Catholic University of America, 1943.

Culver, J. H. *Sacramento Directory 1851.* Edited by Mead Kibbey. Sacramento: California State Library Foundation, 2000.

Daniel, Cletus E. "In Defense of the Wheatland Wobblies: A Critical Analysis of the IWW in California." *Labor History* 19, no. 4 (Fall), 485–509.

Daniels, Robert. *The Politics of Prejudice: The Anti-Japanese Movement in California and the Struggle for Japanese Exclusion.* Berkeley: University of California Press, 1962.

Davis, Winfield L. *Pen Pictures of the Garden of the World: An Illustrated History of Sacramento County, California.* Chicago: Lewis, 1890.

Deverell, William, and Tom Sitton, eds. *California Progressivism Revisited.* Berkeley: University of California Press, 1994.

Diggins, John P. "Mussolini and America: Hero-Worship, Charisma, and the 'Vulgar Talent.'" *Historian* 28, no. 4 (fall 1966): 559–85.

Dinkelspiel, Frances. *Towers of Gold: How One Jewish Immigrant Named Isaias Hellman Created California*. New York: St. Martin's Press, 2008.

Douglass, John Aubrey. *The California Idea and American Higher Education*. Stanford, CA: Stanford University Press, 2000.

Eradicating Plague in San Francisco. Report of the Citizens Health Committee, March 11, 1909.

Everett, Miles Chapman. "Charles Harvey Rowell, Pragmatic Humanist and California Progressive." Ph.D. diss., University of California, Berkeley, 1966.

Ferrell, Robert H. *America's Deadliest Battle: Meuse-Argonne, 1918*. Lawrence: University Press of Kansas, 2007.

Fitzpatrick, John. "Senator Hiram W. Johnson: A Life History, 1866–1945." Ph.D. diss., University of California, Berkeley, 1975.

Foner, Eric. "Class, Ethnicity, and Radicalism in the Gilded Age: The Land League and Irish-America." *Marxist Perspectives* 1, no. 2 (1978): 6–55.

Franklin, William Elton. "The Political Career of Peter Hardeman Burnett." Ph.D. diss., Stanford University, 1954.

Frost, Richard H. *The Mooney Case*. Stanford, CA: Stanford University Press, 1968.

Galarza, Ernesto. *Barrio Boy*. Notre Dame, IN: University of Notre Dame Press, 1971.

George, Henry. *Life of Henry George*. New York: Robert Schalkenberg Foundation, 1960.

Grassman, Curtis. "The Los Angeles Free Harbor Controversy and the Creation of a Progressive Coalition." *Southern California Quarterly* 55, no. 4 (winter 1973): 445–68.

Greenland, Powell. *Hydraulic Mining in California: A Tarnished Legacy*. Spokane: Arthur H. Clark, 2001.

Gribble, Richard. "Peter Yorke and Corruption in San Francisco, 1906–1909." *Journal of the West* 32, no. 3 (June 1993): 87–93.

———. "Peter Yorke and the 1901 Teamsters and Waterfront Strikes in San Francisco." *Southern California Quarterly* 74, no. 2 (1992): 141–60.

Guinn, J. M. *History of the State of California and Biographical Record of Oakland Environs*. Los Angeles: Historical Record Co., 1907.

———. *History of the State of California and Biographical Record of the Sacramento Valley, California*. Chicago: Chapman, 1906.

Gullet, Gayle. "Women Progressives and the Politics of Americanization in California, 1915–1920." *Pacific Historical Review* 64, no. 1 (February 1995): 71–94.

Hamilton, Marty. "Bull Moose Plays and Encore: Hiram Johnson and the Presidential Campaign of 1932." *California Historical Quarterly* 41, no. 3 (September 1962): 211–21.

Hansen, Debra Gold. "Depoliticizing the California State Library: The Political and Professional Transformation of James Gillis, 1899–1917." *Information & Culture: A Journal of History* 48, no. 1 (2013): 68–90.

Hardwick, Susan Wiley. "Ethnic Residential and Commercial Patterns in Sacramento with Special Reference to the Russian-American Experience." Ph.D. diss., University of California, Davis, 1986.

Hennings, Robert E. "California Democratic Politics in the Period of Republican Ascendancy." *Pacific Historical Review* 31, no. 3 (1962): 267–80.

Herman, Paul A. "Religious Identity and 'The Fight for Reform': Catholic and Jewish Responses to the San Francisco Graft Prosecutions, 1906–1909." Master's thesis, Pacific School of Religion, Berkeley, CA, 1996.

Hichborn, Franklin. *Story of the Session of the California Legislature of 1909.* 1909. Reprint, Sligo, Ireland: Hard Press, 2006.

———. *Story of the Session of the California Legislature of 1911.* 1911. Reprint, Ulan Press, 2012.

———. *Story of the Session of the California Legislature of 1915.* San Francisco: James H. Barry, 1916.

———. *The System, as Uncovered by the San Francisco Graft Prosecution.* 1915. Reprint, Montclair, NJ: Patterson Smith, 1969.

History of Merced County, California. Los Angeles: Historic Record Co., 1925.

Hopper, Stanley D. "Fragmentation of the California Republican Party in the One-Party Era, 1893–1932." *Western Political Quarterly* 28, no. 2 (June 1975): 372–86.

Hundley, Norris. *The Great Thirst: Californians and Water, 1770s–1990s.* Berkeley: University of California Press, 1992.

Hurtado, Albert L. *John Sutter: A Life on the North American Frontier.* Norman: University of Oklahoma Press, 2006.

Hutchison, W. W. "Prologue to Reform: The California Anti-Railroad Republicans, 1899–1905." *Southern California Quarterly* 44, no. 3 (1962): 175–218.

Issel, William, and Robert W. Cherny. *San Francisco, 1865–1932: Politics, Power, and Urban Development.* Berkeley: University of California Press, 1986.

Johnson, Linda Ann. "The Invisible Enemy: Epidemic Influenza in Sacramento, 1918–1919." Master's thesis, California State University, Sacramento, 1994.

Jones, J. Roy. *Memories, Men, and Medicine.* Sacramento: Sacramento Society for Medical Improvement, 1950.

Kalisch, Philip A. "The Black Death in Chinatown: Plague and Politics in San Francisco, 1900–1904." *Arizona and the West* 14, no. 2 (1972): 113–36.

Kassis, Ruth Annette. "A Buzz in the Ether: The *Sacramento Bee,* Radio, and the Public Interest, 1922–1950." Master's thesis, California State University, Sacramento, 2010.

Kazin, Michael. "The Great Exception Revisited: Organized Labor and Politics in San Francisco and Los Angeles, 1870–1940." *Pacific Historical Review* 55, no. 3 (August 1986): 371–402.

Kelley, Robert L. *Battling the Inland Sea: Floods, Public Policy, and the Sacramento Valley.* Berkeley: University of California Press, 1998.

———. *Gold vs. Grain: The Hydraulic Mining Controversy in California's Sacramento Valley.* Glendale, CA: Arthur H. Clark, 1959.

———. "Taming the Sacramento: Hamiltonianism in Action." *Pacific Historical Review* 34, no. 1 (1965): 21–49.

Kemble, Edward C. *A History of California Newspapers, 1846–1858.* Edited by Helen Harding Brentnor. Los Gatos, CA: Talisman Press, 1962.

Kinzer, Donald L. *An Episode in Anti-Catholicism: The American Protective Association.* Seattle: University of Washington Press, 1964.

Lagomarsino, Barbara. "Early Attempts to Save the Site of Sacramento by Raising Its Business District." Master's thesis, California State University, Sacramento, 1969.

Laichas, Thomas Michael. "Robbing Peter to Pay Paul: Public Finance and Political Changes in California, 1950–1930, Pts. 1 & 2," Ph.D. diss., University of California, Los Angeles, 1999.

Landino, Tracy Lynn. "The *Sacramento Bee*'s Editorial Policies Towards Organized Labor, 1900–1910." Master's thesis, California State University, Sacramento, 1987.

Larsen, Christian L. et al. *Growth and Government in Sacramento.* Bloomington: Indiana University Press, 1966.

Layne, J. Gregg. "The Lincoln-Roosevelt League: Its Origin and Accomplishments." *Quarterly of Historical Society of Southern California* 25, no. 3 (September 1943): 79–101.

Lee, J. J., and Marion R. Casey, eds. *Making the Irish American.* New York: New York University Press, 2006.

Lehr, Ernest E. "Sutterville: The Unsuccessful Attempt to Establish a Town Safe from Floods." Master's thesis, California State University, Sacramento, 1958.

Lengel, Edward G. *To Conquer Hell: The Meuse-Argonne, 1918.* New York: Henry Holt, 2008.

Lincoln, A. "Theodore Roosevelt, Hiram Johnson, and the Vice-Presidential Nomination of 1912." *Pacific Historical Review* 28, no. 3 (August 1959): 267–83.

Lord, Myrtle Shaw. *A Sacramento Saga.* Sacramento: Sacramento Chamber of Commerce, 1946.

Lotchin, Roger W. *Fortress California, 1910–1961: From Warfare to Welfare.* New York: Oxford University Press, 1992.

Lower, Richard Coke. *A Bloc of One: The Political Career of Hiram W. Johnson.* Stanford, CA: Stanford University Press, 1993.

————. "Hiram Johnson: The Making of an Irreconcilable." *Pacific Historical Review*, 41, no. 4 (November 1972): 505–26.

Lowitt, Richard. *The New Deal and the West*. Norman: University of Oklahoma Press, 1933.

McClatchy, Charles K. *Private Thinks*. New York: Chas. Scribner and Sons, 1936.

McCormick, Richard L. "The Discovery That Business Corrupts Politics: A Reappraisal of the Origins of Progressivism." *American Historical Review* 86, no. 2 (April 1981): 247–74.

McGowan, Joseph A. *History of the Sacramento Valley*. 3 vols. West Palm Beach, FL: Lewis Historical Publishing, 1961.

McKanna, Clare W. *Race and Homicide in Nineteenth-Century California*. Reno: University of Nevada Press, 2002.

McKevitt, Gerald. *The University of Santa Clara: A History, 1851–1977*. Stanford, CA: Stanford University Press, 1979.

McKevitt, Gerald, and George F. Giacomini. *Serving the Intellect, Touching the Heart: A Portrait of Santa Clara University, 1851–2001*. Santa Clara, CA: University of Santa Clara Press, 2001.

Maeda, Wayne. *Changing Dreams and Treasured Memories: A Story of Japanese Americans in the Sacramento Region*. Sacramento: Sacramento Japanese American Citizens League, 2000.

Maguire, James G. *Ireland and the Pope: A Brief History of Papal Intrigues Against Irish Liberty*. San Francisco: James A. Barry, 1888.

Mahan, William E. "The Political Response to Urban Growth: Sacramento and Mayor Marshall R. Beard, 1863-1914." *California History* 69 (winter 1990-91): 354-71.

Margo, Elisabeth. *Taming the Forty-Niner*. New York: Rinehart, 1955.

Melcher, Daniel P. "The Challenge to Normalcy: The 1924 Election in California." *Southern California Quarterly* 60, no. 2 (summer 1978): 155–82.

Melendy, H. Brett, and Benjamin F. Gilbert. *The Governors of California from Peter H. Burnett to Edmund G. Brown*. Georgetown, CA: Talisman, 1965.

Memorial and Biographical History of Northern California. Chicago: Lewis Publishing, 1891.

Mills, Patricia A. "The Anti-Asian Bias in Editorial Cartoons Featured in the *Sacramento Bee*, 1900–1945," Master's thesis, California State University, Sacramento, 1990.

Morris, James McGrath. *Pulitzer: A Life in Politics, Print, and Power*. New York: HarperCollins, 2010.

Mowry George E. "The California Progressive and His Rationale: A Study in Middle-Class Politics." *Mississippi Valley Historical Review* 36, no. 2 (September 1949): 239–50.

————. *The California Progressives*. Chicago: Quadrangle, 1951.

Nagel, Charles E. "A Fight for Survival: Floods, Riots, and Disease in Sacramento, 1850." Master's thesis, Sacramento State College, Sacramento, 1965.

Nash, Gerald D. "Bureaucracy and Economic Reform: The Experience of California, 1899–1911." *Western Political Quarterly* 13, no. 3 (September 1960): 678–91.

Nassaw, David. *The Chief: The Life of William Randolph Hearst*. Boston: Houghton Mifflin, 2000.

O'Donnell, Edward T. "'Though Not an Irishman,' Henry George and the American Irish." *American Journal of Economics and Sociology* 56, no. 4 (1997): 407–19.

Older, Fremont. *My Own Story*. San Francisco: Call Publishing, 1919.

Olin, Spencer C. Jr. *California Politics 1846–1920*. San Francisco: Boyd and Fraser, 1981.

————. *California's Prodigal Sons: Hiram Johnson and the Progressives, 1911–1917*. Berkeley: University of California Press, 1968.

————. "Hiram Johnson, the California Progressives and the Hughes Campaign of 1916." *Pacific Historical Review* 31, no. 4 (1962): 403–12.

————. "Hiram Johnson, The Lincoln-Roosevelt League, and the Election of 1910." *California Historical Quarterly* 45, no. 3 (September 1966): 225–40.

Orsi, Richard J. *Sunset Limited: The Southern Pacific Railroad and the Development of the American West, 1850–1930*. Berkeley: University of California Press, 2005.

Ostrander, Gilbert. *The Prohibition Movement in California, 1848–1933*. Berkeley: University of California Press, 1957.

Owens, Kenneth N. "The Oak Park Redevelopment Area: A Historical Overview." Unpublished manuscript. Sacramento Archive and Museum Collection Center, 1976.

Paterson, Thomas G. "California Progressives and Foreign Policy." *California Historical Society Quarterly*, 47, no. 4 (December 1968): 329–42.

Peterson, Eric Falk. "The End of an Era: California's Gubernatorial Election of 1894." *Pacific Historical Review* 38, no. 2 (May 1964): 141–56.

Pincetl, Stephanie S. *Transforming California: A Political History of Land Use and Development*. Baltimore: Johns Hopkins University Press, 1999.

Pisani, Donald J. "Land Monopoly in Nineteenth-Century California." *Agricultural History* 65, no. 4 (1991): 15–37.

————. "Squatter Law in California, 1850–1858." *Western Historical Quarterly* 1994 25 (3): 277–310.

————. *Water and American Government: The Reclamation Bureau, National Water Policy, and the West: 1902–1935*. Berkeley: University of California Press, 2002.

————. *Water, Land, and Law in the West: The Limits of Public Policy, 1850–1920*. Lawrence: University Press of Kansas, 1996.

Praetzellis, Adrian. "The Archaeology of a Victorian City: Sacramento, California." Ph.D. diss., University of California, Berkeley, 1991.

Procter, Ben. *William Randolph Hearst: The Early Years, 1863–1910.* New York: Oxford University Press, 1998.

———. *William Randolph Hearst: The Later Years: 1911–1951.* New York: Oxford University Press, 2007.

Putnam, Jackson. "The Pattern of Modern California Politics." *Pacific Historical Review* 61, no. 1 (February 1992): 23–52.

———. "The Persistence of Progressivism in the 1920s: The Case of California." *Pacific Historical Review* 35, no. 4 (November 1966): 395–411.

Rogin, Michael. "Progressivism and the California Electorate." *Journal of American History* 55, no. 2 (September 1968): 297–314.

Rolston, Arthur. "Capital, Corporations, and Their Discontents in Making California's Constitutions, 1849–1911." *Pacific Historical Review*, 80, no. 4 (November 2011): 521–56.

Rose, Alice. "Rise of California Insurgency: Origins of the League of Lincoln-Roosevelt Republican Clubs, 1900–1907." Ph.D. diss., Stanford University, 1942.

Sandul, Paul J. P. *California Dreaming: Boosterism, Memory, and Rural Suburbs in the Golden State.* Morgantown: West Virginia University Press, 2014.

Sandul, Paul, J. P., and Tory D. Swim. *Orangevale.* Charleston, SC: Arcadia, 2006.

Sarbaugh, Timothy. "Father Yorke and the San Francisco Waterfront." *Pacific Historian* 25, no. 3 (1981): 28–35.

Scibilia, Dominic. "Peter C. Yorke: The Social Legacy of an American Integralist." *American Benedictine Review* 44, no. 4 (December 1993): 432–47.

Severson, Thor. *Sacramento: An Illustrated History: 1839 to 1874, From Sutter's Fort to Capital City.* San Francisco: California Historical Society, 1973.

Shah, Nayan. *Contagious Divides: Epidemics and Race in San Francisco's Chinatown.* Berkeley: University of California Press, 2001.

Shapiro, Herbert. "The McNamara Case: A Window on Class Antagonism in the Progressive Era." *Southern California Quarterly* 70 (1988): 69–95.

Shepherd, Bernard A. "C. K. McClatchy and the *Sacramento Bee*." Ph.D. diss., Syracuse University, Syracuse, NY, 1961.

Shover, John L. "The California Progressives and the Election of 1924." *California Historical Quarterly*, 51 (spring 1972): 59–74.

———. "Was 1928 a Critical Election in California?" *Pacific Northwest Quarterly* 58, no. 4 (October 1967): 196–204.

Silveira, William. "From Neutrality to Belligerency to Isolationism: C. K. McClatchy and World War I." Master's thesis, California State University, Sacramento, 1996.

Sitton, Tom. "California's Practical Idealist: John Randolph Haynes." *California History* 67 no. 1 (March 1988): 2–17.

Smith, Kathleen. *Mining in Yuba County.* Charleston, SC: Arcadia, 2015.

Staniford, Edward Fawsitt. "Governor in the Middle: The Administration of George C. Pardee, Governor of California, 1903–1907." Ph.D. diss., University of California, Berkeley, 1955.

Starr, Kevin. *Americans and the California Dream, 1850–1915.* New York: Oxford University Press, 1973.

———. *Inventing the Dream: California Through the Progressive Era.* New York: Oxford University Press, 1985.

Steffens, Lincoln. *The Autobiography of Lincoln Steffens.* 2 vols. New York: Harcourt Brace, 1931.

Stevens, Mark H. "The Enigma of Meyer Lissner: Los Angeles's Progressive Boss." *Journal of the Gilded Age and Progressive Era* 8, no. 1 (January 2009): 111–36.

———. "Meyer Lissner and the Politics of Progressive Municipal Reform in the City of Los Angeles, 1906–1913." Ph.D. diss., Claremont Graduate School, Claremont, CA, 1995.

Stoll, Steven. *The Fruits of Natural Advantage.* Berkeley: University of California Press, 1998.

Thomas, Lately. *A Debonair Scoundrel.* New York: Holt, Rinehart, & Winston, 1962.

Thompson, Thomas, and Albert West. *History of Sacramento County.* 1880. Reprint, Berkeley: Howell-North, 1960.

Ullman, Sharon R. *Sex Seen: The Emergence of Modern Sexuality in America.* Berkeley: University of California Press, 1997.

Van Nuys, Frank W. "A Progressive Confronts the Race Question: Chester Rowell, the California Alien Land Act of 1913 and the Contradictions of Early Twentieth Century Racial Thought." *California History* 73 no. 1 (spring 1994): 2–13.

Walsh, James P. "James Phelan: Creating the Fortune, Creating the Family." *Journal of the West* 31, no. 2 (1992): 17–23.

Walters, Donald Edgar. "Populism in California: 1889–1900." Ph.D. diss., University of California, Berkeley, 1952.

Wasserman, Ira M. "Status, Politics, and Economic Class Interests: The 1918 Prohibition Referendum in California." *Sociological Quarterly* 31, no. 3 (1990): 475–84.

Waters, Delmatier et al. *The Rumble of California Politics, 1848–1970.* New York: John Wiley & Sons, 1970.

Wells, Evelyn. *Fremont Older.* New York: D. Appleton-Century, 1936.

Where California Fruits Grow, Resources of Sacramento County, A Souvenir of the Bee. Sacramento: Sacramento *Bee,* 1894.

White, Richard. *Railroaded: The Transcontinentals and the Making of Modern America.* New York: W. W. Norton, 2012.

Whitmer, John Dale. "Knights of Reform: The Knights of Labor in Northern California." Master's thesis, San Diego State University, 1995.

Wiegand, Steve. *Papers of Permanence: The First 150 Years of the McClatchy Company.* Sacramento: McClatchy, 2007.

Williams, Clyde Hu. "Early Populism in California: An Evaluation of the Election of 1894." Master's thesis, California State University, Fullerton, 1970.

Willis, William L. *History of Sacramento County.* Los Angeles: Historic Record Co., 1913.

Wimer, Philip Lee. "C. K. McClatchy and Upton Sinclair's Epic Campaign: The Power of the Press in 1934 California." Master's thesis, California State University, Sacramento, 1995.

Woodbury, Robert Louis. "William Kent: Progressive Gadfly, 1864–1928." Ph.D. diss., Yale University, New Haven, CT, 1967.

Worthen, James. *Governor James Rolph and the Great Depression in California.* Jefferson, NC: McFarland, 2006.

Yanousky, Ronald William. "Seeing the Cat: Henry George and the Rise of The Single Tax Movement, 1879–1890." Ph.D. diss., University of California, Berkeley, 1993.

Index